CONTEMPORARY
ECONOMIC
PROBLEMS 1978

American Enterprise Institute
CONTEMPORARY ECONOMIC PROBLEMS 1978
William Fellner, Project Director

American Enterprise Institute for Public Policy Research
Washington, D.C.

Library of Congress Cataloging in Publication Data

Main entry under title:

Contemporary economic problems, 1978.
   1. United States—Economic Policy—1971–
—Addresses, essays, lectures. 2. United States—
Economic conditions—1971–   —Addresses, essays,
lectures. 3. Inflation (Finance)—United States—
Addresses, essays, lectures. I. Fellner, William
John, 1905–
HC106.7.C675   330.9'73'0926   78-14962
ISBN 0-8447-1330-9

Printed in the United States of America

CONTRIBUTORS

William Fellner—*Project Director*
> Sterling professor of economics emeritus at Yale University, former member of the Council of Economic Advisers, and past president of the American Economic Association. Resident scholar with the American Enterprise Institute.

Phillip Cagan
> Professor of economics at Columbia University, research staff of the National Bureau of Economic Research, and former senior staff economist for the Council of Economic Advisers. Adjunct scholar with the American Enterprise Institute.

Barry R. Chiswick
> Research professor, department of economics and Survey Research Laboratory, University of Illinois at Chicago Circle, and former senior staff economist for the Council of Economic Advisers.

Gottfried Haberler
> Galen L. Stone professor of international trade emeritus at Harvard University, and past president of the American Economic Association and International Economic Association. Resident scholar with the American Enterprise Institute.

Robert B. Helms

Director of Health Policy Studies for the American Enterprise Institute.

D. Gale Johnson

Eliakim Hastings Moore distinguished service professor of economics and provost at the University of Chicago, and past president of the American Farm Economics Association. Member of the Council of Academic Advisers and adjunct scholar with the American Enterprise Institute.

Marvin H. Kosters

Former Associate director for economic policy at the Cost of Living Council. Director of the Center for the Study of Government Regulation and resident scholar with the American Enterprise Institute.

Geoffrey H. Moore

Director of business cycle research for the National Bureau of Economic Research, senior research fellow at the Hoover Institution, Stanford University, and former U.S. commissioner of labor statistics. Adjunct scholar with the American Enterprise Institute.

Herbert Stein

A. Willis Robertson professor of economics at the University of Virginia, former chairman of the Council of Economic Advisers, and former vice president and chief economist of the Committee for Economic Development. Senior fellow with the American Enterprise Institute.

Marina v. N. Whitman

Distinguished public service professor of economics at the University of Pittsburgh, and former member of the Council of Economic Advisers and National Price Commission. Member of the Council of Academic Advisers and adjunct scholar with the American Enterprise Institute.

CONTENTS

4

PREFACE

In the introduction to the 1976 and to the 1977 volume of the *Contemporary Economic Problems* series a brief description was given of this ongoing project. Emphasis was placed on the common elements of our research interests and on the usefulness of our joint meetings in which drafts of our papers are discussed in successive stages of their preparation. Despite the diversity of our areas of work, we have all along shared a common interest in linking the general macroeconomic problems involved in moving back to a sustainable growth path with the microeconomic, structural problems on which the success of macropolicies largely depends. In the present volume this is illustrated by the studies of Phillip Cagan, Geoffrey Moore, Herbert Stein, Marvin Kosters, Gale Johnson, Gottfried Haberler, Marina v. N. Whitman, Barry Chiswick, Robert Helms, and by my own study. There is no reason to repeat the general description of the project on the present occasion. Each individual study begins with a summary, and I will not try to summarize them also at the outset.

In the introduction that follows the preface, I will instead attempt to identify what I consider to be the focal point of the current controversy on anti-inflation policy. Because it is convenient to identify this focal point in macroeconomic terms, my introduction will supplement Cagan's study more directly, or at least more explicitly, than the other studies in this volume. But the work of all contributors to the volume bears quite closely on the problem to which the introduction and Cagan's study are devoted. In these two pieces the concept of the "slack" available for the production of additional output plays a prominent role, and so does the question of what amount of slack may become associated with alternative policies. The now conventional methods of estimating the slack are seriously misleading, and the reasons for this cannot be understood without paying a good deal of attention to the structural problems with which the bulk of this volume is concerned.

W. F.

The Core of the Controversy about Reducing Inflation: An Introductory Analysis

William Fellner

Guide to the reader. *The first two sections of the introductory remarks—those preceding the graphic presentation—may serve also as a nontechnical summary of the content of the introduction. The sections beginning with the graphic presentation relate largely to the technical sections of Cagan's study. That study also begins with a summary expressed in simple language, as do all our papers, and a general discussion of the conclusions derived from Cagan's technical analysis is included in the main body of his contribution to the volume.*

Cracks in the Analytical Foundations of Our Inflationary Policies

Official thinking about the desirable course of the American economy—the course that should be promoted by stimulating demand—is based on the now conventional method of estimating our potential output. For reasons to be discussed later in this volume, this is a misleading method.[1] The estimating procedures consistent with the conventional approach have led to the conclusion that at present our economy has a large slack and that, given the appropriate demand stimuli, we could therefore continue to grow for many years at a rate well above our normal growth rate.

Those employing the conventional approach are inevitably on the way to discovering once more that the approach is unrealistic. Efforts to eliminate the alleged slack by expansionary demand policies must lead once more to a steepening of the inflationary movement and to a thoroughgoing destabilization of the economy. According to Cagan's estimates, based on a conception different from that underlying the con-

---

[1] See pp. 84–89.

ventional procedures, the slack has by now disappeared, if by slack we mean (as we should) unused resources of the required kind that could be drawn upon without steepening the inflationary trend. Indeed, the slack in this essential sense may by now well have become over-exhausted.

Yet neither Cagan nor the other members of our group would base policy on specific numerical estimates of this kind. The conclusion from this is not that our numerical unemployment-rate targets should be reformulated but that our demand-management policies should be directed at preventing a renewed steepening of inflation rather than at numerically specified targets expressed in terms of measured unemployment rates. The basic reason is that it is impossible to determine in advance with anything like the needed precision the effect of structural and institutional factors on the availability of inputs at real supply prices that make their employment rewarding.

I feel convinced also that our policy makers will rediscover the hard way that efforts to stabilize a significant inflation rate—that is, to prevent it from further steepening—are doomed to failure. The markets rightly anticipate that a policy attitude so described will on the next occasion lead the authorities to show the same willingness to accommodate and allegedly to stabilize an even higher inflation rate then prevailing. This results in a steepening of the cost trends and it thwarts efforts to stabilize such rates of inflation.

None of this is as yet generally recognized, but it is sufficiently in the air to have aroused widespread interest in methods available for reducing our inflation rate. That problem does indeed deserve very high priority. I now turn to the current controversy about how to achieve a desired reduction and gradual elimination of the inflation that has developed in the United States.

Propositions Setting the Stage
for the Controversy about Reducing Inflation

Two propositions, neither of which is controversial per se, lend themselves to identifying an area of controversy.

Proposition 1: Empirical investigations, based on American data for the post-Korean War period, suggest that bringing inflation down by monetary and fiscal policy—bringing it down through a reduction of the rate of increase of money GNP—would be associated with an unfavorable mix of effects on output on the one hand, and effects on inflation on the other. The data drawn from the relatively recent past support the hypothesis that the rate of inflation would decrease very slowly and that the depressing effect on output would be much more pronounced.

Those who take the continuation of past relations among the relevant variables for granted are therefore inclined to advocate supplementing monetary and fiscal policy with direct government intervention in the wage and price structure. They believe that without such measures, vaguely described as incomes policies, monetary-fiscal disinflation is in practice not feasible. Hence even if they have no liking for such measures pe se, they tend to be unimpressed by the argument that given the basic characteristics of our economic and political system such interventions are apt to prove unworkable and to cause damage, and that this damage may include major unwanted changes in the characteristics of our society. One is not much impressed by such an argument if one feels that in practice there exists no alternative.

Proposition 2: Those of us who nevertheless favor reliance on disinflation by monetary-fiscal means without renewed attempts to rely on the other devices described above are guided by the conviction that some essential past relations among economic variables would change appreciably if the authorities shifted to a consistent and credible policy of gradually reducing the rate of increase in money GNP. In other words, our position implies a specific reason for the observed fact that in the past—particularly in the second half of the post-Korean War period— the inflation expectations of the public became obstinate and that these expectations survived periods of demand-policy restraint. The implied reason is that the public has not expected anti-inflationary policies to continue for long. The long-run inflation expectations have not been much influenced by the recurring but erratic and short-lasting efforts to stem inflation, and hence neither have cost and price trends been much influenced during these episodes. According to this view, the relation between the adverse output effect and the desired anti-inflationary effect of demand-policy restraint would become much more favorable under a consistent and credible anti-inflationary policy—one that would exert a significant influence on long-run price expectations and hence on cost trends.

There is reasonable agreement that emphasis on one or the other of these two propositions distinguishes different positions of economists concerning the reduction of inflation by monetary and fiscal means. But this is how far the agreement goes. Both analytically and in the area of policy debates a major controversy continues between those stressing Proposition 1, thereby attaching little importance to the promise of the expectations effect described in Proposition 2, and those of us who stress this expectations effect. On the policy level the controversy relates essentially to the existence or nonexistence of a "need" for incomes policy.

Only to those economists is the controversy likely to seem unimportant who, unlike myself,[2] believe that we should not be concerned with reducing the rate of inflation but should aim merely for preventing the acceleration of the inflationary movement and for gearing the economy to a steady and predictable inflation rate. At present reducing the rate of inflation is, however, rightly considered a matter of great importance by most economists, and the controversy may safely be said to relate to a matter of crucial significance. This is not only my personal view[3] but one recently expressed by many economists.[4]

One of the attractive features of Cagan's contribution to this volume is that it facilitates a technical identification of the specific point of disagreement between those who in their appraisal of the outlook for monetary-fiscal disinflation are guided by indications derived from the recent past, and those of us basing our judgment on the expectations effect of a shift to a consistent and credible policy. In Cagan's models estimates derived from past experience support pessimistic appraisals to the extent, and only to the extent, that the coefficients reflect very little confidence on the part of the public in the durability of the authorities' occasional anti-inflationary efforts. The main purpose of the analysis that follows is to explain and to justify this statement.

However, a macroeconomic exploration of these coefficients, or of measures of the slack developing under various types of policy, or of the price level, would be an undertaking of little value if the need were overlooked to relate to that exploration an intensive concern with the structural problems located behind the aggregative concepts. This is a conviction illustrated by most studies in the present volume, and also by those published in the two earlier volumes of this series.

Graphic Presentation of Some Essentials

Figure 1 shows that at $\overline{U}$ the inflation rate neither rises nor declines, or rather that this is the case at the general resource-utilization level to which that measured unemployment rate corresponds. The figure says nothing about the *height* of the inflation rate that remains stable at $\overline{U}$.

---

[2] See pp. 91–93 below.

[3] For my more recent writings, see *Towards a Reconstruction of Macroeconomics: Problems of Theory and Policy* (Washington, D.C.: American Enterprise Institute, 1976), and my study in the 1977 volume of the present series.

[4] For recent contributions, see Martin Neil Baily, "Stabilization Policy and Private Economic Behavior," *Brookings Papers on Economic Activity*, no. 3 (Washington, D.C.: Brookings Institution, 1977), and George L. Perry, "Slowing the Wage-Price Spiral," ibid., no. 1 (1978).

Figure 1

THE RATE OF CHANGE OF THE INFLATION RATE AS A FUNCTION OF THE "SLACK" (MEASURED HERE BY THE UNEMPLOYMENT RATE)

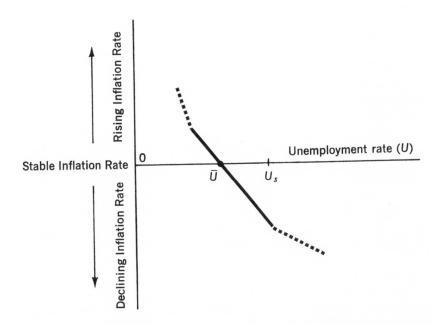

Note: $\bar{U}$ expresses the measured unemployment rate at which the price trend neither steepens nor flattens, that is, the nonacceleration unemployment rate. At U_s there exists (positive) slack measured by the difference between U_s and $\bar{U}$. Only a brief stretch of the function is drawn and, to tie it in with Cagan's simplifying assumptions, the function is made linear in the neighborhood of $\bar{U}$.

The function, a stretch of which is drawn in the figure, does imply, however, that whatever the inflation rate is at $\bar{U}$, market decisions had been made in anticipation of the inflation rate there prevailing. In other words, market decisions have become adjusted to this particular rate of inflation whenever the measured unemployment rate is at $\bar{U}$. As long as this is not yet the case, it is impossible to keep the system at a level of resource utilization at which the rate of inflation would remain unchanged. This is because, given a discrepancy between expected and actual inflation, the public will discover that the current-dollar supply prices of goods and services need to be adjusted to make them correspond to the intended *real* supply prices.

5

The question now arises why we should not be satisfied with stabilizing the inflation rate at $\overline{U}$, whatever this rate may be, and why we should become interested in the controversy concerning specific methods for reducing inflation. Yet it is an ascertainable fact that a high proportion of the public is very much interested in achieving this objective. Why?

One answer may be that inflation would have disadvantages even if market decisions were adjusted to this current rate. But in my appraisal the main point here is that the analysis based on Figure 1 needs to be refined by recognizing that not just *any* price trend *can* be stabilized and that the public distrusts promises to gear the economy smoothly to an "inflationary equilibrium." As said before, willingness of the authorities to accommodate an appreciable inflation rate in order to avoid the difficulties of adopting anti-inflationary policies will generally be interpreted as foreshadowing a future willingness to accommodate *for the very same reason* a higher rate as well. The expected inflation rate and the cost trends will then keep steepening, and the condition that at $\overline{U}$ there should be no acceleration will not be satisfied for long.

Without scrapping a piece of analytical equipment as convenient as Figure 1 is, we shall recognize the difficulties (I would say: the impossibility) of stabilizing an initially observed high inflation rate by interpreting Figure 1 in the following way.

An observed tendency of the inflation rate temporarily neither to have risen nor to have declined when the measured unemployment rate was temporarily at $\overline{U}$ will be interpreted as meaning that in the periods for which we observe $\overline{U}$ the expected inflation rate was temporarily the same as the inflation rate actually prevailing in those periods. This inflation rate was, of course, not the identical rate in the various periods for which $\overline{U}$ was observed and in which the price trend remained temporarily unchanged. We shall assume, however, that if "now" the height of the temporarily stable inflation rate corresponding to $\overline{U}$ is, say, 7 percent, then keeping the economy at $\overline{U}$ would not keep the expected rate at 7 percent for long. The 7 percent rate would describe merely a temporary resting place of the system. The expected rate would soon start rising because, when entering into its commitments for the future, the public would foresee a willingness by the authorities to accommodate more than 7 percent inflation. Substantial variance needs to be assumed around the public's expectations concerning the level of the higher future rate, and this indirectly means substantial variance also around the expectations for the present 7 percent. This variance, or uncertainty, gradually comes to reduce the efficiency of the economic system very greatly. Thus it is a requirement of reasonable policy to reduce the 7 percent inflation rate significantly by demand-policy restraint resulting in a slack (as compared to $\overline{U}$) during a transition period. Indeed, the case for gradually restoring the practically horizontal price trend we had during part of our postwar history is strong.[5]

In Figure 1 the slack is shown for the unemployment rate U_s by the excess of that rate over $\overline{U}$, that is by $U_s - \overline{U}$. The demand-policy restraint resulting in this slack will reduce the steepness of the price trend. It may be added here that there is a good chance that when the postinflationary adjustment is completed the measured unemployment rate at which the rate of inflation remains stable will be lower than $\overline{U}$—a good chance of a leftward shift of $\overline{U}$ on the horizontal axis—because a practically horizontal price trend can be foreseen with very much less uncertainty than one that has a strong tendency to steepen. Productivity trends would therefore be likely to improve, and a somewhat steeper wage trend would then become compatible with the same price trends.

The question may be asked whether such a model contains even traces of the Phillips-curve hypothesis postulating a trade-off between inflation and unemployment. To some extent this is a matter of semantics, but I suggest that the question should be answered in the negative. The sacrifice involved in the measured unemployment rate U_s during the transition period ceases to be a sacrifice over any reasonably defined time horizon if we compare the policy of gradual disinflation with its alternatives. Allowing the inflation rate to remain at 7 percent for a while, then at 8 and 9 percent for a while, with a strong tendency for the intervals to shorten, would soon lead to having to accept much greater sacrifices. The analysis here does not suggest the existence of a Phillips trade-off over any reasonable time horizon. Nevertheless, even over a reasonable time horizon $U_s - \overline{U}$ does measure a slack in the particular sense that after disinflation the resources expressed by this difference between inputs *will* become available for additional production. The system may thereafter return to $\overline{U}$.

Salient Features of Cagan's Models

The two models developed by Cagan suggest that if we want to eliminate inflation gradually, then the length of the transition period during which we need to accept a slack of given size before allowing the economy to settle down at $\overline{U}$ depends on the values of specific coefficients defined in the models. If during the transition period the slack asso-

---

[5] See also pp. 91–93.

ciated with our demand restraint could be kept uninterruptedly at some given level, say, at $U_s - \overline{U}$, then in the first Cagan model the parameter determining the rate of the per-period reduction of inflation would be the algebraic product of the coefficients a and b (equation [5], p. 26). In the second model the rate of price-trend flattening per period would be the sum of the coefficients c (equation [10], p. 31). Given a constant slack, inflation would become reduced period after period in both models.

In the first model the reduction of inflation, from one quarter to the next depends in the successive quarters (1) on the difference between the expected long-run inflation rate and the currently observed (lower) inflation rate of the quarter in question, where this difference needs to be computed first without taking account of the current adjustment of long-run expectations in view of the difference itself, and (2) on the downward adjustment of the long-run inflation expectations in view of the difference. The downward adjustment of long-run expectations results in each quarter from the difference between the expected long-run rate and the currently observed rate as defined in (1), that is, *without* yet taking into account the inflation-reducing effect of the current downward revision of the expected long-run rate itself. We shall describe the difference as defined in (1) as the difference between the as yet *unrevised* expected long-run rate of inflation and the currently observed rate. In each quarter this difference leads to revised expectations and thereby it leads to some further reduction of the inflation rate.

For a slack of given size $(U_s - \overline{U})$, the difference between the as yet unrevised expected long-run inflation rate of the quarter and the current rate depends on the size of the slack $U_s - \overline{U}$ and on Cagan's coefficient a.[6] As long as the demand-policy restraint with which the slack is associated persists, the individual firms would continue to moderate their price trend relative to the hitherto expected long-run trend even if the latter were not further reduced in each quarter. Thus for each quarter we obtain the difference between the as yet unrevised expected long-run rate of the quarter and the current rate of inflation by multiplying the slack by a. This difference $(a\,(U_s - \overline{U}))$ needs to be multiplied by the coefficient b to yield the downward revision of the expected long-run rate in the successive quarters. The downward revision of the hitherto expected long-run rate expresses itself fully in a further reduction of the actual inflation rate as compared to the rate of the preceding quarter. In those Cagan regressions which are the best candidates for consideration the value of b is between 0.20 and 0.25.

---

[6] In Cagan's model a assumes a negative value because he relates a positive slack to the rise of the inflation rate, not to its reduction.

This means that a one percentage point difference between the as yet unrevised expected long-run inflation rate of the quarter and its currently observed rate reduces the expected long-run rate by less than one-fourth of one percentage point. *Only this fraction of the difference between the hitherto expected long-run inflation rate and the currently observed rate carries over into a modification of the long-run expectations and hence into a current change of the inflation rate.*

If in practice the slack is not kept constantly at $U_s - \overline{U}$ but moves between various levels—or if we try to estimate the value of the coefficients from a sample period in which cyclical variations were moving the actual U left and right along the horizontal axis—then we need to take into account that, quite aside from what has been said so far, an *increase* of the slack will have an inflation-reducing effect and a *decrease* of the slack will raise the inflation rate. These effects result from the further moderation of the individual firms' price trend when an addition develops to the slack, or from a steepening of the individual firms' price trend in the contrary case. The effect of changes in the slack on the current rise or reduction of the rate of inflation is measured by the algebraic product of the coefficient a and the change in the slack. The fact that the current steepening and flattening of the price trend thus depends on two terms—the size of the slack and its change—explains why the price trend can steepen in the phases of the cycle when there still is a slack but one that is diminishing. In our discussions Geoffrey Moore had stressed that this usually is the case,[7] and Cagan's results are consistent with this finding.

Regression estimates based on Cagan's first model lead to the conclusion that, if the coefficients should stay unchanged, it would take eight to nine years to reduce the present inflation rate to zero, provided the average slack of that period (the excess of U_s over $\overline{U}$) is about one percentage point in terms of unemployment. $\overline{U}$ itself Cagan estimates at an unemployment rate slightly in excess of 3.5 percent for prime-age males, and he suggests that at present this may correspond to an overall unemployment rate of roughly 6 percent. The slack is defined in relation to the prime-age male unemployment rate.

His second model suggests deceleration at a rate that is even slower by a significant margin. In that model, he modifies the assumption that for a constant $U_s - \overline{U}$ the reduction of the inflation rate proceeds from the preceding quarter in proportion to $U_s - \overline{U}$.[8] Instead, he assumes in the second model that the cumulated $U_s - \overline{U}$ over the preceding four

---

[7] See also Geoffrey Moore's contributions to the 1977 and the present volume of this series.

[8] This proportion, as we have seen, is a times b in the first model.

years (roughly the duration of a business cycle) determines the current reduction of the steepness of the price trend in relation to the average rate of inflation of the same four years. The sum of Cagan's c coefficients in equation [10] determines the rate of this price deceleration in the second model. The model implies that long-run price expectations are revised in view of the experience over a whole cycle, not just a quarter.

Yet as Cagan points out, the real question here is whether a credible policy, pursued with consistency, would not lead to a significant change in the relevant coefficients and to a significant improvement of the outlook. In my writings I have suggested that it would, and I am here repeating that suggestion. A reasonable policy of gradual disinflation by monetary and fiscal means would, of course, raise this question only somewhat indirectly. Such a policy would not try to "fix" the slack in terms of unemployment or other variables but would gradually reduce the rate of increase in money GNP, and the question raised would concern the *implication* of this course with respect to the slack. With the parameter values estimated by Cagan for his first model, the implication for reducing inflation to zero would be an eight- to nine-year long maintained one percentage point excess unemployment over and above the rate required for avoiding a steepening of the price trend, that is, over and above $\overline{U}$; and the one percentage point excess might, according to the same analysis, correspond to a nearly 7 percent overall rate. If with good reason we regard the American price trend of the period 1951–1965—an average yearly increase of consumer prices at a rate of between 1 and 2 percent—as representing "practical price stability," the duration of the transition period needed to get us there shortens from eight or nine years to about six years. Cagan's second model yields much longer adjustment periods. The question is whether consistency and credibility of the policy line would shorten these periods appreciably.

Adjusting the Results to the Credibility Effect of a Consistent Policy

The main reason for believing that under a credible and consistent policy the outcome would turn out to be much less unfavorable is found in Cagan's estimates of the coefficient b. According to his estimates, based on a past period of erratic and inflation-biased policies, a one percentage point shortfall of the currently observed as compared to the hitherto expected inflation rate has reduced the expected rate merely by *less than 0.25 percentage point.* Credibility and consistency of an anti-inflationary policy line would in all probability raise this fraction quite considerably. One would remain far from assuming idealized perfect faith in the permanence of any "currently" observed price trend moderation if one hypothesized a b coefficient of 0.50, instead of less than 0.25, for expressing the adjustment of long-run inflation expectations to current results. This would reduce the duration of the transition from six to less than three years. After three years the unemployment rate would go to $\overline{U}$. If it first took some years of low coefficient values to establish credibility gradually, then the length of time required to get down to practical price stability would, however, exceed three years. But the lengthening of the period of adjustment would be moderate if, after the establishment of credibility by that process, the relevant coefficient reflected reasonably high confidence in the "permanence" of the effort to maintain practical price stability. Even if for the entire transition period we assumed an average value of somewhat less than 0.40 for the b coefficient—a low value at the early stages but one that gradually rises to well over 0.50—the duration would come out at roughly four years.

All this is in terms of Cagan's first model. If one chose a combination of the first and the second model and, in accordance with a hint in the Cagan study, adjusted the result to a high degree of credibility *after* four years (this being the assumed duration of a cycle), one would infer very little reduction of inflation for the first four years but very rapid deceleration thereafter. The entire duration might then come out at somewhat more than five years. To take an unrealistic illustration tilted in the opposite direction: with personalities who could inspire from the outset very high confidence in the permanence of any currently observed results of disinflation ($b = 1$), the assumptions underlying Cagan's first model would suggest completion of the adjustment to practical price stability in about one and a half years. The implied slack in all these exercises is a one percentage point average excess of unemployment beyond the nonacceleration rate ($\overline{U}$), which Cagan defines in terms of prime-age male unemployment.

Regression analysis of the sort discussed here is not a particularly dependable tool, as Cagan would be the first to admit and even to stress. We cannot place a high bet on these estimates of the duration of the span over which a slack of some specific size would develop as a byproduct of a policy aimed directly at a gradual reduction of the rate of increase in money GNP, and thus at a restoration of practical price stability. We can merely come nearer to identifying the parameters on which the magnitude of this byproduct depends and to identifying the ranges over which "optimists" and "pessimists" may move in their tentative judgments. As for the duration of the period with a one percentage point average slack over and above the non-acceleration unemployment rate, Cagan's results, adjusted for the credibility effect of a consistent policy, would suggest to me that three years is an "optimistic" guess and that five years or somewhat more is a "pessimistic" guess. As concerns Cagan's estimate of the unemployment rates relevant to his analysis—somewhat beyond 3.5 percent for the prime-age male rate and roughly 6 percent for the overall rate at the point of non-accelerating inflation, thus perhaps nearly 7 percent for the overall rate including the slack—these rates would become reduced quite a bit if minimum wages were abolished and some of the unemployment-raising features of the unemployment compensation system were modified.

But, as I say in my study in this volume, it would be foolhardy to formulate numerical unemployment-rate targets on the basis of knowledge now available. What can be asserted firmly is this: the slack developing as a byproduct of a policy of gradually reducing the rate of increase in money GNP depends importantly on the credibility and consistency of the anti-inflationary effort. Cagan's work is very helpful in pinning this down, even if in this area all numerical estimates shade over into guesswork.

A closer look at the problem does not tempt us to turn away from strong support of gradual monetary-fiscal disinflation. The unreasonable alternative to that line consists of suffering successive flare-ups of inflation with intervening recessions that do not repair the damage; of again engaging at some stage in unsuccessful experimentation with wage and price controls; and of then adopting even more belatedly and in even more difficult circumstances the monetary and fiscal policy line we should adopt now. This is the alternative unless we should move toward a comprehensively controlled society. Perhaps conditions need to get worse before they get better. But that is not a cheerful thought, nor one in which we should acquiesce calmly.

The Reduction of Inflation by Slack Demand

Phillip Cagan

Summary

The persistence of inflation in the past decade has undermined confidence in our capability of reducing it. To many it appears intractable. While the inflation rate has declined in periods of business recession, it has revived and intensified in the subsequent periods of business expansion. The dissatisfaction with traditional monetary and fiscal measures has brought forth schemes to restrain price increases directly by taxes or subsidies, though these hold no more promise of being effective than have direct controls on prices or incomes policies in the past.

The dissatisfaction reflects in part the failure of inflation, in a business recovery such as 1975–1977, to continue to decline while excess unemployment is reduced. The belief that inflation should decline is based on the presumption that it always tends to decline so long as resources are not fully employed and markets exhibit slack. But that is not an accurate view of historical price behavior. The inflation rate has always fluctuated over the business cycle, falling during business contractions and rising during expansions, invariably beginning to rise early in business recoveries long before economic slack gives way to full-employment output. For a reduction in the inflation rate that outlasts the business cycle, the rate will be lower in corresponding stages of successive business cycles. For such a reduction in inflation, policy must reduce the expected rate of inflation. This rate reflects the anticipated long-run equilibrium trend of prices and underlies explicit and implicit contracts for future payments and the setting of wages and prices gen-

---

I am indebted to William Fellner, John Taylor, and the authors of this volume for helpful comments and to Fred Kittler for computer assistance.

13

erally. The expected rate gradually adjusts when actual rates deviate above or below it for an extended period. Even though the actual inflation rate continues to rise and fall over the business cycle, the expected average rate can still decline if business expansions do not intensify inflationary pressures and the actual rate remains below the expected rate on the average.

Estimates are presented of the effect of slack demand on the expected rate of inflation under two models, one based on adaptive expectations and the other on rational expectations. These two models are formulated to be consistent with the existence of slack markets and the procyclical fluctuations in the inflation rate, but they are nevertheless quite different in their theoretical assumptions and practical implications, though actual behavior may well be a mix of both. The effect of slack demand on the expected inflation rate, though hard to estimate with precision, is confirmed by the evidence. The effect of one percentage point average unemployment in excess of the level at full employment, maintained over a typical four-year business cycle, is estimated to reduce the expected, and therefore the actual, average annual inflation rate by about three percentage points under adaptive expectations, and by about half as much under rational expectations. The latter effect is smaller because rational expectations allow for cyclical fluctuations in the economy and so only an average amount of slack that is larger than expected over an entire business cycle reduces the expected inflation rate.

The small estimates of the effect help to explain the loss of confidence in policies to maintain it. The effect is hidden by the larger cyclical fluctuations in the inflation rate. In assessing an anti-inflation policy, however, the authorities and the public should not be misled by normal cyclical fluctuations in the inflation rate, characterized as "stagflation"; what matters is the noncyclical changes between corresponding stages of successive business cycles.

Expectations are likely to respond more strongly to restraints on aggregate demand once policy makers demonstrate their determination and ability to hold inflation at a lower rate. One reason the effect of excess unemployment is small is that policy has demonstrated the opposite since the mid-1960s by accommodating a rising average rate of inflation. A policy of reducing inflation, coming after a decade of accommodation, is hampered by pessimistic expectations of its capability.

Despite the general pessimism, however, an anti-inflation policy has a good chance of succeeding if it can avoid past errors of overstimulating business expansions to the point of reviving inflationary pressures, which is not an impossible task. Since the economic capability

exists, the pessimism in fact pertains to the political capability of trans-
lating concern over inflation into effective measures of restraint. Here
the recent record has not been encouraging.

Introduction

Current economic policy is directed toward reducing inflation and unemployment. The *Economic Report of the President* in January 1978
states that "We must contain and reduce the rate of inflation as we
move toward a more fully employed economy."[1] That has been the
unquestioned intention of policy since inflation intensified in 1965, and
it was the guiding spirit, even if not always the practical objective, in
the previous years since World War II. The method of achieving the
objective is to stimulate aggregate demand by monetary and fiscal measures to expand production and jobs up to—but not beyond—the point
where new inflationary pressures emerge. The assumption is that it is
possible in theory even if difficult in practice to reduce inflation by
maintaining some slack in labor and product markets in the aggregate.
A period of economic slack is accepted as the cost of subduing inflation.

The maintenance of slack in the economy, with the accompanying
excess unemployment, is not, of course, attractive to policy makers.
Monetary and fiscal measures designed to reduce inflation result in
slack as a byproduct, not as an objective, of anti-inflation policy. U.S.
policy has faced the dilemma of choosing between inflation and unemployment by targeting a path of aggregate demand which, in deference
to political pressures, will produce as little slack as possible and still reduce inflation, even though the reduction of inflation will be slow. The
justification for keeping the slack mild and reducing inflation gradually
is based on the nature of the assumed trade-off between inflation and
unemployed resources. Each addition to the amount of slack is thought
to have diminishing effects in reducing the inflation rate. To avoid en-
during a large amount of slack for little benefit, therefore, a slow reduction of inflation with mild slack has appeared optimal.[2]

In comparison with the precise objectives of policy, the large dis-
crepancies between the results and the targets and the wide swings in
business activity have been discouraging. When the Vietnam inflation

---

[1] *Economic Report of the President*, 1978, p. 5.

[2] The policy argument for reducing inflation slowly is discussed in Phillip Cagan,
"The Reduction of Inflation and the Magnitude of Unemployment," in William
Fellner, ed., *Contemporary Economic Problems 1977* (Washington, D.C.: American
Enterprise Institute, 1977), pp. 41–50.

stepped up in early 1966, it was initially cut down by monetary restraint imposed during the second half of that year. But the monetary authorities, fearful of precipitating a business recession, switched to stimulus in early 1967 and the inflation revived. By 1969 inflation was firmly entrenched and escalating. The monetary restraint applied in 1969 was stronger than in 1966 and this time precipitated a recession in 1970, but the reduction in inflation appeared to be slight up to August 1971 when price and wage controls were imposed. In the meantime, monetary policy stimulated the economy during and following the 1970 recession to remove all but the minimum amount of slack thought sufficient to reduce inflation. The stimulus was carried too far, in part because policy was misled by the umbrella of controls, and by the end of 1972 the overexpansion of domestic aggregate demand was joined by worldwide inflationary pressures to produce an explosion of prices in 1973–1974. The ensuing disruption and confusion in business activity brought on a severe business contraction from the fourth quarter of 1973 to the first quarter of 1975. The considerable slack remaining in the economy after the contraction was viewed as excessive, and policy makers sought to remove most of it, though the recovery of activity in fact proceeded slowly. Despite policy targets which have consistently called for mild slack in the economy to subdue inflation, the amplitude of fluctuations in activity have been large and increasing. The latest business contraction of 1973–1975 was the most severe in the post-World War II period.

Although recovery from the 1973–1975 contraction was slow and appreciable slack continued at least through the end of 1977, the inflation did not continue to decline.[3] To be sure, the explosion of prices in 1973–1974 reflected in part world influences which proved to be temporary, and the rate of inflation fell sharply during the business contraction. But the average inflation rates for 1976 and 1977, based on the consumer price index, remained in the 5 to 6 percent range, well above the 3½ percent for 1971–1972 and on a par with the previous high rates of 1969–1970. At the beginning of 1977 the Council of Economic Ad-

---

[3] Rates of increase of major price indexes in 1977 rose over 1976 but remained below 1975. The following rates in percent are from fourth quarter to fourth quarter, except for the consumer price index (CPI) which is December to December.

	1975	1976	1977
Consumer price index	7.0	4.9	6.7
Deflator for:			
GNP	7.5	4.7	5.8
Private business sector	8.0	4.1	5.6
Nonfarm business sector	8.0	4.9	5.6

visers (CEA) had predicted that the inflation rate would continue unchanged at 5 to 6 percent for the year, which turned out to be accurate.[4] Inflation rose to higher rates unexpectedly during the severe winter months, but it is not clear whether this made any difference for the year as a whole. The positive deviations of the inflation rate from the basic trend in the winter were subsequently offset by negative deviations later in the year.

The CEA's prediction, though correct, departed from the widely accepted view that a slack economy would reduce inflation. The CEA chose to ignore previous estimates of the relation between changes in the rate of inflation and excess unemployment based on post-World War II data. These previous estimates had implied that, given the average unemployment rate of 7 percent for 1977, the inflation rate would decline one percentage point during the year.[5] For 1978 the new CEA again concludes that, apart from the effect of higher social security taxes and minimum wages, "prices would be expected to rise this year at a rate of 6 percent or somewhat above—the underlying rate for the past 2½ years."[6] Unit labor costs are projected to continue rising at an unchanged rate from 1977, and profit margins do not appear large enough to provide room for a decline which would allow prices to rise less than the rise in unit labor costs. Hence no progress against inflation is seen as likely to occur until these basic trends change. The CEA's projection seemed to imply that inflation would not be reduced by the previously accepted policy of maintaining slack in the economy, nor could inflation even be prevented from increasing in the unlucky event of supply shortages or excess aggregate demand.

The theory that economic slack reduces inflation was unquestioned for over a decade but is no longer widely accepted as viable. In recent years forecasters have predicted little or no decline in inflation despite their predictions of continued slack in the economy. Some prominent economists, doubtful of the desirability of traditional monetary restraints and even of straightforward price and wage controls, have proposed a system of taxes and subsidies to induce restraint in wage and price setting.[7] Another prominent economist with experience as a price controls administrator points to the regulatory morass and doubtful

---

[4] Council of Economic Advisers, *Annual Report*, 1977, p. 41.

[5] See Cagan, "The Reduction of Inflation," pp. 21–26.

[6] CEA, *Annual Report*, 1978, p. 80.

[7] Walter Heller, Arthur Okun, Robert Solow, James Tobin, Henry Wallich, and Sidney Weintraub, Letter to the Editor, *New York Times*, March 12, 1978. See also Nancy A. Jianakoplos, "A Tax-Based Incomes Policy (TIP): What's It All About?" *Federal Reserve Bank of St. Louis Review*, vol. 60 (February 1978), pp. 8–12, and the discussions by Gottfried Haberler and Herbert Stein in this volume.

Figure 1

QUARTERLY RATE OF CHANGE OF CONSUMER PRICE INDEX,
1947–1977

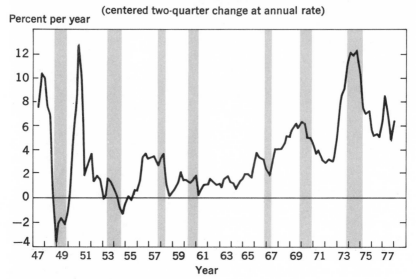

Note: Business contractions are shaded.
Source: Department of Labor, Bureau of Labor Statistics.

success of such a system.[8] The fact that these proposals are even seriously considered is a symptom of the low confidence with which our capability of subduing inflation is now viewed.

Was the previously widely accepted presumption that the inflation rate is related to the amount of economic slack justified? Casual inspection of the post-World War II data does raise doubts. Figure 1 presents two-quarter changes in the consumer price index at annual rates plotted quarterly from 1947 to 1977. The figure shows periods of expansion and contraction in general business activity. The dates of business cycles are those of the National Bureau of Economic Research with the addition of the minor downturn from the fourth quarter of 1966 to the second quarter of 1967, which did not qualify as a full-fledged recession but produced a significant effect on prices. Apart from the upward trend since 1965, the inflation rate displays a typical pattern within each cycle. A steep drop in the rate of change during recessions (even below zero in the earlier cycles) is followed by a sharp

---

[8] Gardner Ackley, "Okun's New Tax-Based Incomes-Policy Proposal," *Economic Outlook USA* (Ann Arbor: Survey Research Center, The University of Michigan, Winter 1978), pp. 8–9.

recovery in the first part of the ensuing business expansion. The recovery in the rate tends to level off in the later stages of expansions and finally to decline, usually before the next downturn in business.[9] This pattern is also characteristic of prices in earlier business cycles.[10]

The latest two recessions display the same pattern but with a delayed peak or trough in the inflation rate. In 1973–1975 the rate rose through most of the business contraction; it then declined well into the business recovery, as it did in 1971–1972. The upturn in the rate in 1971–1972 was delayed partly or wholly by price and wage controls instituted in August 1971. Moreover, most of the price increases prevented by the controls may have been posted later.[11] (The recorded price increases in the data may also understate the actual increases owing to the controls.) When most of the controls were removed in January 1973, prices rose sharply. A substantial part of the rise in 1973 and 1974 reflected temporary world influences on basic commodities (feed grains and metals as well as petroleum). When these influences abated in 1975, the inflation rate came down rapidly, which countered the normal tendency of inflation rates to rise in a business recovery. The rise in the inflation rate in the first part of 1978 suggests that the normal tendency is now appearing, though this rise also reflects a reduction of economic slack to levels that have traditionally marked the beginning of renewed inflationary pressures. The altered timing in the last two cycles may therefore reflect special developments and not indicate a change in cyclical pattern that will be repeated.

Whether the cyclical pattern has changed or not, it is evident from the historical record that the rate of inflation is not to be explained simply by the amount of slack in the economy. Full employment of resources is not normally reached until late in business expansions. If a simple relation existed between the inflation rate and economic slack, the rate would continue to decline until the later stages of business expansions when slack finally begins to disappear. Actually, as the figure shows, the inflation rate fluctuates over business cycles in a procyclical pattern and begins to rise early in business recoveries at or shortly after the trough in activity. The only continuing declines in the

[9] This pattern of price behavior has long been noted by business cycle analysts. For example, see Geoffrey H. Moore, *The Cyclical Behavior of Prices*, Report 384 (Washington, D.C.: Bureau of Labor Statistics, 1971), and "Lessons of the 1973–1976 Recession and Recovery," in William Fellner, ed., *Contemporary Economic Problems 1977* (Washington, D.C.: American Enterprise Institute, 1977), especially pp. 141–158.

[10] See Frederick C. Mills, *The Behavior of Prices* (New York: National Bureau of Economic Research, 1927).

[11] See Michael Darby, "The U.S. Economic Stabilization Program of 1971–74," *The Illusion of Wage and Price Controls* (Vancouver, B.C.: Fraser Institute, 1976).

rate, apart from business contractions, are in 1951–1952 following the sharp run-up of prices at the outbreak of the Korean War and in the early recovery stage of the last two cycles. The first of the latter two exceptions appears to be attributable to price controls and the second to foreign influences.

The theory that the reduction of inflation depends upon the amount of economic slack evolved in the 1960s from earlier theories of price behavior. The 1960s theory was a departure from traditional views and appeared for a time to rectify certain of their deficiencies. Its own deficiencies have in turn led to new theories of price behavior.

Old and New Theories of Price Behavior

Standard economic theory teaches that markets adjust to demand and supply with a rise in prices when demand exceeds potential supply and a decline in prices when demand falls short of potential supply. This was the virtually universal view of price behavior up to the 1930s and is still, with qualifications, commonly held. Strictly interpreted, it implies that the level of prices should generally rise in business expansions and decline in business contractions, propelled by associated fluctuations in aggregate demand. Such behavior is most clearly exemplified by prices sold on organized exchanges, such as agricultural products and basic commodities, and those sold in highly competitive markets. These prices are highly flexible, even volatile, and respond quickly to the shifting forces of demand and supply.

It has long been recognized, however, that prices of many other products, particularly manufactures and services, display considerably less flexibility and often decline quite slowly in the face of slack market conditions. Price inflexibility has often been viewed as somehow unnatural. In the 1930s Gardiner Means gained attention with his theory that inflexible prices were "administered" by producers in disregard of market conditions and thus did not respond to cyclical changes in demand.[12] Such behavior was attributed to the "market power" of producers, which they wielded to enhance their profits (exactly how was never clear). The prime example of inflexibility, of course, is wages, which have always displayed an extreme stickiness in the face of declining employment and even mass unemployment. It was no doubt the

---

[12] Gardiner C. Means, *Industrial Prices and Their Relative Inflexibility*, Senate Doc. 13, 74th Congress, 1st session, 1935. See also *Hearings on Administered Prices*, pt. 9, Senate Subcommittee on Antitrust and Monopoly, 86th Congress, 1st session, 1959, pp. 4745–4760; and National Resources Committee, *The Structure of the American Economy*, pt. 2 (Washington, D.C., 1939), p. 143.

inflexibility of wages in Britain during the mass unemployment of the 1920s that led Keynes largely to ignore cyclical changes in prices and wages in his influential *General Theory of Employment, Interest, and Money*, published in 1936. He assumed that wages and prices were constant when aggregate demand declined; and, though he acknowledged that they often increased when aggregate demand rose, the increase played no role in his theory. As so often happens with an influential work, the assumption made for simplification became widely accepted as fact and extended. For years thereafter theoretical economics usually treated price and wage levels in macro models of the economy as generally fixed until aggregate demand becomes excessive and then pulls them up. This view gained further currency in the 1950s with the notion that downward rigidity characterized wages and many prices—which meant that they never declined, even when markets were slack. Such price behavior was condemned in the 1950s as the major reason for the creeping inflation of that decade. If prices rose in the later stages of business expansions when demand was strong and failed to decline during business contractions, the price level would rise from cycle to cycle, and its long-run trend would be persistently and inexorably upward.[13] Shifts in demand among sectors of the economy, increasing prices in some and failing—because of downward rigidity—to reduce them in others, would have the same effect of raising the overall level of prices.[14] Downward rigidity was thought to be at variance with the normal behavior of prices in competitive markets; it reflected the inertia of custom in economic behavior and, since the 1930s, allegedly the growth of labor unions, product oligopolies, and the institutional rigidities of regulation.

By the end of the 1960s it began to appear that downward rigidity was only half the problem. Prices and wages could continue rising, and not merely fail to decline, when demand was slack. The theory that developed to account for such behavior combined a Phillips curve with price expectations. As described by the Phillips curve, prices respond to excess or deficient demand too slowly to keep markets cleared. A shortfall in aggregate demand, for example, produces a gap at prevailing prices between demand and the potential supply of output. The slack generates pressures for prices to fall below their trend path. Since prices respond slowly, markets in the meantime remain slack. What prevents prices and wages from adjusting rapidly to clear markets and

---

[13] Arthur F. Burns, *Prosperity Without Inflation* (New York: Fordham University Press, 1957).

[14] Charles L. Schultze, "Recent Inflation in the United States," U.S. Congress, Joint Economic Committee, *Study of Employment, Growth, and Price Levels*, Study Paper no. 1, 86th Congress, 1st session (September 1959).

reduce the gap to zero? The main reasons usually given are that changes in market conditions may at first be viewed as temporary, and firms find it costly and awkward to adjust prices to temporary fluctuations in demand and supply; that explicit and more often implicit contracts bind firms to offer their products and purchase resources at a predetermined price or to make changes only under specified conditions, particularly with respect to wages; and that firms in all but highly competitive industries seek to coordinate prices (without overt collusion) so as to avoid the confusion to buyers and the disarray in the market of selling the same product at different prices. For all these reasons prices are constrained from deviating from the expected equilibrium path. Unanticipated disturbances and short-run fluctuations in demand are largely ignored, and firms base selling prices on their unit costs of production at a standard level of output. They rely on these unit costs as an indicator of the long-run equilibrium path of prices likely to prevail in the industry.

The gradual response of prices to a gap between demand and supply is expressed in the Phillips relationship by the dependence of the rate of change of prices upon the size of the gap. But this dependence does not explain why prices rise when demand falls short of potential supply and is deficient by any reasonable measure. Such behavior is explained by expectations. When the growth trend of nominal aggregate demand exceeds that of output, the expected equilibrium path of wages and prices has an upward trend. Economic decisions are geared to this expected upward trend of prices. Deviations of aggregate demand from the expected trend are generally not anticipated. A fall in aggregate demand in a business recession, for example, reduces the actual rate of price increases below the trend rate. Unless the recession is unusually severe, however, most prices continue rising, though at a slower rate. During business expansions prices rise faster than the trend rate. As long as the growth trend in aggregate demand does not change from cycle to cycle, long-run expectations are confirmed and the trend rate is maintained. A persistent deviation above or below the trend would indicate a change in the trend, however, and lead gradually to the revision of expectations.

Expectations are also influenced by the monetary regime and political environment in which monetary and fiscal policies operate. The gold standard was less inflationary than managed currencies, and expectations under the present managed currency system undoubtedly take that difference into account. There is evidence that prices have gradually become less responsive to changes in aggregate demand in the business cycles since World War II. This diminishing responsiveness is caused in part, no doubt, by a decline in the expected capability of monetary and fiscal policies to contain inflation, as demonstrated by the accommodation of higher and higher rates of inflation.[15] Although the statistical analysis reported below ignores changes over time in the way expectations are formed, there is no intention to deny the importance of such changes.

The rate of change of prices at any time, $\dot{p}_t$ (where the overhead dot denotes the rate of change), may therefore be represented by two influences: (1) the pressure of the concurrent gap between demand and potential supply—deficient or excess demand as measured by the difference between the actual rate of unemployment of resources, U_t, and the full-employment rate of unemployment, $\overline{U}$; and (2) the anticipated trend path of prices, $\dot{p}_t^e$, which has been incorporated into wage contracts and past pricing decisions and so raises input costs as it is passed along the production pipeline:

$$[1] \qquad \dot{p}_t = F(U_t - \overline{U}) + \dot{p}_t^e.$$

This is the standard Phillips curve combined with expectations. F is a function which declines as $U_t - \overline{U}$ increases. The coefficient of $\dot{p}^e$ is unity on the assumption that there is no long-run trade-off between inflation and unemployment. The equation summarizes the view that policy can reduce the inflation rate by restraining aggregate demand, in which the amount of restraint is measured by the amount of slack that results. If $\dot{p}$ is thereby kept below $\dot{p}^e$, $\dot{p}^e$ will eventually be revised downward, after which the slack can be removed and $\dot{p}$ and $\dot{p}^e$ will be equal at a reduced rate of inflation.

When applied to experience in 1977, such an equation, as noted earlier, seems to suggest that inflation should have declined. In that year $\overline{U}$ was about 6 percent of the total labor force. This may seem high by past standards, but the rate of unemployment at which inflation neither increases nor decreases has been rising because structural changes in the labor force have added to recorded unemployment. The actual unemployment rate averaged 7 percent in 1977, giving unemployment in excess of $\overline{U}$ of one percentage point. (Most estimates of excess unemployment for 1977 were even higher.) With this excess unemployment the actual rate of inflation should have been below the expected rate, which would then gradually decline, thus reducing the actual rate for any given amount of excess unemployment. But the inflation rate did not decline in 1977. The CPI increased at the same 4.3 percent annual rate from the third to the fourth quarters of both 1976

---

[15] See Phillip Cagan, *The Hydra-Headed Monster: The Problem of Inflation in the United States* (Washington, D.C.: American Enterprise Institute, 1974).

and 1977. Year over year the rate actually rose, from 4.9 percent in 1976 (December to December) to 6.7 percent in 1977. (Most forecasts for 1978, including the CEA's, see no decline in the inflation rate, but, as noted, this is not inconsistent with the above equation. Unemployment fell to the 6 percent level in the first part of 1978, which by the preceding estimate of $\overline{U}$ is the full-employment level and puts the economy at the threshold of increasing inflationary pressures.)

What explanation can be given for a rise in the *rate* of inflation or even constancy early in business recoveries, when aggregate demand still falls short of the potential supply? Prices of crude materials, which are highly sensitive to market conditions, contribute to this rise (see Figure 2). They typically decline sharply in business recessions (that is, have negative rates of change) and then begin to rise as the forces of recovery spread through the economy. They exemplify the behavior that economic theory attributes to competitive prices. Their fluctuations contribute to procyclical movements in the rate of change of a general price index. But they do not dominate the behavior of the general price level and by themselves cannot account for its procyclical fluctuations. The inflation rate for most intermediate and finished goods also displays a procyclical pattern. Crude materials make up too small a part of the total cost of production of most intermediate and finished goods to dominate the movements in their input costs.

One explanation for a rising inflation rate when slack demand exists pertains to the price expectations term in equation [1]. A reduction in $\dot{p}^e$ is presumed to occur whenever $\dot{p}$ falls below $\dot{p}^e$. If $\dot{p}^e$ changes too slowly, however, the cyclical fluctuations in the first term of equation [1] will dominate to produce a procyclical pattern in $\dot{p}$. A slack-induced reduction of inflation that outlasts the business cycle therefore requires that $\dot{p}^e$ respond to $\dot{p}$ and that the net effect be downward. If over the business cycle $\dot{p}$ rises above $\dot{p}^e$ as much as it falls below, there will be no net reduction in $\dot{p}^e$. Inflation has escalated since 1965 because U on the average has been below $\overline{U}$. The reduction of inflation requires that for a while U be above $\overline{U}$ on the average.

This relationship can be expressed in simple mathematical terms which provide a form for regression analysis. If price expectations are revised gradually, an adaptive revision may be described by

$$[2] \qquad \frac{d\dot{p}^e_t}{dt} = b(\dot{p}_t - \dot{p}^e_t),$$

which by [1] equals bF. The coefficient b may change over time, but for simplicity it is assumed to be constant. In theory it can be any positive number. To incorporate such adaptive expectations into the modi-

Figure 2

QUARTERLY RATE OF CHANGE OF WHOLESALE PRICES,
1947–1977
(centered two-quarter change at annual rate)

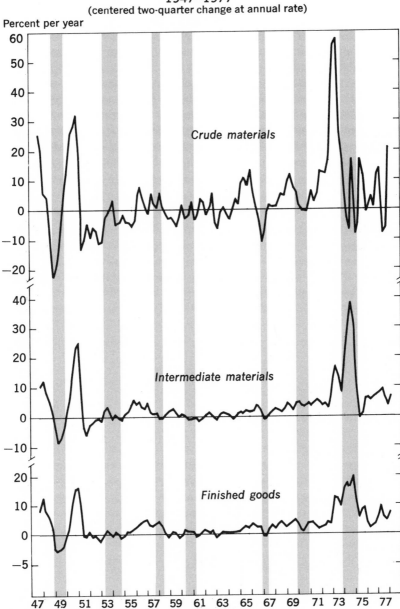

Note: Business contractions are shaded.
Source: Department of Labor, Bureau of Labor Statistics.

fied Phillips relationship, equation [1] is differentiated with respect to time,

$$[3] \qquad \frac{d\dot{p}_t}{dt} = F' \frac{dU_t}{dt} + \frac{d\dot{p}_t^e}{dt}$$

and [2] substituted into [3],

$$[4] \qquad \frac{d\dot{p}_t}{dt} = F' \frac{dU_t}{dt} + bF.$$

If the F function is a simple proportional relationship $F = a(U_t - \overline{U})$, and differentials are treated as discrete first differences, and $\overline{U}$ is constant, then

$$[5] \qquad \dot{p}_t - \dot{p}_{t-1} = a(U_t - U_{t-1}) + ba(U_t - \overline{U}).$$

An indication of the effect of slack demand on the inflation rate that outlasts the business cycle is given by estimates of ba, which is the product of the speed of revision of price expectations, b, and the cyclical effect of slack on the inflation rate, a. Estimates of this effect of slack demand are presented below.[16]

A different way of formulating the effect of slack demand on inflation is suggested by the new theory of rational expectations. This theory starts from the presumption that expectations formed about

---

[16] A similar equation was derived by Lucas Papademos, "Optimal Aggregate Employment Policy" (Ph.D. diss., Massachusetts Institute of Technology, September 1977), p. 23 (equation 23). The equation usually given in the Phillips curve literature is quite different in theory and implications. It has the same right side as [5] above but with the inflation rate rather than its change on the left. (For a review of empirical work on such equations, see R. A. Gordon, "Wages, Prices, and Unemployment, 1900–1970," *Industrial Relations*, vol. 14 [October 1975], pp. 273–301.) Such an equation is unable to explain rising prices in a recession since both variables are then positive, and, given the appropriate negative coefficients, the two terms will be negative. What the standard Phillips curve lacks is a term representing *long-run* price expectations, which equation [5] includes.

Much of the literature finds that the rate of change of wages is more closely related to changes in the unemployment rate than to the rate itself. (See E. Kuh, "A Productivity Theory of Wage Levels—An Alternative to the Phillips Curve," *Review of Economic Studies*, vol. 34, no. 4 [October 1967], pp. 333–360.) In the literature the change in the unemployment rate has been interpreted as reflecting *short-run* expectations of changes in demand. (See William G. Bowen and R. Albert Berry, "Unemployment Conditions and Movements of the Money Wage Level," *Review of Economics and Statistics*, vol. 45 [May 1963], pp. 163–172.) This implies a relation between changes in the rate of change of wages and the second derivative of the unemployment variable. Such a relation has no importance for the effect of slack demand on inflation as formulated here.

economic developments make full use of all available information. Given the incentives to market participants to use information to full advantage, expectations of price changes and other variables will not be subject to repeated errors of forecast in the same direction insofar as available information could avert such biased forecasts, though errors can of course be large because of developments that no one is able to foresee. The theory evolved in reaction to the assumption, commonly made in economic analysis, that expectations adjust slowly to new developments as new information is absorbed gradually through an adaptive error-learning process. Slow revisions of expectations produce a series of similar and avoidable errors during the time in which new information is being acquired by economic agents and behavior has not yet fully adjusted to it. Such lags in response may pertain to habitual behavior, but, when substantial costs can be avoided or profits are to be made by fully utilizing new information, economic agents will try to avoid lags in revising expectations. New information will thus be reflected rapidly in prices that are influenced by expectations of future development. Rapid—virtually instantaneous—use of new information is certainly characteristic of commodity and financial exchanges, where expectations of future movements are critical and new information is extremely important. Analysis of price movements on exchanges indicates that errors of expectations, insofar as they can be measured, are unsystematic, essentially unpredictable, and reflect only new developments which were not foreseen. Such prices are characterized by jumps from one position to another, because everyone is aware of a new development that justifies a change in price, and all transactions occur immediately at the changed price.

In its extreme form the theory of rational expectations requires that prices clear markets at every moment. Since a price that does not equate demand and supply is subject to pressures to change until it does so, market participants acquire and make rational use of information about such pressures and do not transact at a price that they know is subject to further change in a particular direction. Prices so determined always equate all demand and supply offers at the moment. The theory offers no explanations for most prices and wages in the economy, which change smoothly and usually follow the same trend for months at a time in markets often characterized by persistent slack or excess demand. Most prices and wages are either subject to institutional constraints or, if influenced by "rational" expectations, not as yet fully understandable by economic theory.

But a modified form of the theory can be espoused which seems more realistic and accommodates prices which do not clear markets. Faced with a fall in demand, an individual firm or industry, given its costs of production and the desire to maximize profits or minimize losses, will not cut prices far enough to prevent a decline in its sales in real terms and the necessity of reducing its output. Explicit or implicit contracts to supply labor and materials at predetermined wages and prices are one reason for lack of market clearing and a decline in sales, but it seems doubtful that such contracts are the only reason. Another likely reason is the sheer complexity of a full adjustment of the entire price system to changes in demand. The restoration of demand to its original level in real terms only through changes in prices, after a general fall in aggregate demand in a recession, would require a quite large decline in the *general level* of prices and wages, in which each individual firm and industry plays a small part.[17] Individual firms and industries do not know to what extent deflation in the whole economy will reverse a decline in aggregate real demand, and we may suppose that they act on the basis of the demand they face at the moment. There is no reason to suppose that rational expectations of developments elsewhere in the economy, of which individual firms and industries can have only limited knowledge, would significantly affect prices in individual markets, nor that such knowledge would therefore imply an immediate fall in all prices to a level that would restore a shortfall in demand to its original real level. When demand falls, individual firms and industries will cut prices and output, and their action may still be based on rational expectations in that their estimate of sales and the prices that will prevail is neither high nor low on the average. Their reduction of output will, of course, contribute to a continuation of the decline in aggregate demand. With each fall in demand, prices and output will be cut further. If expectations are rational, however, there is no systematic delay in the response of prices to changes in demand. Hence the level of demand will determine the level, not the rate of change, of prices.[18] Such a relationship is formulated below.

Rational expectations may thus be made consistent with the existence of slack markets, but an explanation of rising prices in a recession is still missing. To explain that anomaly, we may also suppose that the anticipated long-run trend of prices is upward, and price changes over the business cycle occur as cyclical deviations from the trend. Then it is

---

[17] This is the implication of the theory of aggregate disequilibrium. The spillover effects of reduced output and employment in one industry make demand lower in other industries. The restoration requires an increase in the purchasing power of money balances through a decline in the price level—an increase sufficient to raise the demand for goods and services to the original level of expenditures in real terms.

[18] A rational expectations model with this relationship is presented in Allan H. Meltzer, "Anticipated Inflation and Unanticipated Price Change," *Journal of Money, Credit, and Banking,* vol. 9 (February 1977), pp. 182–205.

possible that cyclical declines in prices combined with the rising trend can produce prices that rise in a recession—a rise that is less than the trend, to be sure, but a rise nevertheless. The long-run trend would presumably also be subject to rational expectations. The long-run expectations would be based on the anticipated trend of prices from cycle to cycle, after the cyclical ups and downs are netted out. An upward trend would affect prices in recessions as well as expansions for at least two reasons. First, an anticipated rising trend would be incorporated into price and wage contracts for resource inputs and would continue to inflate costs in recessions. Second, the price trend would influence the cyclical price at which storable materials and goods as well as some labor services would be supplied; sellers would withhold supplies as prices in a recession fell further and further below the anticipated trend price. The withholding of supplies would limit the decline in prices during a recession and would even cause prices to continue rising if the anticipated trend were rising fast enough.

Under rational expectations, the anticipated trend of prices would presumably not be influenced by anticipated developments within the business cycle that were reflected in cyclical price changes; rational expectations allow for cyclical fluctuations. But trends can and do change without being clearly foreseen. Rational economic agents will revise their expectations of the price trend when they become aware of a change occurring or about to occur, for example, a business recession more severe or a period of slack demand more prolonged than expected. Hence slack demand may also affect anticipated price trends under rational expectations, but the effect would depend upon the amount of slack in the economy both currently and in the past. Certainly it would not depend upon the current amount only, since the current amount would be largely indistinguishable from expected cyclical fluctuations. This means that the expected trend of prices would be related to the cumulative amount of slack over an extended period. Such a relation contrasts with the modified Phillips equation, in which expected price changes can be related to the discrepancy between actual and expected changes (and this discrepancy can in turn be related to the current amount of slack). The two theories differ because, in accordance with the slow adjustment of prices underlying the Phillips curve, economic decisions are based, not on rational expectations of current price movements, but on an adaptive error-learning process in which current price movements contain relevant unused information for the revision of expectations.

We can express the theory of price behavior under rational expectations in a mathematical form for regression analysis. The theory implies that the *level* of prices depends upon both the expected price level and the *level* of demand or, equivalently, the gap between demand and potential supply as indicated by unemployed resources; namely,

[6] $$p_t = G(U_t - \overline{U}) + p_t^e,$$

where the symbols are the same as those introduced above and G is a function which declines when $U_t - U$ increases. When differentiated with respect to time, the relationship becomes

[7] $$\dot{p}_t = G'\left(\frac{dU_t}{dt}\right) + \dot{p}_t^e,$$

where as above the overhead dots denote the rate of change on the assumption that the price variables are measured in logarithms.

On the proposition that the expected price trend is influenced by the cumulative amount of slack over an extended period,

[8] $$\dot{p}_t^e = [\text{noncyclical trend of prices}] + c_0(U_t - \overline{U}) + c_1(U_{t-1} - \overline{U})$$
$$+ \ldots + c_n(U_{t-n} - \overline{U}).$$

The noncyclical trend of prices may be represented by the average inflation rate over the length of a typical business cycle, which is roughly four years. Whether the average is a little more or less than four years will not materially affect the results. Substituting [8] into [7] and assuming a proportional G function and discrete first differences, we have

[9] $$\dot{p}_t - \sum_{i=1}^{16} \frac{\dot{p}_{t-i}}{16} = a(U_t - U_{t-1}) + c_0(U_t - \overline{U}) + c_1(U_{t-1} - \overline{U})$$
$$+ \ldots + c_n(U_{t-n} - \overline{U})$$

where the average rate of inflation, which has a coefficient of unity, has been transferred to the left side of the equation. The coefficient a of the first term reflects the temporary effect of changes in slack demand on the inflation rate. The lasting effect over a business cycle is given by the sum of the c coefficients.[19]

---

[19] An alternative formulation suggested by other rational expectations models would be to use past monetary growth and other basic determinants of the price level, known to rational economic agents, as indicators of the expected noncyclical trend of prices. Then, in theory, slack demand would be superfluous and would not affect the inflation rate. (For example, see Meltzer, "Anticipated Inflation and Unanticipated Price Change.") In such models, however, a decline of monetary growth and consequent reduction in inflation still produces a period of slack demand. Equation [9] can be interpreted as reflecting the amount of slack which is associated in such models with reductions in the expected trend of prices.

Figure 3

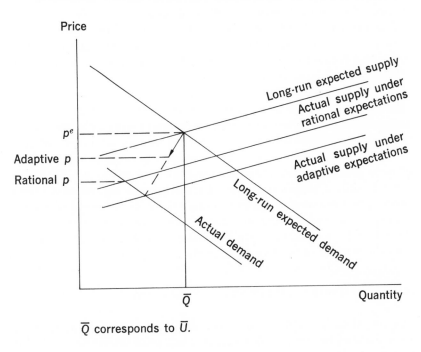

RESPONSE OF PRICE TO DOWNWARD SHIFTS OF DEMAND
AND SUPPLY: ADAPTIVE AND RATIONAL EXPECTATIONS

$\bar{Q}$ corresponds to $\bar{U}$.

Collecting terms into a form suitable for regression analysis, we have

$$[10] \quad \dot{p}_t - \sum_{i=1}^{16} \frac{\dot{p}_{t-i}}{16} = (a + c_0)(U_t - \bar{U}) + (c_1 - a)(U_{t-1} - \bar{U}) \\ + c_2(U_{t-2} - \bar{U}) + \ldots + c_n(U_{t-n} - \bar{U}).$$

In theory n should be the length of a business cycle, but for statistical convenience most of the estimates of this equation, presented below, are based on only six U terms. Results for fifteen and seventeen terms, however, are not dissimilar.

The difference between rational and adaptive price behavior is illustrated in Figure 3. The price at any particular time is influenced by the expected shift in demand and supply schedules owing to inflation and by deviations of the actual schedules from the expected ones. Only one set of expected schedules is shown in the figure, although rational and adaptive expectations would not ordinarily have the same set.

Given the expected price under either theory of behavior, the actual demand and supply will cause the price to deviate from the expected price. The adaptive response will result in a price that partially reflects the actual change in demand and supply in relation to the expected change. The rational response will result in a price which equates actual demand and supply. As argued above, this rational price will not ordinarily prevent a fall in output because contracts predetermine some prices and because supplies may be held off the market in anticipation of more favorable prices in the future.

Therefore, when the earliest and the most recent theories of price behavior are modified to account for procyclical fluctuations in the inflation rate, they are not necessarily inconsistent with a Phillips type of relation between the inflation rate and the amount of excess capacity. As suggested above, however, the correlation between procyclical fluctuations in the inflation rate and in the amount of excess capacity is evidence of only a temporary effect of slack in reducing inflation. For a lasting effect economic slack must reduce the expected trend rate of inflation. Let us examine the record for evidence of an effect of economic slack on price expectations. In estimating this effect, we shall analyze the data in terms of the two theories discussed above.[20]

Statistical Estimates of the Effect of Slack Demand

The two theories formulated above allow for a noncyclical effect of slack demand on the inflation rate through price expectations. In the first theory the *current* amount of slack determines long-run expectations, but in the second it does not because it is largely reflected in short-run expectations and the current price level. Equations [5] and [10], each based on one of the two theories, were designed to distinguish the cyclical and noncyclical effects of slack demand on the inflation rate. Statistical regressions of these equations were fitted to U.S. quarterly data beginning in the first quarter of 1953, which avoids the large price swings associated with the Korean War, and ending in the fourth quarter of 1977, the latest date available, and alternatively in

---

[20] Although equations [5] and [10] have many apparent similarities, they differ crucially in the form of the left-hand variable. Their difference does not, however, provide an acceptable statistical test for choosing between the two theories. The fit of these equations to the data is not sufficiently close to produce a clear preference for one or the other, nor to indicate whether or not certain forms of the variables or their lags should be included in the regression equation. A satisfactory test of the two theories of price behavior requires different techniques and evidence from that provided here. Nevertheless, we may examine the reasonableness of the estimates from the two theories for the effect of slack demand on the inflation rate.

1969 to exclude the last two business cycles. Various series were used to provide a broad indication of how the parameter estimates are affected by different measures of prices and slack demand. The results are presented in the appendix to this chapter.

The regression equations do not in general fit the data closely, as is evidenced by the low levels of significance of many of the regression coefficients. (The total correlation coefficients are high simply because they include an adjustment for serial correlation in the error terms; they have not been reported.) Our principle interest here is the values of the coefficients as estimates of the effect of slack demand on the inflation rate. The lack of a close fit does not appear to bias the estimates of the coefficients and so does not invalidate the statistical results, though it does of course widen the range of error of the estimates.

For equation [5] the estimates of ba represent the noncyclical effect of slack demand on the inflation rate. These are reproduced in Table 1 for the regressions using the unemployment rate to measure slack demand.[21] The estimated effect of slack demand is similar for the consumer price index and wholesale finished goods prices (and is statistically significant, as shown in the appendix, Table 3, except for the wholesale price series over the shorter period). The estimated effect differs for the other price measures. The estimates for wholesale crude and intermediate materials prices are erratic and reflect their lack of regular cyclical pattern. The estimates for average hourly earnings are quite small, reflecting the lower response of wages to the business cycle. The estimated effect for the GNP deflator is also small (and actually nonexistent in the 1953–1969 regression), apparently because of its broader coverage of industries.[22] Many of the results are not strongly significant for the basic reason that moderate slack works slowly and its effect is hard to identify. But it seems to exist overall in these data, and the estimates appear credible in magnitude.

If we tentatively accept the results for the consumer price index and wholesale finished goods, which are statistically the strongest, as the clearest indication of the size of such an effect, the estimates are around 0.2 and imply that excess unemployment maintained at one per-

---

[21] The other measures of slack give a similar result if we note that they register the same slack with two and a half to three times the magnitude shown by the unemployment rate.

[22] Results for the GNP deflator of the private nonfarm sector (not shown) are similar. In a recent study of 1954–1971, Robert J. Gordon ("The Impact of Aggregate Demand on Prices," *Brookings Papers on Economic Activity*, no. 3 [Washington, D.C.: Brookings Institution, 1975], pp. 613–662) also finds, for the GNP chain deflator of the private sector excluding food and energy, that current and lagged changes in the GNP gap affect the inflation rate while the current and past levels do not.

Table 1
ESTIMATES OF CHANGES IN VARIOUS MEASURES OF THE INFLATION RATE FROM EXCESS UNEMPLOYMENT, EQUATION [5]

(change per quarter in annual percentage rate from excess
unemployment of one percentage point)

Measures of the Inflation Rate	Period of Estimate	Total Change (ba)	Total Due to		Estimated Change in Inflation Rate for 1977 over 1976
			a	b	
Consumer price index	1953–69	−0.17	−0.70	0.24	−0.02
	1953–77	−0.23	−0.95	0.24	−0.21
GNP deflator	1953–69	0.01	−0.26	−0.04	—
	1953–77	−0.12	−0.57	0.21	+0.03
Wholesale crude materials	1953–69	−0.43	−0.23	1.87	−0.88
	1953–77	−0.02	−0.06	0.67	+0.33
Wholesale intermediate goods	1953–69	0.02	−0.58	−0.03	—
	1953–77	−0.13	−2.38	0.05	+1.44
Wholesale finished goods	1953–69	−0.20	−0.66	0.30	−0.13
	1953–77	−0.28	−1.22	0.23	−0.10
Average hourly earnings	1953–69	−0.05	−0.56	0.09	+0.10
	1953–77	−0.11	−0.52	0.21	−0.06

Note: The value of b is derived by dividing ba by a. Estimated change for 1977 over 1976 is a $(−0.65) + 4ba$ $(4.6 − \bar{U})$, where $\bar{U}$ for each row is given in Table 3. (The unemployment rate for prime-age men in 1977 was 4.6 percent, and the decline in the average level from 1976 to 1977 was 0.65.)

Dash (—) indicates not calculated because estimates of ba and b are of wrong sign.

Source: Based on regressions in appendix, Table 3, for unemployment rate of prime-age men.

centage point would reduce the annual inflation rate by 0.2 percentage points per quarter and by 0.8 percentage points per year. By this evidence the noncyclical trend of inflation is reduced by economic slack, but quite slowly when the amount of slack is moderate. The slowness of the effect reflects the small revision of the expected price change per period of time, shown by the value of b. The immediate effect, shown by a, is larger, but the part of the effect that has not been translated into a reduction of the expected price change disappears when the slack is removed.

The results in Table 1 seem to suggest that the effect of slack on inflation has increased in recent years; the estimates of ba generally have larger negative values for the full than for the shorter period. This would be consistent with the theory that the increasing variability of inflation rates in recent years has caused fluctuations in aggregate demand to be translated more into prices than into output (which would increase the value of a), contrary to evidence cited earlier that prices have become less responsive to the business cycle. The larger values of ba for the full period can indeed be attributed to a, which may, however, simply reflect the large rise and subsequent decline in the inflation rate in 1973–1975 stemming from the extraneous foreign influences. The estimates for average hourly earnings suggest that b is higher for the full period, but the overall effect shown by ba, though larger, remains low, indicative of the smaller and slower response of wages to economic slack compared with the response of prices. It is therefore doubtful that the effect of slack in reducing inflation has increased much at all, although there is no indication of a decrease either.

The failure of the inflation rate to decline continually when slack exists is reflected in the large negative value of a, which represents the cyclical effect of changes in slack and which dominates the noncyclical effect. In a business expansion the continued existence of slack works to reduce the expected rate of inflation, but, until the decline in slack slows down, the net effect can be no change or even an increase in the current inflation rate. The last column of Table 1 gives the change in the inflation rate as estimated by each regression for 1977. Despite the existence of substantial slack in the economy in 1977, but because of the decline in amount of slack, most of the estimates show a slight decline—practically no change—in the inflation rate for the year. Actually, as noted earlier, the inflation rate increased in 1977; this upward deviation from the equation suggests that the severe winter generated direct upward pressures on prices which were accommodated by aggregate-demand policy but did not affect the measures of excess unemployment.

The implications of the regressions can be derived for 1978, based on estimates of the slack that will exist. The CEA projects an unemployment rate for all workers of 6 to 6¼ percent for the end of 1978.[23] Since the rate in December 1977 was 6.4 percent, the implied average rate for 1978 is only slightly above 6 percent, close to the full-employment rate cited earlier. This would represent a decline of about

---

[23] CEA, *Annual Report*, 1978, p. 79.

Table 2
ESTIMATES OF CHANGES IN VARIOUS MEASURES OF THE INFLATION RATE FROM AVERAGE EXCESS UNEMPLOYMENT, EQUATION [10]

(change per indicated period in annual percentage rate from excess unemployment of one percentage point)

Measures of the Inflation Rate	Period of Estimate	Sum of c Coefficients (1)	Effect per year (0.37 × col. [1])[a] (2)	Effect over Business Cycle, Continuous Adjustments (1.72 × col. [1])[a] (3)
Consumer price index	1953–69	−0.80	−0.30	−1.38
	1953–77	−1.46	−0.54	−2.51
	1953–77	−0.99[b]	−0.37	−1.70
Wholesale finished goods	1953–69	−0.88	−0.33	−1.51
	1953–77	−1.87	−0.69	−3.22
Average hourly earnings	1953–69	−0.84	−0.31	−1.44
	1953–77	−0.78	−0.29	−1.34

[a] See footnote 24.
[b] Estimated from regression with fifteen terms of U.
Source: Appendix, Table 4.

three-fourths of a point from the average rate of 7 percent for 1977. (Although the results in Table 1 are based on the unemployment rate for prime-age men, we may assume that it will change roughly by the same amount as the rate for all workers.) According to the estimates for the consumer price index in Table 1, the decline in the unemployment rate would raise the annual inflation rate in 1978 over 1977 by a half to three-fourths of a percentage point, while the small average amount of excess unemployment in 1978 would reduce inflation very little. According to these estimates we shall have to look beyond 1978 for any progress in reducing inflation.

The results for equation [10], based on rational expectations, are presented in the appendix, Table 4, and summarized in Table 2. The sum of the c coefficients gives the lasting effect of slack demand in reducing the expected trend of prices. The additional c coefficients beyond the first two are not collectively significant statistically, and this remains true when the number of them in the regression is increased. Consequently, the estimate of their sum is subject to a wide range of error. The lack of significance may also mean that rational expectations are an inappropriate basis for describing these data, or it may possibly mean that expectations of the inflation trend cannot be adequately represented by past unemployment. We may nevertheless examine these estimates as an alternative indication of the effect of slack demand on inflation, since they suggest a slower response than does the adaptive expectations model.

The estimates of the sum of the c coefficients in Table 2 vary from 0.8 for the shorter period 1953–1969 to over 1.5 for the full period 1953–1977. The larger sum for the full period probably reflects the unusual fluctuations of 1973–1975, however. As the number of U terms in the regression is increased to provide a longer perspective on the cumulative effect of slack demand, the sum declines toward unity (third row of table). We may therefore take a value of unity or a little lower as the central estimate of the effect. The implications for the average inflation rate are shown in columns (2) and (3) of the table. Column (2) shows the effect per year for an assumed four-year business cycle. Column (3) shows the cumulative effect over a full business cycle of any length, under the likely assumption that adjustments in the expected trend are made continuously.[24] For the central estimate of the sum of c coefficients of unity in the third row, the annual inflation rate would be reduced by 0.37 percentage points per year for each one percentage point of average slack maintained over a business cycle, and reduced as much as 1.70 percentage points over the entire business cycle with continuous adjustments. This effect is about a half or less of the effect estimated above for adaptive expectations over the same length of time. Rational expectations have a smaller effect because it

---

[24] The sum of the c coefficients gives the estimated effect of excess unemployment on the difference between the current inflation rate and the noncyclical trend. For a business cycle of n periods in which this difference is maintained at C,

$$\dot{p}_t - \sum_{1}^{n} \frac{\dot{p}_{t-i}}{n} = \sum_{0}^{n} c_i(U_{t-i} - \bar{U}) = C,$$

the cumulative effect can be expressed by

$$\dot{p}_{t+n} = C\left(1 + \frac{1}{n}\right)^{n-1} \quad \text{and} \quad \sum_{1}^{n} \frac{\dot{p}_{t-i}}{n} = C\left(1 + \frac{1}{n}\right)^{n-1} - C.$$

For $n=16$ quarters, the average rate is $1.48C$ or $.37C$ per year.

The estimate of C is not affected greatly by changes in n beyond a small number, and we may assume C remains the same as n increases. In particular, we may derive the effect for continuous adjustments where the periods approach zero in length and n approaches infinity, for which the limit of $\left(1 + \frac{1}{n}\right)^{n-1}$ is e or 2.72.

Hence the total effect for a full cycle of continuous adjustments, which is independent of the length of the cycle, is $1.72C$.

is assumed that most of the cyclical fluctuation in slack demand is expected and already incorporated in the expected trend, and that only the cumulative amount of slack, if more or less than expected, affects the expected trend of prices.

Although these estimates show a small effect of slack demand, they pertain to the initial effect within the span of a business cycle; the longer-run effect could well be larger. Presumably the slack produced by a business recession will not reduce the expected trend of prices very much if it is expected that the pressure on prices of slack markets in the recession will be offset in the subsequent expansion. The recent cyclical fluctuations, in which the final stages of the expansion have encountered increasing inflationary pressures, give a rational basis for such an expectation. For policy makers to restrain inflation effectively given the recent history of failures, they must demonstrate over the course of a business cycle that the restraint will persist. Once this is demonstrated for one business cycle, however, the effect is likely to be considerably stronger in the next.[25] In the late 1950s the inflation rate was widely viewed as intractable because it was not eliminated by the recession of 1957–1958 (see Figures 1 and 2). Yet the subsequent business expansion did not overshoot, and the inflation rate remained lower than it had been in the previous expansion. Although the inflation stubbornly resisted further decline in the subsequent business contraction of 1960–1961, it rapidly disappeared during the second half of 1961 when the business recovery proved to be mild. With the benefit of hindsight, it appears that the inflation of the 1950s was finally conquered not so much by the business recessions as by the avoidance of renewed inflationary pressures during the business expansions.

The adaptive and rational models imply different time patterns for the effects of slack demand on the expected rate of inflation. The effects under adaptive expectations occur faster and, for a given initial period of excess unemployment, appear to be about twice as large. Given the cyclical fluctuations in slack demand over the business cycle, however, the initial change in the expected inflation rate will be partially or fully offset over a full cycle. Under rational expectations, although slack demand has an immediate effect on price levels, its effect on the expected trend of prices is slight initially, may even be negligible during a recession, and occurs mainly with a lag the length of the business cycle. But the response of the expected rate of inflation to slack demand is likely to be stronger—and this applies to adaptive expectations as well—when a change in aggregate-demand policy demonstrates

---

[25] This is emphasized in William Fellner, *Towards a Reconstruction of Macroeconomics* (Washington, D.C.: American Enterprise Institute, 1976).

that the change will be maintained by outlasting the course of a business cycle.

Although our statistical results slightly favor adaptive over rational expectations, it is not clear which model describes economic behavior more accurately. Actual behavior may well be a mix of both.

The Political Problem of Reducing Inflation

The statistical results add an important qualification to the proclaimed policy goal of reducing both inflation and unemployment. The goal can be accomplished only if the reduction of unemployment is not carried all the way to full employment but stops short of that goal and maintains some excess unemployment for a long period. No such limitation has been evident in the pursuit of the goal over the past decade. Business expansions, whether intended by policy or not, have carried aggregate demand up to and beyond the zone of increasing inflationary pressures. Policy makers have also set up an unattainable goal by claiming that cyclical rates of both inflation and unemployment can be reduced at the same time.

Although there are no economic barriers to reducing inflation, a political problem has erected a barrier. The problem centers on two implications of the economic relation between inflation and slack demand. First, changes in the amount of slack reflect cyclical fluctuations in aggregate demand which produce cyclical fluctuations in the rate of inflation. Restraint imposed on the growth in aggregate demand increases the amount of economic slack and reduces the inflation rate. But while the restraint is being applied the rate declines far more than can be maintained after the economy begins to recover. As the amount of slack declines, the inflation rate increases, which makes it appear as though the hard-earned gains against inflation are slipping away. In fact, however, most of those gains are temporary cyclical fluctuations and cannot be counted as reductions in the long-run inflation rate. The real progress against inflation is to be measured by the rate that prevails after slack has declined to an acceptable level. At that point the inflation rate can be somewhat lower, compared with the average for the previous cycle, because of the cumulative effect of economic slack during the business contraction and recovery. It is conceivable that fluctuations could be avoided by imposing an amount of slack which, once reached, is kept constant thereafter until the long-run rate of inflation has declined to an acceptable level. But fluctuations in business activity owing to policy measures as well as to other sources of cyclical fluctuations in the economy have not been avoided in the past and are well beyond our capability of avoiding in the foreseeable future. Since cyclical fluctuations in the inflation rate will surely continue, a "true" reduction in the rate would mean that the *expected* rate has declined, as implied by a decline in the actual rate between corresponding business cycle stages in which the amount of slack is the same.

A second implication of the relation between inflation and slack demand is an obvious one with touchy political consequences. It is that the reduction of inflation "almost" certainly requires slack demand. The qualification is added to cover the possibility implied by the theory of rational expectations that an announced and widely believed change in policy which reduced the growth path of nominal aggregate demand would immediately reduce the expected growth path and thereby its contribution to the trend of prices. An argument sometimes made for controls is that, if accompanied by announced restraints in aggregate-demand policy, they could help to reduce expected price changes along with the targeted decline in the inflation rate, thus avoiding the period of slack demand produced by a discrepancy between actual and expected price changes. The purpose of the controls would be to make the announced change in aggregate-demand policy believable, though in the light of past experience it is questionable whether they ever have or now would have such an effect. There is no doubt, however, that the stance and credibility of policy affects expectations. Market decisions about wages and prices are guided at least in part by rational expectations of the direction of policy. To the extent that prices behave according to the theory of rational expectations, the persistence of the trend rate of inflation in the face of slack demand is consistent with the proclaimed desire of policy makers to subdue inflation only if they are generally not believed to be capable of carrying it out. Since the evidence suggests that the economic capability exists, the lack of credibility concerns the political capability. In such circumstances and in view of our past experience, the desire to subdue inflation is obviously not enough and must be confirmed by performance. The conclusion appears inescapable, therefore, that the reduction of inflation requires the maintenance of slack demand, and the less that policy hides its intention to maintain it, the faster the reduction will be.

The political incentives to hide the intention have created serious barriers to achieving it. Hidden intentions can mislead economic agents into expecting higher inflation than policy measures are designed to allow, thus slowing down the reduction in the expected rate of inflation and holding back the reduction in the actual rate. In addition, policy makers are trapped into publicly adopting targets of economic slack which are unrealistic and, if pursued, unable to reduce inflation. The 4 percent level of unemployment held as a goal in the Humphrey-Hawkins bill can no longer be considered a reasonable estimate of the noninflationary rate of full employment—if it ever was. Budget projections in 1978 are also based on a full-employment rate of less than 5 percent. More realistic estimates, as noted, indicate that this rate is now close to 6 percent. If these higher estimates are correct and if policy makers mistakenly try to achieve a lower unemployment rate, it will not be possible to reduce the actual unemployment rate much below 6 percent. Nor will the widely deplored high rates for youths and minority groups be reduced much by any degree of economic stimulation that would conceivably be undertaken. But the attempt to achieve these unattainable goals would, of course, push the economy into the zone of increasing inflationary pressures. Even if realism prevails in the adoption of goals and the maintenance of a credible amount of slack demand is acknowledged as necessary, the chances of success are greatly diminished by targeting too little slack, because the slightest disturbance raising aggregate demand or restricting supplies can rapidly eliminate a small amount of slack and set off new inflationary pressures. In times past, when the general price level was relatively stable, such disturbances were not important and the response of prices to them was weak; but in recent years, when experience with inflation alerts everyone to the likelihood of new outbursts, the response is rapid.

Although the maintenance of slack demand is necessary to subdue inflation, the imposition of slack can give the appearance of not working, because it takes time and is dominated by cyclical fluctuations that inevitably accompany the attempt to restrain the growth in aggregate demand. This behavior of the inflation rate is hardly ideal for maximizing political statesmanship or for resisting the political temptation to make promises whose impracticality is revealed much later. But despite all the hand wringing over the political obstacles to subduing inflation, it is still true that avoidance of new outbursts of inflation is viewed as politically acceptable and that the rising trend of inflation has largely reflected the failure of policy to contain new outbursts. The evidence gives more support than denial to the traditional view that, without outbursts and with the maintenance of some slack in the economy, inflation will gradually decline. There is a basis for hope that each of the various kinds of mistakes which allow the economy to overheat will be made only once, and that eventually policy makers will proceed without further serious mistakes to bring inflation effectively under control.

Appendix

For Tables 3 and 4 in this appendix, regressions were fitted to quarterly data by the Cochrane-Orcutt method, which adjusts for first-order serial correlation in the residuals. (The total correlation coefficient is

Table 3
ESTIMATED EFFECT OF ECONOMIC SLACK ON INFLATION ASSUMING ADAPTIVE EXPECTATIONS

Regression Eq. [5]: $\dot{p}_t - \dot{p}_{t-1} = a\left(\dfrac{U_t - U_{t-2}}{2}\right) + ba\left(\dfrac{U_t + U_{t-1} + U_{t-2}}{3} - \bar{U}\right)$

Price Series	Period	Regression Coefficients (and t Values)		
		a	ba	$\bar{U}$
U: Unemployment rate				
Consumer price index	1953–69	−0.70 (2.7)	−0.17 (2.1)	3.9
	1953–77	−0.95 (3.4)	−0.23 (2.6)	3.7
GNP deflator	1953–69	−0.26 (0.7)	+0.01 (0.1)	—
	1953–77	−0.57 (1.8)	−0.12 (1.2)	3.9
Wholesale crude materials	1953–69	−0.23 (0.1)	−0.43 (0.9)	4.0
	1953–77	−0.06 (0.0)	−0.02 (0.0)	8.2
Wholesale intermediate goods	1953–69	−0.58 (1.2)	+0.02 (0.1)	—
	1953–77	−2.38 (2.0)	−0.13 (0.3)	4.4
Wholesale finished goods	1953–69	−0.66 (1.6)	−0.20 (1.6)	3.9
	1953–77	−1.22 (2.0)	−0.28 (1.5)	3.8
Average hourly earnings	1953–69	−0.56 (1.5)	−0.05 (0.4)	3.3
	1953–3/77	−0.52 (1.4)	−0.11 (0.9)	3.7
U: Excess capacity				
Consumer price index	1953–69	−0.07 (1.2)	−0.05 (2.3)	17.7
	1953–77	−0.15 (2.6)	−0.08 (3.4)	17.6
GNP deflator	1953–69	−0.05 (0.7)	+0.01 (0.2)	—
	1953–77	−0.11 (1.7)	−0.04 (1.7)	17.8
Wholesale crude materials	1953–69	+0.01 (0.3)	−0.08 (0.6)	19.0
	1953–77	−0.22 (0.4)	+0.06 (0.3)	—
Wholesale intermediate goods	1953–69	−0.25 (2.4)	+0.01 (0.2)	—
	1953–77	−0.77 (3.3)	−0.06 (0.6)	18.9
Wholesale finished goods	1953–69	−0.16 (1.7)	−0.06 (1.7)	18.0
	1953–77	−0.34 (2.8)	−0.09 (2.0)	17.8
Average hourly earnings	1953–69	−0.11 (1.3)	−0.02 (0.7)	16.2
	1953–3/77	−0.11 (1.5)	−0.04 (1.3)	17.4
U: Potential in excess of actual GNP (CEA)				
Consumer price index	1953–69	−0.17 (1.4)	−0.08 (2.1)	2.7
	1953–77	−0.27 (2.2)	−0.12 (3.4)	2.9
GNP deflator	1953–69	−0.21 (1.3)	−0.01 (0.2)	9.2
	1953–77	−0.19 (1.4)	−0.07 (1.8)	3.1

Table 3 (Continued)

Price Series	Period	Regression Coefficients (and t Values)		$\bar{U}$
		a	ba	
Wholesale crude materials	1953–69	+0.16 (0.2)	−0.14 (0.7)	3.3
	1953–77	−1.12 (1.1)	−0.05 (0.2)	5.9
Wholesale intermediate goods	1953–69	−0.48 (2.2)	−0.03 (0.4)	5.3
	1953–77	−1.36 (2.7)	−0.20 (1.3)	3.2
Wholesale finished goods	1953–69	−0.28 (1.4)	−0.10 (1.7)	2.8
	1953–77	−0.60 (2.4)	−0.16 (2.3)	3.0
Average hourly earnings	1953–69	−0.19 (1.1)	−0.03 (0.6)	1.7
	1953–3/77	−0.07 (0.4)	−0.04 (1.0)	2.8

U: Potential in excess of actual GNP (St. Louis)

Price Series	Period	a	ba	$\bar{U}$
Consumer price index	1953–69	−0.21 (1.7)	−0.08 (2.2)	2.4
	1953–2/77	−0.37 (3.0)	−0.11 (2.9)	3.1
GNP deflator	1953–69	−0.19 (1.2)	−0.01 (0.2)	7.1
	1953–2/77	−0.23 (1.6)	−0.06 (1.5)	3.0
Wholesale crude materials	1953–69	−0.07 (1.0)	−0.12 (0.6)	3.4
	1953–2/77	−1.46 (1.4)	+0.03 (0.1)	—
Wholesale intermediate goods	1953–69	−0.41 (1.9)	−0.01 (0.1)	14.7
	1953–2/77	−1.72 (3.3)	−0.13 (0.8)	3.2
Wholesale finished goods	1953–69	−0.31 (1.6)	−0.08 (1.4)	2.7
	1953–2/77	−0.81 (3.1)	−0.13 (1.7)	3.3
Average hourly earnings	1953–69	−0.17 (0.9)	−0.04 (0.8)	1.2
	1953–2/77	−0.09 (0.5)	−0.06 (1.2)	2.2

Note: The values of the t statistic omit negative signs and were not calculated for $\bar{U}$.

Dash (—) indicates not calculated because of wrong signs.

Source: Consumer price index (all items), wholesale prices, average hourly earnings of production workers (adjusted to exclude overtime and interindustry shifts), and unemployment rate of prime-age men aged twenty-five to fifty-four are from the Department of Labor, Bureau of Labor Statistics. GNP deflator is from the Department of Commerce, Bureau of Economic Analysis. Excess capacity in manufacturing (the complement of capacity utilization) is from the Federal Reserve Board. Potential in excess of actual GNP as estimated annually by the Council of Economic Advisers (logarithmic interpolations used to derive quarterly data) is given in the *Annual Report*, 1978, p. 84, and as estimated quarterly by the Federal Reserve Bank of St. Louis is given in Robert H. Rasche and John A. Tatom, "Potential Output and Its Growth Rate—The Dominance of Higher Energy Costs in the 1970s," *U.S. Productive Capacity: Estimating the Utilization Gap*, Center for the Study of American Business, Washington University, Working Paper no. 23 (December 1977), p. 80.

All series are seasonally adjusted.

Table 4

ESTIMATED EFFECT OF ECONOMIC SLACK ON INFLATION, ASSUMING RATIONAL EXPECTATIONS

Regression Eq. [10]: $\dot{p}_t - \sum_{i=1}^{16} \frac{\dot{p}_{t-i}}{16} = (a + c_0)(U_t - \bar{U}) + (c_1 - a)(U_{t-1} - \bar{U}) + \sum_{i=2}^{5} c_i(U_{t-i} - \bar{U})$

U: Unemployment rate

Period	$a + c_0$ (1)	$c_1 - a$ (2)	Regression Coefficients (and t Values) c_2 (3)	c_3 (4)	c_4 (5)	c_5 (6)	$\bar{U}$ (7)	Sum of cols. (1)–(6) (8)
			p: Consumer price index					
1953–69	0.08 (0.2)	-1.03 (1.8)	0.14 (0.3)	-0.20 (0.4)	0.10 (0.2)	0.12 (0.3)	4.1	-0.80
1953–77	-0.26 (0.7)	-1.00 (2.0)	0.26 (0.5)	0.22 (0.5)	-1.01 (2.1)	0.33 (0.9)	3.9	-1.46
			p: Wholesale finished goods					
1953–69	-0.80 (1.1)	0.27 (0.3)	-0.22 (0.2)	-1.00 (1.0)	1.51 (1.5)	-0.67 (1.0)	3.6	-0.88
1953–77	-0.84 (0.9)	-1.09 (0.8)	1.65 (1.2)	-1.50 (1.1)	-0.17 (0.1)	0.08 (0.1)	3.7	-1.87
			p: Average hourly earnings					
1953–69	-1.24 (2.4)	1.04 (1.3)	-0.67 (0.8)	-0.43 (0.6)	0.48 (0.6)	-0.01 (0.0)	3.3	-0.84
1953–77	-1.10 (2.2)	1.39 (1.7)	-1.01 (1.3)	-0.17 (0.2)	0.09 (0.1)	0.03 (0.1)	3.7	-0.78

Source and note: Same as for Table 3.

made misleadingly high by this adjustment and is not shown.) The period of fit began and ended with the first quarter of the years indicated, with certain exceptions because of unavailability of data. Units of inflation rates are percent per year, and of unemployed resources are percent. Hence units of coefficients are the change per quarter in annual percentage rate for each unit of quarterly change in U for a and for each unit of excess U for ba and the c's. The noninflationary rate of unemployed resources, $\bar{U}$ in percent, is estimated by the constant term of the regressions divided by ba in Table 3 and by the sum of c's in Table 4. The method of calculating the variables was as follows.

$\dot{p}_t$ is the rate of change between quarterly levels of the price series in t and $t-1$ (not the two-quarter change as used in Figures 1 and 2 to smooth the rate).

U_t is an average for the quarter. For equation [5] in Table 3, where the dependent variable is the change in the inflation rate, the two independent variables representing the change and level of unemployed resources have three-quarter spans. Thus all the variables in equation [5] have the same span of coverage. For equation [10] in Table 4, even though $\dot{p}_t$ covers two quarters of data and U_t only one quarter, a comparable span was not necessary because the set of six lagged U variables covers six quarters.

The unemployment rate of prime-age men aged twenty-five to fifty-four years was used in preference to the rate for all workers, because structural changes in the labor force have affected the total rate but are far less important for prime-age men. (See Cagan, "The Reduction of Inflation and the Magnitude of Unemployment.") This rate was about half the rate for all workers in 1977.

The Current State of the International Business Cycle: A New Measurement System

Geoffrey H. Moore

Summary

For many years a system of leading, coincident, and lagging economic indicators, first developed in the 1930s by the National Bureau of Economic Research (NBER), has been widely used in the United States to appraise the state of the business cycle. Since 1961 the current monthly figures for these indicators have been published by the U.S. Department of Commerce in Business Conditions Digest. *Similar systems have been developed in Canada, Japan, the United Kingdom, and a few other countries. Because of differences in content or methodology, however, these independent efforts do not provide comparable materials. In 1973 the National Bureau began a major study to develop an international economic indicator system (IEI) that would provide comparable data, organized in a comparable manner, for a number of industrial countries. The research has demonstrated that such a system can be helpful in tracking an international recovery or recession, in revealing factors that are holding back recovery or leading to recession, in anticipating changes in foreign trade flows, and in providing early warning of new inflationary trends. During 1977 and 1978 the Organization for Economic Cooperation and Development (OECD) and statistical agencies in Canada, the United Kingdom, West Germany, France, Italy, Japan, and the United States have cooperated with the National Bureau in compiling and analyzing the current data for this system of indicators. Some*

Director of Business Cycle Research, National Bureau of Economic Research, Inc., and senior research fellow, Hoover Institution, Stanford University. The research summarized here is the product of a collaborative effort among many individuals and institutions, private and public. A full report, "Monitoring Business Cycles at Home and Abroad," by Geoffrey H. Moore and Philip A. Klein with the assistance of Walter Ebanks, is being readied for publication later this year.

of the practical results of this research program are now available for use.[1]

This chapter explains the functions of the indicator system, summarizes the evidence concerning its strength and weaknesses, and appraises the state of the international business cycle through the end of 1977.

Functions of the IEI System

The National Bureau's first study of business cycle indicators, conducted by Wesley C. Mitchell and Arthur F. Burns, had as its immediate objective the use of indicators to signal a cyclical revival—that is, the ending of a recession, specifically the ending of the severe recession in the United States that began in the spring of 1937. When the work was taken up again after World War II, the objective was broadened to include signals of a cyclical downturn, and NBER studies completed in 1950, 1960, and 1966 as well as a Commerce Department study in 1975 focused on both the beginning and the end of recessions. An international system designed along similar lines should signal both peaks and troughs in each of the countries covered as well as in several countries taken together. In short, an important function of the IEI system is to detect a worldwide recession or recovery promptly. The importance of this function is underlined by the fact that international recessions— those in which many countries participate more or less simultaneously —have been more serious than local ones. The most recent example of a recession that was both serious and international was the recession of 1973–1975.

A second, and closely related, function of the indicator system is to measure the scope, severity, and unusual features of an international recession or recovery while it is in progress. For example, during the 1975–1976 recovery in the United States it became common practice, in reports devoted to the economic outlook, to compare the current recovery with previous recovery periods in this country. News magazines, business journals, annual reports of corporations, government reports, and newspapers used this device as a method of appraisal. But few of the publications made such comparisons for other countries, despite their relevance from a world point of view or their value in the

---

[1] In April 1978 the National Bureau announced that the current data for the individual indicators and composite indexes were available on a monthly subscription basis. Further information can be obtained from International Indicator Project, National Bureau of Economic Research, Inc., 261 Madison Avenue, New York, New York, 10016.

diagnosis of specific problems such as the sluggishness of capital investment in many countries and the persistence of high unemployment and
high inflation. The reason comparisons of this sort are not made is not
lack of concern or interest, I believe, but simply that the information is
not readily accessible. An international economic indicator system
should enable comparisons of this type to be made routinely and kept
up to date.

A third function is to help appraise prospects for foreign trade.
The leading indicators are sensitive measures of the general state of demand. Although many other factors affect the volume of exports and
imports, demand is surely fundamental. The growing trade deficit of
the United States during 1977 has frequently been attributed, in part,
to the sluggish demand for our exports from our trading partners and
our own vigorous demand for imports. Since the leading indicators include such demand-related factors as new orders, inventory change,
hiring rates, and profitability, one can expect that they would relate to
the demand not only for domestic goods but also for foreign products.
Leading indicators for an importing country, therefore, should tell us
something about how much it is likely to import as well as how much
its trading partners are likely to export to it. The international indicators system should help us anticipate changes in the flow of trade to
the countries for which leading indicators are available as well as
changes in the trade balances among these countries.

Fourth, a system of international indicators can provide early
warning signals of an acceleration or deceleration in the rate of inflation. Inflation is in part a demand phenomenon, and, as noted above,
many of the indicators are demand oriented. Inflation is also an international phenomenon. All countries experience it, and waves of inflation often occur at about the same time in many countries. An appropriate set of international indicators should show how the price system
responds to and feeds back upon the rest of the economy, including, of
course, those variables that are under some degree of policy control,
such as the money supply or the fiscal deficit.

Leads and Lags in Recovery and Recession

The NBER's international economic indicator system consists of groups
of leading, coincident, and lagging indicators covering a wide variety of
economic processes that have been found to be important in business
cycles. The leading indicators are for the most part measures of antici-
pations or new commitments. They have a "look-ahead" quality and
are highly sensitive to changes in the economic climate as perceived in

the marketplace. The coincident indicators are comprehensive measures of economic performance: real GNP, industrial production, employment, unemployment, income, and trade. They are the measures to which everyone looks to determine whether a nation is prosperous or depressed. The lagging indicators are more sluggish in their reactions to the economic climate, but they serve a useful purpose by smoothing out and confirming changes in trend that are first reflected in the leading and coincident indicators. Moreover, their very sluggishness can be an asset in cyclical analysis, because when they do begin to move, or when they move rapidly, they may reflect excesses or imbalances in the economy. Hence the lagging indicators can (and often do) provide the earliest warnings of all, as when rapid increases in costs of production outstrip price increases and threaten profit margins, thus inhibiting new commitments to invest, which are among the leading indicators. A conspectus of the U.S. indicators arranged according to the type of economic process they represent and the cyclical timing they exhibit is in Table 1. The compilation for other industrial countries is designed to represent substantially the same processes arranged in a similar manner. The degree of success in accomplishing this varies from one country to another, as shown in Table 2.

The attempt to duplicate the U.S. system abroad does not mean that all countries were thought to be alike or that other indicators could not be found that would serve equally well or better. Duplicating the U.S. system was not an ultimate goal but merely a practicable interim target. The U.S. indicator system had the advantage of being familiar to many users, and both its empirical properties and the economic logic on which it was based have been thoroughly investigated.[2] This logic seems applicable to many countries where free enterprise prevails. Orders placed for machinery that is made to order are likely to lead machinery production in any market-oriented economy, and are likely also to lead the production of the goods the machinery helps to produce. Similarly, in any enterprise economy, changes in the relations between prices and costs influence incentives to expand future output and to make capital investments. In countries where there are markets for common stock, one can expect stock prices to be especially sensitive to changes in profit prospects and to changes in interest rates, and hence to anticipate the effects that these changes produce.

The selection of the U.S. indicator list as a target also advanced the objective of compiling sets of indicators as comparable as possible

---

[2] For a list of NBER publications that explain the behavior of and relationships among particular indicators, see the March 1978 issue of the *NBER Reporter*, pp. 16–18.

across countries. Unless some attention is paid to this, comparisons of cyclical movements in different countries are likely to become hopelessly confused. To cite one example, the index of leading indicators published by the British Central Statistical Office includes a series on interest rates treated invertedly—that is, a rise in rates is counted as a depressing factor, and vice versa. This is not an unreasonable position to take, but in the U.S. classification interest rates are treated on a positive basis and are included among the lagging indicators (see Table 1). It is recognized that at times, as noted above, a rapid rise in such indicators can be interpreted as an adverse development. A straightforward comparison of the U.S. and U.K. leading indexes as published in each country would run afoul of this difference in procedure.

Nevertheless, it is obvious that the system should not be held in a straitjacket, and that adaptations to the way business is done in each country and to the particular statistical data available should be made as more experience with the system accumulates and additional research is conducted. Perhaps two systems will evolve, one in which international comparability is strictly maintained, and one in which each country's own data and cyclical response mechanisms are used to best advantage—always avoiding, as far as possible, arbitrary differences in methodology.

The acid test of the plan to assemble comparable sets of indicators for each country according to the U.S. system lies in whether such data behave in the way U.S. experience has led one to expect. To perform this test long-run trends were fitted to each indicator, including those for the United States, cyclical turning points in the deviations from trend were identified, a chronology of growth-cycle turns for each country was set up to represent the peaks and troughs in aggregate economic activity (after allowance for trend), and the leads and lags of each trend-adjusted indicator were measured with respect to these growth-cycle turns. The trend-adjustment procedure, although subject to difficulties of its own, was essential to the identification of cyclical movements in countries that had experienced almost continuous rapid growth through the period from 1948 to 1973. Computer programs, carefully monitored to rule out dubious results, helped to enhance the objectivity of the data processing. A summary of the findings on cyclical timing is given in Table 3.

The leading indicators, selected and classified on the basis of U.S. data, lead in each of the other countries. The coincident indicators, of course, show virtually no lead or lag, because they are used to determine the growth-cycle chronologies themselves. The lagging indicators lag. Significantly, because the grouping of the indicators is based on U.S. experience only, and not on experience in the country itself, the

Table 1

CROSS-CLASSIFICATION OF U.S. INDICATORS BY ECONOMIC PROCESS
AND CYCLICAL TIMING

Economic Process	Cyclical Timing		
	Leading	Roughly coincident	Lagging
Employment and unemployment	Average work week, manufacturing. New unemployment insurance claims, inverted	Nonfarm employment. Unemployment, inverted	Long-duration unemployment, inverted
Production, income, consumption, and trade	New orders, consumer goods and materials[a]	Gross national product[a] Industrial production Personal income[a] Manufacturing and trade sales[a]	
Fixed capital investment	Formation of business enterprises Contracts and orders, plant and equipment[a] Building permits, housing		Investment expenditures, plant and equipment[a]

Inventories and inventory investment	Change in business inventories[a]	Business inventories[a]
Prices, costs, and profits	Industrial materials price index Stock price index Profits[a] Ratio, price to unit labor cost, nonfarm	Change in output per man-hour, manufacturing, inverted
Money and credit	Change, consumer installment debt[a]	Commercial and industrial loans outstanding[a] Bank interest rates, business loans

[a] In constant prices.

Note: The list and classification is substantially the same as that prepared in 1966 and published in Geoffrey H. Moore and Julius Shiskin, *Indicators of Business Expansions and Contractions* (New York: National Bureau of Economic Research, 1967). The chief modification is that those series marked with [a] are converted to constant prices. The timing classification for each series is the same as shown in *Business Conditions Digest* for all turns (see Table 1, column 1, in any recent issue), except as follows: Unemployment is unclassified (*U*) at all turns in BCD because it leads at peaks and lags at troughs, but here it is classified roughly coincident, as in the 1966 list. Four series that here are in constant prices are shown in BCD only in current prices: change in consumer installment debt, investment expenditures for plant and equipment, commercial and industrial loans outstanding, and change in output per man-hour, manufacturing, inverted, which is the constant price equivalent of labor cost per unit of output. The constant price series are assigned the same classification as the current price series.

Table 2
CONTENT OF ECONOMIC INDICATOR LISTS, SEVEN COUNTRIES

Classification and Title of Series (U.S.)	United States	Canada	United Kingdom	West Germany	France	Italy	Japan
Leading							
Average work week, manufacturing	s	s	s	e1	s	NA	e1
New unemployment insurance claims, inverted	s	s	NA	s	NA	NA	NA
New orders, consumer goods and materials[a]	s	e1	NA	NA	NA	NA	NA
Formation of business enterprises	s	e1	e2	e1	NA	e1	e1
Contracts and orders, plant and equipment[a]	s	e2	e2	e1	NA	e1	e1
Building permits, housing	s	s	e1	e1	s	s	e1
Change in business inventories[a]	s	s	s	s	s	s	s
Industrial materials price index	s	s	s	s	s	NA	s
Stock price index	s	s	s	s	s	s	s
Profits[a]	s	s	s	s	NA	NA	s
Ratio, price to unit labor cost, nonfarm	s	s	s	s	s	NA	s
Change, consumer installment debt[a]	s	s	s	s	NA	NA	s

	1	2	3	4	5	6
Coincident						
Nonfarm employment	s	s	e1	s	s	s
Unemployment, inverted	s	s	s	s	s	s
Gross national product[a]	s	s	s	s	s	s
Industrial production	s	s	s	s	s	s
Personal income[a]	s	s	s	NA	NA	e1
Manufacturing and trade sales[a]	s	e1	e2	e1	e1	e1
Lagging						
Long-duration unemployment, inverted	s	s	NA	NA	NA	NA
Investment expenditures, plant and equipment[a]	s	s	s	NA	NA	s
Business inventories[a]	s	s	s	NA	NA	s
Change in output per man-hour, manufacturing, inverted	s	s	s	NA	NA	s
Commercial and industrial loans outstanding[a]	s	s	s	NA	NA	s
Bank interest rates, business loans	s	e1	s	NA	NA	s

NA: Not available.

[a] In constant prices.

Note: Lagging indicators for France and Italy have not been compiled. The same series is indicated by s. Equivalent series are indicated by e1 (one series) or e2 (two series). For example, for West Germany the series used as equivalent to the average work week is the number of persons working short hours, inverted, and for Japan the equivalent series is an index of overtime worked.

Source: National Bureau of Economic Research.

Table 3

CYCLICAL TIMING OF ECONOMIC INDICATORS DURING GROWTH CYCLES, FIVE COUNTRIES

(mean lead (−) or lag (+) in months)

	United States, 1948–1973	Canada, 1950–1970	United Kingdom, 1951–1972	West Germany, 1952–1973	Japan, 1954–1972	Average, Five Countries
At growth-cycle peaks						
Lagging group, inverted	−14	−19	−21	−17	−23	−19
Leading group	−4	−2	−11	−5	−3	−5
Coincident group	+1	0	0	0	0	0
Lagging group	+5	+6	+6	+10	+3	+6
At growth-cycle troughs						
Lagging group, inverted	−10	−14	−19	−10	−16	−14
Leading group	−2	−3	−5	−3	−5	−4
Coincident group	0	+1	0	0	0	0
Lagging group	+8	+3	+10	+8	+8	+7

Source: Geoffrey H. Moore and Philip A. Klein, "Monitoring Business Cycles at Home and Abroad" (National Bureau of Economic Research manuscript, 1978), tables IV-1 to IV-5. The indicators included in each group correspond with those in Table 2, although at the time this work was done some of the indicators were expressed in current rather than in constant prices. A comparable analysis for France and Italy has not yet been completed.

Figure 1
AVERAGE SEQUENCE OF CYCLICAL TURNS IN THREE GROUPS
OF INDICATORS DURING GROWTH CYCLES, FIVE COUNTRIES

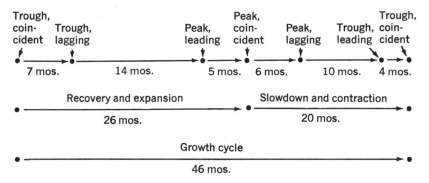

Source: Table 3, last column.

sequence of turns among the leading, coincident, and lagging groups in each country corresponds roughly to the sequence in the United States. The detailed results show that this sequence has been repeated at virtually every turn in each country. Moreover, this consistency includes the tendency for the turns in the lagging group to precede opposite turns in the leading group, corresponding to the economic logic noted above (compare the top line with the second line in each panel of the table). The sequences do not appear to differ systematically from one country to another; hence it is appropriate to average them (see the last column of the table). The average sequence is set forth schematically in Figure 1. Since the growth-cycle chronologies and the recorded leads and lags are based on trend-adjusted data, the rising and falling phases are roughly symmetrical, as are the intervals into which they are subdivided by the turns in the indicators.

Nevertheless, it is true that there are wide variations in the lengths of lead or lag from one cycle to another or from one indicator to another. The system is neither simple nor mechanical. But the historical record is available to help guide current interpretations, and it appears to support the initial hypothesis, namely, that the U.S. indicator system is broadly applicable overseas.

To supplement the analysis of individual indicators, composite indexes of the leading, coincident, and lagging indicators for each country and for groups of countries have been computed, using a method employed for some years by the U.S. Department of Commerce. The indexes are constructed so that their trend rate of growth during 1966–

1976 is equal to that of real GNP for the country concerned during the same period. The procedure corrects for the rather haphazard long-run trends that are likely to result from combinations of indicators that, despite efforts to obtain comparability, are not precisely the same in the several countries. In addition to the indexes with trend equal to the trend in GNP, indexes are available with the long-run trend eliminated. These depict the growth cycles discussed above. The trend rates of growth in the individual indicators are of interest in themselves for the purposes of analyzing and perhaps projecting each country's long-run rate of growth. Finally, short-run rates of growth in the indexes have been compiled, based on changes over successive intervals of six months or twelve months. These rates also depict the growth cycles, but they do not depend upon any trend-fitting procedure and hence avoid the uncertainty that is inevitably attached to bringing such trends up to date.

Figure 2 compares the leading and coincident indexes for the United States and for the six other countries combined (Canada, United Kingdom, West Germany, France, Italy, and Japan) during 1972–1977. Each of the indexes, as noted above, is adjusted so that its percentage growth between 1966 and 1976 is equal to the growth in real GNP between those years. The required adjustment factor, expressed as a constant rate of growth per month, is applied throughout the period and beyond it as well. This is done for each country's index; then the indexes are combined, weighted by the country's GNP in 1970 (expressed in U.S. dollars).

Although this procedure insures that the long-run trend in the indexes will be approximately the same as the trend in real GNP, the fluctuations in the indexes are larger than those in GNP, partly because most of the components are more sensitive than GNP, partly because most of them are monthly rather than quarterly. Another reason is that the average month-to-month change (without regard to sign) in each country's industrial production index is used as a standard by which to adjust the month-to-month change in the index, and industrial production usually undergoes wider swings than GNP. The indexes thus provide measures of economic performance based not on a single indicator but on a group of significant indicators that are relatively homogeneous with respect to cyclical timing. As a consequence of both the cyclical homogeneity and the variety of economic data included, the indexes are relatively free of the month-to-month irregularities that beset most economic time series.

In the latest recession, as Figure 2 shows, the U.S. leading and coincident indexes reached their peaks and troughs virtually simultaneously. Both reached peaks in November 1973, although the lead-

Figure 2

LEADING AND COINCIDENT INDEXES,
UNITED STATES AND SIX OTHER COUNTRIES, 1972–1978

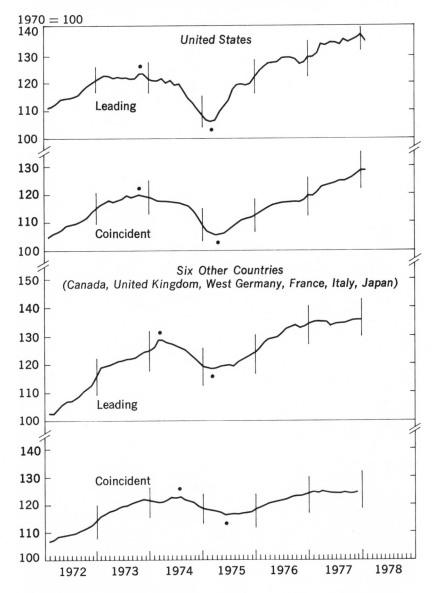

• Specific cycle peak or trough.
Source: National Bureau of Economic Research, March 1978.

ing index had been flat for most of the year. The leading index reached its trough in February, the coincident in March 1975. The six-country indexes displayed more typical behavior. The leading index peaked in March 1974, the coincident index three months later in July. The six-country leading index reached its trough in February 1975, the coincident index three months later in May. The United States and the group of six entered their recessions at about the same time and began their recoveries at about the same time. If the curves were not labeled, even experienced observers would find it difficult to say which represented the United States and which represented the other six countries.

No doubt one of the factors contributing to the downturn late in 1973 and early in 1974 was the embargo on oil shipments and the sharp rise in oil prices. But it was only one of the factors, for the rates of growth in all these indexes began to decline steadily early in 1973, well before the oil embargo (see Figures 3 and 4).[3] Without any obvious exogenous event to account for it, the nearly simultaneous onset of recovery in the United States and in the group of six in the first half of 1975 indicates a high degree of interdependence among these countries, perhaps aided by the coordination of economic policies either by design or by the course of events.

During 1975 and early 1976 the rates of growth reached high levels, as commonly occurs in recoveries from deep recessions. The acceleration began to diminish during 1976. In the U.S. leading index the highest rate, 13 percent, was reached in March 1976. Three months later, in June 1976, the growth rate in the U.S. coincident index began

---

[3] The rates of growth employed in Figures 3 and 4 are a somewhat novel adaptation of the familiar "same-month-year-ago" percentage change. The year-ago figure is not for a single month but is, rather, a twelve-month average centered (approximately) on that month. Thus the rate for, say, December 1977 is the change to that month from the yearly average running from July 1976 to June 1977, a year that is centered (approximately) on December 1976. The rate for January 1978 is the change from the yearly average ending in July 1977, and so on. That is, the average is always for a year ending six months before the current month. The replacement of the single-month-year-ago figure by an annual average avoids the idiosyncrasies that may attach to that figure (such as a strike or unusual weather). It does not, of course, avoid the idiosyncrasies attaching to the current month, but these are generally better remembered, and in any case the procedure avoids the necessity of allowing for special factors in both months. The result is a much smoother rate of change, more representative of the recent trend, hence the term "twelve-month percentage change, smoothed." Greater smoothness than the same-month-year-ago percentage change is obtained, with no loss of currency. Seasonally adjusted data for the current month are required, however. Rates of change computed over shorter intervals, say, six months, are likely to register turning points more promptly (unless the turns are very sharp), but they are more erratic, rendering it more difficult to judge whether a turn will be sustained or will soon be reversed. The twelve-month rates are plotted in the current month. For some purposes, centering the rate six months earlier would be appropriate.

Figure 3
GROWTH RATES IN LEADING INDEXES, SEVEN COUNTRIES, 1972–1978
(Percentage change from same month of preceding year, smoothed)

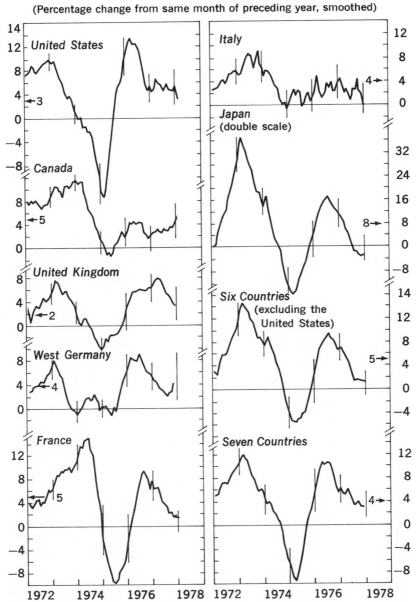

Note: Arrows indicate rate of change, 1966–1976, in the index and in real GNP.
Source: National Bureau of Economic Research, March 1978.

Figure 4

GROWTH RATES IN COINCIDENT INDEXES, SEVEN COUNTRIES, 1972–1978

(percentage change from same month of preceding year, smoothed)

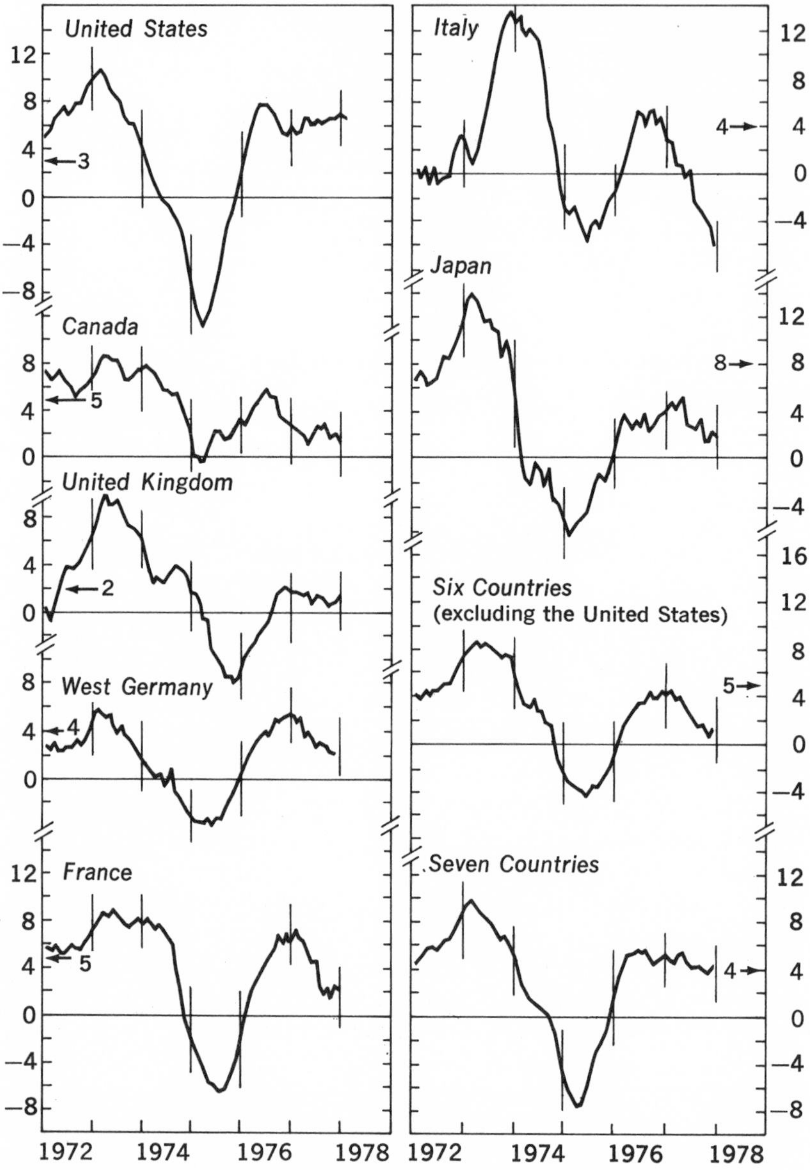

Note: Arrows indicate rate of change, 1966–1976, in the index and in real GNP.
Source: National Bureau of Economic Research, March 1978.

to decline (from 8 percent). In the six other countries combined, the leading index recorded its fastest growth, 10 percent, in July 1976, and half a year later, in January 1977, the growth rate in the coincident index reached its high point of 4 percent. At the end of 1977 the U.S. leading index rate was 5 percent; the coincident index, 7 percent. Both were decidedly higher than the six-country rate of 1 percent for each index. The recovery had faded sharply in the six-country group.

This conclusion is supported by the growth rates for the individual country indexes displayed in Figures 3 and 4. The differences among the countries are considerable, and the relation between the leading and the coincident indexes is not as close as one would like. In general, the differences among countries are greater for the leading indexes than for the coincident indexes. Deficiencies in the coverage of the leading indexes (see Table 2) no doubt have something to do with this.[4] Nevertheless, in every one of the six countries other than the United States, the growth rates in the coincident indexes declined during 1977, and the same was true of the leading indexes in every country but Canada. In nearly every country (again, excluding the United States) the growth rates have declined well below the trend rates of 1966–1976 (indicated by arrows on the charts). In relation to these trend rates, the recovery in the United States has been stronger and has been sustained longer than that in any of the other six countries. According to the data now available, therefore, the situation developing during 1977 resembled the widespread slowdowns that preceded the earlier international growth recessions of 1958, 1967, 1970, and 1974.

Implications for Foreign Trade

The effect upon the U.S. economy of a slowdown in economic growth in other industrial countries is likely to be most visible in U.S. exports. It is customary to assume that exports depend upon the level of economic activity in the country to which the exports go. Ordinarily this level is measured by gross national product or industrial production, both of which are among the coincident indicators. Since the leading indicators, as we have seen, usually anticipate the movement of the coincident by several months, the leading indexes for U.S. trading partners may also anticipate the movements in U.S. exports to them. A number of tests of this hypothesis have been made, using the leading indexes to forecast the rate of change in the volume of trade to and

---

[4] The leading index for Italy is based on an inadequate list of indicators, and that for France is only slightly better.

Figure 5

FORECAST AND ACTUAL PERCENTAGE CHANGES IN QUANTITY OF U.S. EXPORTS
OF MANUFACTURED GOODS TO WESTERN EUROPE, CANADA, AND JAPAN, 1964–1978

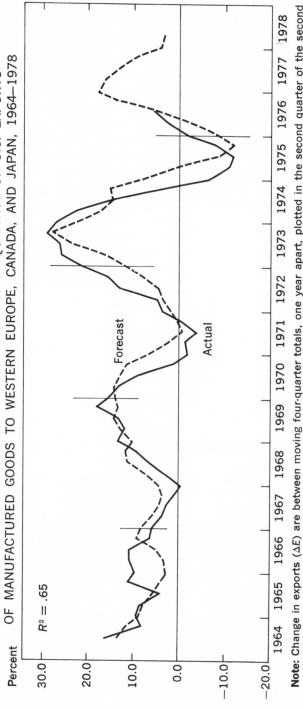

Note: Change in exports (ΔE) are between moving four-quarter totals, one year apart, plotted in the second quarter of the second year. For example, the most recent actual change, between calendar year totals for 1975 and 1976, is plotted in the second quarter of 1976. Forecasts are based upon the percentage change in the leading index (ΔLd) for six countries, GNP weights (Canada, United Kingdom, West Germany, France, Italy, Japan), during the last twelve months before the forecast year, smoothed (see text footnote 3). The regression equation (and t statistics) is: $\Delta E = -0.2 + 2.0 \, \Delta Ld$.
$\quad\quad\quad\quad\quad\quad\quad\quad\quad\quad\quad\quad\quad\quad\quad\quad\quad\quad\quad\quad(-0.1) \quad (9.4)$

Source: National Bureau of Economic Research, Inc., March 1978.

from particular countries or groups of countries, and for trade as a whole as well as for various commodity groupings. This research is still in progress, but the initial results show that from one-half to two-thirds of the year-to-year changes in trade flows can usually be accounted for in this manner. Figure 5 displays the results of one such test, where the percentage rate of growth in U.S. exports of manufactured goods to Western Europe, Canada, and Japan, after allowance for changes in prices, is forecast by the leading index for the six countries outside the United States. Despite the fact that exports are affected by many other factors not explicitly taken account of in this simple model, the forecasts have tracked the major swings fairly well. Late in 1976 and in 1977, however, the index projected larger increases than evidently occurred. (Comparable quarterly data for 1977 are not available at this writing.) That is, the recovery in demand after the 1973–1975 recession, as measured by the leading index for the six major countries, did not produce a commensurate increase in U.S. exports. This shortfall, together with the slowdown in the leading index during 1977, is not a favorable augury.

The same method can be employed to forecast the exports of any country, developed or developing, that trades with the industrial countries for which we have leading indexes. We have already obtained similar results for the exports of the United Kingdom, West Germany, Japan, and for a major group of developing countries (Figures 6, 7, 8, and 9). Naturally this method by itself has serious limitations, since it ignores other factors that influence the quantities of goods exported. Changes in exchange rates, tariffs and other barriers or incentives to trade, supply conditions, and pricing policies are taken into account only insofar as they affect the leading indicators for the importing countries. Yet, in view of the importance of trade flows and trade balances in the economic relations among nations, even a small contribution to our economic intelligence in appraising trade prospects is worthwhile.

Implications for Inflation

Growth cycles are closely associated with the rate of inflation. Indeed, as far as U.S. experience is concerned, declines in the rate of inflation have been associated with virtually every slowdown or contraction in real economic growth and have not occurred at other times. Both parts of this proposition are important. Declines in the rate of inflation have not been as rare as is commonly believed, but they have occurred only at times of slower economic growth, never at times of rapid growth.

Figure 6

FORECAST AND ACTUAL PERCENTAGE CHANGES IN QUANTITY
OF UNITED KINGDOM EXPORTS OF MANUFACTURED GOODS
TO SIX COUNTRIES, 1965–1977

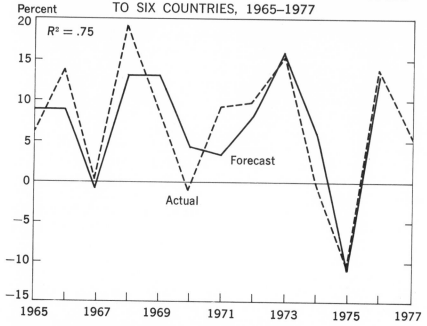

Note: Forecasts are based on the percentage change in the leading index for six
countries, weighted by U.K. exports, over the six months preceding the forecast
year. The six countries and the U.K. export weights (1970) are: United States
(.378), Canada (.117), West Germany (.205), France (.141), Italy (.098), Japan
(.061). The regression equation (and t statistics) is: $\Delta E = 2.6 + 2.4\ \Delta Ld.$
$$(1.7)\quad(5.5)$$
Source: National Bureau of Economic Research, January 1978.

The proposition appears to be true in other countries as well as in the
United States.

The international indicator system is helpful in examining the evidence, and so is the concept of the growth cycle described earlier. This
distinguishes periods of rapid growth from periods of slow growth by
reference to a long-run trend. Trend-adjusted data rise as long as the
short-run rate of growth exceeds the long-run rate. They decline as
long as the short-run rate is less than the long-run rate. The peaks and
troughs in trend-adjusted data, therefore, delineate periods of rapid
and slow growth.

For the United States, a chronology of growth cycles based on
trend-adjusted data for the physical volume of aggregate economic ac-

Figure 7

FORECAST AND ACTUAL PERCENTAGE CHANGES IN QUANTITY
OF WEST GERMAN EXPORTS OF MANUFACTURED GOODS
TO ALL COUNTRIES, 1965–1977

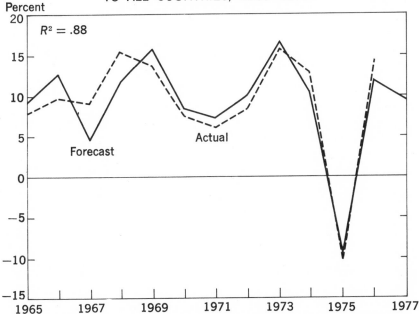

Note: Forecasts are based on the percentage change in the leading index for six
countries, weighted by West German exports, over the six months preceding the
forecast year. The six countries and the West German export weights (1970)
are: United States (.250), Canada (.026), United Kingdom (.098), France (.339),
Italy (.244), Japan (.043). The regression equation (and t statistics) is:
$\Delta E = 4.6 + 2.4\ \Delta Ld.$
    (5.0) (8.6)
Source: National Bureau of Economic Research, January 1978.

tivity is used in Figure 10 as a backdrop against which to examine the
movements in the rate of change in two price indexes. The index of
industrial materials prices—that is, prices of metals, textiles, rubber,
and the like—shows an especially close relation to the growth cycle.
Downswings in the rate of change in these prices occurred in every
period of slow growth or recession, and upswings occurred in every
period of rapid growth. Often, as in 1956 and 1959, the downswings
began before the onset of the slow growth periods. This price index is
one of the leading indicators in Table 1; here it leads not only the
growth cycle but also the rate of change in the consumer price index
(cpi), the bottom line in Figure 10. The cpi, which of course includes

Figure 8

FORECAST AND ACTUAL PERCENTAGE CHANGES IN QUANTITY
OF JAPANESE EXPORTS OF MANUFACTURED GOODS
TO ALL COUNTRIES, 1965–1977

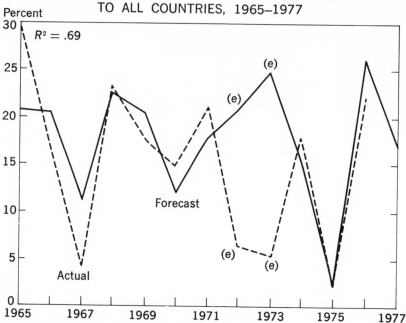

Note: Forecasts are based on the percentage change in the leading index for six countries, weighted by Japanese exports, over the six months preceding the forecast year. The six countries and the Japanese export weights (1970) are: United States (.759), Canada (.071), United Kingdom (.061), West Germany (.069), France (.016), Italy (.024). The regression omits 1972 and 1973 (marked e), which were seriously affected by the dollar devaluation. The regression equation (and t statistics) is: $\Delta E = 15.4 + 1.8\ \Delta Ld$.
(9.7) (4.3)
Source: National Bureau of Economic Research, January 1978.

the prices of services as well as commodities, responds to the growth cycle as well, but often with a lag of a year or more. The lags have been so long, especially in recent years, that sometimes the rate of inflation in the cpi has risen almost throughout the period of slow growth or recession, giving the erroneous impression that slow growth had no influence on inflation.

Watching both price indexes together, and bearing in mind their differences in sensitivity and tendency to lag, enables one to see that growth cycles have pervasive influences upon the price structure. The change one sees in the consumer price index (as, for example, the de-

Figure 9

FORECAST AND ACTUAL PERCENTAGE CHANGES IN QUANTITY
OF EXPORTS OF DEVELOPING MARKET ECONOMIES
TO ALL COUNTRIES, 1964–1977

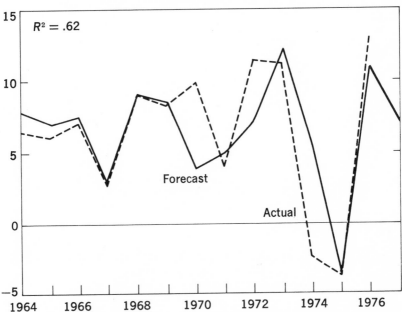

Note: Forecasts are based on the percentage change in the leading index for seven countries, weighted by GNP weights, over the six months preceding the forecast year. The seven countries are: United States, Canada, United Kingdom, West Germany, France, Italy, Japan. The regression equation (and t statistics) is: $\Delta E = 4.2 + 0.6\,\Delta Ld$.
      (3.9) (4.1)
Source: National Bureau of Economic Research, March 1978.

cline in its rate of increase from autumn 1974 to spring 1976) is a lagged response to or reflection of similar developments in commodity markets that react far more promptly to changes in demand pressures or supply conditions.

Corresponding data for the six other countries covered in the international indicator system are employed in Figure 11 to determine whether similar relations are found in these countries. A growth cycle chronology is derived from the trend-adjusted coincident index for the six countries combined. As noted earlier, this index is based upon measures of the physical volume of economic activity, such as real GNP, industrial production, employment, and unemployment. Rates of

70

Figure 10

RATES OF CHANGE IN TWO PRICE INDEXES DURING GROWTH CYCLES, UNITED STATES, 1955–1978

(measured over twelve-month span, smoothed)

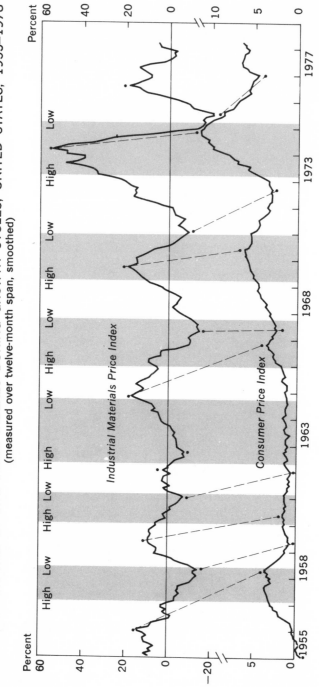

Note: Shaded areas represent slowdowns in economic growth as determined from trend-adjusted measures of aggregate output, income, sales, and employment. Broken lines connect corresponding peaks and troughs in the rates of change in the two price indexes.

Figure 11

RATES OF CHANGE IN TWO PRICE INDEXES DURING GROWTH CYCLES,
SIX COUNTRIES (EXCLUDING THE UNITED STATES), 1955–1977

(measured over twelve-month span, smoothed)

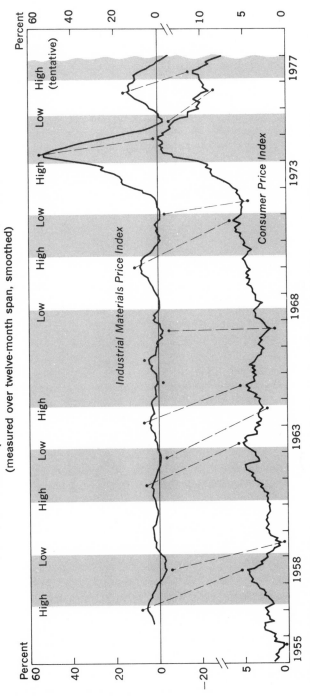

Note: Shaded areas represent slowdowns in economic growth as determined from the trend-adjusted coincident index for six countries combined. The six countries are: Canada, United Kingdom, West Germany, France, Italy, Japan. The indexes are weighted by each country's GNP in 1970, in U.S. dollars. The industrial materials index excludes Italy (data not available). Broken lines connect corresponding peaks and troughs in the rates of change in the two price indexes.

71

change in a composite index of industrial materials prices in five of the six countries (data for Italy are not available) exhibit a sensitivity to the growth cycle similar to that of the U.S. industrial materials price index. Every slowdown in growth has been accompanied by a reduction in the rate of increase in these prices, and often by an absolute decline (where the line on the chart goes below the zero level). Every period of rapid growth delineated by the trend-adjusted coincident index has been accompanied by an acceleration in materials prices. The consumer price index for the six countries exhibits a delayed response, similar to that of the U.S. consumer price index. Nevertheless, when the delay factor is taken into account, it is possible to trace a relation both to the materials prices and to the growth cycle (see the broken lines on the chart, which connect high and low points in the rates of change in the two price indexes).

By comparing Figures 10 and 11 one can observe the close interconnection between the prices of crude materials in the United States and in the six other industrial countries. Most of these materials are traded on world markets, and changes in demand or supply conditions anywhere in the world are registered promptly. It is partly through these markets that slowdowns in growth that are international in scope have international effects on the rate of inflation, notably in 1957–1958 and 1974–1975.

Although Figures 10 and 11 demonstrate that the conditions that produce rates of economic growth in excess of long-run trend are conducive to an acceleration of inflation, they do not suggest what those conditions are, or show why inflation accelerates greatly in some periods of rapid growth while in other periods it accelerates only modestly. Similarly, the conditions that make for slow growth or recession are evidently conducive to a reduced rate of inflation or even to deflation, but further analysis is required to show what those conditions are and how variations among them bring about different results.

It is hardly surprising, of course, that periods of rapid growth produce conditions conducive to rising rates of inflation while periods of slow growth have the opposite effect. When ordering is brisk and order backlogs accumulate, sellers have opportunities and incentives to raise prices, and buyers are less averse to paying them. Costs of production tend to creep up, labor turnover increases, control over efficiency and waste tends to decline. New commitments for investment are made in an optimistic environment, building up demand for limited supplies of skilled labor and construction equipment. Credit to build inventories is more readily available and is in greater demand, even if higher interest rates must be paid for it, thereby raising costs. Labor unions see better opportunities to obtain favorable contract settlements, and their members are more willing to strike to get them. All these conditions apply to more and more firms and industries and produce upward pressure on more and more prices. Indeed, one of the principal factors underlying a rising rate of inflation in the general price level is not just that some prices rise in big jumps but that more prices rise at more frequent intervals.

During periods of slow growth or actual decline in aggregate economic activity, the opposite conditions prevail. Firms and industries cut back their output, reduce or eliminate overtime, shave costs, give bigger discounts off list prices, reduce inventories, repay bank debt, and postpone new investment projects or stretch out existing ones. Quit rates decline and labor demands for pay raises become more conservative. Interest rates drop. As price increases become less widespread and less frequent, and as more price cutting takes place, the rate of inflation declines.

Many of the processes sketched above are represented among the leading and lagging indicators. In an earlier study I showed that in the United States the leading indicators, viewed as measures of demand pressures, were rather effective in accounting not only for the varying leads and lags in the rate of inflation from one growth cycle to another but also for the varying amount of change in the rate of inflation in different growth cycles.[5] This analysis can now be brought up to date for the United States and extended to the other six countries as well.

The record of leads and lags (Tables 4 and 5) shows that, both in the United States and in the other six countries taken as a group, the turns in the trend-adjusted leading index and in the rate of change in industrial materials prices lead the growth-cycle turns (coincident index) by, on the average, four to six months. Furthermore, although the length of these leads varies considerably from one cycle to another, long or short leads in the leading index correspond with long or short leads in the rate of change in materials prices (see the correlation coefficients in the notes to the tables). That is, the turning points in the two series are associated with one another. The tables also show that the rates of change in the consumer price index lag behind the growth-cycle turns by nine or ten months, on the average, and hence follow the turns in the leading index and in materials prices by a year or more. Again, the variation in the length of lag behind growth-cycle turns is partly accounted for by similar variations in the timing of the leading index, or, alternatively, in the industrial materials price index. This suggests that, despite the long lag, the turns in the rate of change in the

---

[5] "Price Behavior during Growth Recessions," *Perspectives on Inflation*, Canadian Studies, no. 36 (Montreal: The Conference Board in Canada, 1974).

Table 4

LEADS AND LAGS DURING GROWTH CYCLES: LEADING INDEX AND TWO PRICE INDEXES, UNITED STATES

Date of Growth Cycle[a]		Date of Turn and Lead (−) or Lag (+) in Months					
		Leading index, deviation from trend[b]		Rate of change in industrial materials price index[c]		Rate of change in consumer price index[c]	
Peak	Trough	Peak	Trough	Peak	Trough	Peak	Trough
July 48	Oct. 49	Jan. 48 (−6)	June 49 (−4)				Jan. 50 (+3)
Mar. 51	July 52	Aug. 50 (−7)	Nov. 51 (−8)	Jan. 51 (−2)	June 51 (−1)	Feb. 51 (−1)	May 53 (+10)
Mar. 53	Aug. 54	Mar. 53 (0)	Jan. 54 (−7)	n.s.c.	n.s.c.	Oct. 53 (+7)	Jan. 55 (+5)
Feb. 57	Apr. 58	Sept. 55 (−17)	Jan. 58 (−3)	Dec. 55 (−14)	Apr. 58 (0)	Mar. 58 (+13)	May 59 (+13)
Feb. 60	Feb. 61	Apr. 59 (−10)	Dec. 60 (−2)	May 59 (−9)	Dec. 60 (−2)	May 60 (+3)	Jan. 62 (+11)
May 62	Oct. 64	Feb. 62 (−3)	June 62 (−28)	Jan. 62 (−4)	Sept. 62 (−25)	n.s.c.	n.s.c.
June 66	Oct. 67	Mar. 66 (−3)	Jan. 67 (−9)	Nov. 64 (−19)	Apr. 67 (−6)	Oct. 66 (+4)	May 67 (−5)

Mar. 69	Nov. 70	Jan. 69 (−2)	Nov. 70 (0)	Sept. 69 (+6)	Jan. 71 (+2)	May 70 (+14)	Aug. 72 (+21)
Mar. 73	Mar. 75	Feb. 73 (−1)	Feb. 75 (−1)	Feb. 74 (+11)	June 75 (+3)	Nov. 74 (+20)	Dec. 76 (+21)

Average lead or lag
at growth cycle

Peaks	−5	−4	+9
Troughs	−6	−4	+9
All turns	−7	−4	+10

n.s.c.: No specific cycle.

Note: The correlation coefficients (r) between the leads of the three series (with coefficients excluding the 1957 peak shown in parentheses) are:

	At peaks	At troughs	At all turns
Leading index and industrial materials price index	+0.54	+0.98	+0.76
Leading index and consumer price index	+0.14 (+0.64)	+0.82	+0.42 (+0.72)
Industrial materials price index and consumer price index	+0.56 (+0.74)	+0.98	+0.56 (+0.67)

a Based on the consensus of turning points in trend-adjusted data for nineteen measures of aggregate output, income, sales, and employment. See Victor Zarnowitz and Geoffrey H. Moore, "The Recession and Recovery of 1973–1976," *Explorations in Economic Research* (Fall 1977), p. 508.

b Commerce Department's index (BCD series 910), trend-adjusted by NBER.

c Change over twelve months, smoothed (not centered). Centering the rates would increase the leads by six months and reduce the lags by six months.

Table 5
LEADS AND LAGS DURING GROWTH CYCLES: LEADING INDEX AND TWO PRICE INDEXES, SIX COUNTRIES (EXCLUDING THE UNITED STATES)

Date of Growth Cycle[a]		Date of Turn and Lead (−) or Lag (+) in Months					
		Leading index, deviation from trend[b]		Rate of change in industrial materials price index[c]		Rate of change in consumer price index[c]	
Peak	Trough	Peak	Trough	Peak	Trough	Peak	Trough
Feb. 57	Jan. 59	Feb. 57 (0)	June 58 (−7)	Dec. 56 (−2)	June 58 (−7)	June 58 (+16)	July 59 (+6)
Mar. 61	Feb. 63	May 61 (+2)	Oct. 62 (−4)	Aug. 61 (+5)	Oct. 62 (−4)	Apr. 63 (+25)	Aug. 64 (+18)
Sept. 64	May 68	Feb. 64 (−7)	June 67 (−11)	Jan. 64 (−8)	July 67 (−10)	June 65 (+9)	Aug. 67 (−9)
June 70	Dec. 71	Nov. 69 (−7)	Feb. 72 (+2)	Dec. 69 (−6)	Dec. 71 (0)	Sept. 71 (+15)	Aug. 67 (−9)
Nov. 73	Aug. 75	Feb. 74 (+3)	July 75 (−1)	Mar. 74 (+4)	June 75 (−2)	Oct. 74 (+11)	June 72 (+6)
Jan. 77[b]		July 76 (−6)		July 76 (−6)		May 77 (+4)	Aug. 76 (+12)
Average lead or lag at growth cycle							
Peaks		−2		−2		+13	
Troughs			−4		−5		+7
All turns		−3		−3		+10	

Note: The correlation coefficients (r) between the leads of the three series are:

	At peaks	At troughs	At all turns
Leading index and industrial materials price index	+0.96	+0.997	+0.95
Leading index and consumer price index	+0.54	+0.61	+0.59
Industrial materials price index and consumer price index	+0.63	+0.65	+0.64

[a] Based on six-country coincident index, deviations from trend.
[b] Tentative.
[c] Change over twelve months, smoothed (not centered). Centering the rates would increase the leads by six months and reduce the lags by six months.

Table 6
TEST FOR TREND IN LEADS OR LAGS, UNITED STATES

	Number of Obser- vations	Regression Coefficients (and t Statistics)			Regression Estimate[a]	
		a	b	r	1948	1978
Leading index	18	−16.8 (−1.4)	+0.18 (0.89)	+0.22	−8	−3
Industrial materials price index	14	−34.9 (−1.6)	+0.49 (1.43)	+0.38	−11	+3
Consumer price index	15	−25.5 (−1.8)	+0.56 (2.52)	+0.57	+1	+18

[a] Lead (−) or lag (+) in months.
Source: Table 4.

consumer price index are associated with those in the leading index and in industrial materials prices.

It is of some importance to determine whether there has been a long-run shift in the length of the lags in prices in relation to the growth cycle. A test of the U.S. data suggests that the lags in the rate of change in the consumer price index have been getting longer with respect to the growth cycle, the leading index, and the materials price index. The leads in the last two indexes may also have been getting shorter, but this is more conjectural. Regressions in which the dependent variable is the length of lead or lag in months and the independent variable is the year in which the turn occurred (for example, 48, 49, and so on) are given in Table 6.

The coefficient for time (under b in Table 6) is positive in all three cases, although it is statistically significant only in the case of the consumer price index. During the thirty-year period from 1948 to 1978, the regression suggests a substantial shift, with the estimated lag for the CPI increasing by nearly a year and a half. The regressions for the leading index and the materials price index suggest a smaller shift in the same direction. In short, the rate of inflation (CPI) lags behind the growth cycle more than it used to, and, to a lesser extent, it also lags farther behind the wholesale prices of materials and the sensitive leading indicators.[6] A possible reason is the increasing relative importance of services in the CPI and their more sluggish price behavior.[7]

The leading index and the materials price index are helpful not only in telling when a turn in the rate of inflation is coming, but also in gauging the magnitude of the forthcoming swing. Tables 7 and 8 show that the size of the upswings and downswings in the leading index are correlated with those in the rate of change in materials prices and in consumer prices, and that the swings in materials prices and consumer prices are also correlated. This is true both in the U.S. data and in the figures for the six other countries. These results strongly suggest that the greater relative weakness during 1977 in the leading index for the six countries as compared with the United States was associated with the fact that the rate of inflation in the group of six was trending down at the end of 1977, while the rate of inflation in the United States was trending up (see Figures 10 and 11).

Further Research and Development

A continuing research and development program is essential if the system of international economic indicators described above is to be preserved and improved. Additional countries should be covered and additional indicators should be included along the lines noted. Greater attention should be given to prompt availability of data, graphic displays, and other analytical tools. Methods of trend-adjusting current data need testing and evaluation, as do methods of using the indicators in trade forecasting models and inflation models. The indicator system is not intended to, nor can it, replace other forecasting methods. But it can supplement them. Its emphasis on monthly data, which are generally more up to date than quarterly data; its capacity to utilize partly redundant information (for example, employment data from two independent sources); its inclusion of variables, such as stock prices, that are known to be relevant but may not fit easily into an existing theoretical model; its adaptability to analysis of units of observation that are of general concern, such as periods of recession or periods of boom;

---

[6] The data in Table 5 for the six other countries do not show a similar trend. The regression coefficients on time are positive for the six-country leading index and for the materials price index, but negative for the consumer price index; none of the coefficients, however, is statistically significant.

[7] Phillip Cagan, however, found a trend toward more sluggish response in the wholesale prices of commodities alone, although he concentrated attention upon the amplitude of price change rather than the length of lag. See his "Changes in the Recession Behavior of Wholesale Prices in the 1920s and post-World War II," *Explorations in Economic Research*, vol. 2, no. 1 (Winter 1975), pp. 54–104.

Table 7

AMPLITUDE OF CHANGE IN LEADING INDEX AND IN THE RATE OF INFLATION DURING GROWTH CYCLES, UNITED STATES, 1951–1975

Date of Growth Cycle		Change in Leading Index, Trend Adjusted[a]		Change in Rate of Change (percentage points)			
				Industrial materials price index		Consumer price index	
High	Low	Low to high	High to low	Low to high	High to low	Low to high	High to low
Mar. 51	Oct. 49	18	−14	108.3	−106.9	11.1	−8.2
Mar. 53	July 52	7	−11	12.5[b]	15.6[b]	0.6	−1.8
Feb. 57	Aug. 54	18	−14	12.2[b]	−27.7	4.1	−2.8
Feb. 60	Apr. 58	15	−17	23.0	−15.9	0.9	−0.8
May 62	Feb. 61	7	−13	9.3	−9.9	0.4[b]	−0.1[b]
June 66	Oct. 64	8	−4	24.2	−30.8	2.3[b]	−1.0
Mar. 69	Oct. 67	10	−9	32.7	−27.4	3.6	−3.0
Mar. 73	Nov. 70	15	−13	62.0	−73.8	8.3	−6.5
	Mar. 75		−27				

Coefficient of correlation (r)	Rises	Falls	Rises and falls[c]
Leading index and industrial materials price index	+0.56	+0.31	+0.40
Leading index and consumer price index	+0.69	+0.52	+0.55
Industrial materials price index and consumer price index	+0.93	+0.90	+0.89

Note: For the dates of highs and lows used to measure changes in the leading index and in the rate of change in prices, see Table 4.

[a] In index points, that is, in percent of trend.

[b] Change to growth-cycle high or low, since there is no corresponding turn in the price series (see Table 4).

[c] The correlation is computed without regard to the sign of the rise or fall.

Table 8

AMPLITUDE OF CHANGE IN LEADING INDEX AND IN THE RATE OF INFLATION DURING GROWTH CYCLES, SIX COUNTRIES (EXCLUDING THE UNITED STATES), 1957–1977

| Date of Growth Cycle | | Change in Leading Index, Trend Adjusted[a] | | Change in Rate of Change (percentage points) | | | |
High	Low	Low to high	High to low	Industrial materials price index Low to high	Industrial materials price index High to low	Consumer price index Low to high	Consumer price index High to low
Feb. 57	Jan. 59		−6.9		−8.8		−3.9
Mar. 61	Feb. 63	8.2	−5.4	6.5	−4.3	4.2	−2.2
Sept. 64	May 68	4.8	−5.0	5.0	−6.1	1.7	−2.6
June 70	Dec. 71	6.4	−9.6	10.2	−9.1	4.0	−0.9
Nov. 73	Aug. 75	11.8	−11.6	53.5	−55.4	9.9	−0.9
Jan. 77		6.9		16.4		1.8	−6.0

Coefficients of correlation (r)

	Rises	Falls	Rises and falls[b]
Leading index and industrial materials price index	+0.89	+0.81	+0.85
Leading index and consumer price index	+0.94	+0.45	+0.69
Industrial materials price index and consumer price index	+0.89	+0.83	+0.82

Note: For the dates of highs and lows used to measure changes in the leading index and in the rate of change in prices, see Table 5.

[a] In index points, that is, in percent of trend.

[b] The correlation is computed without regard to the sign of the rise or fall.

and its reliance, for the most part, upon easily understood relationships, such as those between new orders and output or between the average work week and employment—all suggest a supplementary but nonetheless useful role. Detecting an international recession promptly and measuring its scope and severity, appraising trade prospects, and getting early warning signals of new inflationary trends are matters of vast consequence to the peoples of the world. For that reason it is to be hoped that the relatively modest intellectual and statistical resources required to maintain this new measurement system will be forthcoming.

Structural Problems
behind Our
Measured Unemployment Rates

William Fellner

Summary

The study is concerned with structural characteristics of our unemployment problem and with their bearing on attempts to reduce unemployment by expansionary monetary and fiscal policies.

The analysis starts with a critique of the conventional method of estimating potential output. This method is based on assumed trends in the availability and the productivity of labor and of industrial capacities, but at best only vague assumptions are made about the structural elements determining the supply prices of the inputs and the corresponding commodity price trends. In fact, the conventional estimates of the potential output have served as a basis for inflationary policies. At present they serve as a point of departure for trying to accommodate by monetary and fiscal policy the "basic" or "underlying" rate of inflation which policy makers believe they detect in the money-cost data. Such a policy of accommodation is supposed to move us to a path of higher output with a lower level of unemployment than would a policy of gradually reducing the rate of increase in money GNP. The higher path is alleged to be the path of the potential output.

Yet, in reality, such a policy of accommodation, if continued, will lead to an upward revision of the expected inflation rate and to a steepening of cost trends because the market participants will rightly foresee a willingness to accommodate a higher basic rate of inflation if a higher rate should be detected in the data on the next occasion. If a "potential output" is obtainable only by accommodating such cost and price developments, it is not located on a sustainable output path—nor is it a potential output in any useful sense—because it can be produced only by misleading the suppliers of inputs about the real equivalent of the prices at which the inputs are supplied. Many commitments have already been made for the future each time when inflation expectations steepen anew.

83

Realistically, the potential output, interpreted as being on a sustainable path, depends significantly on the real supply prices of the needed inputs, prominently including labor inputs of all kinds. The real supply prices in turn depend significantly on changing structural and institutional factors that limit the available supply of inputs at supply prices that make their employment rewarding. Some of these limitations could and should be removed or reduced, but in setting our macroeconomic goals it is imperative to make allowances for those structural and institutional rigidities which we do not wish to eliminate or which we are in fact unable to modify. We have been using inflationary techniques to cover up a contradiction between our employment policy goals and our attitude toward rigidifying elements in our economic structure, but this cannot be done for long. These rigidifying elements are clearly reflected in the structural characteristics of our unemployment problem.

Our efforts should be directed at gradually but consistently reducing the rate of increase of money GNP until a noninflationary price trend is restored, and they should be directed at achieving the highest output and employment rate compatible with this course. We should not continue to try for specific unemployment-rate targets when there are no convincing arguments in support of their long-run feasibility in view of the structural characteristics of the unemployment we are trying to reduce. Nor should we further aggravate our problems by resuming experimentation with the administrative direction of the wage and price structure or with euphemistically described equivalents of such controls.

No one can, of course, guarantee that the economy would be recession-proof on the way to achieving a stable price level by successive consistent reductions of the rate of increase in money GNP. But a consistent and truly credible policy so conducted would have a good chance of avoiding significant bumpiness because it would exert a much stronger influence on price expectations, and hence on cost trends, than have the erratic policies of the past. In contrast, along a route described by successive inflationary flare-ups an economy is practically certain to encounter recessions of increasing severity, which do not even clear the ground for a subsequent healthy development. The social and political consequences of remaining on that route would also prove very serious.

The Conventional Concept of Potential Output and the Problem of Rigidities

A Critique of the Conventional Framework. Estimating the potential output of an economy is a much more complex problem than that implied in the conventional estimating procedures.

In its January 1977 Annual Report, the then outgoing Ford administration's last Council of Economic Advisers (CEA) estimated the normal growth rate of the American economy—its growth rate after completion of the cyclical recovery process—at 3.5 percent a year.[1] This estimate is based on conjectures concerning future rates of increase in the labor input as well as in the output per man-hour. For some future span in which the average yearly rate of increase of the labor force is expected to exceed 2 percent, this particular estimate or guess seems reasonable, though admittedly subject to revision. But by itself, this estimate leaves open both the question of the speed at which we can move upward during the present cyclical recovery and, what is equally important, the question of the output base which will be reached at the time of slowing down to the normal growth rate. The 1977 CEA report in fact suggested that the slowing to normal growth will have to happen at the time when our actual output will have caught up with a specific trend line originating in the past and projected into the future. This is the trend line defining the path of the so-called potential output.

This reference trend line displays a 3.6 percent slope per year from 1962 on and its estimated future slope is very similar. Hence these slopes are very nearly the same as the normal growth rate to be achieved after the present cyclical recovery. Moreover, the average yearly rate of increase of the actual output from 1955 to 1965 and from 1965 to 1973 was also about 3½ percent, since in those years the actual output was close to the estimated potential. To put these statements together: we will be back to the potential so estimated when we have returned to a reference trend line that has been sloping upward at approximately 3½ percent annually for a lengthy period. Although for reasonably chosen past periods the actual output path had just about the same slope, the actual output of the years since 1973 has fallen well below the reference trend line in question.

The estimate of the potential output published in the 1977 CEA report represented a downward revision of estimates which had been made by an earlier CEA and which had postulated for the path of the potential output a slope of 3.9 rather than 3.5 percent. In its 1978 Annual Report, from which Figure 1 is extracted, the new CEA of the Carter administration endorsed essentially the 1977 downward revision.[2] Into its estimate of the future slope of the potential output path, the new CEA introduced, however, a narrow band around 3.5 percent. Even the revised estimates suggest that in 1977 we fell short of our potential output by 5.3 percent. They suggest also that in 1978 the pre-

---

[1] Council of Economic Advisers, *Annual Report*, 1977, p. 53.

[2] Council of Economic Advisers, *Annual Report*, 1978, p. 83.

Figure 1

ACTUAL AND POTENTIAL GROSS NATIONAL PRODUCT

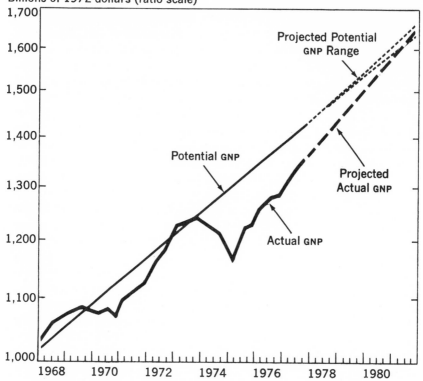

Billions of 1972 dollars (ratio scale)

Source: Department of Commerce and Council of Economic Advisers, *Annual Report*, 1978.

sumptive shortfall will be smaller but still in excess of 4 percent. The reason is that from 1977 to 1978 the potential output will have grown by an additional 3.5 percent, and while the actual output is now expected to grow by more than the 3.5 percent addition to the potential, it is not expected to grow by a margin that would take care of both the 5.3 percent shortfall existing in 1977 and the 3.5 percent further addition to the potential. Taking care of both would require an increase in actual output from 1977 to 1978 of close to 9 percent—more than twice the increase that is now expected to develop. Thus we are supposed to have a significant slack (unused potential), though the behavior observable in the markets contradicts this diagnosis.

During a period of cyclical recovery there is, of course, room for growth by more than the "normal" long-run rate. Yet if we are determined to avoid overexpansion that will soon backfire, then we must recognize that even during a recovery phase there is room for growth only to the extent that it can be brought about by the voluntary supply of inputs at real incomes expressing the value of the output produced. A supply of inputs that is induced by the temporary misjudgment of available real incomes in inflationary circumstances does not result in sustainable output gains. It therefore seems to me unconvincing to assert, as does the now conventional approach, that in real terms the potential output of 1978 will be about 9 percent higher than was the actual output of 1977, and to imply that this assertion can be justified by showing that the 1978 output would indeed be that much higher if since the mid-1950s (or the mid-1960s) we had been growing smoothly at an annual rate of about 3.5 percent. An effort to raise our output in one year by 9 percent beyond its 1977 level would have to involve the use of inflationary techniques that would soon boomerang—the effort would probably be unsuccessful even if that highly unreasonable price were accepted. Indeed, by way of qualification, this much is recognized even by economists employing the conventional concept of the potential output. They point out that, partly because of the short-run limitations of industrial capacity, we could not place ourselves back on the potential path without observing *speed limits* in the catch-up process. Yet, although this qualification concerning speed limits is indeed generally accepted by economists using the conventional concept, it does not eliminate an essential non sequitur from the reasoning developed in the usual conceptual framework.

An essential proposition remains unqualified so long as we remain within the now conventional framework. This proposition is that a monotonically rising line, dating back far into the pre-1973 period with occasional changes in its slope, has continued to be located at some considerable distance above our actual output, and that after the cyclical recovery the economy will tend to grow at its long-run growth rate from an output base represented by the height of that reference line at the time when we catch up with it. Though the measured unemployment rate is not assumed to remain constant along the path, it is claimed that the estimating procedure also provides information concerning the unemployment rate for the successive positions of the path. The 1977 CEA report estimated this unemployment rate at 4.9 percent for the now relevant portion of the line describing the potential output.

Such a conceptual construct glosses over the question whether the guess of a 3½ percent future normal growth rate is to be wedded to the hypothesis that in some predictable future we shall catch up with a trend line originating in a rather distant past, even though we have fallen quite a bit below that reference line during the post-1973 aftermath of a violent inflationary flare-up. Implying an affirmative answer to this question of wedding two hypotheses means deriving conclusions from a non sequitur. Lines connecting the 1973 actual output with that of specific earlier years lending themselves to a comparison with 1973 do have a logarithmic slope of about 3½ percent a year, and our future normal growth rate (after completing the present recovery) might be of similar magnitude; yet we do not know at present whether the output base from which the economy will then again tend to grow at some such rate will be so located that the shortfall that has accumulated in the post-1973 adjustment period in relation to the reference trend line will become fully wiped out. After all, the post-1973 segment of the monotonically rising reference trend line expressing the potential output—a segment that has allegedly been moving since 1973 at a specific distance above the actual output—is a figment of the imagination. Shifts may have occurred from the successive positions indicated by that line.

In fairness it needs to be added, however, that the 1977 CEA report stressed the tentative character of its estimates and the need to adjust them in the future if experience should prove them unrealistic. With respect to the size of the potential output and the 4.9 percent unemployment rate associated with it, the qualifying remarks of the 1977 CEA suggested that realistic estimates of a reasonably defined potential might prove somewhat less ambitious than those derived from the CEA's formal analysis. On the other hand, in the 1978 Annual Report of the new CEA the underlying assumptions were bent slightly in the other direction, and the conclusions became slightly more ambitious, at least for the time when we are supposed to arrive back to the potential output path. For that time the 1978 Annual Report puts the measured unemployment rate at 4.8 percent.

The projections included this year in the documents supporting the 1979 federal budget outdo the 1978 CEA estimates in this regard, though an attempt was made to de-emphasize this difference. According to the budget projections, in the year of catching up with the potential output the output base will be so high that the corresponding unemployment rate will come out at 4.1 percent, but the subsequent discussion in the documents suggests that 4.7 percent may prove to be a more realistic guess. The position taken in the budget documents with respect to this problem is a matter of obvious significance, because fiscal policy is intended to promote the course of events described there. Willingness of monetary policy to supplement such a fiscal policy is a logical implication of the analysis presented in support of the budget policy.

The present study does not make use of the conventional concept of potential output as expressed by monotonically rising lines. An output level admittedly unavailable during any specific period will not here be called the potential output of that period, and ignorance will be pleaded of whether the output base, from which we shall tend to grow at a normal rate of, say, 3.5 percent after the cyclical recovery, will be located on a trend line originating well before 1973. Instead, it will be assumed that, when the appraisals are made within a reasonable time frame, the output and employment potential of any period is determined by the availability of resources at *real* supply prices that can be recovered from the value of the output produced. This statement applies where the supply prices are not falsified by an inflationary process that makes the public misjudge the real equivalent of a current-dollar supply price. Further, the statement takes it for granted that the potential output in the relevant sense must be located on a sustainable output path.

Emphasis will be placed in this study on the role of institutional and structural factors in determining the real supply price of resources on which our output and employment potential depend. Binding limitations of supply have developed largely from institutional and structural factors which any useful concept of potential output must take into consideration. Changes in these factors can shift the potential output up or down, and a basic shortcoming of the conventional approach is that such shifts cannot be accommodated.

The Problem of Rigidities. Institutional elements which limit our output are usually referred to as "rigidities." In principle, we could get rid of all or most of these elements, and it would indeed be very important to press for removing or modifying several. At the same time, a realistic approach must recognize that some of the structural rigidities, such as those developing from the availability of transfer payments, express value judgments widely shared in Western countries, and some other rigidifying factors are very difficult for Western-type governments with limited powers to remove. To the extent that any rigidifying elements are taken for granted, it is imperative to make allowances for them in setting our output goals. Past policies that have jeopardized the functioning of market economies have not concerned themselves with a reduction of structural rigidities. Typically they have allowed them to increase, perhaps partly in response to widely held value judgments, but partly because too little attention has been paid to accommodating these judgments by the least rigidifying arrangements. The conventional procedures for estimating potential output essentially bypass this problem.

The rigidifying elements of our market structures raise a broad spectrum of problems that includes barriers to competition in all markets. The present study, however, calls attention directly to only a limited number of elements bearing particularly on the labor supply. In the present context the emphasis should be placed on these elements because ambitious demand-management policies are motivated mainly by low unemployment-rate targets.

Minimum wage legislation is, of course, a rigidifying factor, and it cannot be reasonably said to reflect widely held value judgments. It limits employment opportunities for the inexperienced, particularly for teenagers, from whose competition it protects the more highly paid. At the same time the value judgment that the young should be enabled to acquire work experience is clearly more generally held than that the wholly inexperienced must immediately earn at least about half the average factory wage or remain jobless. The abolition of minimum wage requirements together with well-focused training programs would in all probability be not only more efficient but also less costly to the government than the largely ineffective job programs whose costs have recently risen very steeply.

Although collective bargaining, unemployment compensation, and the entire system of transfer payments introduce rigidities into the cost structure, they do reflect widely held value judgments. In none of these areas, however, has much attention been paid to finding the least rigidifying solutions that would effectively serve the avowed purpose of the provisions. For example, the present institutional setting makes it possible for the terms of employment reached by specific employers and unions to carry over automatically to employers and workers who would otherwise be willing to agree on different terms involving greater flexibility. Another example is tax-free unemployment compensation. Transfer payments to the unemployed would in any event be tax free to the poor, but when the tax exemption is granted to the nonpoor as well, it becomes unduly tempting for many to extend the duration of their unemployment. Other features of the transfer-payments system strengthen this temptation.

Rigidifying factors have tended to grow. In addition, major changes to which the economy has had to adjust have lent added significance to the given rigidities, by putting the flexibility of the market system to a particularly severe test. Shifts in the composition of the labor force are among the changes that have had this effect, and they are not the only such changes. Demand-management policies, when they imply estimates of the potential output that do not take account of these developments adequately, are thereby disregarding the truly relevant output limits. These limits can be exceeded only temporarily by inflationary techniques, that is, by methods that deceive the public concerning the available real incomes. These methods were in fact used and, as should have been expected, they have left a painful aftermath.

If instead of gradually returning to noninflationary conditions we should continue to rely on such methods, there will be a growing temptation to impose upon the economy a centralized, politically administered organization of essential economic activities in order to suppress the symptoms of steepening inflation. Under such a system the public is faced with the unavailability of many types of wanted goods and with regulated prices for the range of goods made available, rather than with steeply rising prices across the board. Enforcement of such a network of regulations requires governmental powers far exceeding those to which Western nations have become accustomed. This could hardly be regarded as a desirable cure of our difficulties. Unsystematic and sporadic interferences with the wage-price structure under democratic institutions would fail as they have in the past, and meanwhile they would do great harm by creating a high degree of uncertainty. The at present widely discussed idea of providing tax-subsidy incentives for noninflationary cost-price behavior does not get around the basic difficulty of implying an arbitrary wage and price *structure*, not to mention the administrative obstacles standing in the way of such programs.

Maximum Output with Sustainable Behavior of Prices. In my judgment it would be foolhardy to attempt a numerical estimate of the extent to which alternative sets of institutional arrangements would limit output and raise the unemployment rate because of the changing severity of the tests to which the flexibility of the system is exposed as a result of observed major shifts in its basic resource position. Instead of formulating goals in terms of numerically specified rates of growth and of measured unemployment rates, we should try for the maximum output and employment compatible with a behavior of the general price level which does not lead the suppliers of inputs into decisions they will subsequently regret. Only gradually can the employment levels and unemployment rates reflecting such a course be felt out, but the path so described is clearly the best of the *sustainable* paths of the economy.

In principle, any behavior of the price level to which market activities have become conditioned could turn out to be a sustainable behavior, but it is very unlikely that policy makers could prove successful in conditioning market expectations to anything but a gradual return to practical stability of the general price level. For the United States such sustainable "practical stability" is exemplified by the price behavior during the 1951–1965 period. For that period the usual price measures show an average yearly rate of increase of between 1 and 2 percent, but

91

the "all-commodities" component of the Consumer Price Index shows merely a rise at an average rate of less than 1 percent (with the all-services component—essentially a wage component—rising at 2.9 percent).

A return to such a state involves a gradual but consistent reduction of the rate of increase of current-dollar effective demand until the objective is achieved. It is unconvincing to argue that money-cost and price trends would probably not fall in line with such a policy and that the policy would then run a high risk of causing a recession. A *credible* policy of this sort would clearly exert a major influence on price expectations, which in turn have a significant influence on money-cost and price trends. It needs to be stressed that in this regard no valid inferences can be drawn from the experience of the past twenty-five years; during the first half of this period the problem of putting an end to any major inflationary trend did not exist, and during the second half hesitant programs to do so have had no credibility. It is true that even in the event of a credible program, a recession-proof course toward practical price stability could not be guaranteed, but this is beside the point. Along the alternative route of successive inflationary flare-ups there is simply no chance of avoiding recessions. The recessions encountered along the latter route would not even clear the ground for subsequent healthy growth, while any recession that might be encountered on the way to price stability would at least perform that function.

The authorities would be very unlikely to succeed in keeping a significant rate of inflation steady and predictable because the reluctance of policy makers to impose the extra restraints needed to get back to practical price stability would have a decisive effect on cost trends. These trends would then develop in anticipation of a willingness to accommodate an even higher inflation rate in the next phase, if failure to do so would at that time present the same difficulties as those that would have to be faced now by a policy promptly reducing the rate of increase of current-dollar effective demand.

The 1979 federal budget is based on a very different notion. The budget forecast itself suggests no diminution of the large fiscal deficit in a year that is expected to be one of rapid cyclical expansion. The economic projections attached to the budget disclose the intention of the policy makers to accommodate during 1978 and 1979 a proportionate increase in the money GNP that will exceed the increase observed for 1977 over 1976; and to accommodate even for 1980 over 1979 an increase equal to that which occurred from 1976 to 1977. These projections imply a "cooperative" attitude on the part of the Federal Reserve and imply also the belief that the inflation rate, when measured by the GNP deflator, will be somewhat higher in 1978 and even in 1979 than it was in 1977. For unexplained reasons, though, it is suggested that inflation will decline thereafter.

As was said before what matters is not that the official projections include a minor steepening in the deflator's rate of increase in the near future. What matters is that the market participants are being served notice of the intention of the policy makers to accommodate what they now regard as the "underlying" inflation rate corresponding to the present and prospective cost trends, particularly money-wage trends; and what matters is that such a policy is exceedingly likely to lead to the conviction that even steeper cost trends will subsequently also be accommodated. Price expectations and money-cost trends develop upward flexibility which, given the public's growing experience with inflationary processes, may also result at an early stage in an anticipation of the cyclical setback that always follows accelerating inflation, and business decisions will have to be made amidst growing uncertainty concerning future events. Policies running these risks have been adopted mainly with the objective of reducing the unemployment rate. Yet a durable reduction of these rates can be achieved only if inflation is also reduced and gradually eliminated. Even then, the level to which the measured unemployment rate can be reduced depends heavily on structural and institutional factors.

Introducing the Structural Analysis. We now turn to a more detailed analysis of structural and institutional factors bearing on the present and future unemployment rates along the best output and employment path available.

Before surveying the data in some detail, we need to consider four facts that demonstrate the structural nature of the problem—a problem that cannot be dealt with effectively if it is viewed as one of insufficiency of aggregate effective demand. (1) A significant change in the life style of the population is expressed in the rapidly increasing participation of women in economic activity. By the last quarter of 1977 6.8 million more adult women were employed than there would have been if their proportionate representation in total employment had remained the same as in 1956. The great majority of these women live in households with at least one other wage earner. Along with this rise in female employment and with the disproportionate rise of newcomers in the labor force, about 930,000 more adult women were looking for a job and did not yet have one than would have been the case if their unemployment rate had remained the same as in 1956. (2) By the last quarter of 1977 teenagers whose representation in the labor force had risen in an even higher proportion than that of women and whose employment is unfavorably influenced by minimum wage legislation, made up 24.0 percent of our unemployed but only 8.5 percent of total employment. (The discrepancy between weight in unemployment and weight in employment is much smaller for adult women.) (3) At the same time the representation of all nonwhites in unemployment was 23.6 percent, as against their 10.9 percent representation in total employment. (4) One way of raising the question of the impact of age, sex, and race on our unemployment rates is to ask what has been the ratio of the unemployment rate of white prime-age males (twenty-five to fifty-four years) to the overall unemployment rate in recent years. This ratio has typically ranged from 40 to 60 percent. The low unemployment rates of this group have, however, had a declining influence on the overall rates, because the weight of the group in the labor force has become significantly reduced.

The unskilled are clearly more prone to unemployment than are those possessing skills, and the job composition is expected to shift further in the direction of the skilled. However, in appraising this trend it would be difficult to judge the importance of the fact that the temptation to rely on the transfer-payments system must be quite a bit smaller for the skilled than for those who could obtain only jobs requiring no skills.

Some of the structural elements that have caused these developments are best viewed as having resulted from the growth of rigidifying factors. Others are best viewed somewhat differently, as having brought to prominence the effect of rigidities that have been present all along. The steep rise in the labor force participation rate of adult women and thus the rise in the relative weight of new entrants and reentrants into the labor force, illustrates how structural change can intensify the effect of given rigidities. These particular rigidities or imperfections of an economy's flexibility could surely not be eliminated, and generating inflationary pressures is no way to reduce them. New entrants and reentrants into the labor force need some amount of time to find jobs, and, having found their first jobs after entry or reentry, they are apt to change jobs more frequently than workers with a more extended attachment to the labor force. As will be shown in this study, the excess of adult female over adult male unemployment rates is at least mainly, and probably entirely, attributable to this phenomenon. Given the largely inevitable limitations of the speed with which new entrants and reentrants into the labor force can be accommodated, we must conclude that given limitations of flexibility have come to play a more prominent role. The rising participation of women, and thus the rising weight of entrants and reentrants, has put the flexibility of the system to a more demanding test.

On the other hand, the rise in adult male unemployment rates from

1973 to late 1977 is much more likely to reflect in part the *growth* of rigidifying factors connected with unemployment compensation and the general welfare system. However, here, too, the need to go through a transition process after a period of accelerating inflation, with inflationary expectations built into the cost structure, would have placed the economy's flexibility under greater strain even with all rigidifying elements unchanged. As for the high teenage unemployment rates—resulting not *merely* from the high proportion of entrants and reentrants among teenagers—these also have to do with the growth of rigidities brought about by the increasing coverage of minimum wage regulations. But at the same time these specific unemployment rates further illustrate the fact that major changes in the composition of the available resources expose any given degree of flexibility to more severe tests.

It is particularly ill advised to try to attack such a set of problems with analytical equipment derived from grossly simplified textbooks that stress the need to create enough effective demand for achieving "full employment." The monthly census surveys do, to be sure, lead to the conclusion that many millions of persons who have no work during a survey week are jobseekers in the sense defined for the survey. But given collective bargaining, minimum wage legislation, and an extended system of transfer payments, and given also the bearing of the available capital stock on labor productivity, it is impossible to derive from such census data any indication of the relation between the productivity of the jobseekers, on the one hand, and the supply prices of their services on the other.

Structural Factors Bearing on Employment and Unemployment

The Time Span. The data included in Table 1 go back to 1956, but they do not continue beyond the final quarter of 1977. In the early part of 1978 the adult male and adult female unemployment rate declined below the 1977 level shown in the table. The adult male rate declined to about 4½ percent, the adult female rate to below 6 percent, and the overall rate for the labor force as a whole to about 6 percent. The rate of price increase has accelerated, and the high degree of uncertainty surrounding business expectations continues to exert a negative influence on investment plans. But it is impossible to form an opinion at the present writing of whether the most recent brief phase of development is merely a passing episode or whether it is already beginning to bear out our conclusions concerning the consequences of an inflation-

95

Table 1
RATIOS BEARING ON EMPLOYMENT AND UNEMPLOYMENT FOR SELECTED DATES

	E/P (1)	U/NW (2)	LF/P (3)	U/LF (4)	U/P (5)
Total population					
1956	57.5	5.8	60.0	4.1	2.5
1973	57.8	7.0	60.8	4.9	2.9
4th quarter 1977	58.5	10.0	62.7	6.6	4.2
Adult men (20 and over)					
1956	84.6	19.3	87.6	3.4[a]	3.0
1973	78.7	12.3	81.3	3.2[a]	2.6
4th quarter 1977	76.1	15.9	79.9	4.8[a]	3.8
Adult women (20 and over)					
1956	34.9	2.4	36.4	4.2	1.5
1973	42.2	3.7	44.4	4.8	2.1
4th quarter 1977	45.3	6.0	48.6	6.8	3.3
Teenagers of both sexes (16 through 19)					
1956	45.3	10.4	50.9	11.1	5.7
1973	46.0	14.4	53.8	14.5	7.8
4th quarter 1977	47.5	18.2	57.0	16.7	9.5

[a] The prime-age (twenty-five to fifty-four years) male unemployment rates in these three periods were 3.0, 2.5, and 4.1 percent. This relates to all races jointly, as does the table in general.

Symbols: E = Employed; P = Civilian noninstitutional population, aged sixteen years and over; U = Unemployed; NW = Nonworkers (unemployed plus those not in the labor force); LF = Labor force (employed plus unemployed).

Note: Because of changes in the questionnaire used in the monthly surveys in 1967 and in 1970, there are some intertemporal noncomparabilities in the data of the table. The finding that the prime-age male unemployment rate declined from 1956 to 1973 and rose thereafter (see footnote a) does seem to survive any reasonable adjustment. Yet the result that in 1973 the unemployment rate of all adult males was lower than it had been in 1956 (rather than roughly equal to it) is not a dependable finding, nor is the result that the adult female unemployment rate was higher in 1973 than in 1956 (rather than roughly equal to the 1956 rate). However, no reasonable adjustment would eliminate the rise of the adult male and the adult female unemployment rate from 1956 to the last quarter of 1977, nor even from 1956 to the early part of 1978 (at which time the rates were declining). Furthermore, reasonable adjustments would tend to accentuate rather than reduce the rise of the teenage rate from 1956 to the end of the period. As a result of the rising labor-force weight of adult women and of teenagers, the rise of the unemployment rate of the labor force as a whole survives any reasonable adjustment for a comparison not only of more recent periods but even of 1973 with 1956.

Source: Yearly manpower reports of the President and, for recent data, *Monthly Labor Review.*

ary policy posture. The propositions developed in the paper do not depend on this kind of short-run forecasting exercise, and we shall not extend our data into the early months of 1978.

A "Paradox." Some of the numerical information referred to in this section is summarized in Table 1. The note to the table points out some qualifications applying to the intertemporal comparisons.

When tracing the general trends in employment and unemployment observable over the past two decades one runs into an apparent contradiction, and it is advisable to resolve this before trying to appraise the significance of the trends. The appearance of a contradiction arises because the employed percentage of the population as a whole shows a mild upward trend—that of women a sharp upward trend—and because at the same time the unemployed percentage of the population also shows an upward trend as does the unemployment rate in the conventional sense. Before resolving this seeming paradox the following points of terminology must be noted:

(1) The employed, as here interpreted, include the self-employed.

(2) The population to which we relate the civilian employed is the entire civilian noninstitutional population aged sixteen years and over.

(3) The *unemployed* make up merely a small fraction of the *nonworkers* (that is, of the nonemployed part of the population). This fraction consists of (a) those nonworkers about whom the monthly census surveys provide the information that they were available for work during the survey week and were looking for work some time during the preceding four weeks; and (b) those nonworkers who, even if they were not looking for work, will report to work within the next thirty days.

(4) The number of unemployed so defined, expressed as a percentage of the population, does not yield the same ratio as that representing the unemployment rate. The unemployment rate relates the number of unemployed not to the entire population aged 16 years and over but merely to the *labor force*, consisting of the employed and the unemployed (excluding those nonworkers who are not regarded as unemployed).

(5) From the mid-1950s to the present the percentage of the population belonging in the labor force—defined as the labor force participation rate—has risen from 60 percent to about 63 percent, but the behavior of the labor force participation rate has been very different for the various major categories of the labor force.

Trends in the employed proportion of the population (column 1, Table 1) have been favorable, with the result that in 1973, the most recent cyclical peak year, this proportion was somewhat higher than in the most favorable years of the cycle that evolved in the mid-1950s. In 1956, 57.5 percent of the population was employed, and by the last quarter of 1977 this figure had risen to 58.5 percent. Since then there has occurred a further rise.

What at first seems paradoxical is that while nonworkers have thus declined in relation to the population as a whole, the unemployed percentage of the population—the number of those nonworkers regarded as unemployed expressed as a percentage of the population—has also shown an upward trend (column 5, Table 1). The overall unemployment rate, which relates the unemployed to the labor force (to the employed plus the unemployed), rose from 4.1 percent in 1956 to 6.6 percent in the last part of 1977. It had risen even from 1956 to the cyclical peak year 1973 (column 4, Table 1). Most of the unemployment, however, is of very moderate duration. Recently, the average duration of the unemployment has been less than fourteen weeks, more than 40 percent of the unemployed have been out of work for less than five weeks, and less than 25 percent for more than fifteen weeks.

Resolving the Paradox. The apparent paradox is resolved by noting the pronounced upward trend in that percentage of nonworkers which the census surveys show as unemployed, essentially because of the significant increase in the proportion of nonworkers of whom the information is received that sometime during the preceding four weeks they were looking for a job (column 2, Table 1). This upward trend has been quite pronounced, even if the proportion of nonworkers placed in the category of unemployed remains small (only about 10 percent even now, compared with less than 6 percent in 1956). The percentage of nonworkers falling in the category of unemployed has increased in the ratio 1.7 to 1; and in comparison there has occurred only a small proportionate reduction of the nonworking percentage of the population as a whole, corresponding to the increase in its employed percentage. Thus on balance the unemployed percentage of the population rose in a significant proportion of its 1956 level of 2.5 percent. The ratio defined as the unemployment rate also rose in a significant proportion from its 1956 level of 4.1 percent (column 4, Table 1).

If we had no clue whatever to the events that have brought about the increase in the unemployment rate along with the rise of the employed percentage of the population, we would presumably limit ourselves to the conclusion that the labor market has shown a favorable trend for workers in one sense and an unfavorable trend in another. Even in this case there would be reason to add that the favorable trend expressed by the employed percentage of the population is technically a *harder* finding than the unfavorable trend in the unemployment rate.

The reason for this is that population counts are at least moderately dependable, even if nonnegligible errors are occasionally made in them, and whether or not a person is doing work for income is a reasonably clear-cut distinction. It is this type of information that goes into the computation of the employed percentage of the population. But the available information does not make it possible to be reasonably definite about whether a person is looking for a job in any meaningful sense. Yet the unemployment statistics, in contrast to the population and the employment statistics, do imply such a conclusion.

As for the procedure used in the monthly surveys for estimating the number of unemployed, the criterion of having undertaken during the past four weeks some move that qualifies as having "looked for a job" provides in itself merely a very weak indication of effort. The statement that some such move was undertaken does not in itself indicate whether an unsuccessful step was subsequently repeated, nor does it indicate the terms on which a job was sought at least once, nor even what job offers may have been turned down.

Various other pieces of information on responses to job openings and on job search are, to be sure, available, but they add up to what must be regarded as information of a very soft kind. For instance, unemployment compensation is dependent on the readiness of the unemployed person to accept a job corresponding to his work experience and located in his vicinity, but this provision is known to be administered leniently. In many states even persons who have left rather than lost their last jobs are eligible. Also, among those who are included in the unemployment statistics are a considerable number of persons lacking the job experience required for compensation. Those not qualifying for compensation now make up only a small proportion of the labor force but a much larger proportion of the unemployed.

Information beyond that provided by the regular monthly surveys *was* recently published on the intensity of job search, but its evaluation runs into serious difficulties.[3] If these difficulties could be disregarded, the results would suggest that a large proportion of the unemployed search intensively for a job, and it would suggest willingness to accept jobs at wages that are low by the standards prevailing in the American economy. These so-called reservation wages are low

---

[3] Carl Rosenfeld, "Job Search of the Unemployed, May 1976," *Monthly Labor Review* (November 1977), pp. 39–43.

enough to require explanation beyond a reference to the high weight of teenagers, entrants and reentrants in general, and nonwhites among the unemployed.

The data were derived from a special survey undertaken in May 1976 by the Bureau of Labor Statistics in cooperation with the Census Bureau. The report on the special survey was explicit on one of the very serious difficulties of interpretation to which these data give rise. Although the regular monthly census sample taken in May 1976 could be regarded as representative of the month's 6.4 million unemployed, a serious difficulty developed because only from 69 percent of the total did the special survey succeed in eliciting a response to *any* of the questions, and this subset of respondents had to be "blown up" by an arithmetic operation to the size of the entire sample. In addition, those in charge of the survey were faced with quite a bit of nonresponse or response in nonusable form to specific questions, and there is no way of overcoming such obstacles. Also, what one would want to know about the wages acceptable to the job-searching unemployed is not so much how these wages compare with those generally prevailing in the American economy, but how they compare with the wages the same workers earned in their last jobs. The published report contains nothing on this, but data collected during the special survey suggest no tendency to reduce wage demands below the wages last earned.

To the extent that the inference was nevertheless drawn from the special survey that job search of considerable intensity at significantly subnormal wage rates is typical of the unemployed, one would be led to believe that the unemployed belong largely to one or both of two groups. They would then be regarded as belonging to the group of low-productivity workers (and as belonging there not merely because of the high representation of teenagers, of other entrants and reentrants, and of nonwhites) *and/or* as belonging to the group of persons whom pervasive institutional blocks prevent from effectively underbidding the rapidly rising wage rates of the period. The point to be stressed, however, is that information on the intensity of job search on the part of the unemployed is very flimsy. More is known about the meaning of the statement that from the mid-1950s to the present the employed percentage of the population as a whole has somewhat risen and that for adult women this proportion has risen steeply than is known about the meaning of the statement that the unemployment rate has also risen during the interval. The latter statement hinges entirely on the finding that the proportion of the nonworkers "looking for a job" has risen from about 6 to about 10 percent over two decades during which, according to firmer findings, the relative weight of the nonworkers in the population has been declining.

This, of course, does not mean that we may omit exploring the information conveyed by the unemployment rates. Attention needs to be paid also to less firm findings if they are the best available on a matter of importance. We shall therefore now examine whether there exists a reasonable explanation of why the observed increase in the employed proportion of the population should have been associated with an increase in the unemployment rate—an explanation that does not hinge on the ambiguities of our unemployment statistics.

Behind the Paradox: Trends for Adult Women Compared with Those for Adult Men. The reason the behavior of the population at large shows rising unemployment rates along with rising employment-to-population ratios is that in this regard the data are dominated by the adult female population (aged twenty years and over) whose labor force participation rate has been rising very steeply: in twenty-one years it rose from about 36 to almost 49 percent (column 3, Table 1).

Teenagers show this joint rise of the employed proportion of their population and of their unemployment rate only since the mid-1960s, as will be discussed later. More important for the appraisal of the overall trend is that the data relating to all adult men (aged twenty years and over) and to prime-age men (aged twenty-five through fifty-four years) do not show these traits at all. Their weight in the American labor force has been *declining* significantly in the twenty-one years since 1956. From 1956 to late 1977 the labor force participation rate of all adult men declined from about 88 to 80 percent, and that of prime-age males from about 97 to 95 percent. The employed proportion of the adult male population in general and of the prime-age male population in particular has also been declining—in twenty-one years from about 85 to about 76 percent and from about 94 to 90 percent, respectively. Up to 1973 the unemployment rate of adult males showed no tendency to rise; indeed, that of prime-age men showed a declining tendency. Even the rate observed for adult men in general—a rate influenced by the age composition of adults—showed a mild tendency to decline, but this tendency was slight enough to raise doubts as to whether the observation did not result from changes in the questionnaire used in the monthly census survey from the second half of the 1960s on. Later, in the post-1973 period, both these specific unemployment rates clearly rose, and in the present recovery they have so far not declined to the levels of some earlier years of advanced expansion.

To some extent the change in the behavior of the unemployment rate for adult males after 1973 is apt to be the result of the recent significant extension in the coverage of the unemployment compensation system as well as its extension in duration for periods in which the measured unemployment rates exceed specific limits. Additional rigid-ifying factors thus partly explain the post-1973 upcreep of the adult male rates. The additional rigidifying elements, in this case, reflect widely held value judgments, though not much concern was shown for finding the least costly solutions in terms of work incentives and flexi-bility. But even with the degree of rigidity built into the system earlier, the requirements of a transition period after the cost-steepening caused by an inflationary outbreak might well have placed a heavy burden on the existing flexibility of the system. This burden may in any event have been sufficient to account for some rise in all unemployment rates, including the post-1973 adult male rates.

Whatever the full explanation of the post-1973 phase, the data for adult men do not raise the problem of the coexistence of an upward trend in employment ratios with an upward trend in unemployment rates. The reason the data relating to the American population as a whole do raise this problem is that these trends show strongly for adult women. In 1956 this group had an employment-to-population ratio of 34.9 percent, the unemployed made up 1.5 percent of the adult female population, and the group's unemployment rate was 4.2 percent. By late 1977 these figures had risen to slightly above 45 percent for the employment-to-population ratio, to 3.3 percent for the unemployed proportion of adult females, and to 6.8 percent for the adult female unemployment rate. In view of changes in the questionnaire used in the monthly surveys, the unemployment rate of 6.8 percent may, how-ever, have to be reduced by several decimals (perhaps even by as much as half of one percent) to be comparable with the 4.2 percent observed for 1956 (see the note under Table 1).

The weight of adult women in the American labor force was 29.4 percent in 1956 (at that time already appreciably higher than in the late 1940s), and it was about 36.8 percent in the last quarter of 1977; their weight in total employment is described by practically the same two numbers. In contrast, the weight of adult men in the labor force declined from 64.1 to 53.7 percent, and their weight in total employ-ment from 64.6 to 54.8 percent.

One question deserving attention relates to the proportion of the twenty-one year increase in the adult female labor force that has be-come employed, rather than unemployed. This proportion is 90.2 per-cent. The remaining 9.8 percent is a small proportion of the total addi-tion to the labor force. Yet it is a higher proportion than that expressed by the adult female unemployment rate of 1956 (4.2 percent) or of late 1977 (less than 7 percent), this difference reflecting the fact that "marg-inal" magnitudes must exceed the "average" magnitudes when the lat-ter are rising. Furthermore, it is noteworthy that the adult female unemployment rates have all along been quite a bit higher than the adult male rates. The facts thus suggest that in spite of the rising demand for female labor, the rapidly rising adult female labor force participation has created a difficulty in job placement that has not been completely overcome—or has not *yet* been overcome—and that shows in consistent unemployment-rate differentials between adult women and men.

This last statement implies that lags in the employment effect associated with a rising adult female labor force participation rate may be responsible for a rise in adult female unemployment rates that has maintained or possibly even increased the differential (see the note under Table 1). In other words, the rise in adult female unemployment may have developed as a byproduct of that group's rapidly rising employment and may result from a lag in the employment of some of the many newcomers into the labor force. As shown later, a strong case can be made for the assumption that the female-male unemployment differential is in part a lag phenomenon of this particular kind. Even more importantly, the unemployment differential is a somewhat different but similar lag phenomenon, stemming from the fact that a much higher proportion of the adult female than of the adult male population alternates between being and not being in the labor force. The result is that a higher proportion of females is "new" in the labor force (if not literally new, then new in the sense of having rejoined after a period of absence). This finding implies in turn that despite the steep increase in the ratio of adult female to adult male employment and despite the approximate stability of the male-female wage rate differential, the female-male unemployment differential is not explained by any inability of the system to make use of the available female workers. The explanation lies rather in the time it takes fully to absorb continuing additions of large numbers of new job-seekers (in the sense of new entrants *or* reentrants in the labor force). Although the post-1973 rise in the adult male unemployment rate may in good part reflect additional rigidifying factors, the unemployment differential between the sexes is better explained by the greater strain placed on the existing degree of flexibility when many of the workers seeking employment have only recently joined the labor force.

Merely a Lag: In What Sense? The employed proportion of the adult female population and the adult female unemployment rate in 1973 were 42.2 percent and 4.8 percent, respectively. By the last quarter of 1977 the employed proportion of the adult female population had risen from 42.2 to 45.3 percent and their unemployment rate had risen from 4.8 to 6.8 percent. We may now ask how high the employed proportion of the adult female population would have had to be to keep their unemployment rate of the last quarter of 1977 from rising beyond the 4.8 percent level observed for 1973. To answer this question, we shall assume as given the actual 1977 level of all relevant data, except that we shall assume a sufficient "transfer" of unemployed adult women to employment to reduce the number of unemployed in relation to the fourth quarter 1977 labor force from 6.8 percent to 4.8 percent. To achieve this result the employed proportion of the adult female population should have risen by the last quarter of 1977 from its 1973 level of 42.2 percent to 46.3 percent—a level that is only one percentage point higher than the 45.3 percent actually observed for the last quarter of 1977. One percentage point was missing in the employment ratio. It might be concluded that this is not very much, considering that in the recent past it took only about four years to obtain a three percentage point increase, and that (counting from 1956) an increase of more than ten percentage points took place in twenty-one years.

But this argument does not establish the proposition that the employment of adult women has merely been lagging somewhat behind the rise in their labor force participation and that this has been the only or even the principal reason why their unemployment rates have also been rising. We have not refuted the alternative possibility that if at some point the increase in the adult female labor force had stopped, then the increase in the employed proportion of the adult female population would also have promptly come to an end. In this case the employment trend would never have caught up with the trend in labor force participation. Instead the unemployment rate would have become stabilized at the level of the period in which the labor force participation rate stopped rising.

In fact, closer examination leads to the conclusion that an ending of the steeper rise in the adult female than in the adult male labor force participation rate would in itself probably not have put an end to the female-male unemployment differential. But identical trends in the male and the female participation rates together with identical propensities to move in and out of the labor force would have practically eliminated the differential.

The essential part of the reasoning here is derived from three kinds of data: (1) dropouts from the labor force measured as the yearly average of the adult male and adult female workers whom the monthly surveys found to be out of the labor force and to have stopped working sometime during the preceding twelve months; (2) the *net* addition to the labor force; and (3) the yearly average of adult male and adult female workers whom the successive official monthly surveys place in the category of unemployed new entrants or reentrants.[4] It was assumed that if to a year's *net* addition to the adult male or the adult female labor force we add the dropouts of the past twelve months as defined under (1), the sum is a satisfactory approximation of the number of those to be considered entrants and reentrants in that year. In other words, the dropouts, as defined in (1) above, were replaced with workers who were entrants or reentrants, and the net addition to the labor force also consisted of entrants or reentrants. The total number of dropouts was fairly stable during the years covered in Table 2, and a reasonably steady rate of their replacement is implied in our analysis.

We are forced to neglect a presumably small proportion of entrants and reentrants replacing dropouts from the labor force who were not included under (1) in the preceding paragraph. Such dropouts include the members of the labor force who are not found among the persons out of the labor force because they died in the preceding twelve months without first dropping out, and the members who stopped working *before* the beginning of a twelve-month period but remained unemployed members of the labor force during part of that period and dropped out subsequently.

Having thus approximated the number of entrants and reentrants, we deduct them from the adult male and the adult female labor force of the year. By relating to this reduced labor force the number of unemployed, excluding those whom the unemployment statistics identify as entrants or reentrants, we obtain "adjusted" unemployment rates which exclude the entrants and reentrants. Those identified in the unemployment statistics as entrants and reentrants are unemployed persons who have not yet had a job since their entry or reentry into the labor force. No data are available on the unemployment of those entrants and reentrants of a year who relapsed into unemployment after having obtained a job.

Our procedure for excluding the unemployment effect of entry and reentry seems preferable to the alternative used in CEA reports which deducts not only from the unemployed but also from the labor force merely those unemployed who have not yet had a job since their entry or reentry. That procedure has the disadvantage of implying a 100 percent unemployment rate for entrants and reentrants, by regarding as entrants and reentrants only those members of the labor force

---

[4] Data on the dropouts, as defined in (1) above, for the 1967–1976 period, are from U.S. Bureau of Labor Statistics and U.S. Department of Health, Education, and Welfare, *Employment and Training Report of the President, 1977* (Washington, D.C.), p. 157. The data for 1977 and further details were obtained from the Bureau of Labor Statistics.

who are unemployed prior to obtaining a job. In contrast, our procedure has the advantage of not implying that a member of the labor force has ceased to be an entrant or reentrant of the year once he has obtained a job. The procedure here adopted makes it clear that only a fraction—though a relatively large fraction—of a year's entrants and reentrants is unemployed at any time. For instance, for 1977 as a whole, after exclusion of the entrants and reentrants the adjusted unemployment rates of adult men and women were 4.3 and 4.8 percent, respectively, and the unemployment rates for adult male and adult female entrants and reentrants were 19.0 and 17.2 percent, respectively. Without excluding the entrants and reentrants from the labor force and from the unemployed, the adult male unemployment rate of the year was 5.2 percent and the adult female rate was 7.0 percent.

Neither our procedure nor the alternative described above can be carried back beyond 1967 because for earlier years the needed data are unavailable. Further, neither procedure can take account of the indirect unemployment effect of entry and reentry resulting from the merely gradual reduction of the unemployment-proneness of entrants and reentrants after they have been placed in a job. But it is preferable to allow for this by recognizing that our procedure falls short of identifying the *entire* unemployment effect of entry and reentry, rather than to follow the alternative procedure by postulating a 100 percent unemployment rate for new entrants and reentrants.

As can be seen from Table 2, a very high proportion of the female-male differential in the unemployment rate disappears as a result of our adjustment. Although the entire differential does not disappear, the remaining differential would be significantly reduced or eliminated if a dependable method were available for correcting for the more frequent job changes (with intervening unemployment) of the entrants and reentrants of the recent past who had already been employed for a while after their entry or reentry. It is reasonable to assume that the remaining differential would then be negligible.

Some of the numerical relations are worth mentioning, though they are not shown in Table 2. The 1977 yearly average of the previous twelve months' dropouts (as defined above), who were replaced with entrants and reentrants, made up 4.5 percent of the adult male and 13.3 percent of the adult female labor force. To these numbers we need to add the net additions to the labor force. The year over year net addition to the adult male labor force was 1.8 percent in 1977, and the same year's net addition to the adult female labor force was 4.1 percent. The main suggestion derived from the data listed in Table 2 is that while at approximately unchanging wage differentials the number of women in the labor force has greatly increased in relation to

Table 2
ADULT FEMALE AND MALE UNEMPLOYMENT RATES, BEFORE AND AFTER EXCLUSION OF ENTRANTS AND REENTRANTS

Year	UF unadj. (1)	UM unadj. (2)	UF adj. (3)	UM adj. (4)	D unadj. (5)	D adj. (6)
1967	4.2	2.3	2.9	2.0	1.9	0.9
1968	3.8	2.2	2.5	1.8	1.6	0.7
1969	3.7	2.1	2.4	1.6	1.6	0.8
1970	4.8	3.5	3.4	2.9	1.3	0.5
1971	5.7	4.4	4.0	3.6	1.3	0.4
1972	5.4	4.0	3.7	3.2	1.4	0.5
1973	4.8	3.2	3.2	2.6	1.6	0.6
1974	5.5	3.8	3.8	3.2	1.7	0.6
1975	8.0	6.7	6.3	6.0	1.3	0.3
1976	7.4	5.9	5.4	5.0	1.5	0.4
1977	7.0	5.2	4.8	4.3	1.8	0.5

Symbols:

UF unadj. = unemployment rate of female workers aged 20 years and over, with no adjustment for entry and reentry.

UM unadj. = Same for male workers aged 20 years and over.

UF adj. = Differs from UF unadj. in that entrants and reentrants are excluded, as explained in text.

UM adj. = Differs from UM unadj. in that entrants and reentrants are excluded as explained in text.

D unadj. = Difference between UF unadj. and UM unadj.

D adj. = Difference between UF adj. and UM adj.

Source: See note 4.

that of men, the unemployment differential between them is explained primarily (probably wholly) by a lag in the employment of workers newly entering or reentering the labor force.

In interpreting the unemployment differential, the one difference between male and female workers that stands out is the greater frequency with which women move out of and then again into the labor force and the much higher rate at which women who previously have never been in the labor force have entered it. Institutional arrangements which would facilitate these movements are, of course, conceivable, but it would be utopian to conceive of a degree of labor market flexibility that would eliminate the employment lag for entrants and reentrants or even the greater frequency of job changes for those with only brief experience in the labor market.

Teenagers. The representation of teenagers in the labor force has also been rising significantly. In 1956 their weight in the labor force was 6.5 percent, and by late 1977 it had risen to 9.5 percent, that is, in the proportion 1.5 to 1. Their weight in total employment rose during the same period from 6.0 to 8.5 percent, that is, in the proportion 1.4 to 1. These proportionate increases far exceed even the corresponding increase for adult women of 1.2 to 1 for their weight in both the total labor force and total employment.

The rise of the teenage weight in the labor force reflects in large part the rising weight of teenagers in the population (noninstitutional, aged sixteen years and over) from 7.6 percent to 10.5 percent. For the rest it reflects a rise in the labor force participation rate of teenagers from about 51 percent to 57 percent after a decline from the beginning of the period to the mid-1960s. Their employment-to-population ratio at first also showed a downward tendency, but from the mid-1960s on this ratio too has displayed an upward trend, surpassing in the last quarter of 1977 its 1956 level of 45.3 percent by more than two percentage points (see Table 1). The unemployment rate of teenagers has, however, shown a rising trend throughout the period: for teenagers of all races jointly it rose from about 11 to 17 percent in twenty-one years. For nonwhite teenagers, whose labor force participation rate as well as employment-to-population ratio has shown a significant downward trend over the period as a whole, the unemployment rate has risen from about 18 to about 38 percent; for many years it has now amounted to more than twice the white teenager rate.

Adjustments for entry and reentry effects, analogous to those we have undertaken for adult women, do not eliminate or even reduce to negligible size the unemployment rate differentials between the teenage and the adult labor force. Furthermore, compared with adult women, a much smaller proportion of the twenty-one-year addition to the teenage labor force has become employed. In contrast to the 90 percent applying to the adult female addition, slightly less than 80 percent of the entire teenage addition has found employment and only about 40 percent of its nonwhite component (which makes up less than 10 percent of the total teenage addition).[5] Interpretation of the unemployment rate of teenagers, unlike that of adult women, requires emphasis not merely on employment lags connected with entry and reentry but also on the lasting difficulties of accommodating in the labor market a rapidly rising supply of a specific kind of labor with no ad-

---

[5] Because of the significant decline of the nonwhite teenage labor force participation rate, only 9.7 percent of the addition to the teenage labor force is nonwhite. In 1956 about 12.2 percent of the teenage labor force was nonwhite, and this proportion has declined to 10.9 percent.

justment of relative wage rates. As we have seen, a fairly high proportion of this supply—particularly of white teenagers—has nevertheless been accommodated, even though minimum wage legislation has prevented wage flexibility and though the increased coverage of such legislation and the upward creep of the minimum wage relative to other wage rates have produced additional rigidifying effects.

Past fluctuations in the birth rate will soon lead to a reduction of the weight of teenagers in the American population in general, and also in the population aged sixteen years and over which is the definition we have been using for the present purpose. On the way toward a decline, these weights are now going through a stage of virtual stability. But the labor force participation rate of all teenagers has recently been rising in a somewhat higher proportion than the participation rate of the American population as a whole, and so far this has resulted in a continued increase in the weight of teenagers in the American labor force.

Minimum Wage Legislation. Many attempts have been made to estimate the effect of minimum wage legislation on the high teenage unemployment rate discussed above, but the regression techniques usually applied to this problem have led to results that are compatible with a very wide range of conclusions. I will suggest a way of looking at this problem which is in part generally common-sensical but which is supported by the kind of numerical information examined in the preceding sections in other contexts.

I have no numerical suggestions to make concerning the least unemployment-reducing effect that could have developed from doing away with minimum wages. The existence of a noteworthy effect may, however, safely be asserted, and it is clear also that minimum wages represent a much larger source of rigidity for the young than for other major groups in the population. Arbitrary rules as to what a wholly inexperienced teenager must be worth to his employer if he is to get an opportunity to acquire work experience necessarily limit employment of teenagers instead of promoting equity in the labor market. There can be no doubt about the existence of a noteworthy adverse employment effect, even if I will not speculate here about what the least effect might be within a reasonable range of assumptions.

On the other hand, when it comes to appraising high estimates, it would seem unconvincing to me to suggest that by abolishing minimum wage laws alone the unemployment rate of teenagers as a whole could recently have been reduced by more than roughly 40 percent of the number shown in the official statistics. The conjecture that 40 percent is on the high side of the plausible range (or perhaps somewhat beyond it) is based on the supposition that minimum wage legislation has practically no unemployment-raising effect on an age class such as that of thirty-five to forty-four years,[6] and that the unemployment rates of the younger age classes would have remained higher in any event. Unemployment rates would have shown jumps of some size in any event from the thirty-five to forty-four age class to the twenty-five to thirty-four and then to the twenty to twenty-four age class, and particularly as we move further down to the teenage class. The jumps might, however, have been very much smaller in the absence of minimum wage legislation.[7]

Given a reduction by 40 percent of itself, the 1976 teenage unemployment rate would have been just about the same as the 1956 rate, that is, 11 to 12 percent instead of 19 percent. Aside from any effect of the abolition of minimum wages on the teenage labor force participation rate, such a reduction of the unemployment rate of teenagers would have corresponded to an increase of close to 9 percent in their aggregate employment—presumably with a disproportionately

---

[6] Indeed, minimum wages may conceivably lower the unemployment rate of this age class to some extent, and the abolition of such legislation might somewhat raise it, because minimum wages protect this age class from teenage competition. But this would increase rather than reduce the plausibility of the conjecture described in the text.

[7] In 1976 the age class 35–44 had a specific unemployment rate of 4.9 percent, the 25–34 class a rate of 7.1 percent, the 20–24 class one of 12 percent, and teenagers a rate of 19 percent. It would have been astonishing if the abolition of minimum wages had changed the 4.9 rate for the 35–44 class appreciably and if it had reduced the 7.1 rate for the 25–34 class much below 7 percent, thus still leaving a roughly two percentage point differential between these two classes. Given this differential, it would also have been astonishing if the unemployment rate of the 20–24 class had come out at lower than about 9 percent, that is, at a level lower than two percentage points above the 7 percent applying to the 25–34 class, this being a reduction of the actually prevailing five-percentage-point differential to two percentage points between the 25–34 and the 20–24 class. Lastly, even given this greatly reduced unemployment rate of 9 percent for the 20–24 age class, one would not expect the teenage rate to be below 11 to 12 percent, since even this would imply the reduction of the actual 7 percent differential to 2 to 3 percent.
What this implies is that given a roughly two-percentage-point differential between the 35–44 and the 25–34 class, it is difficult to imagine a pattern that would reduce the 1976 teenage rate below 11 to 12 percent, provided abolition of minimum wages is the only change considered. It might be objected that in 1956 the teenage unemployment rate was 11.1 percent, and that at that time too the rate became elevated by minimum wage requirements even if these were less comprehensive than they are now. Hence, assuming no minimum wages, why could the present rate not be lower? Yet the proportionate representation of teenagers in the labor force has grown significantly since 1956, teenagers are distinctly imperfect labor-market substitutes for experienced workers, and it would be farfetched to assume the perfect wage flexibility that would fully compensate employers for the limited use to which a greatly increased teenage labor input could be put.

large impact on the nonwhite component. However, there is more reason to assume that the 40 percent conjecture is on the high side than to assume that the 9 percent conjecture is on the low side. To the extent that in the absence of minimum wages the teenage labor force participation rate would be larger, the unemployment-reducing effect would be diminished, and this strengthens the supposition that the 40 percent estimate is on the high side. On the other hand, given a positive effect on the participation rate, a greater employment-raising effect would have corresponded even to a smaller reduction of teenage unemployment. The total employment-raising effect in the economy as a whole would in any event have included some additional employment of adult unskilled workers and of workers in the old-age classes; and the foregoing way of looking at the problem implies also a noteworthy effect on the twenty to twenty-four age class.

So much for the recent state of affairs. The numerical conjectures concerning a potential 40 percent reduction of the teenage unemployment rate would have been very similar if the argument had been developed for 1975 instead of for 1976. Information now available indicates the 1977 data would also lead to the same result.

All of this is, of course, admittedly speculative. But whatever potential unemployment and employment effect we assume, it needs to be pointed out that an argument frequently used in defense of minimum wage legislation is based on unrealistic assumptions. According to this argument unregulated wages are often below the level that would be determined by a large number of bidders competing for the workers' services, because employers often have some degree of monopsony power (buyer's monopoly power) that leads to lower wages. The argument maintains that these wages could be raised by regulation without any noteworthy reduction of employment. In the case we are considering, monopsony power would exist because workers would become exposed to specific costs or inconvenience if they were to move to another employer. It is these costs or inconveniences which would give employers a leeway in competing with the terms offered by rival employers. For all worker categories, not only for teenagers, the argument suffers from lack of recognition of the fact that a rapid turnover of the work force is costly and inconvenient also to employers. But given the weak attachment of most teenage workers to any given employer, and given the generally large mobility in that segment of the labor market, it would be particularly unconvincing to attach importance to this line of reasoning for teenagers.

Generally speaking, the structural characteristics of the American unemployment problem at large would call for developing efficiently focused training programs with substantial flexibility of wage rates to benefit the presently unemployed. The now prevailing response combines wage-rigidifying arrangements with unfocused and expensive public employment projects and with "demand stimulus" through inflationary demand management. Such a response can only increase the difficulties of adjustment which it will be impossible to avoid and which will further grow if we postpone facing the issue.

Price-Fixing
as Seen by a Price-Fixer:
Part II

Herbert Stein

Summary

Despite official disavowals of an intention to impose mandatory price and wage controls, the possibility of such controls hangs over the American economy. This is partly because such controls were adopted in 1971 despite similar disavowals. This paper considers how the country reached the point at which mandatory controls were imposed, even though almost all responsible public leaders, in and out of government, had been saying for years that they didn't want them. It also examines the proposition that the generally recognized failure of the 1971–1974 controls is not evidence of the basic ineffectiveness of such a policy, but was due to special factors, notably the Nixon administration's distaste for such measures.

Four main factors seem to have contributed to the imposition of mandatory, comprehensive, and long-lasting controls despite the "leadership" opposition to them.

(1) Congress gave the President blank-check, standby authority to impose controls, not because the Congress wanted controls but in order to embarrass a President who had vowed never to use them. The existence of this authority generated a strong temptation and demand to use it.

(2) Unrealistic predictions, mainly emanating from the administration, led the public to expect that conventional measures of fiscal and monetary restraint would work quickly and with minimum increase of unemployment. When these predictions proved incorrect, the whole conventional, gradualist approach was discredited, and the public demanded more radical measures.

(3) Influential leaders of public opinion, mainly outside the administration, while denying any desire for mandatory controls, argued

113

continually for "voluntary" incomes policies, which were, in fact and in public perception, close to mandatory controls, in the sense that they implied the ability of the government to determine the "right" amount of wage or price increase, not only in general but also in specific cases, and the responsibility of government to try to induce conformity to these "right" price and wage increases. Once this is accepted as a legitimate role for government, it is only a small step to accepting the legitimacy of mandatory controls.

(4) The establishment of the controls, which were intended to be very short-lived in any comprehensive form, generated public expectations which made their early termination politically and psychologically impossible.

Despite their determination not to make price and wage controls a permanent feature of the American economy, the officials of the Nixon administration had every incentive to seek the success of the controls while they were in force. Moreover, the management of the controls was largely in the hands of people who did not entirely share the aversion of the White House to them. If it is accepted that the controls were to be temporary, and that the requirements of the control system were not to override all other objectives of economic policy, it is hard to ascribe the failures of the controls to inadequacies of their management. The one charge most commonly made against the management of the 1971–1974 controls is that decontrol came too early. However, there were substantial reasons for the timing of the movement to decontrol, and there is little reason to think that delay would have done any permanent good.

Two lessons of this history are relevant today.

- *Do not think that we can flirt with controls and not get them.*

- *Do not think that the ineffectiveness of controls, which has roots deep in the American economic and political system, can be overcome by sufficiently enthusiastic operators.*

Introduction

Some readers will recognize that "Price-Fixing as Seen by a Price-Fixer" is the title of an article by Frank W. Taussig that appeared in the *Quarterly Journal of Economics* in February 1919. I hope they will not think it presumptuous of me to borrow the title. I do so because it describes precisely what I am setting out to write and because it has a certain nostalgic interest for me. When I was an undergraduate I wrote a senior essay on "Government Price Policy in the United States during the

World War" (I didn't have the foresight to say World War I). Taussig's article was the most professional writing on the subject available.

There are several striking things about Taussig's article when it is looked at from today's perspective. The economic analysis seems archaic, and I suspect that it was crude even from the standpoint of 1918. Most of the discussion is premised on taking as marginal cost the average cost of the bulk-line producer—the producer whose output embraces about the eighty-fifth percentile of all output when producers are ranked by average costs. But, despite the lower level of sophistication in the theory with which Taussig and his colleagues worked, what they actually did was not inferior to what we have recently done or would do now. Our advance in theory since World War I has not been matched by an advance in data or in operating procedures. It should be recognized, however, that the World War I price control was largely confined to the easier cases of standardized commodities. If they had tried to cover a larger part of the economy the inferiority of their capability as compared with ours would have been obvious.

Taussig's detachment about price-fixing is something that few who have been through it recently can equal. The whole area of price control has become "hot." Some participants write about their experience with pride and exuberance, some write to rationalize their failures or put them off onto others, some write to apologize for having been in a place like that at all. Taussig, although he entitles his article ". . . as Seen by a Price-Fixer," hardly lets us know that he was a responsible participant. Indeed, only a footnote on the second page of the article, which lists the members of the Price Fixing Committee, tells the reader what Taussig's role was. He writes with knowledge, but the kind of knowledge that an economist sitting in the corner observing but not participating might have had. He writes as a traveler just returned from a strange country with which he has no emotional connection and which he never expects to revisit, informing his friends but not advising them whether to go there or not.

Taussig's conclusions about the World War I price-fixing experience are moderate and common-sensical. He believes that the controls worked, in the sense of holding down prices, but not much—but, then, they weren't expected to do much. He gently chides his colleagues in the academic practice of economics for thinking that prices are precisely determined by demand, supply, and the quantity of money. These determinations are approximate only, and that leaves room for controls to affect prices without having to contend with strong market pressures or creating shortages.

These conclusions are unsupported by any statistics, let alone econometrics. Probably the basic fact about World War I price control is that there wasn't much of it, either in coverage or in duration, and that contributed to the appearance of effectiveness, especially if attention is confined to the area and period of coverage. Much of the World War I inflation came after the war and the controls were over, and even after Taussig's article was written.

Taussig's paper on price controls did not deal with the question whether we should have the controls again, any more than people writing in 1918 about World War I felt it necessary to deal with the question whether we should have another war. To the economists of 1919 those controls were an unusual experience which might throw some light on economic questions even if the experience were never to be repeated, just as an earthquake would be instructive to geologists aside from the question whether it would, let alone should, be repeated.

Today's situation is different. We live under the shadow of the possibility that the controls will be reimposed. Just as it is necessary for the Jews to reread every year the story of their enslavement under the Pharaohs and their subsequent deliverance, it is necessary to repeat the story of our 1971–1974 price control experience, so that subsequent policy makers, even those who come only four years later, will bear it in mind.

What needs to be retold is not primarily the failure of the 1971–1974 controls. Perhaps that part of the story will have to be repeated for later generations, but every adult now alive must know that the controls did not check the inflation. It is hard to imagine a scenario in which the present price level or inflation rate would have been higher if the controls had not been imposed. When we went into the controls in August 1971 the unemployment rate was 6 percent and the inflation rate about 5 percent. As this is being written the unemployment rate is again 6 percent and the inflation rate is 6 to 7 percent. In the interim (1971 to 1977) the consumer price index has risen 50 percent, or at an annual average rate of 7 percent. The controls repressed inflation in the latter part of 1971 and in 1972, but whatever effect they may have had was washed away by the inflationary surge of 1973–1974.[1]

Not only is our most recent controls experience universally recognized to have been ineffective, but also the administration now in power and everyone else with any authority expresses an immovable determination not to resort to controls. Why, then, does the fear of the restoration of controls hover over the economy, as evidenced by the decline of the stock market whenever the word is breathed?

---

[1] For a systematic evaluation of the effect of controls, see Marvin H. Kosters, *Controls and Inflation: The Economic Stabilization Program in Retrospect* (Washington, D.C.: American Enterprise Institute, 1975).

There are two reasons. One is the memory that the controls were imposed by a government that was in principle deeply opposed to them and that had made promises not to use them at least as strong as those made by the Carter administration. We have learned how quickly and unexpectedly an administration can change its mind on this subject. The second reason for the continuing fear, perhaps less important than the first but reinforcing it, is the belief in some quarters that the failure of the 1971–1974 controls was not inherent in controls but resulted from inadequacies in their management. Thus, there is the possibility that the government will move to controls, despite its vows not to do so, and that it will rationalize this action by saying, and believing, that it will run the controls differently from the way they were run before.

These two reasons lead to two questions. First, how did an administration that was almost religiously opposed to controls come to resort to them? Second, were there deficiencies in the management of controls which caused a failure that could have been averted if they had been managed differently, or by other people?

In the remainder of this paper I will offer the observations of a participant in those controls on some points that are relevant to these two questions.[2]

On the Menace of Standby Authority

Mandatory wage and price controls cannot be imposed in the United States without legislative authority. This authority does not ordinarily exist, and does not exist now.

Mr. Nixon had no specific authority to impose price and wage controls when he came into office. The Vietnam War was under way, and he might conceivably have been able to interpret controls as falling within the President's war powers. He had no desire in those days to impose controls. But even if he had wanted to do so, reliance upon inherent war powers would have been very difficult for him. The war was exceedingly unpopular, his conduct of it was already considered by many to be high-handed, if not illegal, and there would probably have been a furious reaction, in and out of Congress, if he had assumed power over the domestic economy in the name of that war.

As it turned out, the President was given authority by Congress

---

[2] I was first a member and then chairman of the President's Council of Economic Advisers from January 1969 through August 1974, when controls were debated, imposed, redefined, and finally terminated. I was chairman of a committee of the Cost of Living Council, charged with developing plans for Phase II of the controls, and vice chairman of the Cost of Living Council from January 1, 1972, until its extinction on April 30, 1974.

against his will and as a result of a political accident. In August 1970, Congress passed the Defense Stabilization Act, authorizing the President to control prices and wages. The act was a blank check, specifying no standards except that controls imposed under the act should be applied in a nondiscriminatory way. There was no attempt to conceal the fact that the authority was being given to the President to embarrass him. The economy was not in a crisis. The unemployment rate was 5 percent and the inflation rate 6 percent. Hardly anyone wanted mandatory controls imposed at that time. To test this, Representative Benjamin B. Blackburn (Republican, Georgia) introduced an amendment to the bill which would have imposed the controls immediately, rather than giving the President authority to do so. Only five congressmen voted for the amendment. Some members may have wanted controls then, without wanting to take the responsibility for imposing them, but they were probably few. President Nixon said that he would have vetoed the bill if it had not been an amendment to the extension of the Defense Production Act.

The act was passed in the firm belief that the President would not use the price control authority, and the Democratic Congress could place the responsibility for the continuation of the inflation exclusively on the back of the President. This strategy did not depend on any belief by congressmen that controls were an effective or desirable way to stop inflation. It only required the belief that there were a certain number of citizens in the country who did believe that, and who would accept the idea that the President was withholding the sure and painless remedy for inflation. Confidence that the President would not impose controls also relieved the Congress of the necessity of being specific about what was to be covered and what the criteria for establishing maximum permitted prices and wages were to be. If anyone had thought that the authority would be used, the Congress would have been deluged with demands for exemption or for favorable treatment of particular cases.

Although the administration resisted the enactment of the authority, it did not regard passage of the act as marking any significant change in its basic anticontrols stance. Events then moved with what now seems amazing speed. In February 1971, six months after the authority was given, it was used, in the case of the construction industry. The President had asked for voluntary restraint by the construction unions in raising wages. However, national union leaders were afraid of being undercut by rivals within the movement if they accepted wage limitations voluntarily. Their problem was solved by formally invoking the price-wage control authority, which gave the impression that the union leaders had been compelled to agree to the wage restraints. The reliance on the legal authority was only on paper; in fact, everything was done by negotiation. No one in the administration felt that they had crossed the Rubicon to mandatory controls. But still a line had been crossed.

In March the new secretary of the treasury, John Connally, testified in favor of the extension of the control authority. Since the authority was going to be there anyway, he did not want the administration to seem so timid in its anti-inflation policy that it was afraid to have the ultimate weapon in its arsenal. At the same time he assured everyone that the administration had no intention of imposing controls. But still another line had been crossed.

On August 15, 1971, the President, using the authority given him by the Economic Stabilization Act, imposed a total freeze on wages and prices, implementing a decision to which he had been gradually coming during the spring and summer.

If there had been no authority there would have been no controls. Perhaps the President would have obtained the authority even if Congress had not forced it upon him in the politically motivated way it did. He might have asked for the authority, and Congress might have given it to him. But that course of events would have encountered a number of obstacles that might not have been overcome. The President would have had to do much more explaining of his radical change of position about controls. Moreover, the psychological and political aspects of asking Congress for authority would have been quite different from coming down from Camp David and with a single thunderclap putting an end to the inflation. In the latter case he established himself immediately, although not permanently, as a national hero and savior of the economy. In the former he would have entered into a struggle with an opposing and hostile Congress, from which he might not emerge a winner, even if he got the authority. That is, the authority might be so encumbered with restrictions that the President would be left only with the power to anger everyone and please no one. If Congress had believed that the President meant to impose controls it could have become so embroiled in conflict over the terms of the authority that no legislation would emerge. Faced with these prospects there is a strong probability that the President would never have asked for authority, at least unless the economic situation had become more critical than it ever did.

Of course, this is all speculation. But there seems little doubt that the enactment of the authority greatly increased the probability that there would be controls, and that the enactment was not intended by its authors to have that effect. The political situation of 1970 does not exist today. The Democratic Congress is unlikely to give a Democratic President price control authority for the sake of embarrassing him. But the experience is relevant to the idea which arises repeatedly that the President should be given standby authority to impose controls, either as a way of inducing "voluntary" restraint by business and labor, or as a preparation for quick action in some situation that is not present and not expected but is possible, or merely as a means of showing the public that the government is sincerely concerned about inflation.

The lesson of that experience is not to play political games with lethal economic instruments. Chekhov said that a dramatist should not put a gun on the wall in the first act unless he intends it to be fired in the last act. Congress should not provide authority for controls unless it intends them to be used. Probably the greatest assurance we have today against a return to controls is the absence of authority. That condition should be preserved.

On the Importance of Realistic Expectations

The fact that he had authority did not, of course, require the President to use it, although it leaned in that direction. In 1971, when the controls were imposed, Milton Friedman explained them by saying that if 75 percent of the American people believe in witchcraft it is difficult for the President not to practice witchcraft. This is a generous interpretation, and most of the people involved would probably settle for it. However, it deserves to be pushed a little further. What was it the American people believed that made the controls hard to avoid, and why did they believe it?

The belief had two parts. One was that the course of the economy demonstrated that the "natural" solutions—essentially fiscal and monetary policy—had not worked and would not work. The other part was that "supernatural" solutions—some version of wage and price controls—would work.

Certainly by the middle of 1971 there was a general belief in the country that the conventional policy of reducing inflation by fiscal and monetary restraint which would sustain a good deal of slack in the economy was not working. Of course, there were many people who never believed that it would work. The idea that the rate of inflation is influenced by demand is a strange idea, except in the most runaway situations, like all-out war, to the man in the street, and even to fairly sophisticated men in the street. The head of one of this country's largest retail establishments once told me that he never knew a price to be raised because the demand for a product was strong.

But still there had been a common view, beginning in 1968, that slowing down the expansion of the economy, which would involve some increase of the unemployment rate, was the proper way to check the inflation, and would work. This was the rationale behind the enactment of the temporary tax surcharge and ceiling on federal expenditures in 1968 and the policy of gradualism, meaning gradual restraint, preached and followed by the Nixon team in 1969.

Many people who had held this view in 1968 and 1969 were disillusioned by the experience of 1970 and the early part of 1971 and came to believe that the policy of demand restraint would not work. The unemployment rate, which had been 3.3 percent at the end of 1968, had risen to 6 percent, and the rate of inflation, which had briefly touched 6 percent in the early part of 1969, was still around 5 percent, and it was by no means certain that the rate would stay that low. This seemed to many obvious evidence of the failure of the conventional strategy. But it was only obvious if the strategy had implied that the inflation rate would have declined more than that with a smaller rise of unemployment or in a shorter time.

If the commonly held expectation had been that significant reduction of the inflation rate would take three or four years and might involve an increase of the unemployment rate to, say, 7 percent, the policy would not have seemed a failure—at least, not by 1971—and the pressure to move to another solution would have been less. Possibly knowing how long the gradual process of disinflation would take might have convinced some people even earlier of the need to move to controls. But that does not seem to be the most likely reaction. In fact, the country was not suffering any severe injury from the process of gradualism. What soured people on gradualism was not that it took such a long time but that forecasts of what it would deliver in the way of lower inflation were repeatedly disappointed, and this gave rise to the belief that gradualism would never work.

The fault was therefore in large part not in the performance of the economy but in the unrealistic expectations against which the performance was measured.

These expectations came from various sources, but the government was probably the most important. From the time the inflation began to speed up, in 1966, the government repeatedly underestimated the time that would be required to check the inflation. President Johnson's last economic report, published in January 1969, predicted that a brief slowdown of the economy, lasting only until mid-1969, would suffice to get the inflation rate under control. The first statements of the Nixon administration discounted this forecast somewhat, but not much, implying that an economic slowdown lasting throughout the year would be necessary. In January 1970 the Nixon Council of Economic Advisers took the position that an economic decline lasting until the middle of that year, followed by a slow rise, would suffice to get the inflation rate on a downward path. A year later, in January 1971, they said that in view of the slack that then existed in the economy a fairly vigorous recovery during the year would still be consistent with a significant reduction of the inflation rate.

These forecasts all proved to be wrong, and this seriously reduced the credibility of the idea that a continuation of moderate slack in the economy would in time get the inflation rate down, even though this idea might have been, and in my opinion was, correct. The credibility of the idea was reduced for some people in the government, as well as for many outside. These forecasts were based on what seemed at the time a reasonable interpretation of the evidence, including a continuous adaptation to the fact that earlier forecasts had been wrong. With hindsight a number of reasons can be adduced for these errors.[3] What is more relevant today is that even with the forecasts it made, the government should have been more aware of the margin of error that was around them and of the consequences of the expectations that it was generating with these forecasts. If the government had given early warning of the possibility that the disinflation process would be long drawn out there might have been less impatience when that turned out to be the case and less demand for abandoning the policy.

This situation has its counterpart today. Government forecasts are creating the expectation that the inflation rate can be stabilized, that is, kept from accelerating, with what it calls a moderate rate of expansion, which would involve about 4½ percent real growth per annum during 1978 and 1979. It is also fostering the view that if this real growth is not achieved the nation will pay a great price in lost production and excessive unemployment. In this way it is laying the base for a great disappointment with the "moderate" policy and a public demand for stronger and more direct action to hold wages and prices down in order to permit a more expansive policy to be followed.

On the Slippery Slope

For the man in the street it was perfectly natural to think that the most effective way to stop inflation was for the government to tell businesses and unions not to raise prices. The man in the street could not be expected to make much of the distinction between trying to restrain the rise in the average level of prices and trying to restrain increases of particular prices. Neither could he be expected to be a stickler for the distinction between voluntary and mandatory government influence over particular prices.

---

[3] The model of the inflationary process presented in Phillip Cagan's essay in this volume would, I think, have led to more realistic forecasts.

But the demand for controls did not arise spontaneously from the men in the street. It was stimulated and legitimized by the national leadership—the political leadership, the intellectual leadership, and the media leadership. Almost everyone in a leadership position maintained—up to the time mandatory controls were imposed, and in many cases afterwards—that he was against mandatory controls. But the words and actions of these leaders during 1970 and the first half of 1971 were paving the way for mandatory controls.

The grant of authority to impose mandatory controls, which we have already described, is a clear example of this unintended but important miseducation of the public. Even though the congressmen who granted the authority in 1970 said that they did not want controls, their action could not be interpreted as reflecting a conviction that they regarded mandatory controls as beyond the pale, to be ruled out forever. When the President used the authority in the case of the construction industry, even though all the parties regarded that action as window-dressing, outside observers must have gotten the impression that the executive branch considered mandatory controls a respectable anti-inflation instrument. And this idea was enhanced when Secretary Connally testified in favor of extending the authority to impose controls, while denying any intent to use the authority.

The call from respected opinion makers for "some kind of incomes policy"—whether guideposts, a wage-price review board, or whatever—became louder and louder as we went through 1970 and 1971, and was probably even more influential in making the idea of mandatory controls acceptable. These people all insisted that they did not want mandatory controls, but they were relying on a fine and indefensible distinction between mandatory and voluntary. The critical question is whether the government knows best—better than the market—what particular prices and wages should be, from the standpoint of economic efficiency, fairness, or some other criterion. The proponents of incomes policy were saying that the government does know best. Once this is said, it is not convincing to say that it makes a great deal of difference whether the government achieves its preferred prices by mandatory or voluntary means, or that it should not use mandatory means if voluntary means fail. In fact, the distinction between mandatory and voluntary systems in this field is quite loose. The "voluntary" systems can involve a good deal of coercion—in the form of threats of exposure to public calumny, loss of government contracts, or other sanctions—whereas the mandatory systems always have a considerable voluntary element, because they cannot work without the cooperation, or at least the agreement, of the parties.

The largest part of the argument for voluntary incomes policies was also an argument for mandatory controls and helped to create the impression that mandatory controls were an admissible policy. The administration's strategy was to try to appease the mounting demand for incomes policies by making concessions to it, in the hope that the inflation would be checked before the demand escalated into irresistible pressure for mandatory controls. Thus we got the inflation alerts, the National Commission on Productivity, the Government Regulation and Purchasing Review Board, the jawboning of the steel industry, and the Construction Industry Stabilization Committee. These moves did not have the desired effect of slowing down the demand for incomes policy. In fact, they may have intensified that demand, since they were a concession by the administration that to some degree the solution to the inflation problem could be found in the box of government guidance of private price and wage decisions. This was probably true despite the limited scope of the administration's moves and the free price rhetoric with which they were accompanied.

By mid-1971 the President had concluded that further small steps within the area of "voluntary" policies would not satisfy the demands in the country for stronger measures, would not silence his critics, and would not reduce inflation but might accelerate it by inducing people to try to get big price or wage increases before the door was finally slammed shut by mandatory controls. The possibility of avoiding mandatory controls might have been greater if the President had rejected any moves in the direction of "incomes policy" rather than taking homeopathic doses which encouraged the popular belief that the medicine might be of value if taken in larger amounts. The possibility of avoiding mandatory controls would have been still greater if the private leaders of public opinion who were demanding an incomes policy but foreswearing any desire for mandatory controls had paid more attention to the kind of education they were giving the public.

A similar process of public miseducation is going on in the country today. The President and many others are teaching the public that the inflation can be controlled and the operation of the economy improved if leaders of business and labor would follow standards specified by the government, rather than make wage and price decisions in the light of their own conditions as they see them. At the same time the President and most others insist that they do not want to *require* the private parties to abide by these standards. They only want the government to point out what proper behavior is, and persuade the private parties to follow their lead. They sometimes describe inflation as if it were a bad habit, which only needs to be pointed out to be overcome, to the great relief of its former practitioners and of the country at large. But this is simply telling the public that the government knows best, and leaves no convincing answer to the question why the government should not require that people do what is best, for themselves and the country.

The currently favored version of incomes policy, among academics and editorial writers, is the tax-based incomes policy, or TIP. The basic notion is that if an economic unit raises its wages, or prices, by less than some amount which the government specifies it should get a tax reduction, or, alternatively, if the increase is more than the standard it should incur a tax penalty. This is much closer to mandatory controls than most other suggested incomes policies are. It requires legislative authorization. It requires quite precise specification of standards, of a kind that would stand up in court, and does not leave the room for negotiation between the government and private parties that exists in less formal incomes policy. And the TIP would probably have to be of universal coverage, whereas most other kinds of incomes policy are operationally applied only to large economic units. If there is to be a tax benefit for not getting a wage increase in excess of, say, 6 percent, that benefit has to be available to the shoeshine boy in a three chair barber shop as well as to the members of the United Steel Workers.

TIP is mandatory price and wage control in which no one goes to prison. The government would establish standards of price and wage behavior and a financial penalty, in the form of additional tax imposed or tax relief forgone, for failure to conform. Presumably the penalty would be set so as to be powerful.

TIP is, in my opinion, less likely to be adopted than mandatory controls of the conventional sort. However, its proponents feel able to argue for it while denying that they are in favor of mandatory controls. And the argument for TIP is a large part of the argument for controls of the conventional sort.

Proponents of TIP (and other incomes policies) say something like this: The country would be better off if the average of wages, which we will call capital W, rises by 6 percent rather than 8 percent. Therefore let us give a benefit to everyone whose wage rises by less than 6 percent, or impose a penalty on everyone whose wage rises by more than 6 percent. But at this point they have slipped from talking about W to talking about all the hundreds of thousands of little w's which are the specific wages for specific jobs in specific industries and locations. And while it may be correct that W should rise by 6 percent it is by no means correct that all the little w's should rise by 6 percent. In fact, it is neither efficient nor fair that they should. Once the effort is made to specify how much each of the little w's should rise, TIP loses its initial appeal. But if the argument for TIP convinces people either that the government knows how much each little w should rise, or that it doesn't matter how much each of them rises, then much of the argument against mandatory controls is undercut.

The Momentum of Controls

The talk about incomes policy, and the small steps taken in that area, in 1970 and 1971, helped to lead the country to a point that almost everyone had said he didn't want to reach—mandatory controls. Once the controls were adopted they also turned out to have a momentum to lead us in a direction that no one had wanted or foreseen.

When the decision was made, in August 1971, to freeze prices, wages, and rents for a period up to ninety days, there was no clear idea of what would follow the ninety days. However, the quite tentative discussion of that question among the government officials who met at Camp David on the weekend of August 13 suggested a radical reduction in the scope and rigor of controls. Most of the ideas discussed were of the order of the establishment of a Wage-Price Review Board, to examine and form opinions about actions of the largest corporations and unions, possibly with mandatory authority but possibly not.

The initial examination of options for policy to follow the freeze covered a wide range of possibilities, from total decontrol to continuation of something very close to the freeze itself. But it soon became clear that the more far-reaching moves back to the free market were not really possible. The freeze had instantly become the most popular economic action of government that anyone could remember. There was a widespread public rejoicing that at last the government was protecting the people. And it was not, or not only, General Motors and U.S. Steel from whom the public was being protected but also the landlord and the corner grocer. The freeze was a powerful piece of economic education. It taught the people that the government could stop inflation in its tracks. It was not possible to turn people back to the tender mercies of their landlords and merchants. This was not only politically impossible. It was psychologically impossible; the general disappointment at the sudden loss of this new-found protector would have been too wrenching. The danger that this new-found protector might become a nuisance, if not an enemy, referred to a future that most people did not foresee or weigh very heavily.

This became clearest in the case of rent control. This was the area in which the managers of the program were most convinced of the economic folly of continuing the freeze. It was also the area in which the administrative difficulties were the greatest. But it was also an area in which the public—that is, the tenants—most valued having government on their side.

In the end the Phase II program was quite comprehensive and, in principle, entirely mandatory, although it could not literally be enforced on every small economic unit in the country but depended in considerable part on voluntary compliance. This went far beyond any of the possibilities that had been thought of when the freeze was first imposed. And the other options that were most seriously considered when the Phase II decision was made were even more freeze-like than the system that was actually adopted.

This experience is a vivid example of the importance of asking, "What next?" when any step is taken in this field. Every step closes some options.

The Management of Controls

There are, as I have said earlier, some people who deny the value of the 1971–1974 experience as evidence of the ineffectiveness of controls, on the ground that the controls at that time were not properly managed. Among those who think that, the most common argument is not to refer to a specific deficiency of the controls system but to point out that the controls were run by people who did not "believe" in them, as if that contributed to their failure.

I shall indicate later what I think were the reasons for the failure of the controls. My list does not include the fact that they were run by people who didn't believe in them. I recognize that I am not an entirely objective witness on that point, but I will put down some observations which may help others to judge what there is in it.

When it is said that the people who ran the controls did not believe in them, the reference is primarily to Mr. Nixon and to George Shultz, who was chairman of the Cost of Living Council during most of the period. The list probably includes me, since I was vice-chairman of the Cost of Living Council, and have more writing and speeches against controls on the record than anyone else in the government at that time. The questions are, What were our attitudes to the controls, and In what sense did we run the controls?

A distinction must be made between liking the controls and believing in them. Given that there is a controls program to run, there is no advantage in having it run by people who like controls, any more than there is advantage in having surgery performed by surgeons who like to cut or wars commanded by generals who like to bomb. Liking controls can warp judgments and lead to excesses which overstrain the control system as well as interfere with economic efficiency, growth, and other objectives.

It is easy to come to like the controls if one has a position of authority in the system. The price controller has a sense of great power as the heads of large corporations file through his office asking for exemptions or increases in their ceilings. Anyone who has seen J. K. Galbraith on television describing his experience as a price controller in World War II can see the relish with which he still recalls his power over the captains of industry. I observed this attitude in the 1971–1974 period, but we who then ran the controls did not share it.

We not only didn't like controls but we would have preferred not to be in them and we felt that we had gotten there only as a result of strong external pressure. But being there, we believed strongly in trying to use the controls to help effect a transition to a permanently lower inflation rate at high employment.

We did not believe that controls should be permanent. We did not believe that the requirements of the control system should take precedence over all other objectives of economic policy—including the increase of output and employment, and the reduction of unemployment; a high rate of investment, which would contribute to future output; and efficiency in production and distribution. We did not want to establish a huge bureaucracy and enforcement apparatus. We valued economic freedom, including freedom of collective bargaining, highly, not only because of its economic benefits but also because of the underpinning it provides for personal and political freedom. In other words, we did not want to create a permanently and totally managed economy in the United States, and did not believe that the American people expected us to do that.

If those qualifications are not accepted, then the management of the 1971–1974 controls must seem unduly weak. But if these qualifications are accepted, it is difficult to see that the management of the system was inhibited by the ideology of those who were running it. As already noted, the Phase II controls system was much more comprehensive and mandatory than the administration or any one else had expected it to be. Also, the system was kept in operation for a relatively long time. Decontrol during Phase II was quite gradual. Although the move to Phase III in January 1973 had been criticized, I shall argue below that it was a necessary and prudent step. When, nevertheless, inflation accelerated in 1973 the administration made a strenuous, although unsuccessful, attempt to check it by tightening up the system again.

Moreover, in very important respects the price-wage control system was managed by people who did not share the ideological inhibitions of the President and his chief economic officials. During Phase II, the standards and procedures were established, and case-by-case decisions made, by the Price Commission and the Pay Board, and their staffs. In Phase III and IV these functions were largely carried out by the executive director of the Cost of Living Council and his staff, much of which had formerly been Price Commission and Pay Board staff. In December 1973 control over prices of petroleum and its products was shifted to the newly created Federal Energy Administration.

These other agencies were naturally more single-minded in their determination to hold down prices and wages by controls than were the officials with more general responsibilities for economic policy. This was not only, or even mainly, because of the ideologies of the more general officials. The latter had to be more concerned with output, employment, growth, efficiency, and good international economic relations than were the agencies that concentrated exclusively on controlling wages and prices. Moreover, the general officials had to be concerned with what would happen when the controls and the controllers were gone.

There were disagreements between the general officials and the price-wage controllers. However, these disagreements were not usually over matters that were crucial for the success of the program, and the price controllers most frequently had their way with respect to the control standards and their implementation and the administration of the system. The administration recognized the value of leaving a large degree of responsibility for the operation of the controls in bodies that were independent of and somewhat removed from the White House, and it respected that independence.

The Move to Phase III

Insofar as the charge that the 1971–1974 controls were badly run has any content, aside from the complaint that they were run by people who did not believe in them, the content refers to the relaxation of controls in January 1973, when Phase II was followed by Phase III. The rate of price increase began to accelerate sharply in the early part of 1973, and there were many people who believed then, and there probably are some who still believe, that this was the result of the relaxation of controls. Some conclude from this that if the relaxation had not come when it did not only would there have been less inflation in early 1973 but also the whole subsequent course of the inflation would have been different.

Of course, it makes a difference whether one considers the wisdom of relaxation in January 1973 in the context of a policy in which it is possible to have controls forever or in the context of a policy where permanent controls are not accepted as possible or desirable. If, as is almost universally accepted in this country, comprehensive controls are not to last forever, one must ask whether there would have been some better, later, date for taking the step toward decontrol. This question calls for a great deal of speculation, but even in retrospect it is hard to see a better time. Perhaps it would have been wise to keep the controls in their Phase II form until the recession of 1975, when the inflationary pressure of demand would have been less. But this possibility runs into the counterpossibility that prolonging the controls in the Phase II form would have so depressed business investment as to make the recession come sooner than it did. In any case, in January 1973 no one was foreseeing the 1975 recession. And while it is always prudent to expect that there will be a recession within the next few years, the prospect at the beginning of 1973 was that the economy would go through more tightness and demand pressure on inflation before it reached the next recession.

Given a determination to end the controls sometime, the step taken in January 1973 seemed timely and moderate. There were several reasons for acting then:

(1) Some relaxation of the Phase II wage standard was a necessary condition for restoring participation of the labor leadership in the program. The labor members had walked off the Pay Board in April 1972, and while labor had continued to comply with the standards, the absence of the labor leadership seemed a risky condition. Establishment of a new Labor-Management Advisory Committee was a key element in Phase III, and this required movement to a more flexible and negotiated wage-determination process.

(2) Continuation of the Phase II profits limitation as part of the price control system was a threat to business investment. A new standard was desired, which would relax the profit limitation while retaining a fairly firm limit on price increases. Since for most corporations the profit limit was applied on a calendar year basis, it was desirable to announce the new standard early in the year.

(3) As economic activity rose, the price control system was running into an increasing number of cases where the price ceilings were an impediment to production or efficient allocation of output. Revision of the rules to allow more room for adjustment in those cases was in order.

(4) The price control authority would expire on April 30, 1973. There was an advantage in having the new rules in force so that Congress would understand them before it acted on extension of the authority, so that the Congress would not inadvertently make changes in the

authority which would interfere with the new system but would have a chance to modify the system deliberately if it wished to do so.

The changes made in the shift from Phase II to Phase III were not radical. The pricing standards were altered only marginally. The wage standard was made ambiguous, with the idea of case-by-case decisions in the foreground and the Phase II standard of a 5.5 percent limit on increases in the background. Companies were relieved of the requirement to notify the Cost of Living Council of price increases in advance, but they were required to file quarterly reports. The Cost of Living Council asserted its readiness to adopt tougher standards and procedures if necessary.

The rate of inflation was expected not to accelerate significantly in 1973, and not to be visibly greater with the Phase III system than it would have been with the Phase II system. Although the rate of unemployment had come down to 5 percent at the end of 1972, this was thought to signify that there was still a good deal of slack in the economy, even though there would be some cases of shortages at the existing prices. There was confidence that the relations among wages in different unions and sectors had reached a condition of balance in which there would not be a strong drive from any quarter for exceeding the recent pattern of wage increases. The shift from the 5.5 percent wage standard to a more flexible standard was considered to be more formal than real—a concession to the desire of the labor leaders to get credit for wage increases rather than to the desire for larger wage increases. The shift from requiring businesses to notify the government of price increases in advance to requiring reporting after the fact was not expected to change business behavior. Agricultural prices would continue to rise, as they had done in 1972, but this was estimated not to exceed an amount that could be accommodated within an overall price increase of about 3 percent.

Of course, the inflation turned out to be much greater in 1973 than was envisaged when the decision was made to go to Phase III. This unforeseen increase in the inflation rate was not, however, the result of the changes in the standards or procedures of the controls system. The estimate that wage increases would be moderate turned out to be correct. Also, the increase in profit margins was small. The big surge of inflation came in two sectors that had not been under control in Phase II and that are not usually covered by price control systems. These are raw agricultural products and imports. They are typically excluded from controls because price ceilings in these fields have a quick supply response and lead promptly to shortages. The price effects of low food supplies, especially of meat, had been seriously underestimated. So had the effect of the boom in the United States and in the rest of the world on the prices of internationally traded raw materials. The effect on prices of the decline in the exchange rate of the dollar during the first half of 1973 was also underestimated. But the inflationary surge of the first half of 1973 could not have been prevented by the retention of the Phase II controls, as is suggested by the failure of the extreme tightening of the controls in the summer of 1973.

In the middle of 1973 I was asked at a congressional hearing whether, in view of the big rise of the inflation rate, I thought it would have been wise not to shift to Phase III. I replied that I did not think so, except for the fact that by our action in January 1973 we had given decontrol a bad name. There might have been a tactical advantage in not making the shift to Phase III and therefore not taking the blame for the rise of the inflation rate, but that would not have kept the rate from rising.

From the vantage point of 1978 what seems the main problem with the decontrol process was not that it came so soon but that it was incomplete. The system of ceiling prices on domestically produced crude oil established during the controls period remains in effect today, under special price control authority that was enacted before the general authority to control prices expired. The two-tier method, holding down the price of "old" oil and allowing "new" oil to be free, was established in 1973 and is still basically in operation. Even the ceiling price of $5.25 a barrel set in December 1973 for old oil is still in effect. The responsible officials recognized in 1973 that this system was holding back domestic oil production, since the regulatory distinction between old oil and new oil was not identical with an economic distinction between oil that would be produced at the ceiling and oil that would not be produced at that price. Moreover, freeing the domestic oil price after the oil embargo would have eliminated the need for allocations, would have discouraged oil consumption, and would have reduced oil imports. However, the officials feared the immediate effect on the price level if oil was decontrolled and worried about the example that might be set for other prices and the possible reaction of wages to a rise of energy costs. Also there was a strong sentiment in the country and in the Congress against any increase in oil prices.

The oil case illustrates the great tendency of price controllers to be obsessed with this week's price numbers and the inability of anyone to imagine and give adequate weight to the longer-run consequences of today's decisions. It also illustrates the danger that price controls will leave behind a residue which pollutes the economic environment for a long time. The leading example of this danger used to be the rent controls which persisted in many cities around the world after the 1914–1918 war and interfered for decades with the construction of new housing and the efficient use of old housing. But the continuation of oil price controls after other price controls were terminated in the United States in 1974 is probably a more serious example of the residual damage left behind by controls. Possibly we would have had oil price controls if there had not been general price controls, but that is quite uncertain. And if we had never had oil price controls, the economic history of the United States would have been quite different from what it was.

Why Controls Failed

The controls obviously failed in the sense that there was an acceleration of the inflation rate before they ended and an even greater acceleration afterwards. They failed for a number of reasons, some of which are common to most price control experiments, and some of which may have been unusual although not unique.

(1) The underlying rationale of the controls was faulty. If there is to be less inflation after a temporary price control system than before it, something must have changed during the controls period. The postcontrols situation must be less inflationary than the precontrols situation was. The argument for the 1971–1974 controls was that they would exorcise the expectation of inflation and lead people to make smaller price and wage increases than they would otherwise have made in similar conditions. This is the rationale that is now being used to explain a temporary incomes policy. But in fact the controls and the incomes policy do not have that effect. They only create the expectation that when the controls, or the incomes policy, end prices will rise more rapidly.

(2) The controls were accompanied by a strongly expansionary fiscal and monetary policy, and in fact probably helped to make that policy more expansionary than it would otherwise have been. The economic officials of the time were aware of the fact that this had been the cause of the breakdown of controls and incomes policy systems in the past. Being aware of it, they thought they would avoid at least that error. But they did not. They were misled by the apparent success of the controls in their early months into thinking that there was more room for noninflationary expansion than there actually was.

Perhaps this is not an inherent defect of controls. But it has been encountered so often as to suggest that it is in fact an inescapable concomitant of controls, even if not a logical necessity. A government does not ordinarily get into controls in peacetime unless it feels a strong desire to pump up demand close to the inflationary danger point. And when prices are under control it becomes difficult to tell when the danger point is being neared.

133

(3) Prices began to rise sharply in two important sectors where controls are hardest to maintain even for a short while—raw agricultural products and imports. When these prices began to rise sharply it became very difficult to keep the rest of the price structure steady. Any practicable price control system will allow for the pass-through of cost increases, and wage controls will have to respond to the cost of living, so it is quite possible to have a cost-price spiral within the controls system if a few key prices go into motion exogenously. It may be said that the poor crops and the booming world markets were unfortunate accidents which need not have occurred, but they are the kinds of accidents that occur frequently.

(4) The controls failed because they were basically in conflict with the way the American public, or at least powerful forces within it, want the political economic system to work. This is true despite the majority that is commonly revealed by public opinion polls to be in favor of price and wage controls. Once the first flush of enthusiasm has passed, and controls became a matter of continuing regulation that is increasingly detailed, labor and business become more and more resentful and resistant, and a larger and more irritating bureaucratic machine is required in an effort to achieve compliance. This was most obvious in the case of the labor organizations. Although there never was any union defiance of the system, the labor leadership clearly felt that the controls had displaced them from their role as the source of wage increases for their members, and their continued cooperation could be obtained even for a while only by a significant relaxation of the controls. Also businesses were becoming more determined and skillful in trying to find their way through ambiguities and gaps in the regulations. An attempt to make the controls work in those conditions would have required the exercise of government power over the economy on a scale which hardly anyone wanted.

• • •

The history of 1971–1974 is not recounted as conclusive evidence that price and wage controls can never work in a beneficial way. To prove that would require much more historical evidence and analysis than is presented here.

The conclusions I draw from this history are much narrower. The first is that incautious actions and talk did a great deal to lead the country to a policy which hardly anyone had wanted—namely, mandatory controls. The actions included irresponsible provision of legal authority for controls and mild steps in the direction of incomes policy, which were intended to stave off demands for controls, but only sharpened the appetite for them. The talk consisted in part of overly optimistic predictions of the speed and ease with which inflation would be controlled, leading to disappointment with conventional policies when the predictions turned out to be wrong. The talk also included a flood of argument for nonmandatory incomes policy, which turned out to convince the public of the need for controls of some kind—the degree of coercion involved being a secondary consideration.

The second conclusion is that the generally acknowledged failure of the controls in 1971–1974 cannot be convincingly attributed to the lack of enthusiasm of those who ran the control system or other easily remediable deficiencies in the management of the system.

These conclusions suggest two lessons for today. We should not evaluate the possible use of controls under the impression that the difficulties previously experienced will be escaped if the controls are managed by different people or in a different way. More important, all steps taken in this field or words uttered should be carefully considered in the light of the expectations they will arouse, the options they will close, and the momentum they will generate in directions that are unintended.

Wage Behavior and Inflation in the 1970s

Marvin H. Kosters

Summary

*The history of inflation since the mid-1960s includes considerable varia-
tion in rates of increase in prices, with much of this variation associated
with cyclical changes. Yet inflation has been resistant to reduction during periods of cyclical slack, and this resistance has been particularly
evident for wages. As a result, increases in the rate of inflation during
cyclical expansion were only partially reversed by the two recessions
of the 1970s. Without a parallel reduction in average wage increases,
inflation can be suppressed only temporarily. Although average wage
increases subsided during 1975 from the higher rates reached during
1974, there was otherwise little variation in the rate of increase in
average wages throughout the past decade.*

*This relatively stable behavior of average wage increases was ac-
companied by differences in rates of wage increase for major sectors of
the economy that were often quite large. Many factors contributed to
these differences in rates of wage increase among industries, and some
of these factors were specific to the particular industries involved.
Systematic differences in the cyclical responsiveness of industry wages
on the basis of their extent of unionization were also important, however. Wages in the less unionized industries were more quickly responsive to cyclical forces than were wages in the more highly unionized
industries, although this difference in responsiveness and the timing of
its effects were influenced by the spread of cost-of-living escalator provisions in multi-year wage contracts. Changes in rates of wage increase
among sectors of the economy that resulted from differences in cyclical
responsiveness had effects on the overall average that largely offset
each other during most of the past decade.*

The lack of responsiveness to cyclical developments shown by average wage increases in the past may not be a reliable guide to the responsiveness that can be expected in the future. The behavior of average wages did not reflect a uniform lack of responsiveness to cyclical conditions of wages in all sectors of the economy. Consequently, under labor market conditions that differ from those prevailing during the past decade, changes in rates of wage increase for major sectors of the economy could be mutually reinforcing instead of largely offsetting.

The potential for acceleration of the rate of increase in average hourly labor costs in response to cyclical expansion is suggested by three important aspects of current labor market conditions: (1) Wages of many workers under major collective bargaining agreements are closely linked to price performance through cost-of-living escalator provisions; higher prices are quickly translated into higher wages for these workers. (2) With relative wages in high-wage industries currently high by historical standards and subject to little erosion through higher inflation, wages in the lower part of the wage distribution can be expected to be particularly sensitive to rising demand and tightening labor markets. (3) The rise in the minimum wage and the scheduled increases add directly to labor costs, along with such policies as higher payroll taxes, and in addition contribute to pressures for larger wage increases in the lower part of the wage distribution. These aspects of the labor market environment raise the risk that expansionary aggregate economic policies will be translated into higher inflation and smaller increases in employment and production than were intended.

Introduction

Experience with two recessions in the 1970s has led to skepticism about the effectiveness of reducing inflation by restraining increases in demand. This skepticism is based more on the behavior of wages than on the behavior of prices. While both wage and price increases showed some cyclical response, wage increases showed less response than price increases, and the timing and magnitude of the responses partly reflected other short-term developments.

Price increases were smaller from 1970 through 1972 than in 1969, but there was essentially no decline in average rates of increase in wages, and the influence of cyclical slack may have been obscured by the controls that were introduced in 1971. After the sharp recession that began in 1974, there was a pronounced reduction in inflation—from about 12 percent to about 6 percent—and average wage increases also declined significantly. However, this decline in inflation followed the surge in food, energy, and basic materials prices of 1973–1974, and average wage increases subsided only to the 7 percent range, similar to rates that prevailed from 1968 through 1973. Thus, while the reduction in inflation that occurred after both recessions provides evidence of the effectiveness of demand restraint, the extent to which this evidence should be discounted depends on the emphasis that should be placed on special, short-term factors other than demand restraint.

Clearly no more than a temporary reduction in inflation can be achieved without a parallel reduction in average wage increases. The apparent resistance of the average rate of wage increases to decline significantly below the 7 percent range is the major element in discouraging assessments of the effectiveness of demand restraint. This paper discusses factors that have contributed to the apparent insensitivity of average rates of wage increase to cyclical changes in unemployment and inflation during the past decade. The purpose of the discussion is to provide insight into the circumstances that gave rise to observed overall rates of wage change, to consider whether the evidence suggests an underlying stability in wage trends that can be expected to show little response to cyclical conditions, and to assess the implications of recent developments in the labor market and of government policies influencing labor costs for the wage and inflation outlook.[1]

Wage Trends during the Past Ten Years

Despite wide variation in inflation and unemployment rates during the past decade, the rate of increase in the average wage level has shown a remarkable degree of stability. The relative stability from year to year of percentage increases in average wages during most of the past decade is illustrated by the data in Table 1. With the exception of 1974 (and to a smaller extent, 1975) average wage increases have not strayed far from a rate of nearly 7 percent, and variation in annual rates of change has been significantly smaller for wages than for unemployment rates

---

[1] The resistance to decline shown by the average rate of increase in labor costs is the basis for the concept of an "underlying" rate of inflation that can be reduced only at great cost. The concept is referred to frequently in the 1978 *Economic Report:* "An underlying inflation rate of 6 to 6½ percent has persisted since mid-1975 and is deeply imbedded in the wage-cost-price structure," p. 38; "This underlying rate, measured by the consumer price index exclusive of food and energy prices, has remained relatively steady in the range of 6 to 6½ percent during almost the entire 3 years of expansion," p. 46; "For the last 3 years, the underlying rate of inflation has remained in the 6 to 6½ range despite very high rates of unemployment," p. 138; "some longer-term decrease in downward flexibility, especially of wages, seems evident," p. 145; and "the essence of the present inflation problem is that the rate of wage and price increase reacts very slowly to idle resources and excess supply," p. 150. *Economic Report of the President, 1978* (Washington, D.C., January 1978).

Table 1
CHANGES IN WAGES, PRICES, AND UNEMPLOYMENT, 1968–1977

Percentage Changes and Deviations from Average

	1968	1969	1970	1971	1972	1973	1974	1975	1976	1977
Average hourly earnings index										
Percent change	6.8	6.5	6.8	7.1	6.5	6.7	9.4	7.9	6.9	7.0
Deviation from average[a]	−0.1	−0.4	−0.1	0.2	−0.4	−0.2	(2.5)	1.0	0.0	0.1
Consumer price index										
Percent change	4.7	6.1	5.5	3.4	3.4	8.8	12.2	7.0	4.8	6.8
Deviation from average[a]	−0.9	0.5	−0.1	−2.2	−2.2	3.2	(6.6)	1.4	−0.8	1.2
Unemployment										
Average rate	3.6	3.5	4.9	5.9	5.6	4.9	5.6	8.5	7.7	7.0
Deviation from average[a]	−2.1	−2.2	−0.8	0.2	−0.1	−0.8	(−0.1)	2.8	2.0	1.3

Average Percentage Changes and Comparisons of Dispersion

	Average Percent Change[a]	Average Absolute Deviation (in percentage points)[a]	Coefficient of Variation[a]
Average hourly earnings index	6.9	0.28	0.06
Consumer price index	5.6	1.39	0.32
Unemployment rate	5.7	1.37	0.30

Note: Percentage changes in the average hourly earnings index and the consumer price index are for the nonfarm business sector. They are computed from December to December based on data that are not seasonally adjusted. Unemployment rates are yearly averages.

[a] Averages, deviations from the average, and coefficients of variation are computed using the years 1968–1977, excluding 1974.

Source: U.S. Department of Labor, Bureau of Labor Statistics.

and prices.[2] These data lend credence to a view that wage trends are "sticky" and only weakly responsive to cyclical changes in aggregate economic conditions.

There are several reasons why wage trends might be expected to change only sluggishly. Wage adjustments for a significant fraction of the work force take place under previously negotiated contracts in any given year. In addition, for many firms with wages of production workers set under long-term contracts, other workers not covered by these contracts usually receive comparable wage increases. To the extent that terms of new wage agreements are negotiated to maintain historical relationships with wages under other multi-year contracts, established trends tend to be maintained under the system prevalent in the United States because of staggered contract expiration dates so that periods covered by different contracts overlap. Wages for the majority of workers in the economy are set more informally, but these informal arrangements presumably include implicit understandings between firms and their employees that relationships between their wages and wages of related workers will be taken into account. Moreover, many informal wage-setting arrangements make use of area wage surveys, and the principle of comparability is widely and explicitly applied for wage-setting by government. All of these factors contribute to stickiness in wage trends.

It must also be recognized, of course, that these factors have not been sufficient to preclude significant changes in average rates of wage increase. This is illustrated in Table 1 by the notably higher wage increases that occurred in 1974. The rise in annual rates of wage increase from about 3 percent in the early 1960s to the 7 percent range by 1968 also illustrates that established wage trends are not immutable regardless of aggregate economic conditions.

Imitative forces clearly represent only one aspect of wage behavior. If maintenance of historical wage relationships were the main force that led to the stability in average wage trends during the past decade, little short-term change in relationships among wages would be expected. That is, wages in all sectors would rise in tandem at rates similar to the overall average. Moreover, if wages in all sectors were equally responsive to cyclical forces, relationships among wages would remain unchanged over the cycle, and examination of wage develop-

---

[2] There was much less difference between variation in rates of wage and price increase earlier in the postwar period. This change may be attributable in part to the shift that has occurred during the past twenty-five years to longer-term collective bargaining agreements. See, for example, Donald Cullen, "Recent Trends in Collective Bargaining in the United States," *Collective Bargaining in Industrialized Market Economies* (Geneva: International Labor Office, 1972), p. 402.

ments in particular sectors would contribute no insights into the process of wage adjustment that could not be gained by examining the behavior of average wages. Although pressures for maintenance of historical wage relationships may have an important influence on wage behavior, there have been significant short-term changes in relative wages, and these changes have reflected cyclical developments as well as other forces.

Recent Wage Developments

Average Wages. After rising to over 10 percent during 1974, the rate of increase in average wages declined to the 7 percent range during 1975. Measures of wage increases based on the average hourly earnings index and compensation per hour show little trend in their rate of increase during 1976 and 1977 (Table 2). The hourly earnings index rose at rates in the 7 to 7.5 percent range, and hourly compensation rose at a somewhat higher rate, partly because of changes in industry mix and more overtime and partly because benefits rose more rapidly than wages. The employment cost index, which rose by 7.2 percent in 1976 and 7 percent in 1977, also shows little change in trend during these two years.

After rising more rapidly earlier in the cyclical recovery, output per hour rose at rates of about 2 percent or slightly more in 1977. Unit labor costs rose at rates averaging slightly more than 6 percent during 1977 in the nonfarm business sector, while prices in the same sector showed rates of increase slightly below 6 percent. As always, there was significant variation in rates of increase for particular quarters and even for periods spanning as much as a year.

Collective Bargaining. The slowdown in wage increases under collective bargaining agreements after 1974 was more gradual than for broader measures of wage change, such as the average hourly earnings index. Differences in the size and timing of wage increases between these measures could, of course, be expected in view of coverage by major collective bargaining agreements of only about one-sixth of the workers in the private nonfarm sector. In addition, however, the differences in effective wage increases under major collective bargaining agreements are influenced by the size of first-year negotiated increases and deferred wage increases, by the fraction of workers affected by new wage settlements in any given year, and by differences among industries in the average size of negotiated wage increases. First-year wage increases have typically been larger than deferred wage increases, and 1976 and 1977 were both years with relatively heavy bargaining.

Table 2

WAGES, LABOR COSTS, PRODUCTIVITY, AND PRICES, 1975–1977

(percentage change from same quarter a year earlier)

	1975				1976				1977			
	I	II	III	IV	I	II	III	IV	I	II	III	IV
Hourly earnings index[a]	9.7	9.1	8.6	8.2	7.7	7.5	7.2	6.8	7.1	7.1	7.3	7.6
Increase in supplementary benefits as a component of hourly labor costs[b]	0.8	0.9	1.0	0.8	0.8	0.6	0.5	0.5	0.6	0.5	0.6	0.5
Hourly compensation[c,d]	11.4	10.5	9.1	7.7	7.1	8.5	9.0	9.2	9.3	8.8	8.5	8.5
Output per hour[d]	–3.0	1.4	4.4	4.5	5.7	4.4	2.9	3.2	2.8	1.6	1.9	2.7
Unit labor cost[d]	14.9	8.9	4.5	3.0	1.3	3.9	5.9	5.8	6.3	7.1	6.5	5.9
Prices												
Nonfarm business deflator	14.3	10.6	8.6	6.8	5.6	5.3	5.0	4.9	4.6	5.6	5.8	5.6
Consumer price index[e]	10.3	9.3	7.8	7.0	6.1	5.9	5.5	4.8	6.4	6.9	6.6	6.8

[a] The hourly earnings index is based on average hourly earnings of production and nonsupervisory workers in the private nonfarm sector, adjusted for overtime (in manufacturing only) and interindustry employment shifts. Changes in the index differ from actual average hourly compensation changes for the nonfarm business sector because of differences in employee coverage, shifts in relative employment among industries and between production and nonproduction workers, and inclusion of overtime (in manufacturing) and supplementary benefits.

[b] Supplementary benefits include such items as contribution to social security, private pensions, and health and welfare plans. Their effect is computed as the difference between changes in hourly compensation and hourly wages and salaries for all employees.

[c] Hourly compensation is a measure of average hourly compensation for all wage and salary workers and the self-employed in the nonfarm business sector.

[d] Hourly compensation, output per hour, and unit labor costs are for the nonfarm business sector of the economy.

[e] Percentage changes in the consumer price index from the same quarter a year earlier are represented by the third month in each quarter.

Source: U.S. Department of Labor, Bureau of Labor Statistics.

143

Table 3

INCREASE IN HOURLY EARNINGS AND NEGOTIATED WAGE INCREASES UNDER MAJOR COLLECTIVE BARGAINING SETTLEMENTS, 1970–1978

(percentage change)

	1970	1971	1972	1973	1974	1975	1976	1977	1978[a]
Average hourly earnings index, private nonfarm[b]	6.8	7.1	6.5	6.7	9.4	7.9	6.9	7.0	
Effective wage rate change under major collective bargaining agreements[c]	8.8	9.2	6.6	7.0	9.4	8.7	8.1	7.8	
Percentage of workers affected by new wage settlements[d]	43	38	23	52	50	28	45	39	21
Wage settlements[e]									
All industries									
First-year wage changes	11.9	11.6	7.3	5.8	9.8	10.2	8.4	7.9	
Average over life of contract[f]	8.9	8.1	6.4	5.1	7.3	7.8	6.4	5.8	
Deferred wage changes	5.8	7.7	6.0	4.8	5.1	5.2	5.4	5.6	5.1
Construction									
First-year wage changes	17.6	12.6	6.9	5.0	11.0	8.0	6.1	6.4	
Average over life of contract[f]	14.9	10.8	6.0	5.1	9.6	7.5	6.2	6.3	
Deferred wage changes	10.1	13.1	11.6	7.3	5.3	8.0	8.1	6.4	6.5
Manufacturing									
First-year wage changes	8.1	10.9	6.6	5.9	8.7	9.8	8.9	8.4	
Average over life of contract[f]	6.0	7.3	5.6	4.9	6.1	8.0	6.0	5.5	
Deferred wage changes	4.6	4.8	4.5	4.4	4.6	4.4	4.9	5.1	4.6

Nonmanufacturing (excluding construction)								
First-year wage changes	14.2	12.2	8.2	6.0	10.2	11.9	8.6	7.5
Average over life of contract[f]	10.2	8.6	7.3	5.4	7.2	8.0	7.2	5.9
Deferred wage changes	5.2	7.6	7.3	5.0	5.6	5.1	4.9	6.0	5.2

[a] Deferred wage increases for 1978 are estimates of wage increases scheduled to be put in effect during the year, excluding increases that may occur under cost-of-living provisions.

[b] Percentage changes in the average hourly earnings index are computed from December to December.

[c] Effective wage rate changes are wage rate changes actually put into effect during the year. They include wage increases under new settlements, deferred increases under previously negotiated contracts, and increments under cost-of-living escalator provisions.

[d] Percent of estimated workers covered in major collective bargaining situations for which new wage settlements were negotiated during the year.

[e] Data on wage increases are mean percentage changes for collective bargaining agreements covering 1,000 workers or more in private nonfarm industries. First-year wage changes include all changes negotiated during the year and going into effect during the first twelve months of the agreement. Deferred wage increases are increases provided for in agreements after the first twelve months and put into effect during the year, excluding cost-of-living escalator increases.

[f] Averages over life of contracts do not include wage increases under cost-of-living escalator provisions.

Source: U.S. Department of Labor, Bureau of Labor Statistics.

145

Differences among industries in the size of wage increases under collective bargaining agreements have also been significant; the new wage settlements in construction, for example, are lower than the average for other industries since 1974.

Several distinctions must be kept in mind in interpreting the measures of wage increases under major collective bargaining agreements reported in Table 3. Effective wage increases include first-year wage increases, deferred wage increases scheduled under multi-year contracts, and wage increases attributable to cost-of-living escalator provisions. First-year wage increases and increases over the life of contracts include only increments established in contracts that are not contingent on future price behavior (that is, increases under cost-of-living escalator provisions are not included). Increases over the life of contracts include first-year increases, while deferred increases include only wage increases scheduled after the first year. Measures of deferred wage increases include increases under cost-of-living escalator provisions, except for the estimate for 1978. These distinctions, and differences among industries in average lengths of contracts and cost-of-living escalator coverage, are important for the interpretation of these collective bargaining data.

Relative Wages

Dispersion of Relative Wages. The uneven slowdown in rates of wage increase among industries since 1974 is reflected in measures of wage dispersion and in changes in relative wages among sectors of the economy. Slower wage increases were disproportionately concentrated in low wage industries, especially in 1975 and 1976, as shown by the sharp rise in relative wage dispersion in Figure 1. In 1977 the rise in dispersion tapered off, particularly for the broad group of industries included in the private nonfarm sector. If construction wages were included, dispersion for private nonfarm industries would show a decline in 1977, a slower rise during 1975 and 1976, and a considerably different pattern in earlier years when construction wages were rising markedly relative to wages in other industries.

The shift to a less rapid rise in dispersion that occurred in 1977 came at a time when the unemployment rate was declining from the high levels that prevailed in 1975 and 1976. This behavior is broadly consistent with earlier experience, although the relationship between relative wage dispersion and unemployment has been quite loose on a year-to-year basis. Moreover, these broad measures of dispersion do not show the significant changes in relative wages for particular indus-

Figure 1
CHANGES IN RELATIVE EARNINGS AND UNEMPLOYMENT

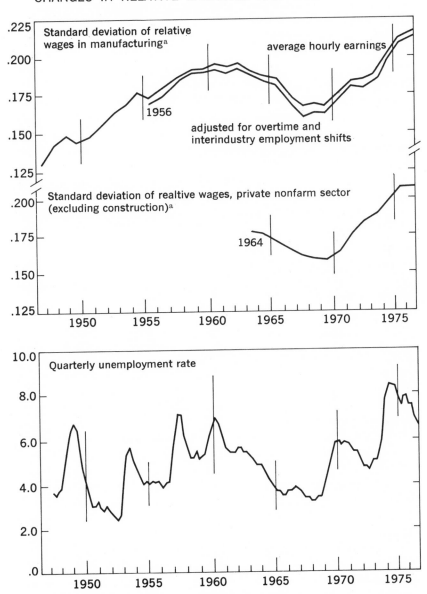

[a] Standard deviation of natural logarithms of average hourly earnings for the industry sectors included.

Source: U.S. Department of Labor, Bureau of Labor Statistics.

147

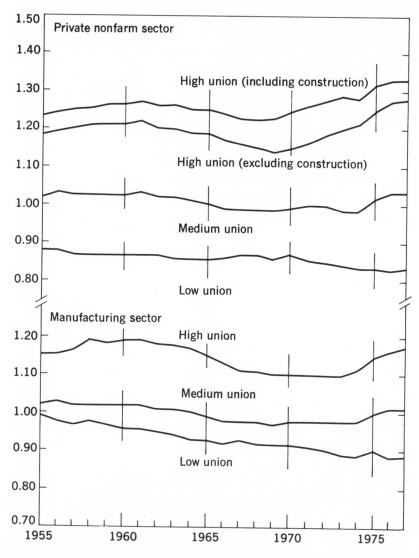

Figure 2

AVERAGE HOURLY EARNINGS RATIOS
BY EXTENT OF UNIONISM, 1955–1977

Note: These ratios are averages of ratios of average hourly earnings for each industry in the categories shown to average hourly earnings in the private non-farm sector. Ratios for manufacturing industries are based on data adjusted for overtime.

Source: U.S. Department of Labor, Bureau of Labor Statistics.

148

tries or for workers under different wage-setting arrangements that have occurred.

Relative Wages by Extent of Unionism. It is clear from Figure 2 that changes in relative wage dispersion have been associated with differences in wage behavior by extent of unionism.[3] (Extent of unionism categories of industries are shown in Table 4.) With the low unemployment rates of the late 1960s, relative wages declined for the more highly unionized industries. The higher unemployment rates of the 1970s were accompanied by a pronounced rise in relative wages in these highly unionized industries, with relative wages declining in less unionized industries. The general pattern of relative wage changes by extent of unionism suggests that differences in wage behavior between union and nonunion wage-setting arrangements contributed to changes in relative wage dispersion.

The phenomenon of significantly smaller average wage increases for nonunion workers than for unionized workers since 1974 is also evident for workers in manufacturing for which data on these two categories of workers are available (Table 5). The gap between union and nonunion wage increases in 1975 and 1976 was considerably wider than it was from 1972 through 1974. It was also wide in the period from 1969 to 1971, particularly for new wage decisions, but larger wage increases for workers in union establishments at that time followed the decline in relative wages of union workers that occurred during the last part of the 1960s. In 1975 and 1976, on the other hand, relative wages in the more highly unionized sectors of the economy rose to new highs. The employment cost index, which covers a broader cross-section of the economy than manufacturing, shows wage increases of 8.1 percent in 1976 for occupations covered by collective bargaining agreements compared with 6.8 percent for other workers. This difference tapered off in 1977, with increases of 7.6 percent and 6.6 percent, respectively, for union and nonunion workers.

Relative Wages for Selected Sectors. Relative wage developments for four sectors of the economy are shown in Figure 3. These sectors were selected because each was subject to conditions of competition, changes in competitive conditions, or sectoral demand shifts that could be expected to influence wage behavior in the sector relative to wages elsewhere in the economy. Collective bargaining was an important factor

---

[3] The measure of relative wages for each category of industry is the average of ratios of average hourly earnings for each industry in the category to average hourly earnings in the private nonfarm sector. For manufacturing industries, the ratios are based on average hourly earnings data adjusted for overtime.

Table 4
EXTENT OF UNIONISM: PRIVATE NONFARM SECTOR

High Union

Metal mining (10)
Bituminous coal (12)
Contract construction (15–17)
Ordnance and accessories (19)
Paper and allied products (26)
Primary metal industries (33)

Electrical equipment and supplies (36)
Transportation equipment (37)
Railroad transportation (4011)
Local and suburban transit (411)
Motor freight (42)
Communications (48)

Medium Union

Food and kindred products (20)
Tobacco manufactures (21)
Apparel and other textile products (23)
Lumber and wood products (24)
Chemicals and allied products (28)
Petroleum refining (291)
Rubber and plastics products (30)

Leather and leather products (31)
Stone, clay, and glass products (32)
Fabricated metal products (34)
Machinery, except electrical (35)
Electric, gas, and sanitation services (49)
Retail trade—food stores (54)

Low Union

Textile mill products (22)
Furniture and fixtures (25)
Printing and publishing (27)
Instruments and related products (38)
Misc. manufacturing industries (39)
Wholesale trade (50)
Retail trade: other (52, 55, 59)

Retail general merchandise (53)
Apparel and accessory stores (56)
Furniture and home furnishings stores (57)
Eating and drinking places (58)
Finance, insurance, and real estate (60-67)
Services (70-89)

Note: Numbers in parentheses are Standard Industrial Classification (SIC) codes. Industries were placed into categories according to the following criteria: *High Union:* All industries that are at least 75 percent unionized according to Bureau of Labor Statistics estimates, or are 50 to 75 percent unionized and at least 60 percent covered by major collective bargaining agreements (as indicated by the ratio of workers covered by major agreements to production worker employment). *Medium Union:* Industries that are 25–75 percent unionized and 10 to 60 percent covered by major collective bargaining agreements. *Low Union:* All industries that are 25 percent or less unionized or are 25 to 50 percent unionized and less than 10 percent covered by major collective bargaining agreements.

Source: Information on unionization and coverage by major agreements is contained in Bureau of Labor Statistics, *Directory of National Unions and Employee Associations of 1973*, p. 81, and Douglas LeRoy, "Scheduled Wage Increases and Escalator Provisions in 1977," *Monthly Labor Review*, January 1977, p. 24.

150

Table 5

WAGE CHANGES FOR MANUFACTURING PRODUCTION WORKERS IN UNION AND NONUNION ESTABLISHMENTS, 1969–1976

(percentage change)

	1969	1970	1971	1972	1973	1974	1975	1976
Mean general wage change put into effect								
Union	5.3	6.4	7.1	5.4	6.4	8.7	8.1	7.8
Nonunion	4.6	4.7	4.0	4.4	6.0	7.7	5.9	6.1
Mean first-year wage change under new general wage decisions								
Union	7.3	7.6	9.2	5.7	6.0	8.1	8.7	8.4
Nonunion	4.6	4.6	3.9	4.4	5.9	7.5	5.7	6.0

Note: Wage changes put into effect during the year include those resulting from current decisions, prior decisions, cost-of-living adjustments, or any combination thereof. First-year changes for union workers include all changes negotiated during the period and scheduled to go into effect during the first twelve months of the agreement. For nonunion workers, they include all changes made under decisions during the period.

Source: U.S. Department of Labor, Bureau of Labor Statistics.

in each of these sectors, and, except for construction, wages or wage patterns established under major collective bargaining agreements were applicable to a high proportion of the workers in the industries included. For industries affected by world market competition, the transition to flexible exchange rates (1971–1973) permitted the decline in the value of the dollar that reduced the impact of competition from important trading partners. The industries engaged in energy production were uniquely affected by the oil embargo and the high cartel prices established by the oil producing countries (1973–1974). Cost-based rate of return regulation contributes to relatively weaker competitive pressures in the regulated industries compared with most other industries in the economy. These sector-specific conditions were apparently reflected by the marked rise in relative wages in these sectors since 1974.

The construction sector shows a very different pattern of relative wage change than either the highly unionized industries or the less unionized industries. After reaching peaks in 1971 and 1973, relative

151

Figure 3

AVERAGE HOURLY EARNINGS RATIOS
FOR SELECTED INDUSTRIES, 1955–1977

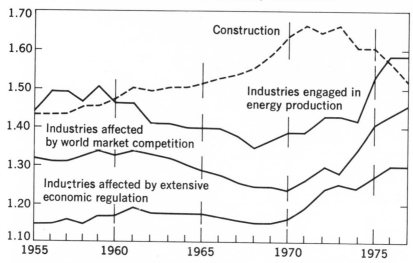

Note: The industries affected by world market competition include motor vehicles (371), metal mining (10), and steel (331); and those affected by extensive economic regulation include railroad (4,011), local and suburban transit (411), motor freight (42), telephone communications (481), and electric, gas, and sanitation services (49); and those engaged in energy production include bituminous coal (12) and petroleum refining (291).

These ratios are averages of ratios of average hourly earnings for each industry in the categories shown to average hourly earnings in the private nonfarm sector. Ratios for manufacturing industries are based on data adjusted for overtime.

Source: U.S. Department of Labor, Bureau of Labor Statistics.

wages in construction show a very pronounced decline. This decline came at a time when construction activity, particularly in the more highly unionized areas of construction activity, showed a sharp decline after a decade of generally strong construction demand. This decline in demand, together with a shift toward nonunion construction that was, in part, a response to high union wages that had been negotiated in construction, apparently contributed to the subsequent slump in relative wages of construction workers.[4] This decline is also evident in

---

[4] A more extensive discussion of construction wage developments appears in Marvin H. Kosters, "Wage and Price Behavior: Prospects and Policies" in William Fellner, ed., *Contemporary Economic Problems 1977* (Washington, D.C.: American Enterprise Institute, 1977), pp. 159–201.

152

collective bargaining settlements for the construction industry (see Table 3).

Cost-of-Living Escalator Provisions and Multi-Year Agreements

Cost-of-living escalator provisions in multi-year wage agreements have become an increasingly important element in wage-setting arrangements during the past decade. The percentage of workers under major collective bargaining agreements covered by cost-of-living escalators rose from about 20 percent in 1967 to 60 percent in 1977.[5] In 1977, about three-fourths of the workers under three-year agreements were covered by escalators. Growth in coverage of escalator provisions, larger payments under these escalators because of liberalized provisions, and higher rates of inflation have all contributed to their greater importance. As shown in Table 6, wage increases under escalator provisions have become a significant fraction, on average, of wage increases for workers covered by major collective bargaining agreements. For workers under agreements with escalator provisions, wage increases attributable to these provisions reflect many factors such as the timing of the payments, the particular escalator formulas in the agreements, and the number of workers with newly negotiated contracts as well as the rate of increase in prices.

In 1976 and 1977 average increases in wages attributable to escalator provisions were in the 3 to 4 percent range when prices were increasing at an average rate of about 6 percent. It should be noted, however, that these average wage increases under escalators occurred at a time when large fractions of these workers received newly negotiated first-year wage increases that were not conditional on price behavior, with the escalator provisions in their contracts mainly applicable to the

---

[5] The spread of cost-of-living escalator provisions in long-term wage contracts since the mid-1960s was preceded by a period in the late 1950s in which a larger fraction of workers under long-term contracts were covered by escalator provisions, but the fraction of workers under long-term agreements was smaller. During the past twenty years, the fraction of workers under major agreements extending for three years or longer rose from about one quarter to about two-thirds. Most of the lengthening of contract durations came during the late 1950s and the 1960s, and by the mid-1970s about one-third of the workers under contracts of two years duration or shorter were in the construction industry.

Information on the duration of collective bargaining agreements is contained in various bulletins and reports published by the Bureau of Labor Statistics and in various issues of the *Monthly Labor Review*. In addition to periodic articles in the *Monthly Labor Review* containing information on contract duration, significant references include: BLS Report No. 17 (June 1953); BLS Report No. 75 (October 1954); and BLS Bulletins No. 1353 (October 1962), 1686 (1970), 1729 (1972), 1784 (1973), 1822 (1974), 1888 (1975) and 1957 (1977), published by U.S. Department of Labor, the Bureau of Labor Statistics.

Table 6
CONSUMER PRICE INCREASES AND WAGE INCREASES UNDER MAJOR COLLECTIVE BARGAINING AGREEMENTS, 1970–1977
(in percentages)

	1970	1971	1972	1973	1974	1975	1976	1977
Increase in consumer price index	5.5	3.4	3.4	8.8	12.2	7.0	4.8	6.8
Effective wage rate changes[a]	8.8	9.2	6.6	7.0	9.4	8.7	8.1	7.8
Adjustment resulting from:								
Current settlement	5.1	4.3	1.7	3.0	4.8	2.8	3.2	2.9
Prior settlement	3.1	4.2	4.2	2.7	2.6	3.7	3.2	3.2
Escalator provisions	0.6	0.7	0.7	1.3	1.9	2.2	1.6	1.6
Wage increases under cost-of-living escalator provisions[b]								
All industries	3.7	3.1	2.0	4.1	5.8	4.8	3.5	3.9
Manufacturing	3.8	3.7	1.8	4.0	7.2	5.2	3.2	4.4
Nonmanufacturing	2.6	1.8	2.2	4.7	2.0	4.1	4.0	3.2
Percentage of workers covered by cost-of-living escalators[c]	26	28	41	39	39	50	58	60
Percentage of workers affected by new wage settlements[d]	43	38	23	52	50	28	45	39

Note: Consumer price increases are from December to December and wage increases are mean percentage increases during the year.

[a] Effective wage rate changes under major collective bargaining agreements are wage rate changes actually put into effect during the year. They include wage increases under new settlements, deferred increases under previously negotiated contracts, and increments attributable to cost-of-living escalator provisions.

[b] Data on wage increases under cost-of-living escalator provisions relate to all workers covered by escalator provisions for collective bargaining agreements covering 1,000 workers or more in private nonfarm industries.

[c] Estimated percentage of workers under major collective bargaining agreements as of the beginning of the year.

[d] Estimated percentage of workers covered by major collective bargaining situations for which new wage settlements were negotiated during the year.

Source: U.S. Department of Labor, Bureau of Labor Statistics.

second and third years of contracts. As a result, simply comparing percentage increases in prices with average percentage increases under escalators does not provide reliable guidance about the extent to which escalators compensate for inflation.

Because of the growth of coverage and liberalized provisions of cost-of-living escalators, data on collective bargaining settlements must be interpreted carefully in order to avoid distortions when historical comparisons are made. Measures of wage increases under collective bargaining agreements negotiated each year are normally reported in terms of the wage increases specified in the contracts, with no allowance for increases under cost-of-living escalator provisions, because the size of escalator payments depends on future price performance and is therefore uncertain. That is, these measures are computed on the basis of an implicit assumption of zero inflation. Failure to take this into account in analysis of collective bargaining data leads to a distortion in interpretation that is more serious the higher the rate of inflation. Distortions are also introduced into analyses that implicitly assume that the fraction of workers covered by escalators is unchanged over time (when it has risen sharply) or that wage payments under escalators for given rates of price increase can be inferred from earlier experience (when provisions have been liberalized or "caps" removed).

The data reported in Table 7 on a selection of collective bargaining agreements negotiated in 1976 and 1977 illustrate the significance of wage increases realized under the escalator provisions of these contracts. Workers under these agreements account for about one-third of all workers covered by major agreements and over half of workers under major agreements scheduled to receive deferred wage increases during 1978.

These data show first-year wage increases that are large compared with increases for subsequent years without taking escalators into account. When escalator provisions are taken into account by assuming a 6 percent inflation rate, the more modest wage increases over the life of the contracts are raised from the 4 percent range to the 8 percent range or higher. And when both wages and benefits are included in addition, all are in the 9 to 10 percent range. All of these are three-year contracts scheduled to expire in 1979 and 1980.

Differential Wage Response and Stability of Trends

Although rates of increase in average wages were quite stable during most of the past ten years, this was not the result of closely parallel rates of increase in wages throughout most of the economy. Differ-

Table 7
SELECTED MAJOR COLLECTIVE BARGAINING SETTLEMENTS, 1976 AND 1977
(annual percentage increases)

	Wages	Wages and Benefits
First-year increases		
Trucking (1976)	9.1	9.9
Electrical equipment (1976)	13.1	11.6
Rubber (1976)	17.1	13.3
Automobiles (1976)	6.1	12.4
Steel (1977)	11.6	12.8
Communications (1977)	8.3	10.8
Increases over life of contracts		
Not including escalator payments		
Trucking	7.2	
Electrical equipment	7.2	
Rubber	8.7	
Automobiles	4.2	
Steel	4.1	
Communications	4.6	
Including allowance for escalator payments[a]		
Trucking	9.7	10.4
Electrical equipment	9.9	9.5
Rubber	11.7	9.9
Automobiles	8.4	9.8
Steel	9.1	9.3
Communications	7.7	9.5

[a] The allowance for escalator payments is computed on the basis of an assumed 6 percent annual rate of increase in the consumer price index during the duration of the contracts.
Source: Executive Office of the President, Council on Wage and Price Stability, *Collective Bargaining*, February 1977; *An Analysis of the Steel Settlement*, June 1, 1977; and News Release, *Analysis of New Contract in Communications*, October 14, 1977.

ences in rates of increase in wages among industries and by extent of unionism were often large. Other factors were also at work, but some of these differences in rates of wage increase apparently reflected cyclical conditions.

Some of the main forces at work during this period may be sketched out, even though the complete pattern of differential rates of wage change among sectors for each of these years was complex. To

Table 8
CHANGES IN THE INDEX OF AVERAGE HOURLY EARNINGS AND MAJOR COMPONENTS, 1969–1976

(annual percentage change)

	1969 to 1970	1970 to 1972	1973 to 1974	1974 to 1976
Index of average hourly earnings	6.6	6.8	8.2	8.0
Components				
Construction	9.4	7.3	6.0	6.7
High union	5.8	8.9	8.7	9.5
Medium union	6.5	6.3	8.3	8.9
Low union	6.5	6.1	8.2	7.2

Note: Annual percentage rates of increase are computed from average annual levels for the index and for the major components. The index of average hourly earnings is adjusted for overtime (in manufacturing) and interindustry shifts, and the components are also based on straight-time average hourly earnings for manufacturing industries. The industries included in the extent of unionism categories are those enumerated in Table 4.

highlight wage developments particularly relevant to the issue of the responsiveness of wage trends to cyclical slack, the discussion is built around wage behavior following the two recessions that occurred. For this purpose, the main focus is on wage behavior during the two-year period from 1970 to 1972 compared with the preceding year and from 1974 to 1976 compared with the preceding year.[6]

In Table 8, rates of increase for the index of adjusted average hourly earnings and four components of the index are shown for these periods. The rates of change reported here do not correspond to those reported in Table 1, because these are based on annual averages to avoid sensitivity to particular months for the components of the index. While rates of increase in the index were higher for the latter period than the former, the response of average wages to the recessions appears to be negligible in each case. The four components of the index, on the other hand, show a mixed pattern of acceleration and deceleration.

A closer examination of the behavior of the components of the index is facilitated by looking at the pattern of changes in rates of increase and their contributions to changes in the overall index shown in

---

[6] If three-year periods following 1970 and 1974 are considered, neither the pattern of changes nor their magnitudes are very much different from those of the two-year periods.

Table 9
CHANGES IN RATES OF INCREASE OF THE INDEX OF AVERAGE HOURLY EARNINGS AND MAJOR COMPONENTS AND CONTRIBUTIONS OF MAJOR COMPONENTS

Changes in Annual Rates of Increase[a]

	From 1969–70 to 1970–72	From 1973–74 to 1974–76
Index of average hourly earnings	0.18	—0.15
Major components		
Construction	—2.1	+0.7
High union	3.1	+0.8
Medium union	—0.2	+0.6
Low union	—0.5	—1.0

Contributions of Major Components to Changes in Rates of Increase in the Index[b]

	From 1969–70 to 1970–72	From 1973–74 to 1974–76
Index of average hourly earnings	0.18	—0.15
Major component contributions		
Construction	—0.13	+0.04
High union	+0.62	+0.13
Medium union	—0.05	+0.12
Low union	—0.26	—0.44

[a] Changes in annual rates of increase are computed from the data in Table 9.

[b] The weights for the major components of the index are sums of the weights for the industries included in each of the major components. The weights are: construction—0.06, high union—0.19, medium union—0.22, and low union—0.53.

Table 9. The pattern of changes in trend that is common to both periods shown in the table is deceleration of wages in the low union sector and acceleration in the high union sector. For industries in the intermediate range by extent of unionism, the changes in average rates of wage increase have opposite signs, but the changes were quite small. For construction, changes in the average rate of wage increase accompanying the recession were small relative to the shift from very large increases in the late 1960s to wage increases significantly smaller than the average in the rest of the economy after 1971. (Average annual increases for construction were 7.9 percent for the five years preceding 1971 compared with 6.2 percent for the next five years.)

The wage behavior for the high union and low union sectors shown in the tables could be viewed as simply indicating modest responsiveness to recessions of wages in the less unionized sector and perverse behavior in the more highly unionized sector. A brief discussion of some of the surrounding circumstances may place these developments in perspective. One reason for expecting slower response in the more highly unionized sector is long-term contracts. Long-term contracts, however, also affected wage behavior during the expansions that preceded the recessions, with their effects dependent in part on whether the contracts contained escalator provisions.

The marked difference in acceleration for the high union sector between the two recessions can be explained by these factors. Prior to the 1970 recession, cost-of-living escalator coverage was less prevalent than later, and payoffs under escalator formulas were often subject to limits. As a consequence, wages in the high union sector were less responsive to the cyclical expansion and to rising rates of inflation than wages in the low union sector. Wage increases averaged 4.9 percent in the high union sector from 1965 to 1970 compared with 6.0 percent in the low union sector. The sharp acceleration of union wage increases from 1970 to 1972 is more appropriately regarded as a "catch-up" phenomenon to compensate for earlier cyclical developments than as a demonstration of sluggish adjustment to recession or perverse behavior.

Conditions affecting the high union sector were very different during the next recession. Widespread introduction of cost-of-living escalator provisions in the interim brought large wage increases for many workers under long-term contracts to reflect the bulge in inflation. In addition, larger-than-average wage increases in the high union sector from 1970 to 1973 had brought their relative wages closer to historical balance than before the preceding recession, so that pressures for "catch-up" increases were less severe.

Wages in the low union sector increased somewhat less rapidly during both recessions, but the deceleration was larger during the deeper recession of 1975. The deceleration that took place during 1970 to 1972 occurred despite average wage increases in the high union sector that were almost 3 percent larger than in the low union sector and a spread between new union wage settlements and average wage increases in the less unionized sector that was even larger. The slowdown in the low union sector during 1974 to 1976 occurred despite average wage increases in the high union sector that were about two percentage points larger and a rise in relative wages in the high union sector to unusually high levels.

The contributions of each of these components to changes in the rate of increase in the overall index are summarized in Table 10. These data show that although the low union sector, which appears to be more responsive to general slack in demand, receives a heavy weight

159

Table 10
FEDERAL MINIMUM WAGE AND AVERAGE WAGES IN MANUFACTURING

Date of Increase in Basic Minimum Wage	Basic Minimum Wage Level (dollars per hour)	Old Minimum Wage[a] (percent)	New Minimum Wage[b] (percent)
October 1945	0.40	31.8	42.4
January 1950	0.75	28.0	52.4
March 1956	1.00	38.9	51.8
September 1961	1.15	44.4	51.1
September 1963	1.25	48.5	52.7
February 1967	1.40	45.3	50.7
February 1968	1.60	47.6	54.4
May 1974	2.00	39.3	49.1
January 1975	2.10	41.9	44.0
January 1976	2.30	40.9	44.7
January 1978	2.65	41.3	47.6
January 1979	2.90	43.7[c]	47.9[c]
January 1980	3.10	43.9[c]	47.0[c]
January 1981	3.35	43.2[c]	46.7[c]

[a] Minimum wage as a percent of average (straight-time) manufacturing wage during quarter preceding change.

[b] New minimum wage as a percent of average (straight-time) manufacturing wage that prevailed during quarter preceding change.

[c] These projections are based on an annual rate of increase in average hourly earnings in manufacturing (adjusted for overtime) of 8.8 percent from the fourth quarter of 1977. This rate of increase was computed on the basis of a ratio of the minimum wage to straight-time manufacturing wages of 44.9 percent by the end of 1980. This ratio represents the midpoint between ratios that would prevail in the quarters immediately preceding and subsequent to the minimum wage change at the beginning of 1981. This ratio of 44.9 percent is the average of the annual percentage ratios that have prevailed since the minimum wage was introduced in 1938, and it is also the average for the percentage ratios before 1979 presented in the table. The average before 1979 for the old minimum wage ratios is 40.7 percent and for the new minimum wage ratios, 49.2 percent.

in the index, the small slowdown in rates of increase was largely offset by different behavior of the other components. The short-term cyclical response of average rates of wage increase consequently reflects a considerably broader range of circumstances than current market slack.

Government Policies Affecting Labor Costs

Persistent inflation cannot be sustained in the absence of demand increases sufficiently expansionary to accommodate continued increases in the price level. However, short-term inflation trends and the amount of unemployment experienced are influenced by government actions with relatively direct effects on labor costs. The responsiveness of price level trends to demand conditions depends in part on microeconomic policies pursued in parallel with aggregate economic policies. That is, resistance to lower inflation under slack demand depends on how extensively government policies contribute in other ways to supporting or pushing up particular wages and prices.

Minimum Wages. The increase in the federal minimum wage at the beginning of 1978 is perhaps the most straightforward example of government action directly influencing labor costs. Labor costs for a significant part of the work force are directly affected by it, and the size of the increase is prescribed in the legislation raising the minimum wage. Despite this information, however, only rough estimates can be made of the direct impact on labor costs. In addition, the full consequences—when adjustments in employment, nonwage conditions of employment such as on-the-job training or other benefits, goods and services produced, profit margins, and possible changes in other related wages are taken into account—are far more difficult to estimate. Nevertheless, a discussion of the implications for inflation of the increase in the minimum wage illustrates the effects of policies that tend to raise short-term labor costs. Because the legislation increasing the minimum wage provides for periodic further increases until 1981, the implications of the minimum wage changes also extend to future labor cost and unemployment conditions.

The federal minimum wage was increased from $2.30 per hour to $2.65 per hour on January 1, 1978. Further increments scheduled for the next three years raise its level to $3.35 per hour by January 1981. Two aspects of the relationship between minimum wages and labor costs will be discussed: the direct effects on the wage bill of increases in the minimum wage; and the rate of increase in average wages that would result if the real minimum wage level were in line with past experience. Effects of the minimum wage on employment and the incidence of these effects will not be discussed here, although these employment-reducing effects are relevant in a broader context to unemployment rates that could be achieved.[7]

---

[7] For evidence on the effects on employment of minimum wages, see Finis Welch, *Minimum Wages: Issues and Evidence* (Washington, D.C.: American Enterprise Institute, forthcoming), and Edward Gramlich, "Impact of Minimum Wages on Other Wages, Employment, and Family Incomes," *Brookings Papers on Economic Activity*, no. 2 (Washington, D.C.: Brookings Institution, 1976), pp. 409–451.

A relatively small fraction of the wage bill is earned by workers directly affected by the minimum wage (because their wage rates are obviously low, because only a small fraction of workers earn low wages, and because a disproportionate fraction of low-wage workers work only part-time). In addition, under partial coverage, uncovered wages are not directly affected by an increase in the minimum wage (and indirectly might even be reduced). For these reasons, the short-term, direct effect on the wage bill is much smaller in percentage terms than the rise in the minimum wage. Thus, even though nearly 20 percent of workers reporting hourly wages apparently earn wages at about the level of the minimum wage or below, many of these workers may not be covered by the legislation, and salaried workers are likely to include a smaller proportion of low-wage workers. Estimates that have been reported suggest a short-term, direct effect on the wage bill of about 0.4 percent as a result of the 15 percent increase in the minimum wage in January 1978.[8] The relatively small estimated direct effect is less significant, however, than is the likely effect of the rise in the minimum wage on other wages in the economy.

Since scheduled increases in the minimum wage are established in the legislation for each year to 1981, it is possible to project the implied rate of average wage increase that would be consistent with the ratio of the minimum wage to average wages in manufacturing remaining at the level that has prevailed in the past. Unless average wages rise sufficiently rapidly, a given schedule of minimum wage increases would lead to compression of wage differentials above the minimum wage and a rising real impact on employment. Resistance to such compression generates pressures for higher wages, which tend to raise the average. The projections indicate that consistency with historical experience would imply an annual rate of increase of 8.8 percent in straight-time average hourly earnings in manufacturing from the fourth quarter of 1977 to the fourth quarter of 1980 (see Table 10). For comparison, the annual rate of increase in straight-time manufacturing wages has been 7.8 percent since the last quarter of 1974 and 7.3 percent during the past ten years.

The 8.8 percent annual rate of increase in average manufacturing wages would be consistent with historical experience in this sense: it would bring the percentage ratio of the minimum wage to manufacturing wages to a level equal to the average of previous levels of the ratio

---

[8] This estimate is reported in Peyton Elder, "The 1977 Amendments to the Federal Minimum Wage Law," *Monthly Labor Review*, January 1978, pp. 9–11. A roughly similar or somewhat larger estimate could be obtained on the basis of evidence reported by Gramlich, "Impact of Minimum Wages," pp. 426–430.

when minimum wage changes occurred.[9] It should be pointed out that these projections are based only on historical experience expressed in terms of the level of the basic minimum wage as a percentage ratio to manufacturing wages. Coverage is not taken into account, and the 1977 amendments raise to the basic minimum wage the lower rates that previously prevailed for sectors that were first covered in 1967. Since estimated coverage has risen from slightly over 60 percent in the early 1960s to over 80 percent, and special rates below the basic minimum have been eliminated, the real effects on the economy would be greater than in the past if the percentage ratio for the basic minimum wage is in line with past experience. Even if these effects are disregarded, however, the path of scheduled increases in the basic minimum wage to 1981 is clearly inconsistent with a deceleration in the rate of wage increase and inflation unless the prospect for a rising real minimum wage and its consequences for employment are accepted.

Other Policies Affecting Labor Costs. Among the other ways in which government policies affect labor costs, some of the most widely noted are taxes imposed on payrolls such as those to finance social security, unemployment compensation, and workers' compensation. Since these taxes are collected by imposing them on employers, they are not included in wage payments to employees. While increases in these taxes raise hourly labor costs, only rough estimates can be made of their initial direct impact, and their long-term influence on labor costs depends in part on their ultimate incidence. Estimates of the short-term effect on labor costs of increases of social security taxes, for example, are only approximate because their effects are offset to some extent by lower employer contributions to private pension plans. On the other hand, since increases in these taxes initially raise labor costs above prevailing compensation trends and lead to correspondingly larger price increases, their impact on inflationary pressures is not entirely captured by estimates of their direct effects.

The impact on labor costs to employers of the social security and unemployment compensation tax increases introduced at the beginning of 1978 is estimated at four- to five-tenths of a percentage point. This estimate of the initial direct impact does not take into account any

---

[9] If the ratio of the minimum wage to straight-time average hourly earnings in manufacturing were to rise by the beginning of 1981 to the average level that previously prevailed immediately after a minimum wage change, the implied annual rate of increase in average manufacturing wages from 1977 to 1980 would be 6.9 percent. On the other hand, if the ratio were to decline by the end of 1980 to the average that previously occurred just prior to minimum wage changes, the implied rate would be 11 percent.

offsetting or secondary effects that may occur, or the effects of other labor cost increases imposed by government, such as those to finance workers' compensation or pension insurance. In addition to the increment to hourly labor costs of slightly more than two-tenths of a percentage point accounted for by employers' share of social security payments, of course, employees' take-home pay is reduced by a corresponding amount. Estimation of the initial, direct impact on hourly labor costs of higher social security payments by taking into account only the share paid by employers may be reasonable for the short term, but it is clearly inadequate and misleading for the longer term. The ultimate incidence of the taxes is largely independent of whether they are paid by employers as a deduction from employees' wages or as the employers' share. If wage and salary levels were unaffected by social security tax rates and by who nominally pays the taxes—which is extremely implausible—inflationary pressures would presumably be reduced by collecting a larger share of social security payments as a deduction from employees' wages.

It is possible to develop estimates of the short-term impact on labor costs of government policies such as increases in the minimum wage or payroll taxes. For government policies of other kinds that also affect labor costs, such as prevailing wage laws, economic regulation, and changes in the legislation establishing the framework for collective bargaining, estimation of their impact is much less straightforward. This distinction should not be overemphasized in assessing the longer-term implications for inflation of government policies affecting labor costs. The initial, direct impact on labor costs of higher social security taxes, for example, may have significant short-term effects, and these effects can be relatively easily measured. Over the longer term, however, these short-term effects are translated primarily into a larger share of employee compensation devoted to social security payments while labor cost trends are established by the terms of wage offers and collective bargaining settlements.

The pervasive influence of the federal government on labor costs can be illustrated in a variety of ways: As an employer, the federal government establishes wages for its own employees, and wages of other workers may be affected in localities where federal workers are a significant proportion of the work force. Federal government authority can also be brought to bear on wage setting for quasi-public entities such as the U.S. Postal Service, and more indirectly, through its procurement and purchasing decisions. The federal government also periodically exerts pressure on wage setting in particular industries—in order to restore service in the case of railroads, for example, or to restore production in the case of coal. The indirect effects on wages of policies that affect competition, such as the establishment of reference prices for imported steel, illustrates another form of federal government influence.

Although federal government policies affecting labor costs are pervasive and can have significant short-term effects, their influence on longer-term labor cost trends is quite limited in an economy in which wage decisions predominantly reflect pressures in the marketplace. Federal employees account for only about 3 percent of total employment, and only a small fraction of private sector employees or employees of other governmental units could be affected by federal government policies. Moreover, wage decisions are reached in response to market forces by taking into account as constraints such government policies as payroll taxes and minimum wages. While constraints of this kind can be expected to influence the composition of overall compensation, the structure of wages, and employment, the overall rate of labor cost increase will reflect conditions in the labor market. If such constraints were imposed in the form of tax incentives (as has been suggested, for example, as an incomes policy approach), they would have differential effects among firms and industries, and wage-setting arrangements would be adapted to benefit from or minimize the costs of these constraints, but long-term average rates of wage increase would respond to the market conditions generated by aggregate demand growth. As long as primary reliance is placed on the marketplace for establishing wages, microeconomic policy actions may have short-term effects on labor costs, prices, and employment, but their principal long-term influence is on efficiency of resource usage (and hence on real wages) instead of on average rates of wage and price inflation.

Conclusion

In this review of wage developments, several aspects of labor market behavior have been discussed to interpret past wage trends and to assess future wage prospects. The main points in the discussion are summarized briefly in this section.

Relatively stable rates of increase in average wages during the past decade have not been the result of closely parallel rates of increase throughout the economy. Instead, significant differences in rates of increase in wages have occurred among sectors of the economy, and these differences have reflected cyclical forces along with other factors. In particular, wages in industries with a relatively low extent of unionization have responded to cyclical forces more quickly than wages in other sectors. On the basis of this review of wage developments the observed past stability in average wage increases provides no assurance that this stability will continue under continued cyclical expansion.

Wage developments during the past decade also illustrate the significance for wage behavior over the business cycle of changes in wage-setting arrangements such as expanded use of cost-of-living escalator provisions in multi-year wage contracts. More extensive use of cost-of-living escalator provisions in recent years has brought relative wages in industries with a high extent of unionization to historically high levels and established a close linkage between price performance and wage behavior in these industries. The spread of cost-of-living escalators has significantly altered structural relationships between cyclical conditions and wage behavior and, as a consequence, has introduced additional uncertainty about the reliability of econometric projections of wage and price behavior under different conditions.

The provisions of major multi-year agreements now in force provide for large increases in wages during the terms of these contracts in a labor market context in which relative wages in the highly unionized sector are already high by historical standards. The data in Table 7 show projected increases in labor costs for these industries in the 9–10 percent range under an assumption of 6 percent inflation. However, the inflation assumption on which the projections are based is inconsistent with hourly labor cost increases in the 9–10 percent range throughout the economy under reasonable assumptions about the productivity growth that can be expected. Higher inflation would result in larger wage increases under these contracts, while inflation in the 6 percent range would imply rising relative wages for workers covered by these contracts in a labor market environment in which their relative wages are already at the highest levels of the postwar period and in which cyclical expansion can be expected to generate pressures for compression of these wage differentials.

In addition to these labor market conditions influencing overall wage developments, the rise in the federal minimum wage will contribute an estimated 0.4 percent to the rate of increase in labor costs during 1978 along with its tendency to introduce pressures for either compression of wage differentials or larger increases in wages in the lower part of the wage distribution throughout the period to 1981. The rise in social security and unemployment taxes at the beginning of 1978 will make a short-term contribution to higher average hourly labor costs that may be in the range of 0.4–0.5 percent, with further increases in social security payments scheduled. These government policies introduce additional short-term costs and labor market pressures into a labor market environment in which the stability or reduction of overall rates of labor cost increase require slower rates of price increase and limited overall labor market pressures.

The Food and Agriculture Act of 1977: Implications for Farmers, Consumers, and Taxpayers

D. Gale Johnson

Summary

American agriculture was subjected to remarkable ups and downs of prices and incomes during the 1970s. The Food and Agriculture Act of 1977 was enacted when total net farm operators' income was the smallest since 1960. But the relatively low level of total net farm income exaggerated the plight of American farm families. In recent years half or more of the income of the families of farm operators has come from nonfarm sources. In 1977 the disposable per capita income of the farm population was a greater percentage of the similar income measure for nonfarm population than in any year prior to 1973 and much higher than during the early 1960s.

Farm debts have increased substantially in recent years, but so has the value of farm assets. At the beginning of 1978 the ratio of farm debt to the value of farm assets at 16.3 percent was slightly less than the same measure for 1970.

The 1977 act was a comprehensive piece of legislation covering all of the major farm crops and dairy products. The act included six major policy instruments—target prices and deficiency payments; commodity loans and support prices; land set-asides and diversions; crop acreage reductions or controls; land diversion payments; and an extended farmer-held grain reserve program.

The policy instruments with the greatest immediate impact upon agricultural prices and incomes are the target prices and support prices. The target prices do not directly affect market prices but serve as a basis for determining deficiency payments which are equal to the difference between the target prices and actual market prices or support prices, whichever are higher. The support prices or loan rates do directly affect market prices, but for wheat, feed grains, and cotton the support prices were set low enough to have minimal effects upon market prices and thus the flow of agricultural products into international trade.

In the 1977 act the target prices were based upon cost of production. This is a serious policy error and will result in misallocation of resources. There can be no meaningful calculation of costs of production of farm products since the return to land is a major component of costs. The price or rent of land is determined by expected future prices of farm products. As a result, within a very wide range, any target price can be justified by cost of production.

The target price for wheat was established much higher relative to support prices or actual farm prices than was true for the feed grains and cotton in the 1977 act. The target price for corn for 1978 was only 5 percent above the support price while for wheat it was nearly 30 percent higher. Yet in May 1978 Congress and the administration agreed on legislation that increased the wheat target price to $3.40 per bushel, or 45 percent in excess of the wheat price support.

American agriculture, especially the grain sector, faces both short-run and long-run adjustments. The feed grain sector faces primarily a short-run adjustment problem, which is relatively modest and could be met by increased feeding of grain and a modest decline in the rate of growth of output. The major long-run adjustment problem is in the specialized wheat growing areas. The 1977 act is not likely to be an effective instrument for assisting wheat producers in their long-run adjustment problems. And much of the adjustment that will occur will impinge adversely upon feed grain producers.

A new feature of the 1977 act is the extended farmer-held grain reserve program. This program is designed to encourage farmers to hold a large percentage of all grain reserves and to make it profitable for them to hold such reserves until market prices increase significantly above the price support levels. Farmers receive payments to cover the cost of storage; these payments will be lost if the grain is sold at prices below those set by the 1977 act for wheat and by the secretary of agriculture for the feed grains. The program is designed to increase price instability and to prevent the use of grain reserves to hold market prices of grain at or near the support levels.

The 1977 act and the changes in it enacted in May 1978 will impose substantial costs upon taxpayers. While farm incomes will be increased in the short run, the legislation is likely to encourage increasing the production of the farm crop that is most seriously out of adjustment, namely wheat. Features of previous farm programs that minimized the effects of direct payments upon current production were ignored in the new act.

Introduction

The economic fortunes of agriculture have undergone dramatic changes during the 1970s. The farmer malaise displayed most dramatically by the small minority who drove their tractors down interstate highways, around state capitals and into the nation's capital city can be understood against the background of the striking changes that have occurred. During the 1970s farm prices first rose dramatically and then declined with equal rapidity; between 1970 and 1973 operators' net farm income per farm, in constant dollars, more than doubled. Just three years later this measure of income had fallen to slightly below the 1970 level, and there was further erosion in 1977.

But it should not be inferred from the actions of a minority of farmers, the concern expressed by members of Congress, or the general picture presented by the national media that the majority of the American farmers are in serious economic distress or are about to have their farms taken away from them through foreclosure. It is not my intention to give the impression that American farm people do not face significant adjustment problems in the years ahead. Clearly, however, the adjustment problems are now no greater than they have been throughout most of the past half century. Unless these adjustments are inhibited and delayed by governmental policy, American farm people will continue to participate in the benefits of a growing national economy.

Recent Economic Developments

Table 1 presents four measures of income from agriculture and the farm population. Each of the measures is in 1967 dollars to permit comparisons over time that are more meaningful than comparisons in current dollars. The first column, farm national income, is a measure of agriculture's contribution to national income. This measure of income displayed a high degree of stability and little growth during the 1960s. But from 1970 to 1973 farm national income increased by 69 percent; by 1977 this measure had returned to the 1970 level.

The second column gives data on the income of farm operators from their own farms. This measure of income was also quite stable during the 1960s and exhibited essentially no growth. However, between 1970 and 1973 net farm operator income doubled, and increased substantially more than farm national income. The difference between farm national income and net farm operator income consists of three components—rent on land owned by nonoperators, interest payments, and wages paid to farm workers. The latter three components of farm

169

Table 1
AGRICULTURAL INCOME AND INCOME OF THE FARM
POPULATION, 1960–1977 IN 1967 DOLLARS

Year	Farm National Income (billion dollars)	Operators' Net Farm Income (billion dollars)	Operators' Net Farm Income per Farm (dollars)	Per Capita Personal Income, Farm Population (dollars)	Disposable Per Capita Income, Farm Percent of Nonfarm (percent)
1960	18.3	12.8	3,230	1,304	53.9
1961	19.0	13.3	3,473	1,430	57.9
1962	19.1	13.3	3,590	1,515	59.4
1963	18.7	12.8	3,582	1,624	62.4
1964	17.4	11.3	3,263	1,640	59.5
1965	19.8	13.6	4,045	1,924	68.2
1966	20.6	14.2	4,373	2,096	71.7
1967	18.9	12.3	3,903	2,102	69.0
1968	18.6	11.8	3,859	2,216	70.5
1969	20.1	13.1	4,372	2,391	74.0
1970	19.5	12.4	4,202	2,473	74.0
1971	19.6	12.4	4,263	2,582	74.7
1972	22.7	15.2	5,288	2,911	83.4
1973	33.0	25.1	8,817	3,856	109.3
1974	25.6	17.5	6,206	3,223	92.4
1975	24.5	14.6	5,203	3,010	88.0
1976	20.8	11.4	4,093	2,888	81.4
1977		10.9	3,960	3,196	84.0

Source: U.S. Department of Agriculture, Economic Research Service, *Farm Income Statistics*, Statistical Bulletin no. 576 (July 1977). The price deflator used was prices paid for family living items. 1977 data from testimony of Howard W. Hjort, U.S. Congress, House, Subcommittee for Agriculture and Related Agencies of the Committee on Appropriations, February 14, 1978.

national income increased very little between 1970 and 1973—by $0.8 billion or 11 percent. In other words, nearly all of the increase in farm national income was retained by farm operators. In the years after 1973 the components of farm national income, other than operator income—especially interest payments and wages—continued to increase. Between 1973 and 1976, while net farm operator income declined by $13.7 billion (55 percent), the other components of farm national income increased by $1.5 billion (19 percent).

Net farm operator income per farm has exhibited a long-term upward trend, despite lower net farm operator income in 1977 than in any year during the 1960s. This is due to the continuing decline in the number of farms—from almost 4 million in 1960 to about 2.7 million in 1977.

The majority of the farm population does not depend solely upon farm income for their total income. Fortunately for the economic welfare of the total farm population, the nonfarm income of the farm population continued to grow from 1970 through 1976, and in 1976 accounted for 57.6 percent of their total income.[1] Per capita personal income of the farm population declined between 1973 and 1977, but only by 17 percent, compared with the 57 percent decline in net farm operator income.

In spite of the recent reversals in net farm income, the growth in the nonfarm income of the farm population has been sufficiently great during the 1970s to permit a significant increase in the income of the farm population relative to the nonfarm population. In 1970 the disposable per capita income of the farm population was 74 percent of the nonfarm population's income, while in 1977 it was 84 percent. Thus the real income of the farm population has increased at a more rapid rate than that of the nonfarm population.

The data in the last two columns of Table 1 relate to the total farm population, which includes the members of farm operator and hired farm worker families. The importance of off-farm income in the family income of farm operator families in 1976 was slightly greater than the importance of nonfarm income, or 58.6 percent, for all families in the farm population.[2] Off-farm income of farm operator families includes some farm income from wages and custom work for other farmers, as well as rent from farm land. It is clear that farm operators, including many with very large farms, have substantial amounts of income from sources other than the farm they operate. In 1976, 5.6 percent of the farms, with sales of $100,000 or more, had family income from off-farm sources averaging $13,310 per family out of a total family income of $69,026.[3] It should be remembered that not all farm operator families have off-farm income, but in 1974 40 percent of the farm operator families with farm sales of $100,000 or more had over $13,000 of off-farm income per family.[4]

Table 2 presents two measures of the parity ratio. The parity ratio is the ratio of prices received by farmers to prices paid by farmers for commodities (living and production), services, taxes, interest, and

---

[1] U.S. Department of Agriculture, Economic Research Service, *Farm Income Statistics*, Statistical Bulletin no. 576 (July 1977), p. 36.

[2] Ibid., p. 56.

[3] Ibid. For farms with sales of $40,000 to $99,999 off-farm income provided 29 percent of total family income of $23,464 in 1976.

[4] U.S. Bureau of the Census, *Census of Agriculture*, 1974.

171

Table 2
FARM OUTPUT PRICES RELATIVE TO PRICES PAID
BY FARMERS, 1960–1977

Year	Parity Ratio	Parity Ratio, Adjusted[a]
	(1910–1914 = 100)	
1960	80	82
1961	79	83
1962	80	83
1963	78	81
1964	76	80
1965	76	81
1966	79	85
1967	73	79
1968	73	79
1969	73	79
1970	72	77
1971	69	73
1972	74	79
1973	91	94
1974	86	87
1975	76	76
1976	71	71
1977	67	68

[a] Includes direct government payments to farmers as though such payments represented part of the prices received.

Source: U.S. Department of Agriculture, Crop Reporting Board, Statistical Reporting Service, *Index Numbers of Prices Received and Prices Paid by Farmers, January 1965–April 1976, Revised*, Pr 1-5(76) (May 28, 1976) and *Agricultural Prices* (January 31, 1978).

wages. The first column gives the traditional ratio; the second column is the adjusted parity ratio which includes government payments to farmers, as a component of prices received. If the traditional measure is used, real farm prices in 1977 were 67 percent of parity, using the 1910–1914 base. This is down from a parity ratio of 91 in 1973 and the lowest since 1960. The 1977 parity ratio is, in fact, the lowest since the Great Depression.

Table 3 includes indexes of prices received by farmers, since 1960, for three groups of agricultural products—all livestock products, food grains, and feed grains—and for all farm products. For comparison purposes, the index of prices and services used in calculating the parity ratio has been included. Food grain prices increased the most from 1970 through 1974 and have fallen most sharply since; feed grain prices

Table 3
INDEXES OF PRICES RECEIVED BY FARMERS, 1960-1977

		Prices Received for			
Year	Prices Paid for Commodities and Services	Livestock and products	Food grains	Feed grains[a]	All farm products
		(1967 = 100)			
1960	88	92	115	87	95
1961	88	91	119	87	96
1962	90	93	128	89	98
1963	91	89	127	94	97
1964	92	86	108	96	95
1965	94	94	93	100	98
1966	99	106	105	105	106
1967	100	100	100	100	100
1968	103	104	91	90	102
1969	108	117	88	96	107
1970	112	118	92	103	110
1971	120	118	95	108	113
1972	125	136	109	101	125
1973	144	183	215	163	179
1974	164	165	300	249	192
1975	180	172	242	232	185
1976	192	177	201	214	186
1977	202	175	156	174	197

[a] Feed grains and hay for 1960-1964.

Source: *Index Numbers of Prices Received and Prices Paid by Farmers, January 1965-April 1976, Revised,* pp. 26, 33, 45, and U.S. Department of Agriculture, *Agricultural Outlook,* January-February 1978, p. 21.

more than doubled between 1970 and 1974. The prices of livestock and their products increased significantly, but much more moderately than did either food grains or feed grains. And by 1977 livestock product prices had nearly recovered to their peak level of 1973, while food grain prices were hardly more than half of the 1974 levels. It is obvious that some farmers have been faced with a high degree of price instability.

During the past year there has been much concern expressed about the increasing debts of American farmers. For all farmers the data in Table 4 indicate that there has been a significant increase in the value of farm real estate and of all farm assets, in current dollars. The amount of debt has increased since 1965 at approximately the same rate as the value of total farm assets. Since 1970 there has been a remark-

Table 4

FARM ASSETS AND DEBTS, SELECTED YEARS, 1960–1978

Year, January 1	Value of Farm Real Estate (billion dollars)	Total Farm Assets (billion dollars)	Total Debt (billion dollars)	Real Estate Debt (billion dollars)	Ratio: Total Debt to Total Assets (percent)	Ratio: Debt to Assets, Largest 15% of Farms[a] (percent)
1960	137.2	210.6	24.8	12.0	11.8	13
1965	167.5	244.0	36.8	18.9	15.1	18
1970	215.9	315.3	53.0	29.2	16.8	18
1971	223.9	326.6	54.4	20.3	16.7	21
1972	241.4	353.2	59.1	32.2	16.7	20
1973	271.0	398.2	65.3	35.7	16.4	18
1974	335.4	486.2	74.1	41.3	15.2	20
1975	378.7	527.5	81.8	46.3	15.5	22
1976	429.1	592.8	90.8	51.1	15.3	20
1977	497.2	670.9	102.1	56.4	15.2	
1978	546.7	729.6	118.7	64.5	16.3	

[a] Estimated by author from data in *Balance Sheet of the Farming Sector*. In 1976 the largest 15 percent of farms, measured by value of sales, accounted for 77 percent of all farm sales.

Source: U.S. Department of Agriculture, Economic Research Service, *Balance Sheet of the Farming Sector 1977*, Agriculture Information Bulletin no. 411 (October 1977). January 1978 data from Division of Research and Statistics, Board of Governors of the Federal Reserve System.

able stability of the ratio of total debt to total farm assets—in the general range of 15 to 17 percent. The debt-to-asset ratio reached a low point in 1974, at 15.2 percent; at the beginning of 1978 the percentage had increased to 16.3 which was slightly below the percentage during the early years of the decade. The last column of Table 4 presents an estimate of the debt-to-asset ratio for the largest 15 percent of all farms. The debt-to-asset ratio has increased somewhat more than for all farms, but remains at a relatively low level.

Obviously there are many farmers who have debt-to-asset ratios greater than the average for all farms. Farmers who have purchased all or most of their land during the past three years will have debt repayment charges (principal and interest) that are large relative to their total net income. However, the farm operators who have bought all of the land in their farms within the last three years are relatively few in number. Less than 3 percent of all farm land is sold annually and in recent years less than 30 percent of the land purchased has represented the land of complete full-time farms.[5] The rest either have been additions to existing farms or were being utilized as part-time farms. Consequently, farms which were created by the purchase of all the land operated within the past three years represent less than 3 percent of all commercial farms. While it is unfortunate that many of this small number of farmers are facing problems due to the purchase of their land at high prices, it hardly seems appropriate to use these problems as a guide for national farm policy.

While there is some evidence of significant financial difficulties among farmers in the Great Plains States and in some adjoining Mountain States (Colorado and Montana), where both adverse weather conditions and low prices have been factors,[6] there had not been an increase in the number of farm foreclosures as of the year ending February 1, 1977. In the first three years of the 1970s farm foreclosures averaged 1.4 per thousand farms. In 1976–1977 there were 1.4 foreclosures per thousand farms.[7]

---

[5] U.S. Department of Agriculture, Economic Research Service, *Farm Real Estate Market Development*, various issues. In recent years approximately 88 percent of all farm real estate purchases have involved borrowing, and for transfers involving borrowing, the debt averages 76 to 77 percent of the purchase price.

[6] U.S. Department of Agriculture, Economic Research Service, *Special Summary of Farm Financial Situation* (April 1977). In the nine states there were 685,000 farms in 1976–1977. Of this number it is estimated that 226,100 were borrowers from banks. Of this latter group it was estimated that 13,900 (6 percent) could not repay their loans, and 59,300 (26 percent) would require refinancing or disposal of assets.

[7] U.S. Department of Agriculture, *Agricultural Statistics*, 1977 (Washington, D.C., 1977), p. 429.

A common complaint by farmers and some of their representatives is that the rate of return on farm land is very low. An estimate by the U.S. Department of Agriculture indicates that for the period from 1960 through 1976 the average annual rate of return was 3.8 percent. This rate of return is calculated as follows: The land rent on land actually rented is divided by the value of the rented land at the beginning of the year. It is thus not a rate of return on original cost, but the base for calculating the return changes as the market value of land changes. From 1960 to 1976 the real or deflated price of land increased at an annual rate of 3.3 percent. Since the value base on which the current rate of return on land is calculated has more than kept pace with the general change in the price level, the 3.8 percent annual rate of return is not a nominal rate of return, such as a 6.5 percent return on a savings certificate. Assuming a rate of inflation of 6 percent, the nominal current rate of return on land has really been at least 10 percent. This is clearly much better than the rate of return on many other forms of investments since 1960, such as savings accounts or common stocks.

The national data that have been presented encompass great diversity of economic fortunes. Some farmers are virtually free of debt; others have large debts and interest payments that amount to a high percentage of net farm income. Farmers who own all or most of their land have very large unrealized capital gains. The increase in the value of farm real estate, in current dollars, between January 1, 1970, and January 1, 1978, was $331 billion. During the same period, real estate debt increased by $35 billion (Table 4). The enormous increase in the value of farm real estate is, oddly enough, one of the sources of the current malaise among farmers. With interest rates on farm mortgages averaging 7.5 percent, farm operators with land valued at $1 million have difficulty understanding why net farm income was less than $60,000 in 1976.[8] In fact, many farmers with land valued at $1 million had net farm incomes in 1976 much less than $60,000. While it is true that at least half the value of the farm land is due to unrealized capital gains of the past six or seven years—and in terms of current income the farmer is no better or worse off than he was when his land had a value half of what it now is—it is not difficult to understand his puzzlement and feeling of having been mistreated by someone or something.

---

[8] The net income from farming of farms with value of sales in excess of $100,000 in 1976 has been estimated as $55,700. The average value of real estate on such farms on January 1, 1976, was $877,000. Sources: U.S. Department of Agriculture, Economic Research Service, *Farm Income Statistics*, Statistical Bulletin no. 576 (July 1977) and *Balance Sheet of the Farming Sector, 1977*, Agriculture Information Bulletin no. 411 (October 1977).

Major Features of the 1977 Act

The Food and Agriculture Act of 1977, which was signed into law on September 29, 1977, was conceived and born of the particular economic setting that I have briefly described. While I believe that the legislation has numerous defects—many of them quite unnecessary and perhaps unrecognized and others the result of pandering to special interests— on the whole it is surprising that the legislation does not have more very serious defects. Vacillation and lack of leadership on the part of the administration undoubtedly contributed to some of the deficiencies that will be noted. Given the posture, or more accurately, the postures of the administration, the Congress deserves a great deal of credit for an act that could easily have been much more costly to taxpayers and which could have contributed more to the misallocation of resources and been more restrictive of consumer choices.

The 1977 act has nineteen titles, including the last title that specifies the effective date of the legislation.[9] This is an omnibus bill, covering a range of programs, from major farm products such as wheat, corn, and cotton to a special program for filberts; it also establishes standards for ice cream, the food stamp program, and grain inspection. The act institutes a dairy indemnity program to pay farmers for loss of milk sales due to nuclear radiation or fallout and chemicals or toxic substances; beekeepers have for some time been indemnified for loss of honey production due to the use of pesticides on adjoining land.

In this essay I shall concentrate on the legislation for the three major farm crops—wheat, feed grains, and cotton. Near the end of the paper there are brief comments on the programs for dairy products, rice, sugar, and peanuts. Thus this summary of the major features of the 1977 act will ignore some interesting aspects pertaining to products that are of minor importance in total farm income. The failure to comment on livestock products other than milk reflects the fact that, for good or ill, the act has little direct relevance to the production of meat animals, other than indirectly through its legislation for feed supplies and prices. Nor are there more than passing references to soybeans since there was no apparent inclination to bring this highly successful crop into the maze of regulations and subsidies that were deemed appropriate for other important crops.

---

[9] The Food and Agriculture Act of 1977 may be found in U.S. Congress, Senate, 95th Congress, 1st session, *Food and Agriculture Act of 1977*, Conference Report no. 95-418. A summary of the major provisions of the 1977 Act may be found in U.S. Department of Agriculture, Economic Research Service, *Commodity Program Provisions under the Food and Agriculture Act of 1977*, Agricultural Economic Report no. 389 (October 1977).

In 1977 the value of cash receipts from farming was approximately $95 billion. Since some of the cash receipts represent sales from one farmer to another, this figure represents an overestimate of the sales from agriculture to the rest of the economy. But the figure can be used to give a rough indication of the share of agricultural output affected by the 1977 act. If soybeans are assumed not to be affected by the legislation because of the very low price support level that has been established, the act quite directly affects nearly 40 percent of agricultural sales. Since many fruits and vegetables are covered by other legislation, the percentage of farm sales directly affected by all farm legislation is greater than 40 percent. In addition, any effects of the legislation upon the prices of feed crops will be felt by livestock and poultry producers.

The 1977 act has six major policy instruments for the major farm products. These are target prices and deficiency payments; commodity loans and purchases (support prices); land set-asides and diversions; crop acreage reductions; land diversion payments; and an extended farmer-held grain reserve program.

Target Prices and Deficiency Payments. The concept of target prices, which was introduced in the 1973 farm legislation, is a major feature of the new act. Target prices are not market prices. The target price is used to determine deficiency payments per unit of eligible production that vary inversely with the market price, if the market price is at or above the loan rate for the commodity. For example, the national average loan rate for wheat for the 1977 crop was $2.25 per bushel; the target price was $2.90 per bushel. The deficiency payment rate that was made was the smaller of the differences between the national average market price of wheat received by farmers during the first five months of the 1977–1978 marketing year or the loan level of $2.25 per bushel and the target price of $2.90 per bushel. Since the national average market price for June through October 1977 was below $2.25 per bushel, the deficiency payment on the eligible production was $0.65 per bushel—the difference between the loan rate and the target price.

The rationale for target prices is to provide income protection for farmers while leaving room for substantial price response to market forces. This is not to say that target prices have no effects upon market prices; the level of target prices clearly influence decisions on production. But once the output has been determined, the target prices leave the market price free to move in response to world supply and demand conditions.

How were the target prices determined? The 1978 target prices were based for each covered commodity on the national average of

1975 and 1976 "cost of production" per unit of output. Cost of production was defined to include normal expenses such as purchased inputs and hired labor, as well as a return to own labor, costs of machinery, and general farm overhead, a return to management (7 percent of gross receipts), and a 4 percent return on land based on its current price.

Agricultural economists had thought that the idea of using cost of production as a method of establishing price supports or fair or reasonable prices had been buried nearly a half century ago. True, the parity price concept, which won out over cost of production in the Agricultural Adjustment Act of 1933, had major defects and has been largely abandoned.[10] This is not the place to show definitely why the use of cost of production data for determining price relationships is wholly inappropriate. However, a few brief points may be made. First, there is enormous variation in production costs on different farms, however such costs are measured. Estimates made by the U.S. Department of Agriculture of production costs in response to a direct demand of the Congress, indicated that in 1974 approximately 11 percent of all cotton had average total production costs of less than 25 cents per pound and 11 percent had costs of 60 cents per pound or more.[11] Second, the price or cost of the services of one major input in the production of crops, namely land, is largely determined by current and expected future prices of the crops grown on the land. As a result, if the price of wheat were $4.00 per bushel, approximately the same percentage of wheat would be produced at an average calculated cost in excess of the market price of $4.00 as would be true if the market price of wheat were $2.50 per bushel. The reason would be that the land rent would increase enough to bring cost of production and price into rough equality. Third, it is not only land return or rent that is affected by the product price, the quantity used of many other inputs, such as fertilizers, herbicides, and insecticides, are determined by the relationships between the prices of the product and the prices of the inputs. Finally, one rather important cost component included is a return for management, which Congress in its wisdom said should be "comparable to the normal management fees charged by other comparable industries." The cost estimates actually used for this economic concept have been 7 percent of

---

[10] See O. B. Jesness, ed., *Readings on Agricultural Policy* (Philadelphia: The Blakiston Company, 1949), pp. 96–97.

[11] U.S. Department of Agriculture, Economic Research Service, *Costs of Producing Selected Crops in the United States—1974*, U.S. Congress, Senate, Committee on Agriculture and Forestry, 94th Congress, 1st session, committee print, January 8, 1976, p. 13. The value of land used in calculating costs was the average acquisition value.

total farm sales, since this is the fee generally charged by farm managers working for banks, insurance companies, and farm management companies.

It was noted earlier that the 1978 target prices were based on the average of 1975 and 1976 unit costs of production. If 1978 crop yields are the same as the average of 1975 and 1976, the target prices in 1978 will be at approximately 85 to 90 percent of the estimated production costs. This estimate assumes that production costs increase at an annual rate of about 4 percent. Why were 1975 and 1976 data used for setting 1978 target prices? It can only be assumed that this was one of the compromises required in order to keep the cost of the legislation at politically acceptable levels. If 1978 production costs had been estimated on the basis of the same formula used for 1975 and 1976, increases in the costs of inputs and the return to land would have increased the 1978 target price for wheat by at least 35 cents per bushel and governmental costs by about $650 million.

The legislation established target prices for wheat and corn for 1977 and 1978 and for cotton for 1978. The secretary of agriculture was authorized to establish target prices for grain sorghums, barley, and oats. Target prices and loan levels are given in Table 5. A formula was specified for changing the target prices for 1979 and later years. This formula does *not* include a factor for changes in land costs, however measured. For the grain crops and cotton target prices will be adjusted for each subsequent year by the difference between the sum of variable costs, machinery ownership cost, and general farm overhead costs for the current year and the second previous year, divided by two.

The wheat target price for 1978 shown in Table 5 is not from the 1977 act. The Emergency Agricultural Act of 1978, signed by the President on May 15, 1978, authorized an increase in the wheat target price to $3.40. The increase in the wheat target price is impossible to justify on economic grounds. The increase will do nothing to assist in resource adjustment or in bringing wheat production more nearly into line with demand at potentially achievable prices. The increase appears to be further indication of the willingness of the national administration to respond to political pressure and to vacillate in its economic policies.

Commodity Loans and Purchases. With respect to commodity loans or price support operations the 1977 act has some innovative features. The act specifies minimum loan rates for 1977 and 1978 through 1981 for wheat and corn. For wheat the minimum loan rates are $2.25 for 1977 and $2.35 for subsequent years; the corn loan rates are $2.00 for all years (see Table 5). Calling these loan rates minimum rates represents an odd use of the English language. An element of flexibility is

Table 5

LOAN LEVELS AND TARGET PRICES FOR WHEAT, FEED GRAINS, SOYBEANS, AND COTTON, 1977 AND 1978 CROPS

(dollars)

Commodity	Loan Levels		Target Prices	
	1977	1978	1977	1978
Wheat (bu.)	2.25	2.35[a]	2.90	3.40[b]
Corn (bu.)	2.00	2.00[a]	2.00	2.10
Grain sorghum (bu.)	1.90	1.90	2.28	2.28[d]
Barley (bu.)	1.63	1.63	2.15	2.15[d]
Oats (bu.)	1.03	1.03	—	—
Soybeans (bu.)	3.50	4.50	—	—
Cotton (lb.)	0.44	0.48[c]	0.52	0.52

Note: A dash (—) means not established.

[a] Loan levels can be reduced to $2.00 for wheat and $1.75 for corn if prices received by farmers in a marketing year are less than 105 percent of the loan level. The maximum reduction in loan levels in any one year is 10 percent. Preliminary 1978 wheat price support of $2.25 announced March 29, 1978.

[b] The Food and Agriculture Act of 1977 set the 1978 target prices for wheat at $3.00 if 1978 wheat production were greater than 1.8 billion bushels and at $3.05 if production were 1.8 billion bushels or less. However, the Emergency Agricultural Act of 1978, signed by the President on May 15, 1978, authorized an increase in the target price for 1978 to $3.40.

[c] The 1978 cotton loan level was to be established on the basis of market prices for the first two weeks of October 1978, but the Emergency Agricultural Act of 1978 authorized a cotton loan rate of $0.48.

[d] Preliminary.

Source: U.S. Department of Agriculture, Economic Research Service, *Feed Situation*, FdS-269 (May 1978), p. 42.

given to the secretary of agriculture to reduce the rates downward to as low as $2.00 for wheat and $1.75 for corn. If the average farm price of wheat or corn for any marketing year is less than 105 percent of the loan rate, the secretary can reduce the price support for the subsequent year by up to 10 percent; however, he may not reduce the price support below the *real* minimums of $2.00 for wheat and $1.75 for corn. The reason for the flexibility in loan rates was that when market prices are at or very near the loan levels, exports are adversely affected.

The establishment of the cotton loan rate in the 1977 act does not follow the same rules applied to wheat and the feed grains. No minimum loan rate was specified. For any crop year the secretary must announce by November 1 a loan rate that is the lesser of (1) 85 percent of the preceding four marketing years' moving average spot market price for a particular grade of upland cotton at average U.S. locations or (2) 90 percent of the average adjusted price for the first two weeks of October of the five lowest price growths of the particular type of cotton c.i.f. Northern Europe. The price in Northern Europe is to be adjusted downward to reflect the average differential between the Northern Europe prices and the prices in the U.S. designated locations.

Clearly, the intent was that the loan program was to assist in orderly marketing and not to result in significant accumulations of cotton by the Commodity Credit Corporation (ccc). The cotton loans would result in acquisition by the ccc only when the market seriously misjudged the demand and supply situation in the weeks following the harvest of the American crop. It may be noted that the two weeks chosen are normally the lowest priced period for the entire year.

The provisions of the 1977 act for the establishment of the cotton loan rates may never receive a trial. The Emergency Agricultural Act of 1978, signed on May 15, 1978, gave authority for a fixed cotton loan rate of $0.48 per pound for 1978. It is not obvious at the time of writing that the loan rate as established will be higher than the one that would have been determined by the formula in the 1977 act.

The legislation imposes limits on the total deficiency payments that can be made to any producer. The prior limitation of $20,000 for 1977 for combined payments under the wheat, feed grain, and cotton programs was changed. However, for 1978 and later years total payments for a single producer of the three crops were increased substantially, ranging from $40,000 in 1978 to $45,000 in 1979. Payments to rice producers are separate and differ; they are somewhat higher for 1977 through 1979 (in excess of $50,000). In 1980 and 1981 the payments for rice must be included in the total of $50,000 for the major commodity programs. However, there is relatively little production of wheat, cotton, or feed grains on rice farms. If the loan rates for wheat and corn are reduced below the levels specified for 1978, the added deficiency payments due to the downward revision are excluded from the payment limitation.

The secretary is required to establish loan rates for grain sorghums, barley, oats, and rye, reflecting appropriate relationships to the loan rate for corn. Primarily the loan rates should reflect relative feeding values, though in the case of grain sorghums both feeding values and transportation costs to market relative to corn are to be taken into account. The effect of including transportation costs in establishing the loan rate for grain sorghums is to reduce the loan rate below what it would be if only feeding values were considered. The effect, however, is likely to be quite small—perhaps about 5 cents per bushel.

The purpose of the commodity loans is to put a floor under market prices.[12] The commodity loans, a major component of farm programs for more than four decades, are an ingenious mechanism. The loans are technically described as nonrecourse commodity loans. To obtain these loans the producer pledges a specific amount of the relevant commodity (wheat or corn, for example) and obtains a loan equal to the quantity multiplied by the loan rate. During a specified period, generally nine or ten months, or by a specific date, the farmer may repay the loan by paying the interest and storage costs. However, if he has not repaid the loan by the maturity date, he satisfies the loan by delivering the commodity to the Commodity Credit Corporation. He pays no interest, though he does have to provide for the storage, either through payment to a storage agency or by providing it himself. The large stocks of grains and cotton have been mainly acquired by the Commodity Credit Corporation in the past through the nonrecourse commodity loans.

A different loan program—the extended farmer-held grain reserve program is discussed below.

Set-asides and Diversions. The secretary of agriculture may require farmers to set aside part of their cropland in order to be eligible for deficiency payments, disaster payments, and loans. The set-aside land must be used in a soil conserving mode and probably little or no productive use of the land will be permitted. For 1978 the set-aside for wheat has been set at 20 percent of the actual acreage of wheat planted and for feed grains at 10 percent. If a farmer produces both wheat and feed grains, he must abide by both set-aside requirements.

If a farmer meets the appropriate set-aside requirements, he will receive the deficiency payment, if any, on a minimum of 80 percent of his actual planted acreage multiplied by his program yield.[13] Deficiency payments, however, can be paid on a larger fraction of adjusted output than 80 percent. The secretary of agriculture is required to establish a national program acreage. If the actual harvested acreage is equal to, or less than, the national program acreage, payments would be made on the product of the planted acreage times the program yield. This assumes, of course, that the set-aside requirements, if any, have been met. The actual percentage of their area on which payments will be made is determined by the national program acreage divided by the number of acres harvested for grain. But as noted, the minimum percentage is 80.

[12] Direct purchases are authorized for the same purpose. However, except for dairy products relatively little use has been made of direct purchases as a technique for price support.

[13] A program yield shall be established for each farm. The program yield for 1978 shall be the 1977 established yield. If a farmer can prove that his actual yield in 1977 exceeded the program yield established by the appropriate authorities, his 1977 actual yield becomes the 1978 program yield.

The legislation assumes that sufficient incentive is provided to comply with set-aside requirements by making these requirements a condition for receiving deficiency payments, disaster payments, and crop loans. For wheat the incentives are significant—the deficiency payments are likely to be substantial and much wheat is grown in areas where crop failure is all too common. But for corn producers, target prices are likely to be very little above loan rates and most corn is grown in areas where the disaster payment provisions are unlikely to apply except occasionally. Many feed grain farmers may be willing to gamble on the fact that enough producers will participate to keep the market price close to the loan rate and that a majority of feed grain producers may not participate in the program. There are provisions in the legislation for payments for additional land diversion.

Crop Acreage Reductions. Farmers can assure themselves of deficiency payments of 100 percent of their normal production on their planted acreage if they "voluntarily" reduce the planted acreage of the crop by at least the percentage specified by the secretary of agriculture. The legislation does not specify how the secretary shall allocate the amount of the reduction of wheat, feed grains, and cotton except that the "limitation shall be applied on a uniform basis to all . . . farms." For the wheat and feed grain programs announced for 1978, the voluntary reduction of planted acreage has been based on the 1977 planted acreage. The 1977 act abolished the acreage allotments that had been a feature of farm programs for two decades.[14] But it may well be that by these few words a new set of acreage allotments has been reinstituted for wheat and feed grains.

Land Diversion Payments. There is one new wrinkle in the 1977 act that could become important in future years. It may well be that the combination of incentives (deficiency and disaster payments and loan rates) and restraints (set-asides and voluntary acreage reduction) provided by the legislation and its administration may result in stocks of major farm products which would be larger than is politically acceptable. The act authorizes the secretary to seek additional diversion of cropland by offering annual payments for land devoted to approved conservation practices; this is not an innovation. Land diversion payments have a long history. The diversion is to be achieved through a bidding process in which farmers indicate the annual payment per acre that they will accept for diversion. In accepting the bids the secretary is

---

[14] For a discussion of acreage allotments, see Willard W. Cochrane and Mary E. Ryan, *American Farm Policy, 1948–1973* (Minneapolis: University of Minnesota Press, 1976), especially chap. 3. The 1977 act retains acreage allotments for rice and introduces a farm poundage quota for peanuts which is closely tied to the previous acreage allotment. The 1978 cotton program has no set-aside requirement.

to take into account the productivity of the land and to accept the lowest bids that will provide the amount of diversion desired. He is admonished not to concentrate such diversion too heavily in particular counties or local communities.

In previous supply management programs that relied upon land diversion, the secretary announced the payment rates that he believed would bring about the desired level of diversion. The new approach, if administered effectively, should be a lower cost method of achieving a given objective.

Payments were instituted for land diversion from feed grains and cotton in 1978. However, the payment rates were not established according to the novel method described above. The lateness of announcing the voluntary land diversion programs (March 29, 1978) probably made it impossible to institute the bidding procedure described above. To participate in the voluntary land diversion program for the feed grains, the farmer must first participate in the 10 percent set-aside and then divert an additional 10 percent of his feed grain area. The 1978 plantings cannot exceed the 1977 plantings for the same crop, and the diverted land must be put into an approved soil conservation use. The payment rates for voluntary diversion are 20 cents per bushel for corn and 12 cents per bushel for barley and grain sorghum. The diversion payment is determined by multiplying the payment rate times the established crop yields for the farm and then times the 1978 acres planted for harvest. The payment for diverting land from cotton production is calculated in the same way and at a rate of two cents per pound.

The payment per acre for diverting land from corn is approximately equal to the expected gross value per acre if corn were actually produced. With a farm yield of 100 bushels per acre, the payment for diverting one acre would be $200.[15] The gross value for an acre of corn yielding 100 bushels, given the loan rate of $2.00, is $200.

---

[15] Assume that a farmer planted 100 acres of corn in 1978. The voluntary diversion required to earn the payment is 10 percent or 10 acres. The payment received for diverting 10 acres would be 20 cents per bushel times 100 bushels per acre times 100 acres or $2,000. This amounts to $200 for each acre voluntarily diverted. In order to receive the voluntary diversion payment, the farmer must have set aside 10 additional acres without payment. In an *Issue Briefing Paper*, issued by the U.S. Department of Agriculture on April 3, 1978, entitled "New Features of Federal Farm Programs" it was estimated that the new diversion program would reduce the feed grain area by 5 to 7 million acres with 4 to 6 million acres being in corn. It was estimated that total diversion payments would be approximately $625 million of which $540 million would be for corn. The estimate of payments for corn diversion seems low. If 5 million acres are diverted under the program, the average farm yield would have to be as low as 54 bushels per acre for a total payment of $540 million. The national average farm yield is likely to be closer to 80–85 bushels per acre resulting in a total payment of at least $800 million for corn if $5 million acres are diverted.

The payment rate for cotton is two cents per pound, and on the basis of a farm yield of 500 pounds per acre the payment rate per diverted acre would be $100. Provisions in the 1977 act that permitted payments for grazing of wheat acreage or cutting wheat for hay were also utilized. The payment rate was established at 50 cents per bushel or the deficiency payment rate, whichever was greater, on the farm yield. The wheat grazing or hay program is another example of imposing some of the wheat adjustment problems upon feed grain producers. Total feed supplies will be increased by this diversion program and feed grain prices decreased as a result. While the small anticipated increase in wheat prices will reduce the feeding of wheat, the net effect will be larger supplies of feed.

Extended Farmer-held Grain Reserve Program. The Commodity Credit Corporation has had the authority to release or sell its stocks of grain and other commodities at prices close to the loan rate then prevailing. At some times the selling price could be as low as 5 percent above the loan rate, though in recent years (since 1971) resales could not occur at less than 115 percent of the current loan rate, except for export sales and other minor exceptions such as the disposition of deteriorated products or for disaster sales. Farmers, at least in principle, are opposed to having large stocks owned by the Commodity Credit Corporation. They argue, with considerable validity, that when stocks are large the loan level becomes a maximum as well as a minimum price.

The 1977 act continues the provision that the ccc cannot sell any commodity that it owns at less than 115 percent of the current loan rate, and this restriction applies to export sales as well as to sales in the domestic market.[16] But the 1977 act provides for a second storage program, namely, the extended farmer-held grain reserve program, and when this program is in effect the ccc selling price is 150 percent of the current loan rate.

The new program provides for loans to farmers to store grain for periods of three to five years. Under this program the farmer receives annual storage payments, and interest on the loan may be waived. If the farmer does not hold the grain until maturity or until a release price has been reached in the market—140 percent of the current loan rate

---

[16] Whether this provision will prevent export subsidies on commodities of the same kind as those held in ccc inventories is not clear to me. Section 32 of the Agricultural Adjustment Act of 1933 authorizes the use of up to 30 percent of U.S. custom receipts for export subsidies and domestic diversions. Other legislation providing funds for export subsidies would sustain the fiction that the ccc was not selling its stocks below the specified level. However, I believe the clear intent of Congress was to eschew the use of export subsidies.

Table 6
FARMER-HELD EXTENDED GRAIN RESERVE PROGRAM: CCC SELLING PRICES, RELEASE PRICES, AND CALL PRICES FOR WHEAT AND CORN FOR 1978
(dollars per bushel)

	Wheat	Corn
Loan level	2.35	2.00
Selling price, if no program[a]	2.70	2.30
Selling price, if program[b]	3.52	3.00
Release price for farmers	3.29	2.50
Call price for farmers	4.11	2.80

[a] Lowest selling price permitted for Commodity Credit Program if there is no farmer-held extended grain reserve program.

[b] Lowest selling price permitted for Commodity Credit Program if there is a farmer-held extended grain reserve program. Such a program now exists.

Source: USDA, *Feed Situation*, FdS-269 (May 1978), p. 42.

for wheat and 125 percent for feed grains—he will be subject to penalties such as repayment of storage payments received and penalty interest or other charges. When the market price reaches 175 percent of the current loan rate for wheat and 140 percent for feed grains, the loans will be called. The objective of the reserve program was to store 17 million tons of feed grains and 8–9 million tons of wheat. These reserves represent about 9 percent of recent annual production of feed grains and about 15 percent of recent wheat production. However, in March 1978 the upper limit on the reserve was eliminated and a 6 million metric ton wheat reserve "to be isolated for international humanitarian and disaster uses only" was announced.

Under the terms of this program the ccc will not be able to dispose of any grain that it acquires under its annual loan program until all of the loans under the farmer-held program are liquidated. Thus it would be possible for the feed grain farmer reserve to have been called but for wheat loans to remain outstanding. This situation would prevent the ccc from selling its stocks of feed grains at less than 150 percent of the current loan rate.

In Table 6 I have tried to illustrate as simply as possible the complex features of the extended farmer-held grain reserve program and the effects of that program upon the minimum price at which the Commodity Credit Corporation can sell any stocks of grains that it may have acquired under the regular commodity loan program. With a loan level of $2.35 per bushel for wheat, the ccc could sell its stocks of wheat at a price of $2.70—if there were no farmer-held grain reserve program. However, in the case of the present farmer-held grain reserve program, the minimum ccc selling price for wheat is $3.52 per bushel. Farmers who have participated in the special reserve program can pay off their loans and retain all storage payments that they have received if the U.S. average farm price is $3.29 per bushel or higher. If the farm price of wheat is $4.11 per bushel or higher, the loans are called and the farmer must repay what he has borrowed plus whatever interest is charged. The features of the feed grain reserve program are illustrated by corn.

Supply, Demand, Price, and Income Prospects

American agriculture is confronted with significant adjustment problems. Some are long run, and some are short run. At the moment, the most serious problems are those that must be faced in the short run. As I tried to illustrate in last year's volume of this series, agriculture had adjusted to its long-run declining position quite satisfactorily.[17] The relative income position of farm families improved substantially during the past two decades. By the early 1970s most of the excess resources engaged in agriculture had been eliminated, in part because of current and previous farm programs. Largely as a result of the increased access to nonfarm jobs, the inequality in the distribution of incomes within the farm operator population had been sharply reduced in the years following 1960.

The sharp increase in farm prices after mid-1972 had a number of consequences that are now being felt. The rate of decline in farm employment slowed. According to the U.S. Department of Agriculture measure of farm employment, there was no decline in employment between 1972 and 1976.[18] The farm population in the age group fourteen to fifty-four years hardly changed between 1970 and 1975; the long term decline reemerged in 1976.[19]

The high farm prices in 1973 and 1974 resulted in increased rates of investment in machinery and other assets with useful lives of several years. But the most dramatic change was the increase in the value of

---

[17] See D. Gale Johnson, "Resource Adjustment in American Agriculture and Agricultural Policy" in William Fellner, ed., *Contemporary Economic Problems 1977* (Washington, D.C.: American Enterprise Institute, 1977), pp. 203–238.

[18] U.S. Department of Agriculture, Statistical Reporting Service, *Farm Labor*, various issues.

[19] U.S. Department of Commerce and U.S. Department of Agriculture, *Farm Population*, Series Census-ERS, P-27, no. 47 (September 1976), no. 48 (April 1977), and no. 49 (December 1977).

farm real estate. Fortunately, as shown in Table 3 above, an increase did not occur in the ratio of debt-to-farm assets; at 16.3 percent at the beginning of 1978 the ratio was lower than in 1940 (18.9 percent) and lower than in 1970 (16.8 percent). The recent low point for the ratio was 15.2 percent at the beginning of 1974. Unfortunately the ratio of debt to assets could continue to increase for the next two or three years because of continuing expansion of debt and slower growth in the value of farm assets.

To a greater degree than is generally realized, American agriculture absorbs a large fraction of the total world supply and demand changes for the grains. This was true during the rapid increase in grain prices after mid-1972.[20] It is now equally true, when grain prices are declining. The same forces, primarily the policies of national price stability, that were responsible for a significant part of the increase in grain prices in 1973 and 1974 have been responsible for the price declines since 1975. A large fraction of the world's grain consumption—more than 50 percent—occurs in countries that insulate their producers and consumers from the worldwide variability of supply and demand. When prices in international markets increase, consumption is not reduced nor are producers provided with incentives to expand production. Similarly when international market prices decline, consumers in such countries are not given the opportunity to increase their consumption because the prices they pay do not change, nor is there any change in the price incentives for producers. Thus it is only the countries that permit their domestic prices to vary with international prices that react and adjust to changing world demand-supply relationships. Barring a change in such policies, it is the major grain exporting countries that must undertake the relevant adjustments. And since the United States is the largest of the grain exporters, much of the adjustment must occur in this country.

One important criterion for evaluating the commodity programs created by the Food and Agriculture Act of 1977 is their effectiveness in facilitating the required short-run adjustments in supply, while not interfering with the long-run adjustments that are required if farm people are to share fully in the income and productivity of our economy. There are a variety of ways of dealing with short-run economic difficulties due to relatively low prices and the resulting low incomes. In fact, several of these ways are illustrated by the different commodity programs provided by the 1977 act. The 1977 act is not really a single piece of legislation, but a collection of legislative enactments.

[20] See D. Gale Johnson, "World Agriculture, Commodity Policy, and Price Variability," *American Journal of Agricultural Economics*, vol. 47 (December 1975), pp. 823–828.

How serious is the short-run disequilibrium in supply and demand? Or put another way, how much reduction in the growth of supply must occur before prices of certain farm products will provide returns for resources engaged in agriculture roughly comparable to those obtained in the rest of the economy? Before continuing, it should be noted that the short-run disequilibrium is not uniform throughout American agriculture. The disequilibrium is primarily concentrated in the grains, though not uniformly so, and in the beef and dairy sectors.

Short-run disequilibrium is nothing new to the beef sector and there is little in the 1977 act that will have significant impacts upon that sector. The dairy sector continues to produce more milk than can be sold in normal markets at the governmentally established prices, but few are claiming that milk producers are suffering from unsatisfactory incomes. As a result of the very large cotton crop in 1977, both in the United States and in the rest of world, the price of cotton has declined by nearly a quarter from the end of 1976 to the end of 1977. However, U.S. and world stocks remain at reasonable levels, and modest production adjustments are likely to result in prices that provide a reasonable return to resources.

By stating that there is a short-run disequilibrium in the grains, I mean, quite simply, that the recent low level of grain prices will not be tenable for very long. The farm price of corn in late 1977, in real terms, was the lowest since the Great Depression, and the same was true of the farm price of wheat.

It is true that the real costs of producing grains has declined during the past three decades and that the 1977–1978 prices are about the same as the real prices in the late 1960s and early 1970s. In terms of 1970 dollars the farm price of wheat was about $1.35 from 1968 through 1971 compared with the 1977–1978 real price of $1.40; the real price of corn was $1.20 compared with a 1977–1978 price of $1.20. Moreover, during the late 1960s and early 1970s wheat producers received direct governmental payments of more than $0.50 per bushel and feed grain producers about $0.20 per bushel of corn equivalent. I have argued elsewhere that about half of these payments represented an increase in net income of farm operators and increased rent to non-operator landlords.[21] It is highly unlikely that real production costs have fallen enough since the early 1970s to justify the 1977–1978 grain prices unless there is a substantial decline in the real price of farm land. Even at these low prices, in real terms, total U.S. grain stocks increased by 15 million tons or 6 percent of the 1977–1978 production. In the

---

[21] D. Gale Johnson, *Farm Commodity Programs: An Opportunity for Change* (Washington, D.C.: American Enterprise Institute, 1973), pp. 48–49.

absence of the price supports and the farmer grain reserve program, farm prices would have been somewhat lower.

There are two reasons why the short-run disequilibrium is concentrated in grains. The effects of national agricultural programs in major consuming and producing nations have already been noted. The other reason is that grain production is widely distributed throughout U.S. agriculture. Grains are harvested on nearly 60 percent of the total harvested area. With few exceptions, grains represent the major alternative to other crops. Thus when cotton profitability is relatively poor, grain is often the primary alternative. Where soybeans are the best alternative to cotton, as is the case in much of the Mississippi Delta, soybeans compete with corn for land and other resources in the Corn Belt and thus impinge on grains. In effect, most of the adjustments in the crop economy impinge quite quickly upon the grains. At times this works to the advantage of grains, but at other times, such as now, grain production is increased because of adjustments in other crop area and output.

How substantial is the disequilibrium in the grain economy? Fortunately it appears to be rather small in terms of quantity, though much larger in terms of price. Unfortunately the disequilibrium appears to be rather significantly concentrated in wheat and correcting that disequilibrium, which is long-run as well as short-run, will increase the supply of feed grains.

My conclusion that the short-run disequilibrium in the U.S. grain economy is rather small follows from some admittedly impressionistic considerations. First, grain feeding in North America and Western Europe has not recovered to the levels of the early 1970s.[22] The slow recovery of grain feeding after 1974–1975 is due primarily to two factors—the slow growth of real per capita income in North America and Western Europe for the past four years and the continued liquidation of beef herds which has resulted in the significant expansion of the supply of meat and in the lowering of meat prices. The liquidation has not been completed, but it should be soon. The percentage reduction in the cattle herd has been the largest in the past three decades. As the liquidation of the cattle herd is being completed, the beef supply is being reduced and beef prices have increased. As the feeding of beef

---

[22] The feed use of grain in North America and Western Europe reached a peak of 264 million tons in 1972–1973. Feed use declined to 224 million tons in 1974–1975, with all of the reduction occurring in the United States and Canada. Feed use has increased but only to 233 million tons in 1976–1977. The U.S. Department of Agriculture projects a further increase to 246 million tons in 1977–1978. But if this is the level of feed use in 1977–1978, it will still be almost 20 million tons below the 1973–1974 use (U.S. Department of Agriculture, Foreign Agricultural Service, *World Consumption of Grain as Livestock Feed*, FG-14-77 [August 23, 1977], p. 4).

becomes more profitable, the supply of beef is reduced, as more animals are moved into feedlots.

Second, the buildup in the world's feed grain stocks from the low levels at the beginning of 1976–1977 year through the end of 1977–1978 will be approximately 27 million tons or about 4 percent of one year's production. Nearly all of the increase has occurred in the United States, where it is highly visible. World wheat stocks will have increased by essentially the same quantity, with somewhat more than half the increase in the United States.[23] During 1977–1978 wheat utilization will exceed supply and world stocks will be reduced. Changes in rice stocks are small and of little importance in total grain utilization.

The short-run disequilibrium in feed grains can be eliminated by a small reduction in the rate of output growth and by a return in feed use to approximately the levels of 1973–1974 in North America and Western Europe. One proviso must, however, be noted. A part of the disequilibrium in the feed grains is due to spillovers from the wheat supply and demand situation. As I argue below, there is little in the 1977 act that will correct the need for the feed grain sector to absorb much of the excess production capacity in the wheat sector. As the market prices of wheat decline relative to feed grain prices, the quantity of wheat used as feed increases. Very little wheat was fed from 1973 through 1976, but the amount of wheat fed in the United States was approximately 6 million tons in 1977–1978, almost double the previous year.

During the last half of the 1960s and the early 1970s the marginal use of wheat in the United States and in the international market was as a feed grain. In most of these years, the average U.S. farm price of wheat was approximately the feed value of wheat, given the market prices of corn. Even with this price relationship, the stocks of wheat owned or controlled by the Commodity Credit Corporation from 1968 through 1972 represented a much larger percentage of annual production than was true of the feed grains.[24] It remains true, in spite of the high wheat prices of 1973–1975, that the international price of wheat has generally been and will be at, or near, its feed value for most qualities of wheat.

Net income from agriculture will remain at a depressed level until there is some slowing of the rate of growth of farm production or a

---

[23] U.S. Department of Agriculture, Foreign Agricultural Service, *Foreign Agriculture Circular: Grains*, FG-23-77 (November 11, 1977), pp. 26, 28–29.

[24] U.S. Department of Agriculture, *1972 Handbook of Agricultural Charts*, Agriculture Handbook no. 491 (October 1972), pp. 105, 121. Beginning of the year stocks of wheat for 1969 through 1972 held by the ccc were over 40 percent of annual production while for feed grains the percentage was approximately half that.

Table 7
TARGET PRICES AND LOAN RATES FOR 1977, PRICES RECEIVED BY FARMERS, DECEMBER 1977, AND ESTIMATED DEFICIENCY PAYMENTS
(dollars)

Commodity	Target Price	Loan Rate	Price Received	Deficiency Payment
Wheat (bu.)	2.90	2.25	2.47	0.65
Corn (bu.)	2.00	2.00	1.98	—
Grain sorghum (bu.)	2.28	1.90	1.77	0.38
Barley (bu.)	2.15	1.63	1.77	0.50
Oats (bu.)	—	1.03	1.03	—
Soybeans (bu.)	—	3.50	5.68	—
Cotton (lb.)	0.52	0.44	0.49	—

Source: U.S. Department of Agriculture, Economic Research Service, *Commodity Program Provisions under the Food and Agriculture Act of 1977*, Agricultural Economic report no. 389 (October 1977), p. 5; various USDA press releases.

significant expansion in the rate of growth of demand. What happens in the next two or three years will have important long-run implications to agriculture and to taxpayers. If the policies followed facilitate the required adjustments, then there will be an increase in real agricultural income, because of the operation of market forces. But if the policies followed result in delaying the adjustments, then political forces will result in continuing and growing subsidies to agriculture. More important, in my opinion, delaying the required adjustments in agriculture will make such adjustments more difficult and painful to farm people.

Some Get More Than Others. The 1977 act and the farm programs that it authorizes can hardly be said to be evenhanded in the distribution of benefits—or potential distribution of the burden of agricultural adjustment. Table 7 compares the target prices and loan rates for 1977 and the average price received by farmers in December 1977 for five grains, soybeans, and cotton.

As noted earlier, deficiency payments are equal to the target price minus the higher of the loan rate or the national average farm market price during the first five months of the marketing year for the grain; the cotton market price is for the calendar year in which the crop is harvested. Since the average farm price of wheat from June through

October, 1977 was $2.10, the deficiency payment on wheat for 1977 was $0.65. The 1977 target prices for grain sorghum and barley were announced January 12, 1978 (by Vice President Mondale) and resulted in substantial deficiency payments.

In announcing the target prices, Vice President Mondale said:

> Establishing these target price levels is important for two reasons. First, it extends the principle of treating all producers of the major commodities fairly and equitably. We are using the same components of production costs for barley and grain sorghum that the Administration used in formulating wheat, corn and upland cotton program proposals to the Congress for the Food and Agriculture Act of 1977.

Second, the vice president stated that barley producers would receive payments of approximately $208 million for barley harvested months earlier.[25]

I find the announcement interesting for two reasons (if the vice president can have two reasons, so can I). First, his explanation of the level of the target prices shows that the administration has fully embraced the cost of production concept in setting target prices. Second, while not a lawyer, I have some difficulty in understanding what authorization there is for target prices for grain sorghums and barley, in excess of the loan rates. Title V of the 1977 act states: "(D) The payment rate for grain sorghums and, if designated by the Secretary, oats and barley, shall be such rate as the Secretary determines fair and reasonable in relation to the rate at which payments are made available for corn." The payment rate for corn (the target price minus the loan rate) is zero, since the 1977 target price and loan rate are the same; the 1978 target price is only $0.10 per bushel more than the loan rate.

The feed values for barley and grain sorghums, per unit of weight, are somewhat less than for corn. Yet the target price per unit of weight is 14 percent greater for grain sorghum and 25 percent greater for barley than for corn. The fact that the 1977 target prices for barley and grain sorghum reflect neither their relative market prices (see Table 7) nor their feeding values relative to corn had no effect upon resource allocation in 1977, since the target prices were not announced until after the grains were harvested. This is not said in criticism. Unexpected political gratuities given after the fact do not waste agricultural resources. But if the same relative target prices are provided in 1978, farmers will be encouraged to substitute grain sorghums and barley for corn at the margin, since the three feed grains are included in the same

---

[25] U.S. Department of Agriculture, *News*, USDA 101-78, January 12, 1978.

set-aside acreage requirement.[26] This will almost certainly reduce feed grain output. Has manipulation of relative target prices and deficiency payments now become a tool of supply management?

The "favored" commodity of the grains included in Table 7 is and has long been wheat. The 1977–1978 farm price of wheat will be approximately the loan rate and just slightly above its feeding value relative to corn. The deficiency payments paid to wheat farmers for the 1977 wheat crop were $1.2 billion or nearly $0.60 per bushel on all wheat produced.[27]

Soybeans and cotton appear to be the Cinderellas among the crops. The soybean loan rate is well below the actual or anticipated market prices, and there are no target price and deficiency payments. It would appear from Table 7 that there should have been deficiency payments for cotton in 1977—the target price is above the loan rate and above the market price (though admittedly one month's market price is not the relevant comparison). But as noted earlier, not only was the cotton price support or loan rate designed to be below market prices, the period for determining the market price to compare with the target price differs from the specifications for the wheat and feed grain programs. For those programs the period is the first five months of the marketing year, which are normally the lowest priced months of the year. But for cotton the period for determining the market price is "the calendar year which includes the first five months of the marketing year for such crop." Thus for the 1977 cotton crop it is the average farm price for the 1977 calendar year that is relevant, and that price averaged more than $0.52 per pound.

Why are soybeans and cotton given such seemingly relative adverse treatment? Primarily because that is what the producers (or their representatives wanted). Basically these producers are more comfortable with having their fate settled by the market rather than by Washington. Soybean producers are rather more secure in their trust of the marketplace than are the cotton producers, since the latter will probably obtain modest benefit from the target price in 1978.

---

[26] In order to receive deficiency payments on the entire acreage planted in 1978, farmers will be required to reduce their planted acreages of corn and grain sorghums by 5 percent and barley by 20 percent below the 1977 acreages. However, if a farmer who grows barley meets the feed grain set-aside requirement (as well as the wheat and cotton set-aside requirements, if applicable) he is assured of the deficiency payment on 80 percent of his planted area times his program yield.

[27] The method of distributing deficiency payments in 1977 differed somewhat from that described earlier for the 1978–1981 crops. In 1977 payments were made on the acreage allotments for wheat. The national acreage allotment was 62.2 million acres, slightly below the 66.6 million acres harvested. See U.S. Department of Agriculture, Economic Research Service, *Wheat Situation*, WS-242 (November 1977), pp. 2, 19.

Supply Management and Resource Adjustment. American agriculture, particularly the grain sector, faces both short-run and long-run adjustments. The major long-run adjustment problems are found in the relatively specialized wheat producing areas, particularly in the Great Plains. Will the 1977 act contribute to appropriate adjustments or will it impede these adjustments, especially the long-run adjustments in the wheat economy? The target price for wheat significantly overvalues wheat relative to the feed grains. Generally prices for most qualities of wheat cannot depart very far from the feed value of wheat. While the feed value of wheat per bushel is approximately 10 percent greater than the feed value of corn, the target price of wheat will be at least 42 percent higher in 1978 and later years than the corn target price. This encouragement of wheat production will delay the required long-run adjustment in wheat production and the effects will be felt throughout the grain sector.

An important objective of the farm commodity legislation in effect from 1961 through 1973 was supply management or, more accurately, supply limitation in order to achieve higher prices and incomes within politically acceptable levels of federal expenditures. There is considerable disagreement concerning the reduction in supply of farm crops due to commodity programs from 1961 through 1973.[28] But there is little doubt that there was some effect.

Are the supply management features of the 1977 act as significant as those in the earlier legislation? As in earlier legislation, the commodity programs depend upon land set-asides, diversion, and reduction of crop acreages. As before, farmers will set aside or divert their least productive land, often after they know output on that area will be low. As before, incentives exist for increasing yields on land actually planted or harvested. Where deficiency payments are important, as for wheat, grain sorghums, and barley, the positive yield impacts of the 1977 act are significantly greater than under the earlier legislation. There are two important reasons. First, in the earlier legislation the yields on which payments were based were determined by average yields for three to five years, and this average was lagged two years. Under the 1977 act, the yield for 1978 payments can be the actual 1977 yield, and for future years, the actual yield for the previous year can be "proven" for purposes of receiving payments. Obviously the value of a yield in-

---

[28] For some indication of the range of estimates, see *Food and Agricultural Policy*, proceedings of a conference sponsored by the American Enterprise Institute, held in Washington, D.C., March 10–11, 1977 (Washington, D.C.: American Enterprise Institute, 1977), articles by D. Gale Johnson, Luther G. Tweeten, and George E. Brandow.

crease for a given year is greater under the 1977 act than under earlier legislation.

Second, under the earlier legislation that provided for payments (under various names), the area on which payment was based was determined by a historical base. This base was generally significantly less than actual acreage. Under the current programs, the area is the actual planted area of the crop. It is true that there are some restraints on planted area through the set-aside requirements, but as long as the set-aside requirements are met, farmers will receive deficiency payments on at least 80 percent of their planted acreage of a particular crop. Where more than one grain is grown on a farm and one of the grains is not eligible for deficiency payments, it is highly likely that most of the set-aside will be absorbed by reducing the area of the grain not eligible for deficiency payments. Since barley and wheat are the grains with the greatest ratio of deficiency payments to the loan rate, it is to be expected that in the long run a continuation of the programs announced for 1978 will fail to have much effect on the acreage of these two crops. In fact, it is quite possible that both acreage and output will be larger than if there had not been programs affecting these crops.

The 1978 programs are thought to avoid one pitfall of earlier programs. In the past, summer fallow could be included in set-aside or diverted land.[29] In those areas where summer fallow is important, this meant that a large fraction of the diversion was fictitious. For the nation as a whole, a third of the diverted acreage represented land in summer fallow, that is, land that would have been summer fallowed whether or not there were acreage limitations. Under the regulations issued for the 1978 wheat program, summer fallow land cannot be included in the set-aside area. It is not clear how another farm practice that originated to "beat the regulations" will fare, namely, the practice of skip row planting of cotton in dry areas as a means of increasing yield on the area counted as planted; the skipped area was regarded as a diverted area.[30]

Only time will tell if the summer fallow loophole has actually been closed. The 1977 act requires that the "set-aside acreage shall be devoted to conservation uses, in accordance with regulations issued by the Secretary, which will assure protection of such acreage from weeds and

[29] Summer fallow is the practice of leaving land idle for a year, but cultivating it to keep it free from weeds and in a manner designed to maximize the retention of moisture.

[30] The Johnson Law is: "Whenever there is a contest between a farmer and the bureaucracy, it can be predicted who will win." The skip row practice was to plant four rows of cotton and then skip the equivalent of four rows. The outside rows, at least, had more moisture available to them and yielded better. Previous administrators were not able to cope with this example of ingenuity.

wind and water erosion." Given the ingenuity of farmers one should not be too surprised if farmers in the areas where summer fallow is an economic practice find some type of conservation use that is almost as good as summer fallow in conserving moisture. For example, might not sparsely planted rows of wheat, spaced at forty-two inches, properly cultivated to keep out the weeds and incidentally to save moisture, constitute a conservation use? It may be very difficult, if not impossible, to write regulations to prevent an even more imaginative and effective means of having your fallow and not having it counted against you.

The deficiency payment for corn will be so low that the feed grain program will have little effect on yields. However, the grain sorghum deficiency payment for 1977 is sizable—20 percent of the loan rate. If the target price for 1978 remains at $2.28 per bushel—or is increased because the target price for corn is increased by $0.10 to $2.10 in 1978—the deficiency payment will encourage farmers to engage in yield increasing practices.

The deficiency payments for cotton could be 20 percent or more of the market price in some years. In any case, farm input decisions will be made in terms of a minimum price, not far from the target price. Farm yields will be influenced to some extent. The objective of the deficiency payments is to increase farm incomes. But the method used for the distribution of the payments is clearly inappropriate, given the assumption that farm output is too large and market prices are too low. Most of the minor effects of land set-asides on acreage will be offset—at least for wheat, barley, and grain sorghums—by the effects of the deficiency payments on yields. These effects will be gradual and may go largely unnoticed for some time, but they will be real, and the long-run disequilibrium will grow, and so will the governmental costs of the programs.

Risk faced by farmers will be reduced by the target prices and loan rates. While most agricultural economists believe that reducing risk has a positive output effect, unfortunately we have not been able to measure the magnitude of the effect.

Stability of Farm Prices. One of the desired consequences of the 1977 act is to *increase* price instability for the major farm crops, in contrast to the situation prevailing for several years prior to 1972. During that period the market prices of wheat, feed grains, and cotton were remarkably stable and, most farmers thought, remarkably low. The primary reason was the nature of the price supports and the large levels of stocks of many farm products owned or controlled by the Commodity Credit Corporation. During most of that time the Commodity Credit Corporation sold its stocks at prices near the loan rate.

198

The farmer-held grain reserve program, described earlier combined with the rules on the sales of grain owned by the Commodity Credit Corporation may permit substantial price variations (see Table 6). When there is any grain in the farmer-held reserve, the Commodity Credit Corporation cannot sell any of its grain for less than 150 percent of the respective loan rates. Thus if any wheat remained in the reserve, even if the ccc held substantial stocks of feed grains, the feed grains could not be sold at less than 150 percent of the loan rate for the feed grains. Somewhat more unlikely, the extended wheat reserves could be exhausted but feed grains remained in the program, and the ccc could not sell the wheat it owned for less than $3.52 per bushel unless the wheat loan rate had been reduced below $2.35.

It should be recalled that the extended grain reserve programs are now in effect. While the feed grains in the reserve can be called when the farm market price reaches 140 percent of the loan rate, the wheat cannot be called until the farm price reaches 175 percent of the loan rate. These price features of the loan and storage programs were designed to give greater freedom to the market and to provide at least some chance that market prices could move above the loan levels. It is still too early to predict what the effects will be upon the amounts of grain stored and the accumulated costs of storage.

On the whole, I believe that these features of the 1977 act are generally desirable, though it would have been better if the call and release prices for wheat had been the same as for corn. How well the system will actually function will depend upon the actual supply and demand situations. If the quantities of the various farm crops in most years are greater than the amount demanded at the loan rates, then stock accumulations will become serious economic and political problems. This prospect makes the output-inducing effects of the commodity programs a very serious matter for both farmers and taxpayers.

The above remarks do not apply to the cotton program. There is no extended reserve program for cotton. Cotton producers did not want as much price instability as the law potentially provided for wheat and feed grain producers. Imports of upland or short staple cotton are strictly limited by an import quota. When the market price of cotton (as defined in the legislation) exceeds 130 percent of the average market price of cotton for the preceding thirty-six months, the President is required to establish a global special import quota "equal to twenty-one days of domestic mill consumption of upland cotton at the seasonally adjusted average rate of the most recent three months for which data are available."

Since a major fraction of U.S. cotton is exported—approximately

40 percent of production during the past five years[31]—and domestic and international prices of cotton are the same if there are no export subsidies, the economic consequences of this imaginative provision are difficult to discern. The special import quota would only affect domestic cotton prices if domestic supply were less than domestic demand and there were no cotton exports, and domestic prices rose above the amount specified in the legislation. It has been a long time—somewhat more than a century—since we had a year when we did not export cotton. But all is not lost; the time spent in devising this ingenious but nugatory section could have been devoted to a section that would have had adverse effects.

Other Farm Programs

Dairy Program. The dairy program in the 1977 legislation differs from previous programs only in detail. It relies on a price support for manufactured dairy products (butter, cheese, nonfat dry milk). The price support is made effective by government purchases. When the market price is at or below the price support level, the government purchases enough of the relevant dairy product to keep the market price at the promised level. There is not now, nor has there been, any effort to limit the output of dairy products. However, the domestic price support program is made possible by tight quantitative controls on the imports of dairy products. Imports are held to less than 2 percent of U.S. milk production.

The 1977 act requires that the dairy price support be at not less than 80 percent of parity until March 31, 1979, when the price support can range between 75 and 90 percent of parity. Under the 1973 act, except for the first few months of its applicability, the dairy price supports were to be between 75 and 90 percent of parity.

The increase of the minimum level of price support to 80 percent until March 31, 1979 may have been an *ex post* justification of President Carter's increase of the dairy price support to $9.00 per hundredweight, effective April 1, 1977. The almost 10 percent increase in the price support (from $8.26) was apparently a response to a campaign promise made at the time of the Wisconsin primary by the then candidate for the Democratic party's presidential nomination. The increase in the dairy price support came at a time that government stocks of dairy products were increasing and feed prices were decreasing. There was no evidence that the profitability of milk production was deteriorating with the then prevailing price support level.

---

[31] U.S. Department of Agriculture, Economic Research Service, *Cotton and Wool Situation*, CWS-13 (November 1977), p. 29.

The consequences of the price support increase were predictable. Milk production increased slightly and consumption was less than it would have been. In just six months—April through September 1977—the government acquired somewhat more milk (in the form of products) than during the full year starting April 1, 1976.[32] On November 1, 1976, governmental stocks of dairy products were nil; a year later the milk equivalent of the stocks held was more than 3 percent of annual milk production. In the fiscal year 1976–1977 (starting October 1, 1976), net support purchases of milk products was $710 million; in the preceding fifteen-month period, net purchases cost $113 million.[33] Keeping campaign promises can be expensive, for many of us.

There is one feature of the calculation of parity prices that favors dairy producers. Parity prices are no longer tied directly to the 1910–1914 prices received by farmers. For all farm products, the parity ratio—the prices received index divided by the parity index—is still based on 1910–1914, but for individual commodities there is an adjusted base (1910–1914) price which is the average price of the commodity for the most recent 120-month average of prices received, divided by the parity index for the same period of time. This calculation is made annually. For the 1978 calendar year the milk adjusted base price is $1.90 per hundredweight, or 18 percent above the actual 1910–1914 price. But for corn the adjusted base price was $0.495 per bushel, 24 percent below the 1910–1914 price.[34] While the corn adjusted base price reflects whatever direct payments were received during the most recent ten years, most of the relative price relationships for the 120-month period reflected the fact that corn prices were determined in the international market, while dairy prices were determined in a highly protected domestic market and as part of a price support program involving substantial governmental purchases and disposal. As long as Congress establishes the minimum level of price support for dairy products in terms of a fixed percentage of parity, present and past price support levels will influence future price support levels. This is probably not what Congress had in mind in revising the parity formula, but it is exactly what has happened and will continue to occur.

Peanuts. The 1977 act changed the peanut program, but not by very much. While governmental costs will be reduced to some extent, the

---

[32] U.S. Department of Agriculture, Economic Research Service, *Dairy Situation*, DS-368 (December 1977), p. 23.

[33] Ibid., p. 24.

[34] U.S. Department of Agriculture, Crop Reporting Board, *Agricultural Prices*, Pr 1(1-78) (January 31, 1978), pp. 4–5.

new program will cost consumers as much as the one it replaces. And that cost can hardly be said to be "peanuts."

The new program establishes a two-price system for peanuts. A national poundage quota is established and is allocated to individual farms that produce peanuts. Acreage allotments are continued, and farmers who market peanuts from an area larger than their acreage allotment face a very substantial penalty—120 percent of the loan level for the quota peanuts.

The legislation establishes minimum national poundage quotas for each year from 1978 through 1981, declining from 1,680,000 short tons in the first year to 1,440,000 short tons in the last year. Even the smallest of the quotas is substantially larger than the domestic use of peanuts for food. In recent years peanuts used for food (peanut butter and peanuts) plus use as seed (included in the poundage quota) has never reached 700,000 short tons. The 1978 poundage quota is only 13 percent below the peak production of the last two decades.[35]

The minimum price support for quota peanuts was set at $420 per short ton (21 cents per pound) of peanuts in the shell. A lower price support is to be established for additional or above quota peanuts. Presumably this price support will reflect price expectations in the export market and/or the value of peanut oil and meal derived by crushing the peanuts. Based on recent prices of oil and meal, the price of the additional peanuts could be in the range of 11 to 13 cents. If the peanuts are sold for export at approximately their crushing value, this would be equivalent to an export subsidy approximately equal to half the support price for quota peanuts.

Since the higher support price will not apply to all peanuts produced, as it has in the past, governmental costs will be reduced since a smaller quantity of peanuts will have to be disposed of in lower priced markets. However, domestic consumers must continue to pay a substantially higher price—on the average—than would be required in an uncontrolled market.

The new program represents some additional improvements over the old one. Under the old program's acreage allotments, farmers were induced by the profitable price of peanuts to emphasize yield increases, thus increasing the cost of producing peanuts. Under the new program's poundage quotas farmers will be in a better position to produce more peanuts at the lowest possible cost. Since the farmers must maintain some control over their peanut acreage, their response will not be an entirely unfettered one. But at least the change is in the appropriate direction. If farmers produce a substantial quantity of additional pea-

[35] *Agricultural Statistics*, 1977, pp. 123, 126.

nuts, we may also obtain a better idea of what it costs to produce peanuts, since such peanuts will receive a price substantially below the price for quota peanuts. If a farmer does not produce enough peanuts to meet his poundage quota in one year, the deficit will be added to his quota for the next year, thereby giving him relatively little incentive to produce more peanuts than is required to fulfill the quota—unless production is profitable at the expected lower price for the additional peanuts.

Rice. The 1977 act continued, with minor adjustments, the program created by the 1975 Rice Production Act. This act introduced the target price concept that had been applied two years earlier to wheat, feed grains, and cotton to rice. Before 1973 the loan rate often resulted in market prices that were above international market prices and rice exports required export subsidies. The target price approach permitted a lower loan rate which was less likely to interfere with exports. In most recent years the United States exported approximately 60 percent of its total rice production and is one of the world's two or three largest exporters of rice.

The 1977 act continues national and farm acreage allotments. Farmers need not limit their acreage to their allotment, but the deficiency payments triggered by the target price as well as the loan rates apply only to production on the acreage allotment.

Rice is produced on a relatively small number of large farms—15,000 farms in 1975. In 1976 the value of U.S. rice production was $776 million or an average of approximately $50,000 per farm.[36]

The target price for 1978 and subsequent years starts from the 1977 target price of $8.25 per hundredweight of rough rice. It is to be adjusted annually by the same formula used for wheat and the feed grains—a moving average of certain costs of production components. It should be noted that for 1977–1978 the farm price of rice will almost certainly be above the target price, though that was not the case in 1976–1977 when deficiency payments of $1.70 per hundredweight were paid. There is also a loan program for rice with a minimum level of $6.31 per hundredweight.[37]

Sugar. The relatively free market for American sugar had a short life. It was born January 1, 1975, and died October 5, 1977, when President Carter announced a program to assure sugar growers 13.5 cents per

---

[36] Ibid., pp. 19, 527.
[37] U.S. Department of Agriculture, Economic Research Service, *Rice Situation*, RS-30 (October 1977), pp. 6–7.

pound of raw sugar. After a number of false starts, a price support loan program was announced on November 8. Loans were to be available for refined beet sugar at 14.24 cents per pound and at 13.5 cents per pound for cane sugar (raw value).

Since the world price of raw sugar has been substantially below 13.5 cents per pound and the prevailing tariff of 1.875 cents per pound resulted in a U.S. price below the loan rate, it was necessary to take further actions to prevent all of the U.S. produced sugar from going under loans and staying there. Section 22 of the Agricultural Adjustment Act of 1933 gives the President authority to impose import fees. On November 11, 1977, he imposed the maximum import fee permitted by the legislation—50 percent ad valorem. But this was not enough, even on top of a tariff rate of 1.875 cents. Thus it was necessary to increase the tariff rate to 2.1825 cents per pound. The effects of these actions were to increase the retail price of sugar by 15 to 20 percent.

To add to the comedy of errors, no one bothered to inform the President that refined sugar sold at a higher price than raw sugar, and since the import fee was the same for raw and refined sugar, increasingly the sugar imported was refined rather than raw. This error was subsequently corrected (if that is the proper description).

The 13.5 cent support price is, in effect, a guarantee to the processors of sugar. In order to receive that price the processors were required to pay at least the following prices per short ton to producers: sugar beets, $22.84; and sugar cane, $17.48. These prices were for products containing specific percentages of sucrose. Prices for Texas and Hawaii were set in terms of the actual amount of sugar, raw value, recovered from the sugar cane; for Texas the price was 8.10 cents per pound and Hawaii, 8.91 cents per pound.[38]

How do the prices for the 1977 crop compare with prices under the earlier sugar acts? From 1967 through 1972 the farm price of sugar beets, in 1967 dollars, averaged approximately $13.20.[39] If the 1977 sugar beet price of $22.84 is deflated by the cost of living index for the first half of 1977, the price in 1967 dollars is $11.59, or some 12 percent below the average price from 1967 through 1972. Similar calculations made for sugar cane result in an average per ton price for 1967 through 1972, in 1967 dollars, of $9.26. If the 1977 price of sugar cane is calculated in 1967 dollars, it is $8.87 or 4 percent below the 1967–1972 average price.

---

[38] U.S. Department of Agriculture, *News*, USDA 2855-77 (October 5, 1977) and *Agricultural Outlook*, AO-28 (December 1977), p. 6.

[39] *Agricultural Statistics*, 1977, pp. 76, 79. Sugar beet prices for 1969 were not included in the average price for 1967–1972 because of low sugar content of that crop. The sugar cane prices exclude Hawaii.

The decline in real returns to sugar producers is even greater than the decline in the real prices. During 1967–1972 sugar beet producers received payments equal to approximately 15 percent of the price they received, while sugar cane producers in the continental United States had payments equal to approximately 11 percent of the farm price. Thus the reductions in real returns per unit of output is more than a fourth for sugar beets and about 15 percent for sugar cane. It is not obvious why the reduction in real price is significantly greater for sugar beets than for sugar cane.

From 1967 through 1972 the tariff on raw sugar was 0.625 cents per pound. In addition there was an excise tax of 0.5 cents per pound on all raw sugar refined in the United States; because of the protection provided for sugar refining by the Sugar Act, virtually all sugar consumed in the United States was refined domestically. If one adds the excise tax to the duty paid price of raw sugar in New York, the 1967–1972 average price of raw sugar, in 1967 dollars, was 7.77 cents per pound.[40] The 13.5 cents per pound of raw sugar for 1977 equals approximately 6.2 cents in 1967 dollars, or almost 20 percent below the average deflated price for 1967–1972.

There may be a number of reasons why the sugar industry, and their congressional supporters, accepted a substantial reduction in the real price of sugar. But an important reason was undoubtedly the development during the early 1970s of an economical method of making high-fructose syrup from corn. With corn at approximately $2.00 per bushel, the production of fructose is profitable at a price of approximately 14.0 to 14.5 cents per pound, dry basis. This large potential source of a sweetener made it desirable to hold the price of sugar at something approximating the price actually chosen.

While the return of a sugar price support program is to be regretted, especially by those who supported the elimination of the sugar program in 1974, the current program is an improvement over the old.[41] As yet, there are no import quotas, so that low cost foreign producers can compete for the American market. Under earlier programs, sugar imports were controlled by country quotas. Further, as noted, the real price of raw sugar has been reduced substantially. But the rate of nominal protection remains very high at approximately 80 percent for the 1977–1978 crop season. It remains a relevant question why the United States should persist in producing a crop at costs so much above

---

[40] *Agricultural Statistics*, 1977, p. 89.

[41] For a description and analysis of sugar programs prior to 1975, see D. Gale Johnson, *The Sugar Program: Large Costs and Small Benefits* (Washington, D.C.: American Enterprise Institute, 1974).

the price at which adequate supplies would be forthcoming. There is nothing in the 1977 act that indicates any reduction in the commitment to produce approximately half of our sugar domestically. The price support level for 1978 is to be not less than the higher of 52.5 percent of parity price or 13.5 cents per pound, raw value. The 1977 act, it should be noted, applies only to the 1977 and 1978 sugar crops.

International Trade Implications

The major farm crop programs—wheat, feed grains, and cotton—as well as the rice program are likely to have relatively little effect upon the movement of these products into international markets. It is essential to the prosperity of American agriculture that governmental programs not interfere with exports of the major crop products. The output from approximately one acre out of every three on which a crop is grown in the United States is exported.

It is the support levels that could have a negative impact upon exports. As noted above, the cotton support level is to be set only after there is a reasonably good indication of what the market price will be for the crop year and then only at 85 percent of the market price. The real minimum price support levels for wheat and corn at $2.00 and $1.75 per bushel, respectively, are sufficiently low to avoid significant interference with exports.

Market prices for our major farm export products are unlikely to be significantly affected by the program. If there is an effect on market prices, the effect is as likely to be to lower prices as to increase them. The programs, through the target prices and deficiency payments, have incentives that will have a positive impact upon production. These incentives may well have a greater effect on production than the set-asides and acreage diversions that are designed to reduce production. The significant reduction of risks due both to the target prices and to the disaster payments will also have a positive production impact.

While there is little likelihood that the programs will have an adverse direct effect upon the volume of agricultural exports, it should be recognized that the differences between the target prices and the export prices leave us open to the charge of dumping and place us in a weaker position to oppose the agricultural price and trade policies of major importing nations. While the target prices are substantially below the support prices in most importing nations or regions, such as the European Economic Community, we cannot argue that American farmers are making their production decisions in response to market prices. While we have used export subsidies before and farmers have received payments in addition to market prices, the fact that deficiency payments are now proportional to production weakens the argument that could be made previously, namely, that the payments represented an income transfer. As noted earlier, in the past, payments were tied to allotments fixed on an historical base, while under the 1977 act payments are related quite directly to current production. While the payments under earlier legislation had some effects on output levels, the effects were much smaller than can be anticipated from the current programs.

Costs: Taxpayers and Consumers. It is too early to estimate what the governmental costs of the 1977 act as modified by the Emergency Agricultural Act of 1978 will be for 1978–1979, either in total or in comparison with the costs if the previous legislation had been renewed. For one thing, significant discretion was given to the secretary of agriculture in the 1977 act, and he used that discretion in a manner that increased costs by more than $1.2 billion over the estimates made by the Congressional Budget Office and by J. B. Penn of the Council for Economic Advisers.[42] The increases in governmental costs made under the 1977 act were due to the substantial deficiency payments for barley and grain sorghums that were unexpectedly introduced for the 1977 crop and will be continued at the same or higher levels for the 1978 crop. The land diversion payments for feed grains and cotton and the payments for the wheat grazing and hay programs were not anticipated. In addition, the Emergency Agricultural Act of 1978 resulted in an increase in the wheat target price, which could increase deficiency payments by more than $650 million.

It is probable that substantial storage costs will be incurred. Storage payments for the farmer-held extended reserve program could exceed $250 million per year. Interest costs are not counted in this figure and under some circumstances could involve the same annual cost. In addition, there will be storage and interest costs incurred in the regular Commodity Credit Corporation commodity loan programs.

Penn's estimates of budgetary costs of the commodity legislation, which seemed reasonable when made in late summer 1977, were that annual outlays would average $4.8 billion for fiscal years 1978 through 1981.[43] As indicated above, budgetary costs for the commodity programs will almost certainly exceed the amounts indicated. Additional costs of at least $1.7 billion have been identified; they are due to the

---

[42] J. B. Penn, "Some Implications of the 1977 Food and Agriculture Legislation," in National Public Policy Committee, *Increasing Understanding of Public Problems and Policies—1977* (Chicago: Farm Foundation, 1977), p. 92.

[43] Ibid., pp. 92–93.

administrative flexibility in the 1977 act and the politically motivated Emergency Agricultural Act of 1978.

Except for dairy products and peanuts, consumer costs will not be significantly affected by the 1977 act. As noted in the discussion of the international trade implications of the commodity programs, market prices will not be affected very much.

Concluding Comments

I conclude this paper with a simple but important observation: In the political management of American agriculture, public officials mislead farmers concerning prospective economic developments that will have an adverse effect upon American agriculture, and these officials hold out hopes of favorable changes, which while remote in prospect may have some small chance of occurring. I do not intend to impugn the integrity or honesty of any of the public officials who have held important responsibilities for the development and execution of agricultural policy and programs. I have known most of them personally and have the highest regard for them.

The fact that we hold elections every other year makes it exceedingly difficult for a public official to be a "bearer of bad news" and puts a high premium upon emphasizing favorable prospects. This can be easily illustrated by the behavior of the last two national administrations. It was rather obvious in 1974 and early 1975 that the relatively high farm prices and incomes that had prevailed since 1972 were a temporary phenomenon and could not last much longer. Yet this was not the message that emanated from Washington, though there was sufficient evidence in studies of the U.S. Department of Agriculture to make it clear that the favorable factors were transitory.

The current administration appears to be behaving in a similar manner. In the latter months of 1977 two high officials of the U.S. Department of Agriculture stated that one of the foundations of our agricultural and trade policies was that the world faces a long-run food crisis which could be of greater significance than the energy crisis. The similarity of language about prospective food shortages in the two speeches, with the implication of much higher farm product prices by reference to energy price changes, suggests that it represents official and accepted views, at least as seen by the department's speech writers.

While one can assume that farmers view with more than a little skepticism the optimistic statements of public officials, more straight forward presentations would be preferable, though it would be unreasonable to expect them. A significant cost of governmental involvement in agricultural production and prices is the reduction in the quality of information provided to the public generally and to farmers in particular.

In the first part of this essay, I noted that the Agricultural Act of 1977, in spite of a number of defects, was a rather better piece of legislation than one might have expected, given the setting in which the legislation was created. In effect, I implied that things could have been worse; the legislation could have been more restrictive and could have imposed greater costs upon consumers and taxpayers; it could have more seriously impeded the necessary short- and long-run adjustments in agriculture. Unfortunately, things have gotten worse since the 1977 act was passed. In response to political pressures, the administration announced relatively high target prices for barley and grain sorghums in January 1978. Congress and the administration increased to $3.40 per bushel the target price for wheat, which had already been too high at $3.00 per bushel to reflect its long-run market value. Establishing the cotton loan rate at a specific figure of $0.48 per pound, rather than permitting it to be largely determined by market forces, represented a backward step.

This is not the place to indicate in detail what agricultural policy measures should have been taken in 1977 and 1978. However, one major point may be made. While the legislation recognized the absolute necessity of minimizing interference with current market prices, the 1977 act and subsequent modifications failed completely to address the long-run adjustment problems facing the grain production sector. The high target prices for wheat contribute not to adjustment but to the maintenance of a situation that is not viable in the long run. The features of previous agricultural legislation that divorced most of the payments from current production decisions were abandoned. The 1977 act is likely to result in a higher level of production of wheat, and perhaps also of barley and grain sorghums, than would have resulted if there were no farm program, or if the target and loan rates in the 1973 legislation had been updated to reflect fully the effects of inflation since 1973. It is surely not in the long-run interest of American farmers to encourage even a modest expansion of grain production at this time.

If the incomes of some farmers are too low to be politically acceptable, it would have been preferable to have addressed that issue directly through income transfers unrelated to current production. Admittedly it is difficult to justify significant income transfers to farm families with assets measured in the hundreds of thousands of dollars, but that is exactly what the current legislation does. Unfortunately the current transfers impede resource adjustments and will, in fact, justify the continuation of the transfers for many years to come.

Reflections on the U.S. Trade Deficit and the Floating Dollar

Gottfried Haberler

Summary

The enormous increase in the U.S. trade deficit in 1977 and the sharp decline of the dollar in the fourth quarter of 1977 and early 1978 came as a great surprise. The heavy emphasis in U.S. official statements on a quick adoption of an energy policy as a remedy for the weakness of the dollar is misplaced and has backfired. On the whole, exchange rate changes have gone in the right direction. The three countries whose currencies have sharply appreciated—Germany, Japan, and Switzerland—have recently enjoyed much lower inflation rates than the United States and large current account surpluses.

Under fixed exchanges a balance of payments deficit is a "burden" because it requires monetary retrenchment. Under floating the situation is much more complicated. The OPEC surplus is not a burden on the rest of the world. On the contrary, it lightens the real burden—the oil price increase—at least temporarily. The large U.S. trade deficit should not be regarded as a drag on the economy but rather as a contribution to the anti-inflation policy. True, a decline of the trade deficit, caused by the depreciation of the dollar or an expansion in the surplus countries, would constitute an expansionary factor for the U.S. economy. But why should this expansion be less inflationary than an expansion through a domestic monetary-fiscal stimulus? The answer could be that there is more slack in the traded-goods industries than elsewhere. This hypothesis is discussed and rejected. Unemployment has led to strong protectionist pressures, to many of which the administration has yielded by imposing import restrictions, which in turn add to inflationary pressure. It is said that the trade deficit undermines the confidence of foreign dollar holders, which depresses the dollar and

211

thereby intensifies the inflation. The dollar is still the world's foremost official and private reserve and transactions currency. The emergence of potential rivals in that role, the German mark, Swiss franc, and Japanese yen, has brought with it the danger of shifts out of the huge foreign-held dollar balances. The basic factor inducing attempts at diversification of international (and domestic) dollar reserves is the large inflation differential between the United States and the three strong currency countries. The market realizes that the currencies of the low-inflation countries have a long-run tendency to appreciate. The incentive to diversify would quickly diminish if the U.S. inflation rate were reduced close to the rate in the rival currency countries by a credible U.S. anti-inflation policy. The so-called locomotive strategy of pressuring the strong currency countries to expand faster is tantamount to an attempt to eliminate the inflation differential by inflating the low-inflation countries rather than disinflating the high-inflation countries. This approach and its latest version, the "convoy" strategy, are criticized on the ground that they would intensify worldwide inflationary tendencies, which would sooner or later lead to another worldwide recession. It is pointed out that the locomotive and convoy strategy is especially ill-advised from the point of view of the policy's strongest advocate—Britain—because simultaneous inflationary expansion in all industrial countries would lead to an unsustainable commodity boom, as in 1972–1973, which would turn the terms of trade sharply against Britain.

The policy of heavy interventions in the exchange market, ostensibly to prevent "disorderly" conditions in the exchange market, is critically examined, and the meaning, under floating, of over- and undervaluation of a currency and "international competitiveness" is discussed. In a Digression on Inflation the tax-based incomes policy (TIP) is subjected to a critical analysis, and finally some conclusions are drawn with regard to the future of the international monetary system.

Introduction

The large increase in the U.S. trade and current account deficit in 1977 and the sharp depreciation of the dollar in the second half of 1977 and in 1978, reflecting mainly an appreciation of the deutsche mark, Swiss franc, and yen, have caught everybody by surprise. The huge increase in petroleum imports is almost universally regarded as the main cause of this development (apart from a cyclical component in the deficit). The U.S. administration, from the President down, emphasizes that cause for political reasons, to sell its energy program. Every official American statement on the dollar intones parrot-like: *Ceterum censeo Energiam esse regulendam.*

The excessive American emphasis on oil has backfired. The theme has been eagerly taken up abroad; more and more foreign official statements complain that the lack of a credible U.S. energy policy is the most important cause of the U.S. trade deficit and of the decline of the dollar, threatening the existing international monetary system. This reaction is not hard to understand. It is always convenient to be able to blame Uncle Sam for every trouble in the world, and, more specifically, the self-admitted failure of the United States to adopt a coherent energy program provides a handy answer to American criticism of other countries' policies. Most private as well as official prescriptions for dealing with the dollar problem list the adoption of an energy policy as the most important step.

It is, of course, true that the enormous rise in the oil price and the resulting large trade surpluses of the OPEC countries had a profound impact on the pattern of international payments. To a large extent the U.S. deficit can be regarded as a reflection of the OPEC surplus.

Nevertheless, the heavy emphasis on the U.S. energy policy as a *remedy* for the U.S. trade deficit is misplaced and unfortunate. For large oil import requirements are likely to continue for a considerable time. Even an efficient energy policy that would rely on market forces to stimulate domestic production (instead of trying—as the policy now under consideration does—to substitute government regulation by a large, self-perpetuating bureaucracy) would take several years to effect a sharp reduction in the import demand for oil.

Actually the dollar value of non-oil imports, especially imports of manufactures from abroad, have grown rapidly in recent years in absolute terms, much more than the growth of oil imports. This fact has one favorable implication: Unlike oil imports, imports of manufactured goods can be expected to be reduced by the depreciation of the dollar.

In the last few years, during the period of widespread floating, exchange rate changes have by and large gone in the right direction. The three strong currency countries, Germany, Japan, and Switzerland, have enjoyed large trade and current account surpluses, and the inflation rate in Germany and Switzerland has been way below the U.S. rate—below 4 percent in Germany, and practically zero in Switzerland. True, until recently the consumer price index has been rising about as fast in Japan as in the United States. But it is well known that in Japan, unlike the United States, the index of wholesale and export prices, especially of manufactured goods, tends to rise much less rapidly than the consumer price index. Measured in terms of wholesale and export prices, inflation has been much lower in Japan than in the United States.

An appreciation of the three currencies was therefore to be expected.[1] In summer and early fall of 1977, many experts, Edward Bernstein and Rimmer de Vries among them, were of the opinion that the dollar was significantly overvalued, and in the third quarter of 1977 the dollar declined significantly. As late as December 1977 the highly respected *World Financial Markets* (Morgan Guaranty Trust, New York) expressed the opinion that "it would appear from the trends in relative prices and current accounts that the recent exchange rate readjustment by and large has been necessary and will bring about balance of payment adjustment, notwithstanding some 'disruptions of exchange markets.' "

Then in the last week of December 1977 and the first days of January 1978 the dollar again fell sharply vis-à-vis the major currencies. This unexpected development led to a shift in the U.S. policy. The Treasury and the Federal Reserve announced on January 4 that they would intervene actively in the exchange markets to check speculation, and two days later the Federal Reserve Board decided to raise the discount rate from 6 to 6½ percent for the expressly stated purpose of supporting the dollar on the foreign exchange markets. This was the first time since the start of floating that money was tightened for balance of payments reasons. But since inflation in the United States is still unacceptably high, we cannot really say that there exists a "dilemma case," that is to say a conflict between the requirements of internal and external equilibrium. Thus the rise of the discount rate can be justified on grounds of domestic policy objectives, that is to say, as a measure to wind down inflation. After all, short-term interest rates *in real terms* are still zero or negative, hardly an equilibrium situation. However, another dilemma, namely that of stagflation, still is unresolved. To that problem I shall return presently.

Most experts are now (early 1978) convinced that at the present rate the dollar is no longer overvalued and may be undervalued—in other words, that the competitiveness of American industries has been restored or more than restored. If that judgment is correct, as it may

---

[1] From 1976 to 1977 wholesale prices of nonfood manufactures rose in Japan by 0.5 percent (November to November) down from 6.6 percent the year before, in the United States by 6.6 percent (December to December) up from 5.5 percent the year before, in Germany by 1.4 percent (December to December) down from 4.2 percent the year before. (See *World Financial Markets* [New York: Morgan Guaranty Trust Company, February 1978], p. 4.) The consumer price index tells the same story: In 1977 and 1978 inflation has decelerated significantly in Germany, Japan, Belgium, and the Netherlands and remained practically at zero in Switzerland, while in the United States it got stuck at 6½ percent in 1977 and is accelerating again in 1978. (See OECD: *Main Economic Indicators* [Paris] and IMF *International Financial Statistics.*)

well be, it should soon be confirmed by a decline in the U.S. trade deficit. But such an improvement will not last very long unless the inflation differential between the United States and the three countries disappears. More on this later.

Current Account Deficits under Floating— Burden or Benefit?

Under fixed exchange rates a prolonged large current account deficit that does not reflect (is not offset by) autonomous capital flows, in other words, a deficit that mirrors (is financed by) a loss of international reserves, is a "burden" or a deflationary factor, because under the rules of the game it forces the central bank to tighten money. Under floating the balance of payments constraint is removed in the sense that the central bank is no longer obligated to react by tightening money. This does not mean, however, that under floating a country cannot have a prolonged large current account deficit or that a run of such deficits cannot be the subject of legitimate concern.

There is much confusion or even contradictory reasoning on these points. The emergence of a large deficit is regarded by some as a failure of the floating rate system to adjust the balance of payments and as a serious drag on the U.S. economy. As a result, the U.S. government has been urging Germany and Japan to reduce their surpluses or develop deficits by fiscal and monetary expansion in order to lighten the "burden" of weaker neighbors and less developed countries, which have been carrying, it is said, a disproportionately large share of the irrepressible oil deficit. In this connection the United States has been praised as a shining example because it has permitted a deficit in its own balance of payments.

In reality the OPEC surplus is not a burden on the rest of the world, but the opposite. The fact that the OPEC countries have not stepped up their imports *pari passu* with their swollen receipts lightens what is a burden—the oil price increase—at least temporarily. This is implicitly acknowledged when it is urged that the petrodollars should be recycled from the lucky recipients to other less fortunate countries. Recycling is the opposite of relieving the beneficiary countries of the burden of a deficit; it is meant to benefit them by allowing them to run a deficit.

In general, for a less developed country, in fact for any country that wishes to speed up its growth by supplementing domestic capital formation by importing capital from abroad, a trade deficit, however financed, is not a burden but a means of furthering its legitimate or at any rate rational aspiration. It is possible that public or private investment projects financed by borrowing abroad are ill-conceived or over-ambitious and thus turn out to be a burden, or that countries borrow abroad to finance excessive consumption, but that does not change the principle that capital imports if properly used constitute a potentially beneficial option.

Why should the American current account deficit be judged differently from that of other countries? From a cosmopolitan standpoint it can be argued that a rich country should export capital and not import it. But from the national standpoint, from the standpoint of maximizing American GNP or economic welfare, why should the importation of capital be a negative factor? Surely, the statement that the oil importers are better off if the oil exporters do not insist on being paid instantaneously in terms of real goods but accept IOUS instead, applies to rich as well as to the poor oil importer. Furthermore, why should capital imports from other countries such as Japan be judged differently from capital imports from OPEC countries?

There are several possible answers to this question which raise important issues. The straightforward Keynesian answer was given by Edward Bernstein and Paul McCracken. McCracken puts it very lucidly this way:

> From 1975 . . . to 1977, our merchandise trade position has shifted from a $9 billion net export surplus to a $30 billion net export deficit. This is another way of saying that the total demand for output during these two years increased $39 billion more than demand for domestic output, because a part of the . . . increase in [total] demand took the form of enlarged purchases from abroad. . . . If that $39 billion had been spent on [domestic rather than foreign ouput] employment would have been substantially larger. It is probably safe to assume that this deterioration in our trade had an employment cost of at least a million jobs.[2]

My trouble with this analysis is the following: True, if our trade balance disappeared, for example because Germany and Japan follow the American advice to inflate or simply because of the depreciation of the dollar, aggregate demand for U.S. output would increase. But can we be sure that this increase in nominal GNP will result in larger output and employment and will not be absorbed by higher prices (inflation)?

---

[2] Paul W. McCracken, "The Dollar and Economic Growth," *Wall Street Journal*, January 26, 1978. On the basis of an essentially similar type of reasoning Edward Bernstein, focusing on the balance of goods and services and GNP rather than on trade and employment, reached the conclusion that the real GNP growth (and therefore employment) has been significantly reduced by the deterioration of the balance of payments.

The orthodox Keynesian answer, adopted by Bernstein and McCracken, is that with much unemployment and underutilized capacity there is no need to worry about inflation. But if that is so, why wait for a change in the balance of payments? Why not simply adopt a more expansionary monetary or fiscal policy?

Here we encounter the problem of stagflation, the coexistence of inflation and unemployment. I have expressed my views on stagflation on other occasions.[3] To repeat briefly: The experience of the last few years has shown conclusively that comparatively high rates of measured unemployment and underutilization of capacity are not incompatible with inflation. Unlike some extreme monetarists, I do not doubt that in the very short run monetary expansion, however brought about, would increase output and employment, in other words would not go entirely into higher prices. But I do believe that because of the long experience with inflation and the resulting high sensitivity of inflationary expectations we are now closer to the extreme monetarist than to the Keynesian position. It follows that we should look at the trade deficit while it lasts as a (small) contribution to the fight against inflation and not as a threat to employment. If and when the trade deficit declines a somewhat tighter monetary-fiscal policy would be required to prevent inflation from accelerating.

Let me put the argument in a somewhat different form. Suppose a current account deficit had not developed in the first place, for example because Germany and Japan had followed the American advice to inflate their economies or to appreciate their currencies sufficiently to keep their emerging surpluses and our deficit at a minimum, or because the United States (horrible thought) had restricted imports.[4] Then demand for U.S. output would have been that much higher. Can we be sure that this increase in nominal demand would have gone wholly or predominantly into quantities (real output and employment) and not into prices? In 1976 and 1977 the United States had a respectable *real* expansion. Monetary and fiscal policy was, and still is, engaged in a delicate balancing act. It tries to expand nominal demand sufficiently to keep *real* expansion going, but at the same time it seeks to restrain inflation by preventing an excessively fast rise in nominal aggregate demand. Nobody can be quite sure that the actual speed of expansion is the optimal one. But two things should be kept in mind: First, the actually prevailing rate of inflation of 6.5 or 7 percent is gen-

---

[3] See, for example, William Fellner, ed., *Contemporary Economic Problems 1976* (Washington, D.C.: American Enterprise Institute, 1976), pp. 255–272, and William Fellner, ed., *Contemporary Economic Problems 1977* (Washington, D.C.: American Enterprise Institute, 1977), p. 277.

[4] I abstract here from possible foreign reaction to such a policy.

erally regarded as too high and unsustainable. Second, moderation in the speed of real expansion is widely viewed as essential for sustained real recovery. Thus, by moderating the speed of expansion the U.S. trade deficit has made a contribution to long-run stability and growth.[5]

It seems wrong to pick out one factor—the foreign balance—and to declare categorically that if it increased then real GNP and employment would be that much larger, without even asking the question how such a change would fit into the present balancing act of overall demand management.

Are there any reasons to believe that an expansion in aggregate demand for "domestic output" brought about by an improvement in the trade balance is in some way more desirable, more effective, and less inflationary than an equal expansion brought about by a domestic monetary-fiscal stimulus? There may be special conditions suggesting an affirmative answer, such as a higher rate of unemployment in the export- or import-competing (traded-goods) industries than elsewhere. This is probably a more important consideration for countries that depend to a much greater extent on international trade than the United States does. Thus, there has been much discussion in Britain on the advantage of "export-led growth" as compared with domestically induced growth. This alleged advantage depends partly on the balance of payments constraint under fixed exchanges (and is therefore no longer relevant) and partly on structural factors such as sectoral unemployment in traded-goods industries due to lack of labor mobility or potential increasing return to scale in the traded-goods industries. The classical balance of payments constraint does not exist under floating, and I doubt that the structural factors are of much importance for the United States.

Much more important is the following consideration: It is generally assumed that the large trade deficit has been a major factor responsible for the speculation against the dollar. The decision of foreign dollar holders to change the currency composition of their reserves is thought to be the consequence of the deficit. Thus, the dollar is pushed down, which intensifies the inflation. This raises the crucially important problem of the implications of the fact that the dollar still is the world's foremost official reserve and official intervention currency: it is the currency most widely used for private transactions all over the world, and, as a result, there are huge foreign official and private dollar

---

[5] For an excellent general discussion of the problem of the relation between national stability and growth on the one hand and the degree of openness (degree of "international interdependence") on the other hand, see Richard Blackhurst, Nicolas Marian, and Jan Tumlir, *Trade Liberalization, Protectionism, and Interdependence* GATT Studies in International Trade, no. 5 (Geneva, 1977), pp. 34–38.

holdings (dollar overhang). In the following two sections we take a closer look at the structural problem and that of the dollar overhang.

Structural or Sectoral Aspects and the Protectionist Threat

From a broad global ("Keynesian" or "macro") viewpoint of aggregate output and unemployment (which does not differentiate different sectors of the economy), it makes no difference whether an expansion comes from an improvement in the balance of payments (decline of the external deficit) or from internal monetary-fiscal measures.[6] In the longer run this may be a reasonable position. But how about the short and medium term?

In Europe, especially in Britain, it is widely assumed that there is a significant difference between the foreign trade sector, especially the export industries on the one hand and the domestic, nontraded-goods sector ("sheltered industries") on the other. Industries in the export sector are progressive and competitive, often subject to increasing return to scale (because of external or internal economies), while the sheltered industries are less progressive, often monopolistic, and comparatively backward.[7] There probably is some truth in these statements as far as Europe and Japan are concerned because of the small size of those economies compared with the American economy. But whether true or not in the long or short run, it is, I believe, not possible to argue that in the huge American economy traded-goods industries *as a group* are more competitive, more progressive, and more likely to enjoy increasing returns to scale than the rest of the economy. Nor is there any evidence that there is more cyclical unemployment in the traded-goods industries than in the rest of the economy.

What is true is that there are some comparatively unprogressive, inefficient protected industries and that the impact of the recent surge of non-oil imports on different industries has been uneven, resulting in spotty, above-average unemployment in some areas. Steel, color tele-

---

[6] It is true, however, that with rigid wages any expansion of real GNP whether resulting from domestic factors or from the foreign sector, requires an accommodating monetary expansion.

[7] See, for example, Nicholas Kaldor, "Conflicts in National Economic Objectives," *Economic Journal*, vol. 81 (March 1971), pp. 1–16. Kaldor advocated export-led growth through devaluation or floating which he contrasts with consumption-led growth stimulated by domestic fiscal-monetary measures. Similarly, the so-called Scandinavian model of inflation, which enjoys much popularity on the European continent, is based on the alleged backwardness of the nontraded-goods sector. (See, for example, Helmut Frisch, "Inflation Theory 1963–1975: A 'Second Generation' Survey," *Journal of Economic Literature*, vol. 15, no. 4 [December 1977], p. 1305ff.)

vision, and shoes come immediately to mind. Predictably, this has led to strong protectionist pressures, and the government has given in to many of them by imposing import restrictions in various forms—such as "voluntary" restraints imposed on foreign exporters, also deceptively called "orderly market agreements" (OMAs), and "trigger prices" in the case of steel. If and when the trade balance improves, as a consequence of the depreciation of the dollar in foreign exchange markets or of a more rapid expansion abroad, the import pressure on some of these industries could be expected to abate somewhat.

Nobody can be sure, however, how much relief from import competition the particular industries mentioned will get when the trade deficit declines. The change in the trade balance may come more through an increase in U.S. exports than a decrease in imports. The difficulties of the industries that have been given protection from foreign competition are largely due to long-run structural weaknesses, to a loss of comparative advantage, rather than to temporary cyclical factors. The steel industry probably requires structural changes, a shakeout of high-cost obsolescent facilities which simply cannot compete with the efficient Japanese steel mills. A special self-imposed handicap of the steel industry is an outsize wage increase which the union of steelworkers obtained early in 1977. This contract put steel workers' wages at the top of the American scale. With this out of the way, unions and management appeared arm in arm in Washington clamoring for protection from foreign competition, as Arthur Okun aptly described the procedure.[8] The protection was duly provided by the notorious price trigger scheme, which went into effect in February 1978 and has already reduced imports and raised domestic steel prices for countless steel users (a fine contribution to the fight against inflation!).[9] The United States is, of course, not the only sinner, nor is it the worst. Neither the European Community (Common Market) nor Japan are models of liberal trade policy—far from it.

At the root of the rising protectionism is (as demonstrated in the above mentioned GATT report, *Trade Liberalization, Protectionism, and*

---

[8] Okun has spoken of a new variant of the wage-price spiral as follows: "A big wage hike is followed by a major price increase and then by a joint pilgrimage of business and labor executives to Washington to demand that the government stop foreign sellers from increasing their share of the American market" (see Arthur M. Okun, "The Great Stagflation Swamp," *Challenge*, vol. 20 [November–December 1977], p. 9).

[9] See the article "Anti-Dumping Measure Cuts into Foreign-Steel Flows: Domestic Prices Firming," in the *Wall Street Journal*, February 23, 1978. According to news reports the American move was not unwelcome in Brussels because it made it easier for the Commission of the European Community to institute similar protectionist measures.

Interdependence) the increasingly stubborn resistance to adjust to changing conditions. This resistance to adjust can be observed in many areas, but it is especially pronounced, for obvious reasons, when the change takes the form of additional imports. Thus when the American steel industry became less competitive internationally after the large wage increase in 1977, it was hardly mentioned that the wage boost had anything to do with the larger imports, and nobody dared to suggest that the wage hike be rescinded. Let me mention one example from another area: When grain prices fell back from the record level that they had reached in 1972–1973 (as a consequence of a crop shortfall and Russian wheat purchases) farmers organized heavy political pressures to force the government to "protect" them. The government complied by raising price supports and acreage restrictions. For good measure import duties and fees for sugar were sharply raised (another contribution to the fight against inflation). But the farmers are not satisfied and even try to organize a "farmer strike."[10] This situation has the elements of a vicious circle. Refusal to adjust reduces the rate of growth, and slower growth makes adjustment more difficult. Trade restrictions are, of course, only one factor among many that slow growth, but they are becoming an important factor. The growing readiness to impose restrictions when imports rise creates uncertainty and inhibits investments that are necessary to exploit fully opportunities of trade and further division of labor.[11]

To summarize: As far as the United States is concerned, a disaggregated analysis that distinguishes between the traded- and the nontraded-goods sectors does not support the proposition that an expansion resulting from an improved balance of goods and services is less inflationary than an expansion resulting from a domestic monetary-fiscal stimulus. For broadly speaking there is no evidence that the two sectors are different with respect to the volume of unemployment, the chance of developing increasing returns to scale, or other relevant attributes. There exist, of course, some industries that have suffered from large imports—steel, shoes, color television, and some others. But the troubles of these industries are largely of a long-run structural nature, because of a change in the comparative cost situation, and not merely temporary and cyclical.

---

[10] The farmer strike need not be taken very seriously. While the government subsidizes and finances strikes of industrial workers by generous welfare payments, food stamps, and unemployment benefits for workers idled by strikes (including, in some states, the striking workers themselves), we have not yet reached the stage where striking (that is, nonproducing) farmers can apply for welfare and unemployment benefits.

[11] See the above mentioned GATT report in regard to all this.

However, to say that the steel industry suffers from an adverse shift in the comparative cost situation does not mean, as protectionist propaganda would make one believe, that in the absence of protectionist measures, steel production in the United States would be radically slashed. What it does mean is that there would be marginal adjustments, rationalizations, specialization, a shakeout of some high-cost production facilities, and greater resistance to wage pressure.

In this connection it is well to call attention to a highly significant development in the structure of world trade—the rapid growth of what has become known as intra-industry trade, especially of manufactures: Industrial countries increasingly exchange—that is, export and import simultaneously—variants of the same type of manufactured goods. Among the many examples that could be cited, Irving B. Kravis and Robert E. Lipsey have discovered

> a number of cases in which the size of the U.S. market enables U.S. producers to reach a large volume production for relatively specialized product variants for which markets are thin in any one of the smaller, competing economies. In the antifriction bearing industry, for example, the United States imports commonly used bearings which can be produced in large volume both here and abroad, but the United States has nevertheless enjoyed a net export position in bearings owing to exports of specialized kinds capable of meeting precision needs, resisting heat or rust, or bearing great weight.[12]

Modern trade in manufactures is an enormously complex structure, and the fact that seemingly similar products are simultaneously exported and imported, often through the same ports, is at first blush a baffling phenomenon and gives the impression of wastefulness and inefficiency. But the private actors in the market, manufacturers and dealers, know what they are doing. The research economist may require a major effort to find out what is going on, and the correct solution often eludes him, but the market if left alone solves the most intricate problems with reasonable dispatch and efficiency. The clumsy hands of government regulators and protectionists are bound to play havoc with that delicate mechanism.

---

[12] Irving B. Kravis in *The Technology Factor in International Trade*, Raymond Vernon, ed. (New York: National Bureau of Economic Research, 1970), p. 289. Other examples can be found in Irving B. Kravis and Robert E. Lipsey's massive monograph *Price Competitiveness in World Trade* (New York: National Bureau of Economic Research, 1971). See also H. G. Grubel and P. J. Lloyd, *Intra-Industry Trade* (New York: Halsted, 1975), and the GATT Report, *Trade Liberalization, Protectionism, and Interdependence* for an evaluation of the phenomenon of intra-industry trade.

The Problem of the Dollar Balances Held Abroad

As mentioned above, the U.S. external deficit is widely regarded as the principal factor undermining the confidence in, and triggering speculation against, the dollar; the decline of the dollar feeds inflation, and it is therefore very important, it is said, to staunch the leak even though, mechanically, the trade deficit has an anti-inflationary effect.

This argument raises several broad issues. If we substitute for speculation the less emotive words portfolio adjustment or currency diversification of international reserves then the question of the huge dollar balances abroad is raised. These balances are the legacy of the past and the consequence of the fact that the dollar is still the foremost official reserve, official intervention, and private transactions currency. Another issue is whether it is the trade and current account deficit as such that undermines confidence, or the American economic policies that are perceived as the root cause of the deficit.

Well over $100 billion are held by foreign official agencies (central banks) as their countries' international reserves and many more billions are held in liquid form by private individuals and national and multi-national corporations. The magnitude of private dollar holdings is open-ended, for the line between foreign- and domestically-held dollar balances that are potentially subject to diversification is hazy and liable to shift.

Official dollar reserves are probably fairly safe. There is little danger that the large dollar holders, Germany, Japan, Saudi Arabia, and Britain (yes, Britain is, for the time being, one of the large dollar holders) will massively shift into other currencies. They don't want to rock the boat, and they have no place to go with their dollars. (Gold is of no use any more, and SDRs have not yet taken gold's place as a store of value.) But marginal, incremental currency diversification of official portfolios, especially of lesser countries, is not out of the question. The fact that Switzerland recently has extended the 40 percent negative interest charged for deposits of private foreigners to apply also to official deposits of foreign central banks suggests that such shifts have actually taken place on a large scale.[13] Even more important, the shift of a comparative small percentage of the large private dollar holdings into some other currencies can produce turmoil in the foreign exchange market and large swings in exchange rates.

That does not mean, as is sometimes asserted, that purchasing

---

[13] It seems that central banks of several less developed countries and OPEC countries have taken advantage of the intermittent interventions of the strong currency countries to switch from dollars into deutsche marks, yens, and Swiss francs.

power comparisons, international competitiveness of industries, comparative inflation, and money growth rates are totally irrelevant, that it is capital movements and portfolio adjustments and nothing else that matters. On the contrary, comparative inflation and money growth rate, the resulting changes in international competitiveness, and the policies perceived behind these factors are of paramount importance, because the operators in the foreign exchange markets, especially the large ones who count the most, are highly sophisticated and pay close attention to actual and prospective inflation rates, money growth rates, and all that. But the possibility of short-run disturbances and large overshooting of long-run equilibrium exchange rates, which may snowball into major turbulences, cannot be excluded. Something like this seems to have happened late in 1977 and early in 1978. If the possibility of significant overshooting due to destabilizing speculation and band wagon effects is accepted—and it is difficult to rule out that possibility altogether—the case for large-scale official interventions in the exchange market, going beyond smoothing "disorderly" fluctuation, seems to become stronger. This is a widely accepted conclusion.

There are two problems here, a short-run technical one and a long-run problem. The short-run technical problem is how interventions are managed (or mismanaged), how "overshooting" and "disorderly fluctuations" are defined and identified under floating exchange rates. The long-run problem is this: It is widely held, also by those who favor large-scale intervention, that interventions alone even on a large scale "cannot influence basic trends" unless accompanied by policies that tackle "fundamental" factors.[14] I take up the long-run problem first.

To begin with, it is not quite true that no interventions, however large, could solve the problem. If the surplus countries intervene on a very large scale—and they can always do it because they can print their money ("the sky is the limit" as President Klasen of the German Bundesbank once put it during the fixed rate system)—they would inflate their economy enough to eliminate their surplus and the U.S. deficit.[15]

Second, for reasons already stated, adoption of a sensible energy policy, which would be very desirable on other grounds, is not a solution of the U.S. balance of payments problem (except perhaps in the very

---

[14] This formulation which reflects widely held views comes from a speech by Henry C. Wallich at the joint luncheon of the American Economic Association and American Finance Association, New York, December 28, 1977.

[15] Interventions by U.S. monetary authorities, financed by borrowing of surplus countries' currencies in some form, has the same inflationary effect in the surplus countries. The only difference is that the exchange risk is shifted from the surplus to the deficit country.

long run) although it may have a favorable short-run psychological effect because it has been played up so much.

Third, the really fundamental factor is the large inflation differential between the United States and the three countries whose currencies have emerged as potential rivals for the dollar. The three currencies the mark, the yen, and the Swiss franc are fit for the role of an international official and private reserve and transactions currency because they are fully convertible, in other words because they are not of a mousetrap variety, which are easy to get into but difficult to get out of again. So long as there exist such rivals for the dollar with a significantly lower inflation rate than in the United States, there will be a continuous or recurrent pressure on the dollar. For the market will realize that the currencies of the low inflation countries have a long-run tendency to appreciate. Thus there will be a continuous incentive to diversify the large foreign-held dollar balances and increasing danger that domestic dollar balances will be shifted abroad. Theoretically one can imagine the exchange rate adjustment, the depreciation of the dollar, proceeding in a more or less steady, orderly fashion, with the volume of diversification of dollar balances being held in check by an appropriate interest differential. If the inflation rate is, say, 3 percent in Germany and 5 percent in the United States, and it is expected to stay at approximately that level, an interest rate two percentage points higher in the United States than in Germany may discourage large shifts from dollars into marks.

In practice, with the prevailing high-inflation rates and large inflation differential it is most unlikely that the process of adjustment will work so smoothly. For one thing high-inflation rates are inherently unstable; they have a strong tendency to accelerate. For another there are likely to be policy reactions. All this creates a great deal of uncertainty which is bound to make diversification of dollar balances look advisable, despite existing interest rate differentials. The most likely outcome will be recurrent waves of diversification causing turmoil in the exchange market, at least until the dollar balances have been diversified to a high degree. Given the large volume of these balances and the danger that domestic balances may begin to be shifted, and given further the fact that Germany, Switzerland, and Japan have shown no inclination to assume the role, along with the United States, of a repository for official and private reserves and have taken measures to resist the inflow of funds, the process of diversification will probably take a very long time. That does not mean that there cannot be periods of comparative calm. What it does mean is that so long as there is a large inflation differential between the United States and some other financial centers, such tranquil periods will not last long.

225

I have been asked the question: Is it plausible that comparatively small inflation differentials between the United States and the three rival reserve currency countries would have such far-reaching consequences? The answer is yes. In the first place, as we have seen, the differences in the inflation rates are not so small. Second, if the dollar were not the world's foremost reserve currency the situation would be very different. If it were not the United States but, say, Brazil, there would be no foreign holdings of the currency subject to diversification, and domestic currency holdings would be comparatively small in relation to domestic transaction requirements, so that the danger of a flight from the currency would be small.[16]

Third, expectation of future exchange rate developments and comparative confidence in different currencies depend not only on current and recent inflation rates but also on the stance of those economic policies in the countries concerned that are generally perceived as principal determinants of the rate of inflation. To these policy implications I shall turn presently.

The upshot is that we have to expect trouble, excessive fluctuations in the exchange markets, with the danger of overshooting of the equilibrium rate,[17] so long as there exist large inflation differentials between the United States and other important countries whose currencies qualify for the role of international reserve and transactions media.

The best solution of the problem would be to bring the American inflation rate down close to the rate of inflation in the surplus countries. If that could be done, not only would it have a direct effect on the balance of goods and services, it would also remove or drastically weaken the incentive to diversify dollar balances. Even if the inflation rate is not significantly higher in the United States than in rival financial centers, there may occur from time to time large changes in the current account, or a series of deficits due to shifts in international demand of a cyclical or structural nature. But there would be no presumption of long-run changes in exchange rates all in one direction, as there is now.

A change in U.S. policy in the right direction—that is, toward the adoption of a credible anti-inflation program—could be expected to have a beneficial, calming effect on the foreign exchange markets long before the inflation differential actually has been whittled down. The

---

[16] This situation would, of course, change if the inflation rate became very high. A comparison between a hyperinflation, such as the German inflation after World War I, and the Brazilian or Argentinian inflation in recent years would make this clear.

[17] Equilibrium rate is to be defined in this connection as that rate which would obtain in the absence of bursts of diversification.

difficulty will be to make the anti-inflation policy credible. After years of stop-and-go, of shifting policy priorities from unemployment to inflation, from inflation to unemployment, and recently back to inflation again (for how long?), it will take a while before a fresh start inspires confidence.

Unfortunately no such change in policy is in sight. On the contrary, everything points toward faster inflation—a mounting budget deficit, short-term real interest rates being at zero (or decidedly negative after allowing for taxes), wages rising more than three times as fast as would be compatible with price stability, the wage rise showing no signs of deceleration, and an ongoing series of price raising measures initiated by the government (sharp boost of the minimum wage, import restrictions, increase in farm support prices for several products, a large hike of payroll taxes, and the like). To be sure, monetary policy by gradually reducing monetary growth could bring down inflation, despite the handicaps just mentioned. But unless some of the inflationary developments such as the excessive wage rise are checked, and price boosting government policies are changed, monetary restraint will create so much transitional unemployment that it is most unlikley to be carried to a successful conclusion.

The so-called locomotive policy pushed by Britain, the United States, and the OECD secretariat can be regarded as an attempt to eliminate the inflation differential, not by reducing the rate of inflation in the weak currency countries, but by raising it in the strong currency countries. This can be described as a policy of curing the healthy rather than the sick,[18] but it could be an effective cure of the U.S. balance of payments disequilibrium.

Of course, the advocates of the locomotive policy do not put it that way. They point to unemployment, slack, and slow growth in Germany and Japan, and assert that these countries can apply an expansionary monetary-fiscal stimulus without accelerating inflation.

The argument is, however, unconvincing. In the first place it ignores the stagflation dilemma or assumes that Germany and Japan are exceptions. Up to now Germany has been more successful than the United States and the United Kingdom in limiting the stagflation syndrome. But for fairly obvious reasons its past comparative immunity to the stagflation disease has become weaker and will probably further diminish. And for well-known reasons sensitivity to inflation is much

---

[18] It will be recalled that this was the favorite phrase used by German officials—inappropriately—when they resisted appreciation of the mark and asked for depreciation of the dollar instead under the Bretton Woods system, before it became generally accepted that, in an inflationary world, price stability cannot be achieved without floating.

greater in Germany than in the United States and Britain. Germany may be willing to pay a somewhat higher price in terms of temporary unemployment and slack for greater price stability. The difference is not large. Actually there exists no government in the present day world that is not terribly afraid of unemployment.

Second, if Germany succeeded in reducing unemployment and accelerating growth without faster inflation, the inflation differential between the United States and Germany would persist, and the mark would still have a long-run tendency to appreciate.

Third and most important, Germany and Japan can make the same contribution to reducing their surpluses and the U.S. deficit, and thereby to stimulating the world economy, by letting their exchange rate float up as by expanding internally. The difference is that the continuous appreciation of the mark exerts a continuous pull on the outstanding dollar balance, a continuing incentive to diversify. However, this aspect of the problem has not been mentioned by the locomotive drivers.[19]

Much has been made of the fact that in Germany the appreciation of the mark (as in the case of the Swiss franc and the yen) is a depressing as well as an anti-inflationary factor which, if not counteracted by expansionary measures, could impede the reduction of the trade surplus and thus reduce the stimulus to other countries. It has been said that this factor has been overlooked by the governments concerned. This is obviously not the case. The three governments fully realize that the appreciation of their currencies is a hard blow to their export industries, which account for a very high percentage of total output and employment.

The problem should be viewed in the context of the overall stance of monetary policy, which in Germany is still aimed at further reducing the rate of inflation. Otmar Emminger, President of the German Bundesbank, has stated on several occasions that German monetary policy has been shaded in the direction of greater monetary ease to allow for the depressing effect of a possible further appreciation of the mark.[20] Like the U.S. government, the governments of the other locomotive countries are confronted with the difficult task of winding down inflation without creating too much unemployment. The stagflation dilemma afflicts all industrial countries although the intensity of the

---

[19] This follows from the fact that they assume that the locomotive countries can expand without accelerating inflation, which would leave the inflation differential unchanged and would not eliminate the pull it exerts on the dollar balances.

[20] See, for example, *Ausszüge aus Presseartikeln* (Frankfurt: Deutsche Bundesbank), no. 10, January 30, 1978; no. 12, February 2, 1978; no. 18, February 28, 1978; and no. 24, April 4, 1978.

dilemma and the relative weight attached to price stability and full employment vary somewhat from country to country.

An important aspect of the locomotive policy which has not received any attention on the part of the policy's proponents, is its impact on the terms of trade.[21] A rapid simultaneous inflationary expansion in all important industrial countries would almost certainly lead to a commodity boom, as in the early 1970s, shifting the terms of trade sharply in favor of the raw material exporting countries. This would be a matter of great importance for Britain. It makes the British insistence that Germany, Japan, and the United States expand faster look decidedly ill-advised.[22] As Max Corden pointed out, there is "in this world of flexible exchange rates . . . no need . . . to wait for an American or German boom before inflating the British economy, if that is what the British government wants."[23] Britain would be much better off if it alone expanded, because in that case it would enjoy much better terms of trade.

The locomotive policy makes more sense for the less developed countries (LDCs). But before somebody replies that the locomotive policy has been proposed mainly to help the LDCs and not the weaker industrial countries,[24] he should ask himself the question how much good an inflationary boom would do to the LDCs if the boom is again followed, as it surely would be, by a severe recession. At the Economic Summit in London in May 1977, the assembled heads of state declared: "Inflation does not reduce unemployment. On the contrary, it is one of its major causes." The Germans evidently still believe that a nation cannot inflate itself into a stable full employment equilibrium, while the proponents of the locomotive theory have retreated to the Keynesian

---

[21] It has been mentioned, however, in Max Corden's article "Expansion of the World Economy and the Duties of the Surplus Countries," *The World Economy*, vol. 1, no. 2 (January 1978), p. 126.

[22] The strange notion and morbid fear of deflation among British economists is illustrated in a letter to the *London Times*, February 15, 1978 by Nicholas Kaldor (answering a letter by F. A. Hayek of February 11, 1978) in which he characterizes Chancellor Brüning's policy in 1930–1932 of severe deflation (sharp contraction of the money supply causing a large decline of the price level) and stubborn refusal to devalue or float the mark as "monetarist policies" and says that "the economics of Chancellor Schmidt and his advisors are very similar to those of Dr. Brüning and in this country [Britain], too, there is a return to the views prevailing at the time of Montague Norman and Philip Snowden."

[23] W. M. Corden, *Inflation, Exchange Rates and the World Economy* (Chicago: Chicago University Press, 1977), p. 132.

[24] Actually, the proponents of the locomotive policy usually mention the weak industrial countries along with the LDCs as the beneficiaries of the policy. It has even been said that German expansion was important to check communism in France and Italy!

position, which assumes that money illusion is substantially intact and that inflationary expectations present no serious problems. However, as argued earlier in this paper, it has become more and more difficult to ignore the fact that many years of inflation have eroded money illusion, have sensitized inflationary expectations, and have made Keynesian policies increasingly ineffective except in the very short run.

According to newspaper reports, the locomotive theory has recently been expanded by the OECD secretariat and by key U.S. officials into the convoy theory, a proposal for coordinated fiscal-monetary expansion in a large number of countries led by, but not confined to, the three largest (locomotive) countries—the United States, Germany, and Japan. The main advantage claimed for the new approach seems to be that if many countries expand at the same time, there is less danger that some of them will run into serious balance of payments problems.

The convoy strategy seems to me subject to even more serious objections than the locomotive theory. First, if in addition to the strong locomotive countries with low-inflation rates other weaker countries with high-inflation rates expand, the overall inflationary effect of the new approach becomes stronger. Accelerating worldwide inflation does not improve the chances for sustained world prosperity. Second, the emphasis on an improved pattern of current account balances is out of place in a world of floating exchange rates. Moreover it is not clear why current account deficits should decline if simultaneously with the surplus countries the deficit countries take expansionary measures. This would make the current account imbalance under the convoy policy larger, and not smaller, than under the locomotive policy.[25]

To summarize briefly: So long as the United States has a much higher rate of inflation than other potential reserve currency countries, the market will conclude that the dollar has a long-run tendency to depreciate vis-à-vis the mark, Swiss franc, and yen, providing a strong incentive for official and private dollar holders to diversify their currency holdings and thus putting heavy pressure on the dollar. This would change if the United States adopted a credible anti-inflation policy to bring the inflation rate down close to the level of the strong currency countries. The so-called locomotive policy pushed by the United States and Britain would reduce the inflation differential not by reducing inflation in the weak currency countries but by raising it in the

---

[25] If the locomotive countries expand internally, or alternatively if they let their currency appreciate, the deficit countries will be stimulated and their deficits will decline. It will perhaps be argued that they will have to support this increase of real demand from abroad by expansionary monetary-fiscal measures and that this supporting expansion is the real meaning of the convoy policy. But this argument would ignore the fact that the deficit countries still suffer from high inflation.

strong currency countries. This would lead to higher world inflation, which is not likely to restore stability in the world currency markets.

I now come to the short-run problem of how interventions are conducted, how "disorderly" market fluctuations and "overshooting" are defined and identified under floating. Since the end of 1976, there have been very large official interventions in the exchange market. In 1977 foreign central banks in Western Europe and Japan bought some $35 billion to moderate the rise of their currencies. U.S. interventions, too, have been stepped up but are still comparatively small.[26] The U.S. interventions have been accompanied by repeated emphatic statements to the effect that the purpose of these operations is to prevent or offset "disorderly" fluctuations and not to peg the dollar to any particular rate; medium- and long-run movements of exchange rates are to be determined by market forces.

The usual criteria of disorderly markets are "thinness," "widening spread" between bid and ask quotations, and "imbalance between demand and supply" in the sense that there is no demand or no supply. Since these are hardly operational concepts, in practice the meaning of disorderliness comes down to excessive short-run fluctuations, during the day, from day to day, or possibly from week to week.[27] It is, indeed, fairly generally accepted that there are no objections to this kind of intervention.[28] By and large American interventions seem to have conformed to this rule. But it is clear that the massive foreign interventions in support of the dollar have gone way beyond anything that could be described as merely ironing out short-run fluctuations.[29] The policy must be assumed to be based on the belief that the market has badly "overshot" the equilibrium, in other words that the dollar is undervalued, reflecting overvaluation of the deutsche mark, Swiss franc, and Japanese yen. Is it possible in a world of floating exchange rates, to attach a precise meaning to these statements, which are widely bandied about by policy makers and others on both sides of the Atlantic (and

---

[26] On March 8, 1978, the New York Federal Reserve Bank reported that in the quarter ending January 31, 1978, the Federal Reserve and the Treasury sold foreign currencies, mostly German marks, equivalent to $1.5 billion—a record amount for a three-month period—in the New York exchange market.

[27] The "Guidelines for the Management of Floating Exchange Rates," enunciated by the IMF in 1974, draw the line between short and medium run between the week and the month. (See IMF, *Annual Report for 1974* [Washington, D.C., 1974].)

[28] See Leland B. Yeager, *International Monetary Relations: Theory, History and Policy*, 2d ed. (New York: Harper and Row, 1976), pp. 278–292, for a thorough discussion, references to the literature, and a contrary position.

[29] However, the Joint Statement of the U.S.–German Agreement on Exchange Market Policies of March 13, 1978, says: "Both sides reaffirm that continuing forceful action will be taken to counter disorderly conditions in exchange markets" (see *IMF Survey*, March 20, 1978, p. 86).

the Pacific)? And if so, how can the approximate magnitude of the over- and undervaluation be ascertained?

The answer to the first question is, if the current exchange rate continues and there are no major changes in the underlying conditions (that is, no burst of inflation or recession in the United States and no recession in the surplus countries), the U.S. deficit and the Japanese, German, and Swiss surpluses are expected to decline sharply in a reasonable period, say within a year. Such expectations are supported by more or less elaborate price and cost comparison and econometric exercises.

The definition of the envisaged balance of payments goals is rather vague. Surely balancing of current account cannot be the goal; allowance must be made for some types of capital movements. Rich countries should be net capital exporters, implying a surplus on current account. But then there are the "irrepressible" OPEC surpluses. How will they be, or should they be, distributed? Beyond all that, there are now the capital flows resulting from the attempts of dollar holders to diversify their currency portfolios. Presumably it is primarily these capital flows that should be financed, at least to a large extent, by official interventions.

All this is rather vague and has never been clearly formulated officially, let alone agreed upon internationally. Similarly inconclusive and unreliable are attempts to ascertain and quantify the alleged over- and undervaluations by price and cost comparisons and econometric simulations.

The conclusion to be drawn from this analysis is that the case for large official interventions in the exchange market is not so strong after all. The implicit assumption of the policy of massive intervention is that the interventions are skillfully performed in full knowledge of the relevant facts, including more or less correct projections of future developments, that only unnecessary, reversible fluctuations are ironed out, leaving the broad underlying tendencies undisturbed.

This is an overly idealistic and highly unrealistic assumption. Actually the record of balance of payments management has been anything but encouraging in recent years. Even important countries such as Australia and Mexico have acted erratically and have thoroughly mismanaged the float of their currencies. Major powers have a bad record. The British pound was propped up for a long time by huge official and semi-official borrowing abroad. Then early in 1976 sterling was allowed to plunge and to become clearly undervalued. Later it was stabilized by huge interventions in the exchange market, resulting in an enormous accumulation of reserves from $3.6 million at the end of 1976 to $17.5 billion in November 1977, the highest level on record. Still later in 1977 the interventions stopped and sterling sharply appreciated vis-à-vis the dollar.[30] The Italian policies were equally erratic.

It is no exaggeration to say that most recent disturbances in the exchange market were the consequences of government interventions, apart from the responsibility of governments for sharply divergent inflation rates, which are the root cause of turbulence in the exchange markets.

Some Policy Conclusions

The main conclusion that emerges from the foregoing analysis is this: The single most important, nay indispensable, measure to prevent a further weakening of the dollar and of the whole international monetary system is that the United States bring down its rate of inflation close to the level in other important industrial countries whose currencies can vie with the dollar as a repository for official and private international reserves. There is almost general agreement that from the domestic standpoint, too, winding down inflation is imperative. Sustainable full employment output is impossible in a highly inflatonary environment.

A Digression on Inflation. Here is not the place for a thorough discussion of how to wind down inflation. The problem is discussed in some detail in other contributions to the present volume and in the 1976 and 1977 editions of *Contemporary Economic Problems*. (See especially the contributions of William Fellner and Phillip Cagan.) But I would like to make a few remarks on what seems to me some of the basic issues.

There is almost general agreement that an indispensable condition for winding down inflation is a gradual reduction of monetary growth. Most experts, including many monetarists, add fiscal restraint (reduction of government deficit spending) to monetary restraint. There is, however, disagreement on whether monetary-fiscal restraint is not only a necessary but also a sufficient condition for regaining price stability. Monetarists insist that monetary-fiscal restraint is all that is needed and all that can be done to bring down inflation, while many others believe—with some justification in my opinion—that exclusive reliance on monetary-fiscal policy would create so much unemployment, at least in the short and medium term, that the policy of disinflation is unlikely

---

[30] The sharp policy-induced fluctuations of the sterling/dollar rate and of the trade-weighted exchange rate of the pound in 1975–1978 is vividly depicted in *The Economist* (London), March 4, 1978, p. 35.

to be carried to a successful close. Monetarists and nonmonetarists should be able to agree that monetary restraint to bring down inflation would work much better with less transitional and permanent unemployment if it were possible to bring the economy closer to the competitive ideal, if there were no powerful labor unions which, with the help of government policies, are able to push up wages even in the face of heavy unemployment, if there were fewer other pressure groups such as the farmers or the steel industry which force the government by political pressures to raise their incomes by restricting imports or output, if there were no mimimum wages which are raised from time to time, and the like.

It is understandable that policy makers are looking desperately for means to break out of a vicious wage-price spiral: prices cannot be stabilized because labor costs are rising too fast and wage push cannot be eliminated because the cost of living is going up rapidly. Incomes policy is again being recommended with increasing urgency as a way out of the dilemma. But incomes policy means different things to different people. On several occasions I have proposed to distinguish two basic types of incomes policy, incomes policy I and incomes policy II.[31] The first type is what usually is called incomes policy, ranging from comprehensive wage and price controls, wage freezes, and price stops to guidelines for noninflationary wage and price setting. The second type of incomes policy is defined as a collection or bundle of policies of different kinds designed to bring the economy closer to the competitive ideal. It includes such diverse measures as freer trade, antimonopoly policies, restraint of union power, deregulation of industry, and elimination of minimum wages.

Incomes policy in the usual sense (incomes policy I) has never worked for any length of time. Incomes policy II is an entirely different matter. It is the type of incomes policy that the present writer favors.[32] A particular kind of incomes policy that has found impressive sponsorship recently will be briefly analyzed in the next few pages. It is the so-called tax-based incomes policy (TIP), which tries to attack the problem of inflation with a combination of taxes and subsidies.[33] Henry Wallich and Sidney Weintraub have proposed that firms that grant

---

[31] Gottfried Haberler, "Incomes Policy and Inflation: Some Further Reflections," in *American Economic Review*, vol. 62 (May 1972), pp. 234–241, available as Reprint No. 5 (Washington, D.C.: American Enterprise Institute, 1972); and Gottfried Haberler, *Economic Growth and Stability* (Los Angeles: Nash, 1974), chapter 7.

[32] This type of incomes policy (with some concessions to the first type) was recommended by Arthur Burns. For references see the publications mentioned in the preceding footnote.

[33] I briefly discussed TIP in "Tax Measures against Wage Push," in Haberler, *Economic Growth and Stability*, pp. 132–133.

wage increases exceeding a certain norm be subjected to an excess wage tax, and Arthur Okun has turned the Wallich-Weintraub penalty into generous tax incentives, which would benefit employers who avoid widening gross profit margins and employees who keep their wage demands below a clearly defined noninflationary standard.[34] The proposal of the "carrots" and "sticks" cure for inflation has been endorsed, in principle, by an impressive group of experts.[35]

In my opinion it would be a great mistake if policy makers in their desperate search for a way out of the stagflation dilemma were to embrace the gadget of the tax-subsidy scheme instead of applying monetary-fiscal restraint, grasping the nettle of standing up to the various pressure groups, and changing government policies which are at the root of the trouble.

Although ingenious and greatly superior to direct wage and price controls (because it does not destroy the price mechanism), TIP is subject to two very serious objections: First, as Gardner Ackley has convincingly demonstrated, the administrative complications and costs of the scheme would be formidable, hardly less than those of full-blown wage and price controls.[36] Ackley's paper is so convincing because he is, in principle, for an incomes policy and because his paper is based on personal experience as a price controller during World War II and again during the Korean War. Passages from Ackley's paper indicate the complexities of the problem.

> I retain keen, and sometimes bitter memories [from my wartime experience] of great ideas about ways to restrain wage and price increases for which the fine print could never be written—or, if it could be written, filled endless volumes of the *Federal Register* with constant revisions, exceptions, and adjustments necessary to cover special situations that could never have been dreamed of in advance by the most imaginative economists, accountants, and lawyers. Okun's proposal raises some of these old problems. . . . For example, Okun's firms must be told how to define each wage rate, and thus how to measure its increase—presumably to include all benefits,

---

[34] See Okun, "The Great Stagflation Swamp"; Henry C. Wallich and Sidney Weintraub, "A Tax-Based Incomes Policy," *Journal of Economic Issues*, vol. 5 (June 1971); see also A. P. Lerner "Stagflation—Its Causes and Cure," *Challenge*, vol. 20 (September–October 1977), for still another version of TIP.

[35] See, for example, a letter to the *New York Times*, March 12, 1978, signed by Walter Heller, Arthur Okun, Robert Solow, James Tobin, Henry Wallich, and Sidney Weintraub.

[36] See Gardner Ackley, "Okun's New Tax Based Incomes Policy Proposal," *Economic Outlook*, Winter 1978 (Ann Arbor: Survey Research Center, University of Michigan), pp. 8–9.

including pension rights, dental-care plans, executive stock options, and changed eligibility for overtime pay. Whose estimates of these costs would be accepted? How would cost-of-living escalators in contracts be evaluated? Instructions must then be given as to how to compute an average wage rate increase. . . . How does one visualize a union bargaining with an industry composed of many firms differently affected by a given wage increase? How could an employer assure a union that a proposed agreement would or would not qualify its workers for the tax rebate, until much bookkeeping (and IRS review) had been completed? Indeed, could it give any assurances before its tax year was finished? . . . Are exceptions to be made for that portion of wage increases that merely lets workers "catch up" with wage increases already granted to other workers, or that remove long-standing "inequities"? Is it possible to deny all exceptions to the wage standard? . . . It [would take] a growing army of economists, commodity experts, statisticians, and lawyers to deal with the question and the problems that [arise] not about the general principle, but about how to define, apply, and measure it in all the infinite variety of its applications. . . . And would it [Congress] not need to write into the tax code the equivalent of a complete wage control system in order to define the wage increases which would qualify workers for their tax rebates?

It will perhaps be said that the administrative costs, though high, are small compared with the enormous costs of inflation which the tax-subsidy scheme is supposed to eliminate. But will it achieve its objective? This brings me to the second basic objection to the scheme.

The wage tax is supposed to stiffen the employers' resistance to excessive wage demands. The proponents of the tax-subsidy scheme are surely right that one of the principal causes of stagflation is the power of labor unions to impose by threat of crippling strikes wage increases that far exceed what would be compatible with stable prices. The proponents of the scheme are also right that monetary-fiscal restraint alone does not offer a completely satisfactory solution of the stagflation problem; it can stop inflation but only at a high cost of unemployment. True enough, but it must be asked: Why should excess-wage taxes succeed where tight money fails? I see no reason why unions would moderate their excessive wage demands if the resistance of the employers stems from a wage tax and not from tight money, which prevents an increase in overall demand that would enable the employer fully to pass on higher costs to the consumers. If union pressure for higher wages persists despite the wage tax, the employer has no choice but to pass on to the consumers the tax along with the higher wage costs in the form of higher prices, an expansionary monetary policy permitting; or to cut output and employment if tight money prevents the pass-through of the tax to the consumer. It follows that TIP cannot do anything that cannot be done cheaply, efficiently, and without any red tape and administrative cost by monetary-fiscal restraint.

In addition, TIP is bound to have a distorting, growth reducing effect on the economy because it would penalize expanding, dynamic, innovating firms and industries that have to bid labor away from other less dynamic sectors of the economy. Since the dynamic, innovating firms and industries are saddled with an additional cost—the wage tax—output and employment are bound to suffer. The proponents of the wage tax will perhaps answer that exceptions will have to be made for innovating, expanding firms and industries. But that presents formidable administrative problems as described by Gardner Ackley. It means substituting decisions of a government bureaucracy for the price mechanism.[37]

The basic objection to the subsidy scheme is somewhat different. The tax benefits are supposed to persuade unions to moderate their wage demands and business firms to refrain from utilizing monopoly power they may possess. Wages are now rising more than three times as fast as would be compatible with price stability. To make it worthwhile for unions to moderate their wage demands sufficiently to reduce appreciably inflationary wage pressure, very large tax subsidies would be required. This would create a formidable budgetary problem, in addition to the enormous administrative costs and the distortions any such scheme is bound to produce because it would be practically impossible to apply it generally in a uniform, nondiscriminatory manner.

The first reaction to this criticism may well be that it is defeatist. Since the costs of unemployment and inflation keep piling up and nothing else seems to work, isn't it worth trying the tax-subsidy approach? This type of argument always reminds me of the story of the man who during the Lisbon earthquake walked the streets trying to sell anti-earthquake pills. When somebody argued with him that pills could not possibly protect anyone from earthquakes, the man answered: "But my dear fellow, what would you put in their place?"

Fortunately, even in the form of stagflation, inflation is more amenable to remedy than earthquakes, but unfortunately, from a certain point on, inflation has a strong tendency to accelerate. If inflation

---

[37] Wage guidelines, if strictly enforced, freeze the wage structure, which leads to increasing distortions when the underlying situation changes. The excess-wage tax does the same, although to a lesser extent. The higher the tax the more closely its effects approximate the effect of enforced guideposts.

is not curbed now it will become worse and more difficult to deal with later. The only remedy that can be applied quickly is monetary-fiscal restraints. These restraints should be applied immediately to prevent a further acceleration of inflation, although this policy will cause some transitional increase in unemployment. These side effects can be minimized by applying the restraint gently and gradually. By making it clear at the same time that the policy will be firmly pursued, it will be possible to dampen inflationary expectation. The side effects on employment can be further reduced by avoiding price and wage boosting measures and by eliminating as many as possible of those that have been taken earlier, thus making the economy more competitive and flexible.[38] Although it would be unrealistic to expect quick results from such reforms, the application of monetary-fiscal restraint should not be delayed, or else we would find ourselves in an even more difficult situation a year later.[39]

After this digression on inflation I return to international problems.

International Problems. If the United States adopted a credible anti-inflation policy combined with measures, mainly in the tax area, to stimulate productive private investment, the pressure on the dollar would quickly abate. American industries would gradually become more competitive on international markets, and the incentive to diversify dollar holdings would diminish and disappear. The existing interest differential between the United States, Germany, and Switzerland, if preserved, would attract capital.

On the other hand, if inflation is not checked, or if as many fear it accelerates, we must expect continuing attempts to diversify the currency composition of reserves on the part of foreign and domestic dollar holders, resulting in further pressure on the dollar.

The locomotive strategy, the attempt to persuade the surplus countries to inflate and thus to reduce the inflation differential, is bound to fail, or if it succeeded, it would heat up world inflation. It might reduce the pressure on the dollar, but it would not provide a solid basis for world prosperity.

The locomotive strategy is objectionable also from the political point of view. There is no government in the modern world that is not deeply committed to full employment and growth, although there are differences in the relative weight they attach to price stability, employ-

---

[38] Arthur Okun has proposed a moratorium on new cost raising measures. He evidently regards it as hopeless to try to change existing cost raising policies. Okun, "The Great Stagflation Swamp," p. 12.

[39] See the essays by Phillip Cagan and William Fellner in this volume.

ment, and growth. Some countries are prepared to tolerate a little more slack than others to bring down inflation. But there is no government in the modern world that will accept mass unemployment without fighting back with expansionary measures. To continue an acrimonious debate in order to induce others to change their policy mix a little bit is not conducive to international harmony and cooperation. International negotiations should concentrate on exchange rate management and commercial policy. The legitimate subjects for complaints are the manipulation of exchange rates and protectionist measures, not the attempts of some countries to maintain price stability by allowing a little more slack than others would prefer. In a highly inflationary world, putting pressure on the few oases of stability to join the inflationary convoy is a perverse policy.

Inevitably, the question of reform of the international monetary system is again being raised. Proposals are made for an expanded role of special drawing rights (SDRS), for substitution of SDRS for the dollar, and for linking together some of the major currencies, especially the dollar and the deutsche mark—a transatlantic "snake," as it were, analogous to the European snake (common float, an arrangement now in force between Germany, the Netherlands, Belgium, Sweden, and Denmark).

All such schemes of linking together major currencies, either rigidly or in the form of target zones, are entirely utopian so long as large inflation differentials exist. The arrangement would require enormous interventions and would be what the Germans call an "Inflationsgemeinschaft," an engine for world inflation. Even after the inflation differential has been eliminated, preferably by reducing the rate of inflation in the more inflationary countries, a rigid link would make little sense unless it were accompanied by safeguards against future inflationary escapades. It is difficult to see how this could be accomplished without introducing an international base money whose quantity is firmly controlled, a sort of modified gold standard, and a binding commitment by all participants to abide by the rules of the game. Surely, the time has not come for such grandiose reforms.

There remains the question of massive interventions in the exchange market. On the occasion of his departure from the Federal Reserve Board, Arthur Burns called on the U.S. government to mobilize huge sums of foreign currencies—$40 billion was mentioned in news reports—to "defend" the dollar. For this purpose the United States should sell some of its gold, issue bonds denominated in foreign currencies, perhaps as much as $10 billion, and utilize SDRS and the credit tranch in the IMF. Not all the news reports have made it clear that Burns regards such interventions in the exchange market as a bridging operation until the anti-inflation measures which he proposed have taken hold.

This makes all the difference. If inflation in the United States is not brought under control, interventions in the exchange market would fail, unless they were on a truly gigantic scale. Nobody can be quite sure of the approximate size that would be required. Forty billion dollars would—in the absence of a credible anti-inflation program—almost certainly be inadequate. But we can be sure that interventions of sufficient magnitude to stabilize the dollar for an indefinite period would be highly inflationary in the low currency countries and thus for the world at large.[40]

On the other hand, if the United States launched a credible anti-inflation program, large interventions would probably not be necessary. From the political standpoint it must be doubted that it is wise to combine the two steps. For if huge sums for interventions are available, the politicians may well drag their feet in implementing meaningful anti-inflation measures, which are bound to be unpopular.

Postscript

Since this paper was written, the so-called convoy strategy that was criticized above (p. 230) has been embraced and escalated by the International Monetary Fund (IMF). At the meeting of the IMF Interim Committee in Mexico City, April 29–30, 1978, H. Johannes Witteveen, then the IMF managing director, presented a "scenario for coordinated growth and payments adjustment." In this scenario the growth rates for real GNP in "the medium term" (1978–1980) are laid out for the seven leading industrial countries—4 percent for the United States, 4.5 percent for France and Germany, 4 percent for Italy, and 3.5 percent for the United Kingdom. The scenario is called "a desirable one in the sense that countries are assumed to expand *domestic demand* so as to reach a rate of real GNP growth judged to be appropriate from the standpoint of absorbing available slack with account being taken of interdependence of the various countries through flows of foreign trade." (Emphasis added.) The concomitant expected changes in the current account balances of the seven countries are specified with due allowance for factors such as "temporary disturbances," "fall in the OPEC surplus," "recent relative price changes," and "cyclical developments." The scenario is "characterized as cautious" because "all indus-

---

[40] The only exception, which Burns cannot have had in mind (or else he would have mentioned it), would be to conduct the interventions in such a way that they have a deflationary (anti-inflationary) effect in the United States.

trial countries except the United States presently have large amounts of slack," which is said to minimize the danger of rekindling inflationary pressures. This approach has been very aptly described as "international fine-tuning" and subjected to a trenchant critical analysis by Herbert Stein.[41]

Mr. Witteveen and the IMF staff are, of course, fully aware of the dangers of inflation.[42] In scores of cases the condition of IMF financial support to various countries has been more or less stringent monetary measures against inflation. But there has been a marked change in emphasis since 1976. At the annual meeting of the IMF in Manila, October 1976, speaker after speaker emphasized the overriding importance of checking inflation, even at the cost of temporarily reducing the rate of growth and accepting higher rates of transitional unemployment. Witteveen in his opening speech said: "The social and economic costs of inflation, though less immediate and less obvious than those of unemployment, can prove to be even more corrosive." In his closing remarks he summed up the sentiment of the gathering by saying: "There is a clear and general view that the path to sustainable economic growth and to the reduction of unemployment lies in the elimination of inflationary psychology and the restoration of a reasonable degree of price stability."[43] The theme was reiterated in May 1977 at the economic summit meeting in London. The assembled heads of government declared: "Inflation does not reduce unemployment. On the contrary, it is one of its major causes."

At the IMF annual meeting in Washington in September 1977 the emphasis shifted from fighting inflation to promoting growth and employment by expanding domestic demand. Witteveen said that in a number of industrial countries the anti-inflationary fiscal measures had

---

[41] See Herbert Stein, "International Coordination of Domestic Economic Policies," *The AEI Economist*, June 1978 (Washington, D.C.: American Enterprise Institute, 1978). The Mexico speech by Witteveen was published in IMF *Survey*, Washington, D.C., May 8, 1978.

[42] It would be strange if this were not the case. It was, after all, the IMF staff which first developed the monetary approach to the balance of payments, which directs the analyst's attention to rates of inflation. See International Monetary Fund, *The Monetary Approach to the Balance of Payments: A Collection of Research Papers by Members of the Staff of the International Monetary Fund* (Washington, D.C., 1977). The basic essay in that collection is J. J. Polak's seminal paper, "Monetary Analysis of Income Formation and the Payments Problem," which appeared in 1957. The IMF version of the monetary approach was, as the introductory essay by Rudolf R. Rhomberg and H. Robert Heller points out, developed under the guidance of E. M. Bernstein. It thus clearly antedates the academic version of the monetary approach which is associated with the names of H. G. Johnson, Robert Mundell, and Jacob Frenkel.

[43] International Monetary Fund, *Summary of Proceedings, Annual Meeting 1976* (Washington, D.C., 1976), pp. 13, 243.

"turned out stronger than intended. The growth of domestic demand has been significantly less than that required by our strategy [to fight inflation], particularly in countries with strong external position. This lag in demand growth should now be decisively corrected."[44] In other words the time for vigorous reflation, especially in the locomotive countries, has arrived.

What can be questioned is, of course, not the continued dedication of the IMF to promoting noninflationary growth, but the judgment that the time has come for more rapid expansion of "domestic demand." As was argued earlier in this paper, the existence of unemployment and slack does not guarantee, in the age of stagflation, that expansionary fiscal-monetary measures will promote growth without accelerating inflation. The dangers of premature reflation are highlighted by recent U.S. experience. In his Mexico speech Witteveen himself said that in the United States, while "the growth of output since the recession has been relatively strong . . . the inflation picture has now become more worrisome." That puts the inflationary dilemma rather mildly. There is now widespread agreement that in the United States the inflation picture is rather grim. A continuation of the stop-and-go policy is bound to strengthen inflationary expectations.

True, as mentioned earlier in the present paper, since about 1976 inflation rates in Germany and Japan have been lower than in the United States and have continued to decline. But the two countries are still far from zero inflation. It is therefore difficult to agree with Witteveen's statement that "inflationary expectations have been blunted" so that "expansion of domestic demand" could be speeded up without accelerating inflation. Witteveen did not say which countries he had in mind, but it cannot have been any other than Germany and Japan. In fact, however, the only country where inflation has been really eliminated—for more than two years now—is Switzerland.[45]

How to achieve noninflationary, high-employment growth cannot be further discussed here. The papers by William Fellner and Phillip Cagan in this volume wrestle with that problem. But a few general remarks on the IMF's new, intensified approach to the problem of international coordination of domestic macroeconomic policies may be permitted.

As Herbert Stein, speaking from extensive personal experience, points out in considerable detail, international discussions of domestic economic policies and problems among high officials and even among

---

[44] IMF, *Summary of Proceedings, Annual Meeting 1977*, pp. 14, 15.

[45] See Emil Küng, *The Secret of the Swiss Economic Success*, translated from the German by Eric Schiff (Washington, D.C.: American Enterprise Institute, forthcoming).

heads of government can be very helpful. Such discussions have in fact been going on for a long time on many different levels—for example, in the European Economic Community, OECD, and in the IMF itself. What must be questioned, however, is the new escalation of the coordination effort by the IMF. Instead of telling every country how fast it should grow and bringing pressure on the few oases of relative price stability to join the inflationary convoy, the IMF would be well advised to focus its effort on surveillance of exchange rate policies and on elimination of dirty floating and of contradictory interventions in the exchange market. (I distinguish sharply between dirty floating—split exchange rates and the like—and merely managed floating in the sense of influencing exchange rates by judicious intervention in the exchange market.) When making that suggestion one is usually told that the IMF has very little influence on exchange rate policies of its members, especially those of the major countries. This seems to me excessively defeatist. But whatever the limits of the IMF's influence, it surely is better to aim at a sensible target than at a highly questionable one.

The Locomotive Approach
to Sustaining World Recovery:
Has It Run Out of Steam?

Marina v. N. Whitman

Summary

Against a background of increasing dissatisfaction with the pace of global economic recovery, and of growing concern about the development of "vicious circles" of depreciation and inflation in countries with initially high rates of price increase and weak external positions, the general call for increased coordination of macroeconomic policies among the leading industrialized countries has taken a more specific form. This is the so-called locomotive argument, the crux of which is that a satisfactory pace of global recovery can be achieved only if those major industrialized countries with relatively low inflation rates and strong external positions—that is, initially, Germany, Japan, and the United States—take the initiative in adopting a stimulative stance for domestic stabilization policy. By adopting such expansionary policies, the argument goes, the "strong" countries would not only support export-led expansion in the weaker countries but would also loosen the domestic policy constraints imposed on the latter by fears regarding the impact on their payments positions and exchange rates of adopting a policy stance more stimulative than those of their stronger partners.

Underlying the sometimes heated debate that has surrounded the locomotive approach are two fundamental points of controversy. One has to do with the nature and existence of the Phillips curve: how to resolve differences of opinion among countries as to what constitutes the most desirable—or least undesirable—combination of inflation and unemployment and, indeed, whether such a trade-off exists at all, except perhaps in the very short run. The alternative view, that more in-

I am most grateful to Amor Tahari, formerly a graduate student at the University of Pittsburgh and currently an economist on the staff of the International Monetary Fund, for his valuable assistance.

flation will over the longer term make the achievement of satisfactory levels of output and employment more difficult rather than less so, has gained considerable currency recently. A second issue has to do with the sectoral composition of demand growth; if, as it sometimes appears, strong and weak nations alike regard export-led stimulus as more desirable than an equivalent dose originating at home, a genuine conflict of interest emerges. Furthermore, positions regarding these two issues interact in complex ways, and divergent views on these questions complicate efforts to agree on common criteria for the conduct of national stabilization policies.

Recent theoretical work suggests one possible route to resolving or minimizing the locomotive controversy by adapting the monetary-fiscal mix of macroeconomic stimulus to meet the needs of both strong and weak countries. Specifically, the suggestion is that fiscal-led expansion combined with monetary caution in a locomotive economy will produce an increase in the interest rate, an inflow of capital, and an appreciation of the exchange rate which reduces both the country's trade surplus and the rate of inflation associated with any given level of domestic output relative to potential. The effect on the country's trading partners will be to cause outflows of capital, depreciation of their exchange rates, a consequent improvement in their trade balances, and thus an expansion of demand and income. For a variety of reasons, such export-based demand stimulus is thought to carry less risk of touching off a vicious circle of cumulative inflation and depreciation in the weaker countries than would the unilateral introduction by their own governments of more stimulative domestic policies.

The evaluation of this policy-mix version of the locomotive approach involves a host of issues, both theoretical and empirical. Among them are the degree of flexibility possessed by governments in varying the monetary-fiscal mix of demand-management policy, the sign and magnitude of the relationship between changes in the domestic interest rate and in net international capital flows, the impact of exchange-rate appreciation on the domestic rate of inflation associated with any given level of excess capacity, and the duration of upward pressure on the exchange rate arising from a policy-induced increase in the interest rate. In particular, because the available evidence suggests that this last effect is likely to be relatively short-lived, a change in the policy mix can be expected to have a durable impact on the relationship between inflation and excess capacity in the domestic economy only to the extent that the inflation-reducing impact of an appreciating exchange rate persists for some time after the rate has in fact ceased to appreciate. The existence of such an "echo effect" turns out to depend crucially on the way in which expectations about the future path of prices are formed;

only to the extent that such expectations are "sticky" can the period during which a shift in the policy mix is likely to benefit both the locomotive economies and their weaker partners be prolonged.

An overview of actual policies and developments in Germany, Japan, and the United States since 1974–1975 suggests that all three did indeed initially follow the "locomotive policy mix" of fiscal-led expansion, although for domestic rather than international reasons, and the exchange rates of all three in fact appreciated until mid-1976. After the "summer pause" in economic recovery experienced by all three during that year, however, divergences in policy stance, pace of recovery, and external position began to emerge, divergences which were intensified—and politicized—during 1977.

In Germany and Japan, current-account positions strengthened, inflation rates declined, and the exchange rates of both appreciated substantially, while in both countries the growth rate remained consistently below expectations and the degree of economic slack increased. In the United States, in contrast, domestic demand strengthened, the degree of excess capacity shrank as real growth targets were met, the rate of inflation proved stubbornly persistent, the current account experienced a sharp negative swing, and the weakening of the dollar exchange rate became an increasing source of concern and controversy. This depreciation persisted and accelerated into the early months of 1978, despite shifts in the policy mix toward monetary tightening in the United States and monetary ease in Germany and Japan which produced the expected interest-rate differential in favor of the United States. At the same time, massive exchange-market intervention to dampen the appreciation of their currencies was undertaken not only by Germany and Japan but also by two of the most conspicuous of the "weak" OECD partners, Italy and the United Kingdom.

Despite inevitable ambiguities, the experience of the past three years sheds some light on the analytical issues raised in the first part of this paper and suggests certain conclusions regarding the effectiveness and limitations of the locomotive approach to stimulating global recovery. First, there is a somewhat surprising absence of any clear-cut relationship between the degree of policy stimulus exerted in each of the locomotive countries and the strength of domestic economic recovery. Second, as the policy mixes pursued by the three countries diverged, the associated movements in exchange rates were quite different from those implied by the simple analytics of flexible exchange rates: the currency of the United States, which intensively pursued a locomotive policy mix of fiscal stimulus and monetary tightening, depreciated, while those of Germany and Japan, which abandoned that prescription in favor of increasing monetary ease, appreciated more sharply than ever. Third, the impact effects, both internal and external, of an exchange-rate change, are likely to be quite different from the long-run effects and may cause short-run difficulties in both appreciating and depreciating countries even when the ultimate effects are beneficial to both. Thus, it is perhaps not surprising that the behavior of both strong and weak countries in 1977 suggests that neither are likely to view with equanimity rapid changes in the real (that is, inflation-adjusted) exchange rates of their currencies.

Finally, over the past three years, the distinction between "locomotive" and "nonlocomotive" economies has become increasingly blurred, suggesting the obsolescence of policy prescriptions based on this distinction. More fundamentally, our survey of both theory and experience has revealed no new means of reconciling differences of opinion regarding the relationship among policy stimulus, inflation, and real growth or of eliminating conflicts of interest regarding the optimal composition of demand expansion. Until and unless the current uncertainty regarding the impact of the traditional tools of demand-management policy in an environment of persistent stagflation can be significantly reduced, it is likely to remain a serious barrier to significant further progress in the international coordination of macroeconomic policies.

Background: Oil Deficits and Stagflation

The massive economic "coup" staged by the oil-exporting (OPEC) countries in the form of a five-fold increase in petroleum prices in 1973–1974 left, in the wake of its immediate and stunning impact on the price levels and terms of trade of the oil-consuming countries, two persistent problems that have occupied the attention of economists and policy makers ever since. The first is the question of how best to distribute the current-account (or, more accurately, goods-and-services) deficits that are the counterparts of a declining but still substantial, OPEC surplus. The second is how to respond to the global contractionary effect of large transfers of income and wealth to countries with higher than average savings propensities.

During the severe global recession in which the world found itself in 1975, the industrialized countries returned to a collective position of current-account surplus. The massive oil-consumers' deficit was thus experienced primarily by the developing countries and the more developed primary-producing nations, particularly those European nations ringing the Mediterranean. This situation appeared to threaten both the creditworthiness of the two latter groups of nations and their continued economic growth, as well as raising the specter of a world-wide financial crisis. With the uneven economic recovery of 1976–1977, however, this pattern changed: the current-account deficit of the less-developed countries as a group shrank substantially (although that of the more-developed primary producers did not), while the industrialized nations moved collectively into current-account balance. Within the industrialized group, moreover, divergent patterns developed: while some—particularly Germany and Japan—remained in or moved toward surplus, others—including France, Italy, the United Kingdom, and the United States—either remained in or moved toward deficit positions.[1] Meanwhile, the pace of global recovery remained sluggish, at least in light of the steepness of the preceding recession, and substantial excess capacity persisted in many countries along with the continuation of historically high, although significantly reduced, rates of inflation.

To the extent that the shifts just described transformed the issue of current-account imbalances into one internal to the industrialized nations, whose currencies are at least partially free to perform an equilibrating function (in cases where offsetting movements on capital account do not render such exchange-rate changes unnecessary), the first of the two problems described in the opening paragraph might appear to have been alleviated. However, a new concern now appeared on the horizon. This was the possibility that high-inflation countries, unable to attract capital inflows to offset their current-account deficits, would find themselves trapped in a self-reinforcing process of depreciation and inflation, along with an erosion of their creditworthiness and borrowing capacity. Low-inflation countries with strong external positions, in contrast, would have their efforts to contain domestic inflation assisted by a chronic upward tendency of their currencies. The fear is that such "vicious" and "virtuous" circles, once they got started, would drive countries with initially different inflation rates along ever-diverging paths and thus create cumulative instability in exchange rates and in the world economy.[2]

---

[1] By the end of 1977, Italy and the United Kingdom had moved into current-account balance.

[2] See, for example, Bank for International Settlements, *Forty-Sixth Annual Report* (Basel: BIS, 1976), pp. 8, 30–32; Rudiger Dornbusch and Paul Krugman, "Flexible Exchange Rates in the Short Run," *Brookings Papers on Economic Activity*, no. 3, 1976 (Washington, D.C.: Brookings Institution, 1976), pp. 568–573. For a skeptical critique of various versions of this argument see Thomas D. Willett, *Floating Exchange Rates and International Monetary Reform* (Washington, D.C.: American Enterprise Institute, 1977), pp. 59–67, and for the assumptions that generate such a process in a formal model, see Giorgio Basevi and Paul De Grauwe, "Vicious and Virtuous Circles: A Theoretical Analysis and a Policy Proposal for Managing Exchange Rates" (University of Bologna, 1977, mimeo.).

Although the analytical foundations of this "vicious and virtuous circle" argument remain highly controversial, it has unquestionably become a focus of attention for policy makers and their economic advisers at both national and international levels. And the experiences of the past few years, together with the implications of recent advances in macroeconomic theory as applied to open economies, have combined to give widespread credence to a related, more general point. That is that flexible exchange rates do not fully insulate an economy from external disturbances in a world of capital mobility, and that exchange-rate changes do have "real" effects, at least over any time horizon relevant to a policy maker's decision process. Thus, both exchange-rate adjustment *and* the coordination of stabilization policies may be required to minimize economic instability in an interdependent world.

Against a background of increasing dissatisfaction with the pace of global economic recovery, this general call for the coordination of macroeconomic policies, at least among a few major countries, took on a more specific form: the so-called locomotive argument. The crux of this position is that a satisfactory pace of global recovery can be achieved only if those major industrialized countries with relatively low inflation rates and strong external positions—that is, initially, Germany, Japan, and the United States—take the initiative in adopting a stimulative stance for domestic stabilization policy. The behavior of these three nations is crucial, in this view, because other industrialized nations with higher rates of inflation and weaker external positions could not afford to "get out ahead" with stimulative demand management policies of their own, however high their levels of excess capacity, for fear of jeopardizing their financial viability and plunging themselves into a vicious circle of depreciation and inflation.

One version of this argument holds that domestically based expansion in the three locomotive countries could generate sufficient export expansion in the weaker countries to relieve their difficulties and increase significantly the pace of world recovery.[3] In this form, the question is simply one of the size of the relevant intercountry income multipliers, empirical estimates of which vary too widely to inspire

---

[3] For a sympathetic view of the locomotive argument based on this approach, see Robert Solomon, "The Locomotive Approach," paper prepared for seminar on "The Locomotive Theory" at the American Enterprise Institute, April 13, 1978 (1978, mimeo.). For a critical view based on the same reasoning, see Norbert Walter, "The Role of Big Countries in International Stabilization Policies," presented at the Conference on the Economic Crises of the 1970's: Lessons for Stabilization Policy, Baden, Austria, September 15–17, 1977, pp. 5–6.

much confidence.[4] A more sophisticated version of the argument is that, by adopting expansionary policies themselves, the "strong" countries would also loosen the domestic policy constraints imposed on their weaker partners by fears regarding the impact on their external positions and exchange rates of adopting a policy stance more stimulative than those of other countries, particularly the largest and strongest ones.

Glimmerings of the locomotive argument began to appear as early as mid-1975, when the OECD's annual Economic Surveys for the three countries already mentioned each stressed the importance, for international as well as domestic reasons, of domestic demand-management policies consistent with vigorous recovery.[5] By mid-1976, the changes were being rung on this theme in a variety of prestigious settings. For example, the same 1976 Annual Report of the Bank for International Settlements that apparently coined the term "vicious circle" in the sense just described also stressed "that Germany, Japan and the United States were well placed to lead the world out of recession. Indeed, they can well afford to do so."[6]

During 1977, the positions in the debate shifted significantly. By then the United States was clearly out ahead of other major industrialized nations in the pace of domestic recovery and its current-account position had moved sharply into deficit. This shift was rooted in a trade deficit of unprecedented magnitude and, while estimates vary, it appears that at least a third of the 1977 trade deficit (which totaled almost $30 billion) is attributable to the disparity in the rates of cyclical expansion between this country and its major trading partners.[7] The

---

[4] See Allan V. Deardorff and Robert M. Stern, "International Economic Interdependence: Evidence from Econometric Models," seminar discussion paper no. 71 (Department of Economics, University of Michigan, 1977, mimeo.) and the references cited there. The OECD has utilized its own model to generate such multipliers for internal use, some results of which were cited in *Newsweek*, February 27, 1978, pp. 63–64.

[5] OECD, *Economic Surveys*: Germany (May 1975), Japan (July 1975), United States (July 1975).

[6] Bank for International Settlements, *Forty-Sixth Annual Report*, p. 7. See also, OECD, *Economic Outlook* 20 (December 1976), pp. 11–12, and the "McCracken Report": OECD, *Towards Full Employment and Price Stability* (OECD, June 1977), p. 237.

[7] Robert Z. Lawrence, "An Analysis of the 1977 Trade Deficit," *Brookings Papers on Economic Activity*, no. 1, 1978 (Washington, D.C.: Brookings Institution, 1978), p. 182. Governor Henry Wallich of the Federal Reserve Board estimates that "the U.S. trade deficit of about $30 billion might be $10–20 billion lower if there were full employment in major industrialized countries" ("Reflections on the U.S. Balance of Payments," remarks at the joint luncheon of the American Economic Association and American Finance Association, New York City, December 28, 1977, p. 7).

United States took the position that it had fully discharged its locomotive function, and that the responsibility now rested squarely on Germany and Japan to do the same, that is, to increase the stimulative stance of their own policies to an extent consistent with elimination of their current-account surpluses. The general line of their response was, in essence, that they were doing all they could, that to undertake additional domestic stimulus would risk undermining their continuing battle against inflation.

As this thumbnail history indicates, the somewhat arcane "locomotive" hypothesis has become the basis of a controversy which, rather than being fought out in the pages of scholarly journals, has produced heated, if somewhat stylized, debates among national delegates at international meetings, has heightened tensions in economic relationships among the leading nations of the "Western" alliance, and has become the major topic of discussion at summit meetings of their heads of state.[8] It seems worthwhile, therefore, to examine the nature of the controversies associated with the locomotive economies argument, explore any possibilities for a reconciliation of divergent views, and evaluate the analytical underpinnings of the discussion in the light of the policies actually followed by the three locomotive countries during the current recovery and concurrent developments in their external positions.

Points of Controversy: Phillips Curves and the Composition of Demand Growth

In simplest terms, the issue can be seen as a divergence of views regarding what is the most desirable, or least undesirable, combination of inflation and unemployment (or excess capacity in general)—the optimal point on the Phillips curve.[9] If the locomotive economies have a lower tolerance for inflation and a greater tolerance for excess capacity than do the countries on the other side of the argument, then the problem is one of differences in preference functions and becomes the province of the negotiator rather than the economic analyst.

From another point of view, it can be argued that conflict among preference functions is not the issue at all and that, in fact, there can

---

[8] For a lively presentation of the argument in dialogue form, see W. M. Corden, "Expansion of the World Economy and the Duties of Surplus Countries," *The World Economy*, vol. 1, no. 2 (January 1978), pp. 121–134.

[9] This section draws heavily on Marina v. N. Whitman, "Coordination and Management of the International Economy: A Search for Organizing Principles," in William Fellner, ed., *Contemporary Economic Problems 1977* (Washington, D.C.: American Enterprise Institute, 1977), pp. 322–325.

be only one definition of the optimal macroeconomic policy, whether the point of view taken is national or global. That policy is to achieve the degree of economic stimulus that will maximize the real growth of the domestic economy over some reasonable time frame, say, the next three to five years. If full account is taken, in establishing policy goals consistent with this criterion, of what the policy stances of other nations are likely to be, then any greater degree of stimulus would only serve to exacerbate inflation, internationally as well as domestically. From this perspective, the locomotive controversy must be grounded simply in divergences in forecasting, differences of opinion regarding the actual policy stance most likely to achieve the generally accepted goal.

Unfortunately, this "harmony of interests" view is itself based on a highly controversial assumption: an implicit denial that there exists, except perhaps in the very short run, a Phillips-curve trade-off that enables a country to achieve higher rates of output and employment at the cost of tolerating a higher rate of inflation. The alternative view, that more inflation will over the longer term make the achievement of satisfactory levels of output and employment more difficult rather than less, has gained considerable currency as a result of the stagflation of recent years.[10] At present, views regarding this issue are both widely divergent and strongly held, and must inevitably complicate efforts to agree on common criteria for the conduct of national stabilization policies.

Another possible source of controversy relates to the sectoral composition of demand growth. Central to the "locomotive economies" hypothesis is the belief that, since the oil-consuming countries must collectively run a deficit for some time to come, a satisfactory global rate of recovery can be achieved only if the three strongest industrialized nations, by maintaining sufficient domestic stimulus and refraining from intervention in the foreign exchange market, reduce the role of the export sector and increase the role of domestic sectors in supporting the expansion of their own output.[11] It is this reasoning that makes a shift from current-account surplus to current-account deficit the test of whether a country has adequately discharged its locomotive obligations. All this reflects the widespread support the weaker nations have marshalled for their belief that their own expansions must be coordi-

---

[10] For this view, see the April 29, 1977 communique of the Interim Committee of the IMF's Board of Governors (IMF *Survey*, May 2, 1977, p. 130), and Milton Friedman's "Nobel Lecture: Inflation and Unemployment," *Journal of Political Economy*, vol. 85 (June 1977), pp. 451–472.

[11] The OECD notes that, under this prescription, "the rates of total output—and, hence, demand pressures—would not differ between countries as much as the growth of domestic demand, because revaluing countries would see their net exports decrease and devaluing countries would see theirs develop" (OECD, *Economic Outlook* 20 [December 1977], p. 9).

nated with, and in fact led by, expansion in the stronger countries if they are to avoid the weakening of payments balances and accompanying exchange-rate depreciation that would both threaten their financial viability and exacerbate their domestic inflationary problems. If, for any one of a variety of reasons, the stronger nations also regard export-led stimulus as more desirable than an equivalent dose originating at home, a genuine conflict of interest emerges. We shall return later to the question of why, and to what extent, resistance to changes in the sectoral composition of demand may have affected the behavior of the locomotive economies.

If, in fact, it is a universal preference for export-led rather than domestically based output expansion that lies at the heart of the locomotive controversy, an impasse is inevitable, and we are back to the world of the zero-sum game. For there is no mechanism that will allow all the industrialized nations to run a current-account surplus at the same time when, for the near future, they must collectively run a current-account deficit, with the OPEC countries acting as net lenders to the rest of the world.[12] But the controversy is never phrased explicitly in these terms; rather, it appears to center on the relationship between expansion of domestic demand and continued progress against inflation.

Unfortunately, the issues cannot be so neatly separated. Disagreements arising from different views regarding the nature and existence of a Phillips curve interact with those arising from conflicts of interest regarding the optimal composition of demand expansion. To those who believe that a Phillips curve operates over the medium to long run, and that under present conditions the increased global utility to be derived from greater demand stimulus would outweigh the costs of any associated acceleration of inflation (which, most such expansionists argue, would be negligible as long as substantial excess capacity persists), export-led growth appears as a zero-sum game in global terms, while real growth originating in the domestic sector benefits one's neighbors as well as oneself. To those holding the alternative view, any efforts to stimulate domestic demand beyond the point of maximum real growth can only serve to exacerbate inflation, globally as well as domestically.

Obviously, in a world of complete information and perfect forecasting, such questions would be resolved immediately and definitively. In the real world of uncertainty, however, estimates and forecasts are bound to be influenced by the biases of their originators, and differ-

---

[12] In principle, the OPEC countries and the industrialized nations might serve jointly as net lenders to the oil-consuming primary-producer countries. In fact, however, the magnitude of the debt-increase of the latter group implied by such a configuration would not be manageable. It was such a situation that gave rise to fears of a worldwide financial crisis in 1975.

ences of opinion based on inconsistent assumptions and divergent forecasts will inevitably shade over into differences based on perceived conflicts of interest. Recognizing the impossibility of separating the points
at issue into watertight compartments, it nevertheless seems worthwhile to explore analytically the conditions under which the locomotive
economies might expand domestic demand in a manner consistent with
a reduction in, or at least no acceleration of, the domestic inflation rate.

Changing the Policy Mix: A Means of Reconciliation? A possibility for
resolving the controversy is implied in a recent article by Dornbusch
and Krugman, who argue that the mix of macroeconomic policies
utilized to stimulate expansion can and should be adapted to meet the
needs of both strong and weak countries.[13] The argument is based on
the observation that, in a world of flexible exchange rates and high international mobility of capital, fiscal-based expansion of income in one
country will be transmitted to other countries as well, while an expansion based on monetary stimulus will, on the contrary, tend to exert a
contractionary effect on the incomes of other countries.[14] The mechanisms producing these results are perhaps most easily seen if we assume for the sake of exposition that a country introduces a mix of
tighter monetary policy and more expansionary fiscal policy just sufficient to hold aggregate demand (domestic plus foreign) for domestic
production constant. The result will be an increase in the domestic interest rate, an inflow of capital, and an appreciation of the exchange
rate which reduces the country's trade surplus (or increases its deficit).[15]
The effect on the country's trading partners will be to cause outflows of
capital, depreciation of their exchange rates, a consequent reduction of
their trade deficits (or increase of their surpluses), and thus an expansion of demand and income. A monetary expansion-cum-fiscal contraction in the mix-shifting country would, in contrast, cause an outflow of
capital and a depreciation of its exchange rate, shifting demand away
from the goods of partner countries and thus reducing total demand
and income in their economies.

The terms on which this line of reasoning has been set forth are
not those in which the locomotive position is usually put. The aim, as

---

[13] Dornbusch and Krugman, "Flexible Exchange Rates."

[14] These results hold strictly in the extreme case, when domestic and foreign finan-
cial assets are perfect substitutes. See Robert A. Mundell, *International Economics*
(New York: Macmillan, 1968), chaps. 11, 17, 18, and J. Marcus Fleming, "Domestic
Financial Policies Under Fixed and Under Floating Exchange Rates," IMF *Staff
Papers*, vol. 9 (November 1962), pp. 369–379.

[15] The terms "trade balance" and "current-account balance" are used more or less
interchangeably here. The two moved in essentially parallel fashion in the major
industrialized countries during the period under discussion.

generally stated, is not to hold aggregate demand constant, but rather to increase it in a way that minimizes the domestic inflationary impact, as well as maximizing the positive effect on incomes of partner countries. The policy-mix prescription does not necessarily imply, therefore, the adoption of monetary and fiscal policies that operate in conflicting directions on the domestic economy—a prescription that, in view of a growing perception of severe limitations on the ability of governments to fine-tune the impact of stabilization policies, might well be greeted with extreme skepticism. Rather, the suggestion is that fiscal policy rather than monetary policy be the main instrument of stimulus in the locomotive economies.[16]

Whether one talks about the question in terms of maintaining constant aggregate demand and output with an appreciating exchange rate or of expanding aggregate demand with less depreciation (or more appreciation) of the rate than might otherwise be expected to occur, the purpose of utilizing the policy mix to affect the exchange rate is twofold: to reduce inflationary pressure in the country in question by lowering (absolutely or relatively) the domestic prices of imported goods, and to shift the composition of demand in such a way as to exert a stimulative impact on the incomes of partner countries. It can be argued, of course, that there is an alternative way of achieving the same results. That is, the locomotive economy might utilize whatever mix of monetary and fiscal policies it found most desirable and effective from the domestic point of view, and then intervene directly in the foreign exchange market to limit the resulting depreciation—or reinforce the resulting appreciation—of its exchange rate.

There are several objections to this argument. First, the recent behavior of exchange rates casts severe doubt on the notion that a sustained appreciation of the currency could be achieved simply by exchange-market intervention. At the least, the magnitudes involved might be astronomical, and the effects on the domestic economy would be quite different from those created by a change in the policy mix.[17]

---

[16] In urging "that during a world recession a synchronized expansion is appropriate," Dornbusch and Krugman argue ("Flexible Exchange Rates," p. 574) that countries should "apply fiscal expansion to stimulate aggregate demand and an accommodating monetary policy to maintain the rate of interest and therefore exchange rates." Under present conditions, with differential rates of inflation in strong and weak countries, such a policy mix would be more likely to produce appreciation in the former and depreciation in the latter.

[17] Using a standard two-country model with perfect capital mobility, Lehment has shown that monetary expansion via exchange-market intervention (purchases of foreign currency) will have a greater contractionary impact on foreign income than will an equivalent monetary expansion achieved by domestic open-market policy. Harmen Lehment, "Exchange Market Interventions and Open-Market Operations as Instruments of Active Employment Policy Under Flexible Rates," paper presented

Furthermore, if one takes the view that the international monetary system can function most effectively if exchange-market intervention by governments to alter trends in the rate is minimized, to base a policy on such intervention, whatever the motive, would be counterproductive even if it were technically feasible. At the same time, of course, the logic of this policy-mix argument certainly requires that the locomotive economies refrain from intervening in the exchange markets in the opposite direction, that is, to reduce the resulting upward pressure on their currencies.

Some Analytical Issues

Buried in the stark theory of the impact of different policy mixes under flexible exchange rates are a host of questions, both theoretical and empirical, regarding the impact of macroeconomic policy instruments, both domestically and internationally. Unfortunately, all the major efforts so far to estimate econometrically the intercountry impacts of various policy combinations have been based on pegged-rate assumptions, with the exchange rate either held constant or varied exogenously as a policy variable.[18] Because the international transmission process is believed to operate quite differently under flexible rates, we cannot evaluate the propositions just outlined directly against the results of an econometric model. Rather, we must examine the theoretical and statistical evidence piecemeal, one step at a time, and use the insights thus derived to assist our general evaluation of the locomotive argument, and the proposed policy-mix resolution, in the light of actual developments in the world economy. Furthermore, in view of the inevitable variation in estimated coefficients among studies, each of whose authors utilizes a somewhat different model and different data from the others, the emphasis here will be on the robustness of qualitative results obtained from such studies, rather than on the range of point-estimates of quantitative relationships that have been generated in econometric work.

---

at the Conference on the Economics of Flexible Exchange Rates, Vienna, March 29–31, 1978.

[18] A major exception is the Federal Reserve's new multicountry model, which is designed to apply to both pegged-rate and managed floating regimes. See Richard Berner et al., "Modelling the International Influences on the U.S. Economy: A Multi-Country Approach," International Finance Discussion Papers No. 93 (Washington, D.C.: Board of Governors of the Federal Reserve System, November 1976, mimeo.), and "Multi-Country Model of the International Influences on the U.S. Economy: Preliminary Results," ibid., no. 115 (December 1977, mimeo.). Estimates of intercountry policy multipliers generated by this model are not yet available. Several flexible-rate models have also been developed for Canada.

Interest Rates, Capital Flows, and the Exchange Rate. Although it is not generally spelled out precisely, what the policy-mix prescription must amount to is that the governments of the locomotive economies should rely more heavily on debt-financing and less heavily on monetization of the government budget deficits associated with fiscal stimulus. This means creating a permanent increase in the flow supply of government bonds (as contrasted with the one-shot increase involved in open market-operations) leading, *ceteris paribus*, to a permanently higher domestic interest rate in a growing economy. Any serious consideration of this prescription presupposes, first, that it is indeed possible to alter the monetary-fiscal mix utilized to achieve a particular degree of stimulus and, second, that the increase in the domestic interest rate will indeed lead in the short run to an inflow of capital and an appreciation of the exchange rate.

The first of these assumptions has been challenged by the monetarist proposition that debt-financed fiscal expansion can have no net stimulative impact, since the resulting increase in the interest rate will ultimately force a decrease in private investment spending equal to the initial increase in government spending. However, recent theoretical work suggests that such complete crowding out is by no means inevitable and depends, in fact, on special assumptions about the relative responsiveness of private spending and the demand for money to changes in wealth and the interest rate.[19] Evaluating the evidence from leading industrialized nations in recent years, the OECD's 1976 "McCracken Report" concluded, furthermore, "that the link from fiscal to monetary policy is less close than is sometimes implied" and that "the structural linkages offer the opportunity of substantial freedom in the policy mix actually selected."[20]

The conventional view that an increase in the level of domestic interest rates will attract an inflow of capital from abroad has recently been challenged by the proposition (also of monetarist origins) that differences among countries in the real rate of interest are insignificant (as well as being unaffected in the short run by policy changes of the sort discussed here), so that observed differences in nominal rates of interest are determined primarily by differences in expected rates of inflation.[21]

---

[19] See Allan S. Blinder and Robert M. Solow, "Analytical Foundations of Fiscal Policy," in *The Economics of Public Finance* (Washington, D.C.: Brookings Institution, 1974), p. 53.

[20] OECD, *Towards Full Employment and Price Stability*, pp. 123–124. The authors note that this conclusion is qualified by the important role of expectations in financial markets and the adverse consequences of too great a "twist" in the policy mix.

[21] See, for example, Jacob A. Frenkel, "A Monetary Approach to the Exchange Rate: Doctrinal Aspects and Empirical Evidence," *Scandinavian Journal of Eco-*

An increase in the nominal interest rate, in this view, must reflect an increase in the expected domestic rate of inflation, leading to an expected depreciation of the currency, and thus to a capital outflow that produces an actual depreciation.

A reconciliation of these conflicting hypotheses has been suggested in a recent paper by Frankel, who obtained excellent econometric results by introducing into the equation explaining the deutsche mark/dollar exchange rate *both* the differential in short-term money market rates (as a proxy for the relative "tightness" of the money market) *and* the differential in long-term government bond rates (as a proxy for differences in expected rates of inflation) in the two countries.[22] The expected negative sign on the short-term rate differential and positive sign on the long-term rate differential were obtained, both consistently significant, and the fits were far better than those obtained in equations based on either of the alternative simple hypotheses described above.

Since, in actual operation, monetary and fiscal instruments have their primary and most direct impact on short-term rates, this evidence offers support for the conventional view that a shift from monetary to fiscal stimulus will indeed produce a capital inflow and an appreciation of the exchange rate. It should be noted, however, that the existence of international capital mobility sufficient to produce these results also implies that such an increase in debt-financed fiscal stimulus cannot be achieved without any increase in the monetary growth rate; some degree of monetary "accommodation" is required. This is because inflows of capital from abroad will limit the increase in domestic interest rates associated with the expanded flow supply of bonds, thus reducing also the increase in money velocity that, in a closed economy, would have made possible an increased growth of aggregate demand with an unchanged monetary growth rate.

Finally, a growing body of empirical evidence suggests that an appreciating exchange rate does indeed reduce the domestic rate of inflation associated with any given level of excess capacity by reducing

---

nomics, vol. 78, no. 2 (1976), pp. 200–224, and John F. O. Bilson, "The Monetary Approach to the Exchange Rate—Some Empirical Evidence," IMF *Staff Papers*, vol. 25, no. 1 (March 1978), pp. 48–75.

[22] Jeffrey A. Frankel, "Explaining the Mark: A Theory of Floating Exchange Rates Based on Real Interest Differentials" (Massachusetts Institute of Technology, 1977, mimeo.). These results may help to explain the failure of other researchers to find a strong systematic relationship between interest rates and exchange rates. See Ira J. Kaylin et al., "The Effect of Interest-Rate Changes on Exchange Rates during the Current Float," in Carl H. Stem et al., eds., *Eurocurrencies and the International Monetary System* (Washington, D.C.: American Enterprise Institute, 1976), pp. 223–234.

(or lowering the rate of increase in) import prices.[23] Although the magnitudes of the coefficients vary substantially from one study to another, they are both significant in the statistical sense and nonnegligible in the economic sense for most major industrialized countries. The one puzzling exception is Germany, for which the relevant elasticities have generally been both implausibly low and statistically insignificant.[24] This result is the more puzzling in view of the generally accepted view that the appreciation of the mark has made a major contribution to Germany's remarkably low inflation rate in recent years. This unresolved conundrum is generally attributed to some structural misspecification of the estimating equation for Germany; certainly it has not been taken seriously enough to become a part of the arsenal of antilocomotive arguments, either in Germany or anywhere else.[25]

The question of how long the upward pressure on the exchange rate resulting from a policy-induced increase in the interest rate is likely to persist is crucial to the discussion. This is especially true in view of the fact that there appear to be substantial lags in the response of trade flows to changes in exchange rates.[26] If this is so, the immediate impact of an appreciation in one of the locomotive countries on the trade balances of its trading partners, measured in current prices, will be perverse (the so-called J-curve), and the stimulus to aggregate demand in these countries, stemming from an improvement in the trade balance measured in constant prices, will be delayed. If the exchange-rate impact of a higher interest rate in the locomotive country does not persist

---

[23] That is, there is a two-step relationship between changes in import prices and in the domestic price level. Most of the models referred to below ignore the additional impact of exchange-rate changes on the domestic prices of exportable goods and import-substitutes.

[24] See, for example, Dornbusch and Krugman, "Flexible Exchange Rates"; Morris Goldstein, "Downward Price Inflexibility, Ratchet Effects, and the Inflationary Impact of Import Price Changes: Some Empirical Tests," IMF *Staff Papers*, vol. 24, no. 3 (November 1977), pp. 569–612; Erich Spitäller, "An Analysis of Inflation in the Seven Main Industrial Countries, 1958–76" (International Monetary Fund, 1977, mimeo.).

[25] Dornbusch and Krugman suggest that "part of the explanation is likely to come from the automatic adjustment of agricultural prices in response to exchange-rate movements" under the Common Agricultural Policy ("Flexible Exchange Rates," p. 570).

[26] For a survey of this literature, see Stephen P. Magee, "Prices, Incomes, and Foreign Trade," in Peter B. Kenen, ed., *International Trade and Finance: Frontiers for Research* (New York: Cambridge University Press, 1975), pp. 175–252. Studies conducted at the Federal Reserve Board indicate that "the full impact of the rate change would normally be expected to occur over a period of two years following the exchange rate change" (Henry C. Wallich, member, Board of Governors of the Federal Reserve System, statement before the U.S. Congress, Senate, Subcommittee on International Finance of the Committee on Banking, Housing, and Urban Affairs, February 6, 1978).

long enough for trade flows to respond, the impact of a mix-shift becomes problematic, and, at the very least, efforts to evaluate the applicability of the argument in the light of actual events will be severely complicated.

Modern portfolio theory tells us that an increase in the domestic interest rate relative to interest rates in other countries will produce a one-shot inflow of capital as existing wealth portfolios are reallocated in the light of the change in relative rates of return. In addition, there will be a much smaller continuing inflow resulting from the fact that a larger share of additions to the stock of wealth will now be allocated to investment in the home country. Under the assumption of a unitary wealth-elasticity of demand for foreign bonds, the ratio of this continuing flow effect to the one-shot stock effect will be equal to the growth rate of the relevant stock of wealth.[27] The continuing impact on the balance of payments will be affected in addition by higher interest payments to foreigners and smaller interest receipts; thus the size (and sign) of this impact depends on the growth rates of wealth at home and abroad relative to the levels of foreign and domestic interest rates, as well as on the substitutability between domestic and foreign securities in response to changes in the interest-rate differential.[28]

A number of empirical investigations of the response of international capital flows to interest-rate differentials have indicated that reallocation of portfolios takes place relatively rapidly, and that the stock-

---

[27] William H. Branson and Thomas D. Willett, "Policy Toward Short-Term Capital Movements: Some Implications of the Portfolio Approach," in Fritz Machlup et al., eds., *International Mobility and Movement of Capital* (New York: Columbia University Press for the National Bureau of Economic Research, 1972), pp. 287–310.

[28] The formula for the flow or continuing impact on the balance of payments $(d\dot{R}_t)$ of a change in the home interest rate (r^h), holding the foreign interest rate (r^f) constant, is as follows:

$$\frac{d\dot{R}_t}{dr^h} = W_t^h \frac{\partial \lambda^h}{\partial r^h} (g^h - r^f) + W_t^f \frac{\partial \lambda^f}{\partial r^h} (g^f - r^h) - W_t^f \lambda^f$$

where: h, f = superscripts representing the home and the foreign country, respectively

W_t = the stock of wealth at time t

λ = the wealth-allocation function

g = the growth rate of wealth

The signs of the first two terms, representing the net impact of reallocations of new additions to the stock of wealth and of the changed streams of interest receipts and payments resulting from wealth-reallocation, depend on the signs of the terms in parentheses, that is, on the growth rates of domestic and foreign wealth in comparison with the levels of foreign and domestic interest rates, respectively. However, the third term, representing the effect of higher interest payments on the stock of foreign wealth invested in the home country on the basis of the pre-existing wealth-allocation, is always negative. See Robert F. Stern, *The Balance of Payments: Theory and Economic Policy* (Chicago: Aldine Publishing Co., 1973), p. 231.

adjustment process is essentially completed within one year or less.[29] These findings, together with the small size and uncertain sign of the continuing balance-of-payments impact, lend support to the conclusion that

> the clear lesson for policy-makers is that attempts to influence capital flows through changes in monetary policy will have a much stronger impact in the short run than in the long run. Thus, unless the monetary authorities are prepared to change policy continuously in the same direction, monetary policy is better regarded as a means of influencing the stock of foreign exchange reserves than as a means of influencing the longer-run pattern of capital flows.[30]

As the language of this quotation suggests, however, the studies just mentioned relate to the pre-1973 era of pegged exchange rates. And there is reason to believe that the response mechanisms to international differences in interest rates are significantly different under different exchange-rate regimes. Under a pegged-rate system, government intervention in the exchange markets guarantees the availability of whatever currency an investor requires to carry out his portfolio-reallocation process. Under a pure flexible-rate regime, in contrast, such accommodation is not provided, and the necessary deutsche marks (taking Germany as an example) will not be immediately available to would-be investors in German bonds. This implies that, because available supplies are fixed in the very short run, a change in the price of marks must alone clear the market. As trade flows adjust with a lag to the appreciation of the mark, the resulting current-account deficit will generate the supply of marks desired by the would-be investors, allowing the capital inflow to take place.[31]

---

[29] See, for example, William H. Branson and R. D. Hill, "Capital Movements in the OECD Area: An Econometric Analysis," in OECD *Economic Outlook, Occasional Studies* (December 1971); Richard J. Herring and Richard C. Marston, *National Monetary Policies and International Financial Markets* (Amsterdam: North-Holland Publishing Co., 1977); Norman C. Miller and Marina v. N. Whitman, "A Mean-Variance Analysis of United States Long-Term Portfolio Foreign Investment," *Quarterly Journal of Economics*, vol. 84 (May 1970), pp. 175–196; Norman C. Miller and Marina v. N. Whitman, "Alternative Theories and Tests of U.S. Short-Term Foreign Investment," *Journal of Finance*, vol. 28 (December 1973), pp. 1131–1150.

[30] Herring and Marston, *National Monetary Policies*, p. 127.

[31] This sharp distinction between fixed and flexible exchange-rate regimes will be blurred, even in the absence of any official exchange-market intervention, to the extent that private speculators substitute for the government in making foreign exchange available and thus obviate the need for the "overshooting" described in the next two paragraphs.

There are two alternative explanations of how the short-run market-clearing mechanism operates under these conditions. One is the so-called portfolio rebalancing effect, according to which foreigners' demands for an increased proportion of mark-denominated assets in their portfolios initially cause an appreciation of the mark sufficient to satisfy this demand entirely through a "capital gains" or "valuation" effect on the existing mark-denominated assest in their portfolios. Gradually, as marks become available and investors can increase the actual volume of mark-denominated assets in their portfolios, the mark will fall back somewhat from its initially large appreciation, and the valuation effect will be correspondingly reduced.

The second and more plausible explanation of the market-clearing mechanism is that an increase in the interest-rate differential and the resulting incipient capital inflow cause the mark to appreciate above its new equilibrium value (that is, to "overshoot") to the point where the interest-rate differential is exactly offset, according to Keynesian interest-parity theory, by the forward discount on the mark engendered by its expected future depreciation. The implication of this hypothesis is that, paradoxically, while the exchange rate responds immediately (and, indeed, over-responds) to a change in the interest-rate differential, the actual capital flows associated with portfolio-reallocation will occur more slowly than under pegged rates. Indeed, in this framework, the period over which the stock-adjustment capital inflow takes place must of necessity coincide with the period required for trade flows to respond to changes in relative prices, since it is the latter response which generates the supply of marks that makes the former possible.

Empirical studies of the determination of exchange rates during the recent years of managed floating generally reveal a substantial and prompt (with very short lags) response of these rates to policy-induced changes in interest-rate differentials.[32] The evidence regarding over-shooting is mixed, however, with some models suggesting that the lagged response of the exchange rate is in the opposite direction from the initial response and others indicating the opposite. Thus, the econometric evidence is far from conclusive regarding the question whether the observed response of exchange rates to interest-rate differentials under managed floating is caused by prompt completion of the stock-

---

[32] See, for example, Jacques R. Artus, "Exchange Rate Stability and Managed Float-ing: The Experience of the Federal Republic of Germany," IMF *Staff Papers*, vol. 23 (July 1976), pp. 312–333; Bilson, "The Monetary Approach to the Exchange Rate"; John F. O. Bilson, "The Current Experience with Floating Exchange Rates: An Ap-praisal of the Monetary Approach," *American Economic Review*, vol. 68 (May 1978), pp. 392–397; Jeffrey A. Frankel, "Explaining the Mark"; Susan Schadler, "Sources of Exchange Rate Variability, Theory and Empirical Evidence," IMF *Staff Papers*, vol. 24 (July 1977), pp. 253–296.

adjustment capital inflow or by overshooting and a more gradual completion of the portfolio-reallocation process.

In any case, leaving the overshooting issue aside, upward pressure on the exchange rate of the locomotive economy will persist only until the stock-adjustment capital inflow is completed. The sign of the continuing flow effects of the interest-rate change on the rate is uncertain; in any case, its absolute magnitude is unlikely to be significant. Thus, unless the locomotive economy continues to shift its policy mix so as to increase the interest-rate differential—a policy that could hardly be sustainable for very long—the appreciation of the exchange rate will be a short-run phenomenon.

Exchange Rates, Domestic Prices, and the Phillips Curve. Under the conventional formulation of the Phillips-curve relationship, the favorable impact of an exchange-rate appreciation on the rate of domestic inflation associated with a given level of excess capacity will be a direct one, operating solely through its effect in holding down the rate of price increase of the imported component of GNP (or the consumer's market-basket), and will cease promptly when the exchange rate stops appreciating.[33] To see this, assume that the process of price-formation is represented by equations of the following type,

[1] $$\dot{p} = a_o + a_1 \dot{w} + a_2 (\dot{e} + \dot{p}^*),$$

and

[2] $$\dot{w} = b_o + b_1 u,$$

where:

$\dot{p}$ = domestic inflation rate
$\dot{w}$ = rate of wage increase
$\dot{e}$ = rate of change of the exchange rate
u = unemployment rate (as a proxy for the level of excess capacity)
$\dot{p}^*$ = foreign rate of inflation (assumed to be zero in this analysis).

The reduced-form expression for the domestic rate of inflation is given by

[3] $$\dot{p} = a_o + a_1 b_o + a_1 b_1 u + a_2 (\dot{e} + \dot{p}^*),$$

in which the effect of a changing exchange rate is represented by the coefficient a_2, and the effect vanishes when $\dot{e} = 0$.

If, however, it is assumed that the rate of wage increase is affected

---

[33] This is partly because, again, such models do not incorporate the additional effects of exchange-rate changes on the domestic prices of exportables and import-substitutes.

not only by the level of excess capacity in the labor market but also by expectations regarding the rate of inflation, then a reduction in the actual inflation rate because of an appreciating exchange rate may bring about a reduction in the expected rate of inflation as well, a shift that may persist for a time even after the exchange rate itself has ceased to appreciate. Such a lowering of inflationary expectations would, as long as it persisted, make it possible to achieve a higher level of capacity utilization, and thus a higher rate of output growth, for any given rate of inflation.[34] Under such circumstances, the locomotive economies would be able to enjoy more rapid real expansion with no increase in domestic inflation rates, and impart more stimulus to the deficit economies and to the world as a whole at unchanged exchange rates, for a period of time after the effect of a policy-mix shift on exchange rates has been completed. Such an "echo" effect arising from the impact of lowered inflationary expectations would thus stretch out in time the period during which a shift in the policy mix could be expected to benefit both the locomotive countries and their weaker partners.

It turns out, however, that the existence of such an echo effect depends heavily on the particular assumptions made about the processes by which expectations are formed. To see this, let us substitute for equation [3] two reduced-form equations for the rate of inflation generated by alternative versions of an expectations-augmented Phillips-curve equation.[35] First, assume that expectations are formed adaptively, according to a Koyck distributed-lag process:

[4] $$\dot{p}^e - \dot{p}^e_{t-1} = \lambda(\dot{p}_{t-1} - \dot{p}^e_{t-1}),$$

so that

$$\dot{p}^e = \frac{\lambda}{1-(1-\lambda)L} \dot{p}_{t-1},$$

and

[5] $$w = b_o + b_1 u + b_2 \dot{p}^e,$$

where

$\dot{p}^e$ = the rate of inflation expected to prevail at time t,

$0 < \lambda < 1$ = speed-of-adjustment coefficient,[36]

and L = lag operator.

---

[34] This result, incidentally, will hold independently of whether a stable negatively sloped Phillips curve exists over the medium- to long-run or not.

[35] See Helmut Frisch, "Inflation Theory 1963–1975: A 'Second Generation' Survey," *Journal of Economic Literature*, vol. 15, no. 4 (December 1977), pp. 1301–1302.

[36] Note that when $\lambda = 0$, $\dot{p}^e = \dot{p}^e_{t-1}$ (constant expectations), and when $\lambda = 1$, $\dot{p}^e = \dot{p}_{t-1}$ (myopic expectations).

Combining equations [1], [4], and [5] yields

[6] $\quad \dot{p} = a_0 + a_1 b_0 + a_1 b_1 u + a_2 (\dot{e} + \dot{p}^*) + a_1 b_2 \dfrac{\lambda}{1-(1-\lambda)L} \dot{p}_{t-1}.$

Substituting for $\dot{p}_{t-1}$, we have

[7] $\quad \dot{p} = A + a_1 b_1 u + a_1^2 b_1 b_2 \lambda u_{t-1} + \dots$

$\qquad\qquad\qquad\qquad + a_2 (\dot{e} + \dot{p}^*) + a_1 a_2 b_2 \lambda (\dot{e}_{t-1} + \dot{p}^*_{t-1}) \dots.$

In this case, we see that lagged prices do indeed enter into the determination of the price equation [6]. Since these lagged prices are themselves functions of lagged rates of exchange-rate change, the echo effect postulated above indeed exists, as is made explicit in equation [7]. How quickly it fades away depends, of course, on the size of λ, the speed-of-adjustment coefficient in the equation determining price expectations.

In our alternative version, the price and wage equations [1] and [5] remain unchanged, but we assume that expectations are formed rationally, that is, with full knowledge of the structure of the system represented by our equations. In effect, this means that the rate of inflation expected to prevail in period t differs from the one that actually occurs in that period only by a random variable. That is,

[8] $\qquad\qquad\qquad\qquad \dot{p}^e = \dot{p} - v,$

where v is the error term in the price equation.[37]

The reduced-form expression for the rate of inflation obtained by combining equations [1], [5], and [8] is

[9] $\qquad\qquad \dot{p} = \dfrac{a_0 + a_1 b_0}{1 - a_1 b_2} + \dfrac{a_1 b_1}{1 - a_1 b_2} u + \dfrac{a_2}{1 - a_1 b_2} (\dot{e} + \dot{p}^*)$

In this case, the coefficient on the rate of change of the exchange rate is larger than it was in the previous cases,[38] since in addition to affecting the rate of inflation directly, the rate of currency appreciation or depreciation has an additional, indirect impact through its effect on inflationary expectations. No lagged values of any of the variables appear in this expression, however; the echo effect has vanished. If, in other words, people know that the domestic rate of inflation has been temporarily dampened by an appreciating exchange rate, their demands for wage increases will return to preappreciation rates instantly when the exchange rate ceases to rise further.

---

[37] The error terms in equations [1]–[3] and [5]–[7] have been omitted for simplicity.

[38] This is because $a_1 < 1$ and we assume that $b_2 \leq 1$ (that is, that the Phillips curve does not have a positive slope).

It appears, therefore, that the favorable effects of a policy-mix shift in the locomotive countries will last longer than the impact of the resulting capital flows on the exchange rate only if people's expectations regarding the rate of inflation are sticky, that is, affected by what happened in past periods, when the rate of price increase was dampened by an influence which is in fact no longer operating. Little is known about the relative importance of "adaptive" and "rational" components in the actual processes by which expectations are formed. However, some observers suggest that, at least in the United States, the responses that determine expectations-formation have been shifting over the postwar period. That is, as the public's knowledge about the nature of government policies and their impact on the economy has increased, the role of the "distributed lag" component in expectations-formation has shrunk, and the role of the "rational" component has increased.[39] To the extent that this is true for the locomotive economies generally, it weakens the possibility of prolonging the desired impact of a shift in the policy mix beyond the period during which it has a direct impact on the exchange rate.[40]

Effects on Partner Countries. We have been focusing so far on some of the conceptual issues involved in trying to resolve the locomotive economies argument by means of a shift in the monetary-fiscal policy mix, primarily in terms of the structure of economic relationships in the countries undertaking such a shift in the mix of demand-management policies. Before attempting to evaluate some of these issues in the light of recent events, however, we must inquire in more detail than we have so far into the impact such a strategy might be expected to have on the economies of the weaker "nonlocomotive" industrialized countries.

The basic thrust of the locomotive approach is that only if the strongest economies take the lead in stimulating domestic expansion will their weaker partners be able to introduce policies of their own sufficiently stimulative to reduce excess capacity without running the risk of setting off a vicious circle of depreciation and inflation which threatens to become explosive. But to the extent that the strong countries are improving the domestic relationship between inflation and the reduction in excess capacity by a shift in the policy mix that leads to an exchange-rate appreciation and thus a reduction in their current account surpluses, there must be a symmetrical deterioration in this rela-

[39] Martin N. Baily, "Stabilization Policy and Private Economic Behavior," *Brookings Papers on Economic Activity*, no. 1, 1978 (Washington, D.C.: Brookings Institution, 1978), pp. 11–50.
[40] Indeed, in a world of "rational expectations," no temporary policy (including demand-restraint) could be expected to have durable effects.

tionship for those countries which trade with the locomotive countries and whose currency depreciations are the other side of the latters' appreciations. If the weaker industrial countries are simply optimizing their own trade-off between inflation and excess capacity, they should welcome the additional net demand from the locomotive countries only if it is somehow less inflationary than the additional demand they could create domestically through unilateral fiscal-monetary stimulus. But there is no *a priori* basis for assuming that the depreciation associated with any given total increase in aggregate demand will be smaller, or that each percentage point of depreciation will be less inflationary, when it arises from a policy-mix shift in the locomotive countries than it is when caused by a policy of increased domestic stimulus introduced unilaterally.

If this were the whole story, the strategy of a policy-mix shift could offer no reconciliation of the divergent objectives that underlie the locomotive controversy, at least not without appeal to asymmetries in structural relationships that are not revealed by the analysis at the level of abstraction utilized so far. Why, then, do the weaker countries appear to prefer a depreciation of their own effective exchange rates caused by an appreciation of the locomotive countries' currencies to one arising from increased domestic stimulus introduced unilaterally? One reason may be simply a new version of the old "burden of adjustment" argument heard so frequently toward the end of the Bretton Woods era. That is, from the point of view of an individual country confronting great uncertainty regarding the length of J-curve lags and the magnitudes of structural relationships both within and among countries, the danger of "overshooting" must appear far greater when depreciation results from the introduction of more stimulative domestic policies than prevail in the rest of the world than when it occurs simply as the mirror image of a policy-mix-induced appreciation in a few strong countries.

A second point may be more fundamental. That is, while the magnitude of depreciation associated with a given expansion of aggregate demand may be the same whatever its origins, differences in the composition of that demand have important implications. In the case of a policy-mix shift in the locomotive economies, the depreciation of the weaker country's currency is accompanied by a current-account surplus; when the depreciation is caused by domestic stimulus, it is not (since it occurs precisely in response to the emergence of a potential or actual current-account deficit). Because the weaker countries tend to be concerned about their borrowing positions and continued financial viability, they are likely to regard the first situation as less threatening than the second. Indeed, there is a pervasive tendency in financial circles to define the "strength" or "weakness" of a currency primarily in terms of its trade and current-account positions.[41] To the extent that this is the case, the implicit view of the weaker countries that a vicious circle of depreciation and inflation is more likely to be touched off by a depreciation arising from domestic stimulus than by one induced by a policy-mix shift abroad may indeed have a rational basis.

Economic Trends and Policy Developments in the Locomotive Countries

A variety of difficulties confronts any attempt to survey actual policies and developments in Germany, Japan, and the United States in order to shed light on some of the analytical questions discussed so far. For one thing, the instruments of monetary policy differ significantly among the three countries, making generalization both difficult and risky.[42] For another, the criteria for determining whether a particular policy stance is stimulative or contractionary—and in which direction it is moving— are fraught with ambiguity, especially in the case of monetary policy. This ambiguity is compounded when the period under consideration is one of declining actual and expected rates of inflation and weakening credit demand in the private sector. Finally, the purpose of this brief discussion is not to provide a definitive description of the course and impact of macroeconomic policy developments in the three largest industrialized countries during the current recovery, but rather the much narrower one of seeing whether these developments can illuminate the particular issues at hand. With this purpose in mind, the discussion that follows will focus on the broad outline of policy developments, doubtless suppressing in the process many detailed differences in implementation among the three countries, as well as a number of temporary zigs and zags in the conduct of macroeconomic policy in each one.

There can be little doubt that the shift from contractionary to stimulative demand-management policies in response to the sharp recession of 1973–1975 was fiscal-led in all three countries. Indeed, the most striking contrast between the years immediately following 1973 and those just preceding it is the increase in public sector deficits to unprecedented heights (not simply in money terms, but as a percentage of

---

[41] Some observers argue that this was particularly true in 1977. See, for example, Council of Economic Advisers, *Annual Report*, 1978, pp. 119–120.

[42] In Germany, as in the United States, the primary focus of the monetary authorities is on the growth rate of monetary aggregates (rather than on interest rates or credit flows). Japan, in contrast, relies more heavily on the use of quantitative credit restrictions, along with the discount rate and bank reserve requirements.

gross national product) in all three countries,[43] "reflecting the effects of expansionary fiscal measures as well as automatic stabilizers,"[44] along with a sharp decline in the growth rate of monetary aggregates. The latter development, it is true, was accompanied by a significant decline in interest rates and rates of inflation, giving rise to the ambiguity regarding the evaluation of monetary policy already mentioned. It is also true that the importance of claims on the treasury as a source of monetary expansion increased as compared with the 1970–1973 period, but this appears to have been due to the sharp contraction of private credit demand in all three countries and certainly was not evidence of pressure from monetization of the government debt.[45]

Although the timing of the move from a restrictive to an expansionary policy stance differed significantly among the three countries, in each one monetary policy remained restrictive for some time after the fiscal policy stance had shifted in an expansionary direction. And, when restrictive monetary policy was finally abandoned, it was in favor of a cautiously accommodating rather than an aggressively easy monetary stance. Thus, the "locomotive policy mix" outlined earlier was indeed followed by the three largest industrialized countries during the early stages of the current recovery. The reasons were domestic rather than international in nature; in the face of persistent stagflation, the policy mix reflected the prevailing view that monetary caution was essential to continue exerting downward pressure on rates of price increase, while fiscal stimulus should be directed at the expansion of real growth.[46]

---

[43] This is true in virtually all the major industrialized countries. Corden argues (in "Expansion of the World Economy") that these large public deficits are the offset to the increased public savings of OPEC countries and the increased private household savings and reduced private investment in OECD countries.

[44] OECD, *Towards Full Employment and Price Stability*, p. 111.

[45] "Had such [public-sector] deficits not emerged—or increased—and had they not been financed through the banking system, the rate of growth of the money supply could in some cases have fallen well below acceptable levels" (Bank for International Settlements, *Forty-Sixth Annual Report* [Basel: BIS, 1976], p. 37).

[46] The analytical basis for this widely held view is by no means clear, that is, why an increase in aggregate nominal demand stimulated by expansionary monetary policy should, *a priori*, result in a division between real output and price components that differs from an equivalent increase produced by fiscal stimulus. Two possibilities suggest themselves: (1) exchange rate effects: expansionary monetary policy is more likely to be associated with a depreciation of the exchange rate than is an equivalent fiscal expansion, and this depreciation is an additional source of inflationary pressure; and (2) expectational effects: if expansionary monetary policy is defined as an increase in the growth rate of the money supply, it may produce expectations of a permanent increase in the rate of inflation, while fiscal stimulus is more likely to create expectations that the increase in the inflation rate is only temporary. I have not seen any explicit discussion, however, of these or any other rationales for the position under discussion.

Meanwhile, data on reserve holdings for Germany and Japan indicate relatively little net intervention in foreign exchange markets during 1974 and 1975;[47] the dollar and the deutsche mark both experienced some effective appreciation between the end of 1973 and the end of 1975, while the Japanese yen underwent some effective depreciation over the same period. At the same time, some of the industrialized countries with persistently high inflation rates and weak current-account positions experienced sharp effective depreciations of their currencies, giving rise to the concerns with which this whole discussion began.

The conduct of macroeconomic policy became less expansionary in most industrialized countries in 1976, although this turn toward caution was less pronounced in the locomotive countries than in nations with higher rates of inflation and weaker external positions. The stance of monetary policy in Germany, Japan, and the United States was little changed from the previous year; interest rates remained low and demands for credit were readily accommodated. The degree of fiscal stimulus was reduced significantly in all three, a change that was in part the result of automatic stabilizers, including fiscal drag (as inflation continued to push money income up more rapidly than real income) and—at least in Germany and the United States—of unanticipated shortfalls in public expenditures. And in each of the three countries, the pace of real growth slowed significantly as the year went on.

Despite these similarities, divergences in policy stance, pace of recovery, and external position among the three strongest industrialized economies began to emerge in 1976, divergences which were to become intensified—and politicized—in 1977. The reduction in fiscal stimulus was accompanied in Germany and Japan by a general weakness of domestic demand, while export growth provided the main source of economic strength, particularly in Japan, where the current account moved sharply into surplus. In the United States, on the other hand, domestic demand strengthened, while the current account made a substantial negative swing, from a large surplus to a small deficit. The currencies of all three countries appreciated (with the dollar reaching its peak in June 1976), but the upward movement was far greater for the deutsche mark than for the other two, while the appreciation of the yen was dampened by Japanese intervention in foreign exchange mar-

---

[47] Increases in German holdings of foreign-exchange reserves in 1974, 1975, and 1976 were due entirely to intervention within the European "snake," that is, to obligatory purchases of other EEC currencies (in excess of net sales of other currencies). It might be argued, however, that Germany's policy of discouraging other EEC countries from acquiring deutsche marks as reserves is an indirect method of dampening the appreciation of that currency.

kets, as evidenced by an increase in Japan's foreign exchange reserves of more than $3 billion.

Divergences among the three locomotive economies with respect to the development of economic aggregates, which had begun to emerge in 1976, became pronounced in 1977. While all three had experienced a "summer pause" in economic recovery in mid-1976, this was followed in the United States by a resumption of above-trend real growth and continuing, albeit gradual, reductions in excess capacity and the unemployment rate, despite a negative shift in the trade balance of more than $20 billion. In Germany and Japan, in contrast, actual growth remained below potential during 1977, and the degree of economic slack increased somewhat in both, as was true for most major industrialized countries outside the United States and for the OECD area as a whole. In Japan, this stagnation occurred despite an increase of nearly $10 billion in the trade surplus, reflecting a sharp weakening of domestic demand. The sharp divergence in patterns of real economic growth among the three countries is perhaps best dramatized by comparing the growth targets agreed on at the June 1977 "economic summit" meeting with what actually occurred. The United States, which had projected a year-over-year real growth of GNP of 5 percent, ended the year roughly on target. Germany, whose projection for the same period had also been 5 percent, had a realized growth rate only half as great (2½ percent), while Japan, whose target for the fiscal year had been 6.7 percent, actually experienced 5 percent.

To what extent these divergent movements in 1977 are attributable to differences in the overall stance of demand-management policy in the three countries is not entirely clear, although differences in the policy *mix* prevailing in Germany and Japan on the one hand and in the United States on the other became increasingly evident as the year progressed. In Germany, what was apparently intended originally as a modest degree of fiscal stimulus turned out to have a net contractionary effect, owing to the impact of built-in stabilizers and further shortfalls in expenditures. New expansionary measures were initiated in the final quarter of the year, and preliminary figures indicate a significant upturn in the growth of real income for that quarter. The 8 percent growth target for central bank money, unchanged from 1976, represented an effective easing of monetary conditions, in view of the continuing decline in inflation and weakening of real growth. The monetary growth target was in fact overshot, as it had been in 1975 and 1976, partly as a result of exchange-market intervention and partly in response to developments in the domestic economy.

In Japan, the degree of fiscal stimulus remained roughly the same as in 1976, despite the announcement of a "reflationary package" for fiscal 1977 (beginning April 1), while the degree of economic slack increased. The growth of monetary aggregates slowed somewhat from 1976 but, in view of the weakening private demand for funds, this was consistent with an easing of money-market conditions. In both Germany and Japan, there was some further deceleration of inflation, while interest rates declined significantly in both nations during 1977. By the latter part of the year, both countries were actively encouraging this decline in order to moderate the upward pressure on their exchange rates.

In the United States, as in the other two locomotive countries, the fiscal measures proposed for 1977 were a good deal more expansionary than the actual impact of fiscal policy turned out to be once the books were closed on the year. This was partly because not all of the stimulus package proposed early in the year by the new administration was actually enacted and partly, as in 1976, the result of the operation of automatic stabilizers and unanticipated shortfalls in public expenditures. As in Japan, the degree of fiscal stimulus remained roughly unchanged from the previous year; the federal budget deficit in 1977, calculated on a high-employment basis, was essentially unchanged from 1976. In the United States, however, the unemployment rate and the output gap were reduced during the year, while in Japan (and in Germany) they increased.

On the monetary side, the U.S. pattern was in sharp contrast to what occurred in Germany and Japan. The growth of monetary aggregates accelerated significantly and interest rates rose markedly, particularly on short-term instruments. Taken together with the underlying stability, or at most slight acceleration, of the inflation rate, these developments reflected a significant expansion of demand for private credit, leading to a tightening of money-market conditions.

Differences in domestic economic trends among Germany and Japan on the one hand and the United States on the other were not merely reflected, but magnified many times, in dramatically diverging external positions. The dramatic increases in the United States' current-account deficit and Japan's current-account surplus have already been mentioned, while Germany's current-account surplus remained essentially unchanged from 1975 and 1976 (it was in the range of $3½–4 billion in each of those three years). The exchange rate of the dollar, which had already declined slightly from its June 1976 peak, declined by 5½ percent on a trade-weighted (effective) basis between December 1976 and December 1977.[48] The effective appreciation of the deutsche

[48] CEA, *Annual Report*, 1978, p. 111. This measure is derived by weighting currencies by countries' shares of total trade of the ten-country group. If the weights used reflect bilateral trade with the United States, the depreciation is only 2.4 percent, because of the much larger share of the weak Canadian dollar in the latter index.

mark and the yen were also sharp; as a result, the yen appreciated by more than 22 percent vis-à-vis the dollar over the year, and the German mark by nearly 11 percent, with roughly half of these increases occurring in the final three months of the year. These sharply divergent movements of exchange rates, which continued in the first quarter of 1978, occurred despite contrasting movements in interest rates, already mentioned, which created a substantial and growing interest-rate differential in favor of the United States, roughly reflecting the different trends in inflation rates among the three countries. They occurred, too, in the face of massive intervention by some of the major industrialized countries in foreign exchange markets to limit the appreciation of their currencies. Whereas in 1976 the only significant acquisition of reserves by industrialized countries resulting from dollar intervention had been Japan's $3 billion, in 1977 such intervention totaled nearly $35 billion, with Japan's share amounting to more than $6 billion and Germany's to more than $5 billion, again, concentrated heavily in the last quarter of the year.

Ironically, the largest net intervention of all—estimated at nearly $17 billion—was undertaken by the United Kingdom, one of the most important of the "weaker partners" in whose behalf the locomotive strategy was proposed in the first place. And the net acquisition of the dollar reserves by Italy, originally regarded as the other leading beneficiary, was not much smaller than Germany's and Japan's. Presumably, the purpose of such intervention was partly to rebuild depleted reserve stocks. But, at least in the case of the United Kingdom, there is no question that the aim was also to limit or slow down the appreciation of the pound sterling. Although it appears that these massive interventions had little lasting effect on exchange-rate developments, the very fact that they were undertaken not only by "strong" countries but also by two of the most conspicuous of the "weak" OECD partners might well make proponents of the locomotive argument feel as if they had walked through Alice's Looking Glass.

Some Lessons of Recent Experience

What light is shed on the analytical issues discussed in the first part of this paper, and what conclusions regarding the effectiveness and the limitations of the locomotive approach to stimulating global economic recovery are suggested by the experience of the past three years, summarized briefly in the preceding paragraphs? Inevitably, the data are subject to conflicting interpretations. The inductive process is complicated by the fact that there are two sets of issues involved: the first relates to the relationship between the stance of macroeconomic policy and the developments in the aggregate economy of each of the locomotive economies. The second has to do with the relationship between these developments in the domestic economy (as well as the nature of the policy mix utilized) in each of these countries and changes in external positions—current-account balances, exchange rates, and reserve movements—through which such developments affect the economies of other nations and the global economy as a whole.

At the outset, we are confronted by the absence of any clear-cut, unambiguous relationship between the degree of policy stimulus exerted in each of the locomotive countries and the strength of domestic economic recovery. In all three countries, stimulative measures have been applied relatively cautiously during the present recovery, owing to the persistence of high rates of inflation, and it is not obvious that the stance of monetary and fiscal policy over the period 1975–1977 as a whole can be characterized as more stimulative, in an absolute sense, in the United States than in Germany and Japan. During each of the past three years, for example, the rate of money supply growth has been lower, and the budget deficit of the federal government a smaller proportion of GNP, in the United States than in either of the other two countries.[49] Yet recovery from the 1973–1975 recession continues in the United States, while it has been seriously interrupted in Germany and Japan (and in all other major industrialized countries as well).

Many factors, it appears, intervene to prevent the emergence of a predictable relationship between the stance of macroeconomic policy and the progress of economic recovery in a large industrialized country. For one thing, the composition of a debt-financed fiscal deficit is apparently significant. In Germany, in particular, fiscal stimulus in the early part of the recovery was focused on short-term "pump-priming" measures, particularly temporary tax reductions. Later, when it appeared that the resulting increases in disposable income were being offset by increases in the private savings rate–that is, that the marginal propensity to hoard such temporary increases in income is extremely high–the focus was shifted toward increasing public expenditures, with particular emphasis on longer-term public investment projects. These, however, encountered unanticipated expenditure shortfalls (a phenomenon that occurred also in the United States and, to a more limited ex-

---

[49] The usefulness of such comparisons is limited by institutional differences among the three countries, particularly those affecting trends in money velocity, by differences in rates of inflation, and by the fact that the growth rate of potential output is higher in Japan than in the other two countries. The purpose of using them here is simply to raise questions about dogmatic assertions regarding the relative "stimulativeness" of demand-management policy in the three countries.

tent, in Japan),[50] and clearly failed to impart the expected stimulus to domestic aggregate demand, as evidenced by the growing discrepancy between forecast and actual real growth rates. In Japan, the situation is somewhat different; here expenditure shortfalls have been much less of a problem, and "the authorities have not yet discerned any weakening in the capacity of fiscal policy to influence aggregate demand"[51] (although here, too, government expenditures appear to be a more effective form of stimulus than is tax reduction). Yet the expansion of domestic demand has, again, been consistently below expectations in recent years; the gap between expected and actual real growth in 1977 was less in Japan than in Germany, but this was because the current-account balance improved sharply in the latter and remained constant in the former.[52]

One of the factors interfering with the effectiveness of traditional demand-management policies in affecting the actual growth of domestic demand in the locomotive economies may be that the traditional instruments of such policies—the growth of the money supply and the size of the government budget deficit—are themselves becoming policy *objectives*, that is, arguments in the national economic welfare function. Certainly, the substantial reduction or actual elimination of the federal budget deficit has become an explicit medium-term policy target in all three countries. This may, if anything, be a more important constraint in Germany and Japan, where deficit spending is a relatively new phenomenon, than in the United States, where its use is of longer duration, and government debt instruments have a longer-established and more prominent place in domestic financial markets. In Japan, in particular, the rule that deficit spending should not exceed 30 percent of total government (general account) expenditures was regarded as having almost constitutional sanctity, and the fact that it was breached for the first time in the budget for fiscal year 1978 has been described by some observers as tantamount to a "fiscal revolution." On the monetary side, "the view that increased rates of monetary expansion would raise inflationary expectations even under depressed conditions"[53] has

---

[50] In some cases, apparently, newly mandated spending programs may have the perverse effect of reducing (or postponing) actual government expenditures. See Edward M. Gramlich, "State and Local Budgets the Day After It Rained: Why Is the Surplus So High?" *Brookings Papers on Economic Activity*, no. 1, 1978 (Washington, D.C.: Brookings Institution, 1978), p. 209.

[51] Bank for International Settlements, *Forty-Seventh Annual Report* (Basel: BIS, 1977), p. 27.

[52] It is interesting to note that official German and Japanese forecasts of real growth rates have consistently been more optimistic than those generated by private forecasters or the OECD Secretariat.

[53] CEA, *Annual Report*, 1978, p. 103.

clearly limited the utilization of monetary policy to stimulate recovery of real growth rates from the 1973–1975 recession.

The possibility that intensive use of macroeconomic policy instruments to stimulate the economy may kindle inflationary expectations directly (that is, apart from their effect on demand) and thus produce a perverse reaction in private spending—a possibility which appears to be of particular concern in Germany—is relevant to two of the points of controversy raised at the beginning of this paper.[54] First, to the extent that such responses are significant, they raise doubts about the existence of a stable Phillips-curve relationship between the rate of inflation and the level of unemployment (or excess capacity). They are consistent, rather, with the alternative view that, in an inflationary environment, increased monetary-fiscal stimulus may tend to retard rather than encourage aggregate real growth, even under conditions of less-than-full employment. Just where this "saturation point" lies is, of course, the heart of the issue. Second, the existence of such responses might help to explain the apparent preference of many countries for export-led growth over that engendered by domestic policy stimulus (a preference that has no rational basis in terms of conventional analysis) on the grounds that expansion of demand originating in the private sector is less likely than increased stimulus by the government to provoke such perverse reactions.

The particular version of the locomotive argument analyzed in this paper involves questions relating not only to the relationship between the overall stance of demand-management policy and the state of the domestic economy, but also to the impact, both internal and external, of changes in the monetary-fiscal mix. In terms of conventional Keynesian analysis, the effect of fiscal-led stimulus would be to encourage expansion of consumption at the expense of investment, as compared with a mix consisting of less fiscal and more monetary stimulus. In view of the particular weakness of investment in all three of the largest industrialized economies during the current recovery, and the strong likelihood that "stagflation" cannot be effectively alleviated without an increase in the share of output devoted to the expansion of productive capacity, such an effect would clearly be undesirable.

In fact, however, the impact of the policy mix on the composition of domestic output is by no means as simple as the conventional wisdom suggests. Some observers suggest that there has been a weakening of the effectiveness of monetary stimulus in encouraging increased investment, presumably because of its impact on expectations regarding

---

[54] For a skeptical view of this argument, see CEA, *Annual Report*, 1978, p. 314.

inflation.[55] At the same time, the term "fiscal policy" encompasses a variety of different policy measures and thus considerable flexibility in focusing on different components of aggregate demand. Clearly, an increase in the investment tax credit, a reduction in the corporate profits tax, or some form of tax break for home construction would have substantially different effects on the investment-consumption mix than would an increase in the individual income-tax exemption or a reduction in personal income-tax rates, for example. On the public-expenditure side, the fiscal components of stimulative "packages" introduced recently in Germany and Japan have emphasized infrastructural investment "designed to complement and encourage private fixed investment."[56]

In the light of recent experience, some observers are also questioning the effectiveness of fiscal-led stimulus in expanding imports (at an unchanged exchange rate, that is, apart from the effects of the exchange-rate appreciation it produces through capital inflows) and thus exerting downward pressure on the current-account surplus of the country undertaking it. It has been suggested that, in view of the emphasis in both Germany and Japan on social infrastructure as the major focus of increased government expenditures, the marginal import propensities associated with such expenditures are likely to be significantly lower than the average propensities for the economy as a whole.

In fact, it appears that the experiences of the two countries have been quite different in this respect: public spending in Germany has sustained a higher import-content (relative to the average level for the whole economy) than in Japan and, at least partly as a consequence, the volume of German imports has expanded significantly during the present recovery, while Japan's import volume was actually lower in 1977 than in 1974. Thus, the impact of fiscal-led stimulus on the composition of domestic demand, in terms of both the consumption-investment mix and the mix of imported and domestically produced goods, appears to follow no simple universal laws. Rather, the relationship seems to differ significantly from one country to another, and governments appear to have some discretionary leeway to determine, or at least modify, the compositional effects of their fiscal policies.

Finally, there are the issues or uncertainties surrounding the effects, both internal and external, of an exchange-rate change. Earlier in this paper we noted that, in terms of most of the models of wage-

---

[55] The picture is clouded, however, by a secular decline in rates of return on capital assets and by the current coexistence of low interest rates with low rates of capacity utilization in most major industrialized countries.

[56] Bank for International Settlements, *Forty-Seventh Annual Report* (Basel: BIS, 1977), p. 27.

price determination currently in use, exchange-rate appreciation can be expected to exert downward pressure on the rate of inflation associated with a given level of aggregate demand. If this is in fact the case, why do we not observe "competitive appreciation" among nations anxious to dampen inflationary expectations, rather than the resistance to appreciation that is observed, at least intermittently, even in those nations with the strongest anti-inflationary convictions and policies?

The answers offered to this question frequently involve some general reference to the "political power of exporters." Without poaching on the realm of political science or sociology, however, there are also some economic considerations that bear on this issue. There is the perennial question of demand-shift inflation which, if it were a significant enough factor in the shift of demand from tradable to nontradable goods associated with appreciation, might actually swamp the anti-inflationary effects of appreciation cited earlier. Arguments regarding the existence of demand-shift inflation have not generally been supported by systematic empirical evidence,[57] but certain conditions might be regarded as increasing the likelihood of such a phenomenon. In particular, the existence of higher levels of excess capacity in tradable-goods than in nontradable-goods industries might have this effect. This does indeed appear to be the case at present in both Germany and Japan, where excess capacity is a more severe problem in manufacturing than in nonmanufacturing industries. More than 25 percent of German output is exported, and one of Japan's major current economic problems is "an overexpanded manufacturing sector, the physical side of its excessive export orientation."[58] As a result of these structural characteristics, the short-run effects of an appreciating exchange rate on the domestic economies of these two countries are negative: severe pressure on profits in the export sector, accentuating a secular decline in profit shares and further weakening the already-lagging investment sector.[59]

---

[57] The most comprehensive recent study of "ratchet effects" associated with downward price rigidities found no evidence of such asymmetrical responses of domestic prices to changes in import prices in pooled regression equations for five large industrial countries (the United States, the Federal Republic of Germany, Japan, the United Kingdom, and Italy) for the period 1958–1973. For individual countries there was no evidence of such asymmetries for Germany and the United Kingdom, and mixed (inconclusive) evidence for the United States, Italy, and Japan. Morris Goldstein, "Downward Price Inflexibility, Ratchet Effects, and the Inflationary Impact of Import Price Changes: Some Empirical Tests," IMF *Staff Papers*, vol. 24 (November 1977), pp. 569–612.

[58] Lawrence B. Krause, "International Economic Outlook," *Economic Research*, January 1978 (New York: Goldman Sachs, 1978), p. 12.

[59] There is dramatic evidence of these pressures in the rapid rise recently of corporate bankruptcies in Japan.

The fact that the immediate impact of an exchange-rate change on the trade balances of both the appreciating and the depreciating countries is likely to be perverse—the so-called J-curve effect—is well known. This is because the immediate "valuation effect" of an appreciation is to lower the domestic-currency prices of a country's imports (or raise the foreign-currency prices of its exports), and to have the opposite effect on a depreciating country. The reallocation of expenditure patterns and of resources in response to changes in relative prices (or the changes in the relationship between income and expenditure caused by a change in the real value of money balances when the exchange-rate changes, as postulated by the monetary approach to balance-of-payments analysis) is likely to occur gradually and with significant lags.

In the case of economies heavily dependent on exports, and with excess capacity concentrated particularly in the tradable-goods sectors, this J-curve effect may be even more pronounced. This is because of the effects on profits and investment already mentioned; in such economies, "stagnation in foreign sales cannot be easily offset by greater domestic absorption in the short run."[60] Thus, the effect of rapid appreciation may be a slowdown in the rate of aggregate real growth, adding a negative "income effect" on the volume of imports to the already-mentioned valuation effect, which causes the immediate impact of an exchange-rate change on the balance of trade to be perverse. Thus, while the ultimate effect of an exchange-rate appreciation should be to improve the relationship between inflationary pressure and excess capacity in the domestic economy, and to cause a negative shift in the balance on current account which should stimulate demand and improve the current-account positions of partner countries, the short-run effects, both internal and external, may be in the opposite direction. In a depreciating country, on the other hand, the immediate effect is to increase domestic prices; the beneficial effects on domestic output and employment are likely to occur only after some delay.[61]

How Best to Carry World Recovery? Where do things stand, then, as regards the locomotive argument in general and its policy-mix variant in particular? Interestingly enough, this prescription was most closely followed in the early stages of the current recovery, even before it was articulated in the publications of expert groups or international organizations. All three of the locomotive economies did indeed undertake fiscal-led stimulus late in 1974 or early in 1975, while maintaining a

---

[60] Krause, "International Economic Outlook," p. 9.
[61] Dornbusch and Krugman, "Flexible Exchange Rates," pp. 573–574.

tighter rein on monetary policy throughout most or all of the latter year. Although the reasons for adopting such a policy mix were primarily internal rather than external—an effort to stimulate real growth while continuing to reduce inflation, rather than the pursuit of specific current-account or exchange-rate goals—all three countries did in fact experience effective appreciations of their currencies between mid-1975 and mid-1976. After that, however, internal and external economic developments in the three countries began to diverge, and, with them, so did the policy-mix pursued by each. By late 1977 and early 1978, Germany and Japan were deliberately creating easy conditions in money markets in order to hold down the rapid appreciation of their currencies, and were intervening substantially in foreign exchange markets—which in itself contributed to the growth of monetary aggregates—for the same purpose. The United States, on the other hand, confronted by an unprecedented trade deficit and a rapidly depreciating dollar, actively pursued the "locomotive" policy mix, relying on fiscal stimulus to support real growth and allowing interest rates to rise significantly, particularly on short term instruments, in an effort to slow the dollar's depreciation.

In fact, as this is written, the degree of fiscal stimulus is expected to be greater in 1978 in all three countries than it was in 1977—and there is already preliminary evidence of a pickup in real growth in Germany and Japan. But, for different reasons, the locomotive argument in its simple form has become increasingly irrelevant for all three. The United States, the only one of the three in which industrial production is today significantly above its 1973–1974 peak and the output gap is narrowing, has clearly done its share in this respect—and more. Its current-account deficit and the rapid depreciation of the dollar have become a source of concern to the world economy. Recent changes in the real (that is, inflation-adjusted) effective exchange rate of the dollar should, in fact, bring about a lagged adjustment in the form of a reduction in the U.S. trade deficit this year or next, a development that most of our trading partners, strong and weak alike, would prefer to see reinforced by means of an effective U.S. energy policy and further containment of domestic inflation rather than by continuing depreciation of the dollar.

Germany and Japan, with decelerating inflation rates, widening output gaps, and strong current-account positions, are clearly in a better position, both internally and externally, to pursue strong expansionary policies than is the United States. But, as regards Japan, it is increasingly felt that the most direct routes to improving its domestic "trade-off" between inflation and unemployment and reducing its burgeoning surplus on current account may lie in the realm of trade-

281

liberalization and nonintervention in exchange markets; discussions have focused increasingly on these issues and commensurately less exclusively on the setting and meeting of domestic growth targets.

Germany appears to be the country to which the locomotive argument remains most applicable in 1978. Even critics of the approach acknowledge that "additional stimulating impulses are primarily suitable in those 'strong' countries where the growth of real public expenditure remained below the rate of potential GNP growth in 1976—like in West Germany—or where it is going to undershoot the respective rate for 1977."[62] Nonetheless, the indications of perverse reactions in the private sector to increased government stimulus, and the distinctly negative response of the German government to American efforts early in 1978 to urge more stimulative policies on it, suggest strongly that their are no painless resolutions of genuine disagreements regarding the existence of a Phillips curve or the selection of an optimum position on such a curve. And, as might have been expected in any attempt to "bargain" about such differences in the face of widespread uncertainty, national sovereignty has apparently prevailed.

The behavior in 1977 of the most important "weak" industrialized countries also suggests the obsolescence of the simple locomotive view. As already noted, Italy and the United Kingdom both purchased dollars in substantial amounts, and, at least in the case of the latter, the motivation was in part a desire to dampen the appreciation of the pound sterling. This suggests that neither strong nor weak countries are likely to view with equanimity rapid changes in the real exchange rates of their currencies, because of the adverse short-term effects of such changes on the domestic economy. Thus, policy prescriptions predicated on significant effective changes in real exchange rates, and thus in international competitive positions, occuring over a relatively short period of time are likely to meet with strong resistance.[63]

Finally, over the past three years, the clear distinction between "locomotive" and "nonlocomotive" economies has become increasingly blurred. The divergent paths taken by the economies of the United States on the one hand and Germany and Japan on the other have already been described. On the other hand, the largest of the "weak" industrialized nations—France, Italy, and the United Kingdom—have recently experienced noticeable improvements in their rates of inflation, current-account positions, and exchange rates. Thus, for a variety of

---

[62] Walter, "The Role of Big Countries," p. 17.

[63] The Dornbusch-Krugman policy-mix argument was, in fact, directed toward maintaining rather than altering real exchange rates. "Flexible Exchange Rates," p. 574.

reasons, it seems more appropriate at this juncture to spread the responsibility for global "reflation" more thinly among a larger number of countries, rather than expecting more intensive stimulus from a few. Indeed, as this article was being completed, such a shift in strategy became official OECD policy with the announcement of the so-called convoy approach, envisaging the coordination of policies to stimulate real growth among all six of the countries mentioned in this paragraph and some smaller ones as well.[64]

Finally, our intensive perusal of the road map of the locomotive approach has revealed no undiscovered high road, no simple and painless means of reconciling differences of opinion regarding the relationship among policy stimulus, inflation, and real growth or conflicts of interest regarding the most desirable composition of demand expansion. The root of the problem is, it seems to me, the tremendous uncertainty that currently prevails regarding the impact of the traditional tools of aggregate demand policy in an environment of persistent stagflation. Until some general consensus on this critical issue emerges, and until reliable ways are found to sustain or stimulate real growth while continuing to hold down or further reduce inflation rates, divergent views and preferences are likely to stand in the way of significant further progress in the coordination of macroeconomic policies.

This does not imply any relaxation of the struggle to avoid protectionism, exchange-rate manipulation (whether direct or indirect), or other beggar-my-neighbor solutions to domestic problems. But it does suggest a certain caution in giving advice to others, and considerable restraint on our expectations from locomotives, convoys, or other sophisticated modes of transport in a world where, for the moment, there are no maps or navigational charts of generally accepted reliability. Only when such aids become available will it prove feasible for the leading nations in the world economy to chart a common course, even if failure to do so increases the difficulty of the journey for everyone.

---

[64] The formal name of this new growth strategy, as reported in the *New York Times* of February 28, 1978, is the Coordinated Reflation Action Program, which perhaps explains why it was promptly dubbed the "convoy" approach by its originators.

Immigrants
and Immigration Policy

Barry R. Chiswick

Summary

This chapter is concerned with immigrants to the United States—their economic progress, their impact on the native population, and immigration policy.

The review of U.S. immigration policy indicates that it was changed fundamentally only twice. From colonial times until 1921 there were no quantitative restrictions, except against East Asians. From the 1920s until 1967 the national origins quota system restricted immigration from Eastern and Southern Europe, Asia, and Africa. Since then, a more liberal immigration policy has been in effect, and the proportion of immigrants from Asia, Africa, and Latin America has increased. The 1965 amendments also placed greater emphasis on family reunification as a criterion for rationing immigrant visas. Currently, about 400,000 legal immigrants and an unknown number of illegal immigrants enter the United States each year.

The economic progress in the United States of white male immigrants and the white sons of immigrants is examined. Whether measured by earnings or occupational status, the relatively low economic position of immigrants when they first arrive is temporary. The earnings of immigrants reach parity with those of native born men with similar characteristics after ten to fifteen years, and afterwards they have higher earnings. The native born sons of immigrants have higher earnings than the native born sons of native born parents. These findings suggest that immigrants are self selected on the basis of high innate

I appreciate the comments I have received on earlier drafts of this paper from the participants in the *Contemporary Economic Problems 1978* project, as well as from Terry Anderson, Carmel U. Chiswick, Melvyn Krauss, David North, Dan Usher, and the participants in the Stanford University labor economics seminar. I alone, however, am responsible for its contents.

ability and work motivation. Mexican-Americans, however, earn less than other white men of the same immigrant status.

There have been illegal aliens as long as there have been restrictions on immigration. The number of illegal aliens living in the United States is unknown. Data on apprehended illegal aliens indicate that they have essentially the same earnings and earnings-related characteristics as legal aliens from the same country who have been in the United States the same length of time. This suggests that U.S. immigration policy is largely neutral with respect to skills and earning potential in the issuance of immigration visas.

The theoretical analysis of the impact of immigrants on the native population is concerned with both the aggregate level and the distribution of income. It is shown that as long as they are not substantial recipients of welfare benefits or do not impose a substantial net cost on publicly provided goods and services, immigrant workers increase the aggregate income of the native population. Although the native born skill groups closest to those of the immigrants experience a decline in income, this can be mitigated through income transfers from the native groups that experience an increase in income. These findings suggest that a liberal immigration policy can effectively increase the economic well-being of the native population by placing greater emphasis on earning potential in rationing immigrant visas.

Introduction

There has been renewed public debate in recent years regarding U.S. immigration policy. This has arisen in part from the large, and apparently increasing, number of persons entering the United States illegally each year. In addition, the sluggish performance of the economy and the persistent high unemployment rate have led some to feel that reducing immigration, legal and illegal, would ease some of the domestic economic problems. Yet, an understanding of the issues has lagged behind the public policy debate—there has been little research on the economic progress and impact of immigrants to the United States. The purpose of this chapter is to provide an analytical background, both empirical and theoretical, for the consideration of U.S. immigration policy.

Currently, about 400,000 legal immigrants enter the United States each year, composing about one-fourth of the annual growth in the population.[1] The number of persons entering illegally each year who

---

[1] This does not include persons entering the United States on student, tourist, diplomatic, or other temporary visas. In addition, approximately 170,000 Southeast Asian refugees have been admitted to the United States since 1975 under a "parolee" rather than immigrant status. Data do not exist for the number of legal immigrants who subsequently emigrate from the United States.

successfully evade detection is, of course, unknown.[2] In 1977, the Immigration and Naturalization Service apprehended and deported over 1 million illegal aliens. Most of the arrests, however, were made along the border and were among persons who had just crossed or were in the United States for only a few days. Clearly, in spite of all the obstacles, many more people want to immigrate than the United States will allow to enter the country legally.

Although Americans have always had conflicting feelings about immigration, basic U.S. immigration policy has changed fundamentally only twice. Until 1921 the United States had a policy of essentially unrestricted immigration, except for periodic restrictions on paupers and convicts and the racist Oriental exclusion acts and agreements starting in the late nineteenth century. From the 1920s to 1967 an ethnocentric national origins quota system was in effect, originally introduced to limit the immigration of persons from Southern and Eastern Europe. With the Immigration Act of 1965, the national origins quota system was scrapped as of 1968, and the emphasis on "preferences" for admission was shifted to family reunification. As a result, the composition of the immigrant population changed. An increased proportion of legal immigrants now come from Asia, Africa, and Latin America.

This chapter is concerned with the economic progress and impact of immigrants, and the "optimal" immigration policy for the United States. As it is the native population (native born and naturalized citizens) that is the decision maker, optimal will be defined relative to the native population's well-being. However, well-being needs to be defined broadly to include real money income (that is, goods and services) and the psychic income derived from family reunification and refugee relief. The chapter begins with a brief review of the history of U.S. immigration policy. A historical perspective is important because the policy issues of today are not very different from the policy issues of the past. The economic progress in the United States of recent immigrants is then examined through a summary of empirical research on their earnings and occupational mobility. The current illegal alien situation is then discussed. This is followed by a largely theoretical analysis of the impact of immigrants on the aggregate level and the distribu-

---

[2] The euphemism undocumented alien has recently been substituted by some for the previous designation, illegal alien. Persons in the United States without legal rights to be here are in violation of U.S. law. Some crossed the border without going through an immigration service checkpoint (entry without inspection, or EWI), others entered legally but overstayed their visa or violated the conditions of their visa (visa abusers), while still others entered the United States through immigration service checkpoints but with fraudulent documents. The term illegal alien is used here to apply to all three categories of persons whose presence in the United States violates U.S. law.

tion of income among the total and the native population. The chapter explores the effects of immigrants on the native population when there is a welfare system and a large public sector in which goods and services are financed by taxes rather than user-charges. A synthesis of the findings of the previous sections, and their policy implications, closes the chapter.

U.S. Immigration Policy

From colonial times to the present, two persistent views have been articulated regarding immigrants to the United States. One view is that immigrants increase the well-being of the native population, as they engage in productive work that needs to be done. They were productive in colonial times by helping to extend the frontier beyond the Appalachian mountains, in the nineteenth century by building canals and railroads and helping to close the frontier, and in recent years both by doing some highly skilled work and by engaging in lower skilled or unskilled jobs that native born workers would not accept.[3] The second persistent view is that immigrants would alter the cultural or ethnic composition of the native population, or that they would lower the standard of living of native workers, if not the entire nation. These seemingly conflicting views were (and are) often held by the same person. For example, in a 1753 letter concerning German immigrants to Pennsylvania, Benjamin Franklin wrote:

> Those who come hither are generally the most stupid of their own nation, . . . it is almost impossible to remove any prejudices they may entertain . . . I am not against the admission of Germans in general, for they have their virtues. Their industry and frugality are exemplary. They are excellent husbandmen and contribute greatly to the improvement of a country.[4]

American immigration policy has been concerned with protecting the well-being of the native population through qualitative restrictions on the immigration of criminals, paupers, and persons with contagious diseases. When numerical limits were imposed in the 1920s, a mechanism was needed to ration visas among those wishing to immigrate. A two-step rationing mechanism was adopted—country quotas and

---

[3] "Involuntary immigration," the importation of slaves, was legal from the seventieth century until 1808. The Constitution permitted Congress to abolish the slave trade as of 1808, but undoubtedly slaves were imported illegally until the Civil War, though on a smaller scale.

[4] Letter quoted in Marion T. Bennett, *American Immigration Policies: A History* (Washington, D.C.: Public Affairs Press, 1963), p. 5.

a preference system for ranking applicants within each country. There are numerous mechanisms for rationing immigration visas—they can be distributed by lottery, sold by auction, given to those with the most human capital (skills)[5], given to those with the closest relatives already in the U.S. (family reunification), or distributed in some other way. As will be shown below, current U.S. policy emphasizes family reunification as the rationing mechanism, with the worker's skills having a smaller role.

An immigration policy based on family reunification is likely to have a smaller favorable impact on the aggregate income of the native population of the United States than one based on the skills and likely economic success of the immigrants. The similarity in earnings and in earnings-related characteristics between legal immigrants and apprehended illegal aliens (a nonrandom sample of persons wishing to enter but who are denied immigrant visas) suggests that the distribution of immigration visas is not related to skill level. Presumably the kinsmen in the United States of prospective immigrants would place a greater weight on family reunification as a goal of immigration policy than would those who have no close relatives in other countries. Even the latter, however, would presumably view the humanitarian aspects of family reunification as beneficial. Whether they view these benefits as outweighing the forgone economic benefits is, however, an important policy issue beyond the scope of this study.

Period of Qualitative Restrictions. Franklin's view that on balance immigrants have a favorable impact on the country has been the dominant theme in American immigration policy.[6] From the time of the first

---

[5] Since liquid assets are, by definition, fungible, and land cannot be moved from country to country, the only form of capital that necessarily moves with an immigrant is his skills. In practice, an effective policy of rationing admissions on the basis of the capital the immigrant brings with him means rationing on the basis of human capital.

[6] For a more detailed treatment of U.S. immigration policies, see Bennett, *American Immigration Policies*; U.S. Department of Justice, *Domestic Council Committee on Illegal Aliens, Preliminary Report* (Washington, D.C., December 1976); and Elizabeth J. Harper, *Immigration Laws of the United States*, 3rd ed. (Indianapolis: Bobbs-Merrill, 1975). For histories of immigration to the United States, see Leon Dinnerstein and David Reimers, *Ethnic Americans: A History of Immigration and Assimilation* (New York: Harper and Row, 1975); Leo Grebler et al., *The Mexican-American People* (New York: Free Press, 1970), chap. 4, "The Ebb and Flow of Immigration"; Marcus Lee Hansen, *The Immigrant in American History* (Cambridge, Mass.: Harvard University Press, 1940); Marcus Lee Hansen, *The Mingling of the Canadian and American Peoples* (New Haven: Yale University Press, 1940); Marcus Lee Hansen, *The Atlantic Migration, 1607–1860* (Cambridge: Harvard University Press, 1940); and Shirley Hune, *Pacific Migration to the United States*, RIIES Bibliographic Studies No. 2 (Washington, D.C.: Smithsonian Institution, 1977).

colonial settlements until World War I, there was a largely free and open immigration policy, with several "qualitative" exceptions. Concerns for the health and safety of the population and prejudice against various ethnic groups did influence immigration policy during this long period. In the Colonial era, for example, at various times the separate colonies enacted restrictions on the immigration of paupers and convicts (although some colonies, particularly Georgia, were at times used by the British as penal colonies) and on Scotch-Irish, Catholic, and other immigrant groups.

The Constitution gave Congress, rather than the states, the power to regulate commerce with foreign nations and among the states. However, as the Constitution did not specifically grant Congress sole authority over immigration policy, some states continued to enact immigration restrictions based on their police powers. Because of unrestricted interstate mobility, state laws presumably had limited impact. By the 1870s, Supreme Court decisions made it clear that the formation of immigration policy was limited to the federal government. Attempts at restrictive state legislation regarding immigrants may have been in part a consequence of the virtual absence of federal legislation. Except for the Alien and Sedition Act of 1798, which for two years gave the President authority to deport undesirable aliens, there was no direct federal legislation limiting or restricting immigration, or providing a mechanism for the deportation of undesirable aliens.[7]

The first restrictive federal legislation was enacted in 1875, in part as a response to court decisions prohibiting state restrictions (for example, California legislation against forced Chinese immigration). Concerns over the "exploitation" of Chinese workers led to prohibiting the forced immigration of Chinese and Japanese men and women, and prohibiting contracts to supply unskilled ("coolie") labor. Although the legislation was intended to eliminate forced labor among Chinese immigrants, and partially to satisfy those who wished to ban all Chinese immigration, substantial immigration from China continued.[8] The 1875 act also included the first federal qualitative restrictions, as it pro-

---

[7] Federal legislation was passed, starting in 1819, concerning the living conditions aboard the ships bringing immigrants to the United States and the recording of immigrants who arrived by ship. During the first decade of record-keeping, 1821 to 1830, 143,000 immigrants arrived. The decade of peak immigration was 1901 to 1910, 8,795,000 immigrants.

[8] Immigration from China was negligible prior to the 1850s, but was 41,000 in 1851–1860, 64,000 in 1861–1870, and 123,000 in 1871–1880. With the passage of more restrictive legislation against Chinese laborers in 1882 it fell to 62,000 in 1881–1890 and to 15,000 in 1891–1900. U.S. Department of Justice, *Immigration and Naturalization Service, 1976 Annual Report* (Washington, D.C., 1978), table 13. (Data rounded to nearest thousand.)

hibited the immigration of convicts, other than political prisoners, and prostitutes.

After several attempts, the Chinese Exclusion Act became law in May 1882. This was the first federal legislation restricting the immigration of persons who wished to come and who had not engaged in illegal or immoral activities. The law barred the immigration of Chinese laborers for ten years, but it was extended periodically and made permanent in 1904. It also provided for the deportation of Chinese who were not in the United States lawfully, and it barred foreign born Chinese from citizenship. Subsequent amendments extended the definition of the excluded group and barred re-entry of Chinese living in the United States who visited China. The first illegal aliens in the United States were those who attempted to evade this act. It was not until World War II (in December 1943) that the Chinese Exclusion Act and its amendments were repealed and foreign born Chinese were made eligible for citizenship.[9]

In August 1882, the first general immigration restrictions were enacted. They were modeled after the state laws that had been declared unconstitutional in the 1870s, which themselves were based on colonial laws. The Immigration Act of 1882 barred from entry convicts, the insane, and those likely to become a public charge, and it provided for the deportation of such immigrants. The Alien Contract Labor Act of 1885 made contracts for the immigration of unskilled workers unenforceable and illegal. Subsequent legislation culminated in the Immigration Act of 1917, when the list of those barred included persons who are insane, carriers of contagious diseases, criminals, prostitutes and procurers, professional beggars, polygamists, anarchists, those likely to become a public charge, children unaccompanied by or not joining a parent, those not literate in any language (with certain exceptions), and persons from nearly any part of Asia.[10] Except for the restrictions on the immigration of Asians, there were no quantitative limits on immigration.

---

[9] Starting with the so-called Gentlemen's Agreement of 1907 between Japan and the executive branch of the U.S. government, with few exceptions Japanese laborers were barred from immigration to the United States. Immigration from Japan started in the 1890s, reached 130,000 in 1901–1910, and then declined to 84,000 in 1911–1920 and to 33,000 in the 1920s. Ibid. (Data rounded to nearest thousand.) The exclusion remained in effect until 1952.

[10] During the period 1892–1920, 309,000 aliens were denied admission to the United States, including 12,000 as criminals or immoral persons, 67,000 as persons with mental or physical defects, 168,000 as persons likely to become a public charge, 34,000 as contract laborers, and 5,000 as illiterate adults. During the same period 43,000 aliens were deported. Ibid., tables 21, 23. (Data rounded to nearest thousand.)

National Origins Quota System. The poverty created by famines, wars, and revolutions in Europe have historically encouraged immigration to the United States. And, just as often, nativist groups would attempt to bar this immigration, particularly during periods of slow United States economic growth. The largely anti-Irish sentiments of the Know-Nothing Party gained it considerable support in the 1850s, following the increased immigration from Ireland. However, the impending North-South conflict and the increased demand for labor during the Civil War thwarted efforts to restrict immigration. After the war, the emerging labor unions were joined by largely rural nativist and populist groups concerned with the impact of the new large influx of immigrants from eastern and southern Europe (Table 1). The anti-foreign sentiments reached a peak in the 1890s, but their influence waned with the better employment opportunities at the turn of the century. The tradition of a more liberal immigration policy, supported by the industrialists and by recent immigrants, prevailed until the 1920s, when concern heightened over the alleged adverse impact on employment and on society of immigrants from eastern and southern Europe.

The Quota Law of 1921, an addition to previous immigration law, instituted the first limit on the number of immigrants that could legally enter the United States in any year. Essentially, the law applied only to Europe, as most Asians were still barred and no limits were placed on the immigration of persons from Western Hemisphere countries. The quota was to be an annual limit of 3 percent of the foreign born persons of that nationality living in the United States as reported in the 1910 Census of Population. Approximately 358,000 aliens would be admitted under the quota, 200,000 from northern and western Europe and 155,000 from southern and eastern Europe. Although up to the 1880s the overwhelming majority of immigrants entering the United States each year were from northern and western Europe, from the 1890s the majority were from eastern and southern Europe (Table 1).[11] The new law substantially reduced immigration from Europe, primarily eastern and southern Europe, but had little binding effect on northwestern Europe.

The Immigration Act of 1924 placed further restrictions on the

---

[11] The data in Table 1 are for gross immigration. Net immigration is the difference between immigration and emigration. Data on emigration from the United States, particularly for the foreign born, are scarce. Return migration has been common for immigrants from some countries (for example, Canada and Mexico) and was more frequent in some time periods (for example, the 1930s) than in others. See Bernard Axelrod, "Historical Studies of Emigration from the United States," *International Migration Review*, vol. 6, no. 1 (Spring 1972), pp. 32–49; Hansen, *The Mingling*; and Grebler, *The Mexican-American People*.

immigration of persons from southern and eastern Europe. The quota was reduced to 2 percent of the foreign born based on the census of 1890. This was temporary, however, because a quota based on the "national origin" of all persons in the United States in 1920, rather than just the foreign born, was introduced in 1929. The total annual quota, applicable primarily for Europe, was reduced from about 358,000 under the 1921 law, to 165,000 under the temporary 1924 provisions to 154,000 under the 1929 national origins system. The relative number of immigrants permitted from eastern and southern Europe declined with each revision, and this affected the distribution of immigrants by country of origin. In practice, however, various exemptions permitted more persons to enter, particularly from southern and eastern Europe, than would have been allowed solely on the basis of the quotas (Table 1).

The ethnocentric national origins quota system served as the basic U.S. immigration policy for thirty-five years.[12] During this time, however, various amendments removed the exclusion of Asians and gave the Asian countries small quotas (for example, 105 for China), provided for admitting war and political refugees over and above quota limitations, and increased immigration preferences based on family reunification and scarce skills.

Current Immigration Law. By the 1960s attitudes towards immigrants, particularly those from countries outside of northwestern Europe, had changed substantially. With the decline in the foreign born from 13.2 percent of the population in 1920 to 5.4 percent in 1960, fears that foreigners would over-run the country and change the character of the society had diminished. The change in public attitudes towards minorities that produced the Civil Rights Act of 1964 and the Voter Registration Act of 1965 carried over into the area of immigration. The ethnic and racial discrimination inherent in the national origins quota system was now viewed as an embarrassment, internationally and domestically. The 1965 amendments to the Immigration and Naturalization Act made two fundamental changes—they abolished the national origins quota system and sharply altered the system of "preferences" or priorities used to ration the distribution of immigrant visas.

Under the 1965 amendments, starting in 1968, a total of 170,000 immigrant visas per year were to be given to persons from Eastern Hemisphere countries, with no more than 20,000 for each country. The

---

[12] The Immigration and Nationality (McCarran-Walter) Act of 1952 recodified existing law in addition to introducing several modifications. Subsequent legislation are amendments to this act.

Table 1

IMMIGRATION TO THE UNITED STATES BY PLACE OF ORIGIN, 1820–1975

(in thousands)

Year	Total	Average Annual as a Percent of U.S. Population[a]	Europe Northwest[b]	Europe Other	Western Hemisphere Canada	Western Hemisphere Mexico[c]	Western Hemisphere Other	Asia[d]	Africa	Australia and Oceania	Country not Specified
1820–1830	143	0.15	99	8	2	5	5	—	—	—	33
1831–1840	599	0.47	484	12	14	7	13	—	—	—	70
1841–1850	1,713	1.00	1,574	23	42	3	18	—	—	—	53
1851–1860	2,598	1.12	2,385	68	59	3	12	42	—	—	29
1861–1870	2,315	0.74	1,889	176	154	2	11	65	—	—	18
1871–1880	2,812	0.71	1,831	441	384	5	15	124	—	11	1
1881–1890	5,247	1.05	3,128	1,607	393	2	32	70	1	13	1
1891–1900	3,688	0.59	1,291	2,264	3	1	35	75	—	4	14
1901–1910	8,795	1.16	1,435	6,621	179	49	133	324	7	13	34[e]
1911–1920	5,736	0.62	997	3,325	742	219	182	247	8	13	1
1921–1930	4,107	0.39	1,087	1,376	925	459	133	112	6	9	—
1931–1940	528	0.04	184	164	109	22	29	16	2	3	—
1941–1950	1,035	0.08	457	164	172	61	122	32	7	19	—
1951–1960	2,515	0.17	864	462	378	229	319	150	14	16	12

1961–1965	1,450	0.16	314	215	243	228	323	107	10	9	1
1966–1970	1,871	0.21	219	376	170	226	526	321	19	12	3
1971–1975	1,936	0.19	125	297	80	319	479	590	28	12	6

Note: Data are rounded to the nearest thousand persons. Detail may not add to total because of rounding.

a Resident population of the United States in the census year at or prior to the start of the period.

b Includes Belgium, Denmark, France, Germany, Great Britain, Ireland, Luxembourg, and the Netherlands.

c No record of immigration from Mexico, 1886–1893.

d Includes Turkey and Southwest Asia.

e Includes nearly 33,000 returning to their homes in the United States in 1906.

Source: U.S. Department of Justice, *Immigration and Naturalization Service, 1976 Annual Report* (Washington, D.C., 1978), table 13. U.S. Bureau of the Census, *Statistical Abstract of the United States: 1975* (Washington, D.C., 1975), table 1.

Table 2
PREFERENCE SYSTEM FOR IMMIGRATION
UNDER THE 1965 ACT

Preference	Characteristic	Maximum Proportion of Total[a]
First	Unmarried adult children of U.S. citizens[b]	20 percent
Second	Spouse and unmarried children of permanent resident aliens	20 percent plus any not required for first preference
Third	Professionals, scientists, and artists of exceptional ability	10 percent
Fourth	Married children of U.S. citizens	10 percent plus any not required for first 3 preferences
Fifth	Siblings of U.S. citizens	24 percent plus any not required for first 4 preferences
Sixth	Workers in occupations for which labor is scarce in the U.S.	10 percent
Seventh	Refugees	6 percent
Nonpreference	Any applicant not entitled to a preference	Numbers not required for preference applicants
— — —	Spouse and children of any preference applicant can be classified within the same preference if a visa is not otherwise available	Charged to appropriate preference

[a] Applicable to immigrants from the Eastern Hemisphere since 1966 and the Western Hemisphere since 1977.
[b] The spouse and minor children of U.S. citizens and the parents of citizens over age twenty-one may enter without being charged to the hemispheric limitation.
Source: U.S. Department of Justice, Immigration and Naturalization Service.

spouse and minor children of U.S. citizens and parents of U.S. citizens over age twenty-one could enter without being charged against the quota. As under the national origins system, a set of preferences was adopted to ration the visas. The preferences under the 1965 act (Table 2) placed greatest emphasis on family reunification (at least 74 percent of visas), but gave some preference to professionals (up to 10 percent),

Table 3
IMMIGRANTS ADMITTED BY CLASS UNDER THE
IMMIGRATION LAW, FISCAL YEAR 1975

Class	Total
Immigrants Subject to Numerical Limitations of the Eastern Hemisphere	160,460
Relative preferences	95,945
1st preference (unmarried adult children of U.S. citizens)	871
2nd preference (spouse and unmarried adult children of resident aliens)	43,077
4th preference (married children of U.S. citizens)	3,623
5th preference (siblings of U.S. citizens)	48,374
Occupational preferences	29,334
3rd preference (professionals)	8,363
6th preference (other workers)	6,724
Their spouses and children	14,247
Refugee preference (7th preference)	9,129
Nonpreference	25,961
Adjustment of status of aliens in United States	91
Immigrants Subject to Numerical Limitations of the Western Hemisphere (including special program for Cuban refugees)	121,101
Immigrants Exempt from Numerical Limitations	104,633
Immediate relatives of U.S. citizens	96,561
Others (including ministers, refugees, employees of U.S. government abroad)	8,072
Total	386,194

Source: U.S. Department of Justice, *Immigration and Naturalization Service, 1975 Annual Report* (Washington, D.C., 1976), table 4.

to other workers with scarce skills (up to 10 percent), and to refugees (up to 6 percent). The family ties of immigrants admitted under the preference system, particularly the fifth preference (regarding siblings and the siblings' immediate family) can be quite remote.

The occupational and refugee preferences tend to be fully subscribed (Table 3). Entry under the occupational preferences requires prearranged employment and a labor certification from the Department of Labor. Once the immigrant worker enters the United States he is not required to stay at the job indicated on his visa application. Family members that accompany workers entering under occupational preferences are charged to the occupational preference.

The emphasis on family reunification in the 1965 amendments is in contrast to the previous system of preferences. Before the 1965 amendments, professionals and skilled workers who had prearranged employment were classified as first-preference immigrants (as were their immediate family members), and were allocated 50 percent of each country's quota. Current U.S. policy also differs from those of the other major English-speaking countries that receive immigrants (Canada, Australia, and New Zealand), which place a much greater emphasis on education and labor market skills in rationing immigration visas.[13]

The United States imposed a numerical limit (120,000 visas per year) for the first time on immigrants from Western Hemisphere countries in the 1965 amendments. Immigrants were accepted on a first-come first-serve basis, with no country limits or preferences. Because of the 1976 amendments, the preference schedule used for the Eastern Hemisphere now also applies to the Western Hemisphere, as does the annual limit of 20,000 immigrants per country.

As a result of the 1965 act, immigration increased from about 300,000 persons per year before 1965 to about 400,000 per year— 290,000 authorized under the two hemispheric quotas and about 100,000 from parents, spouses, and children of U.S. citizens exempted from these quotas (Table 3). The distribution of immigrants by country of origin has also changed. The number of immigrants from northwestern Europe has shown the sharpest relative decline while the proportion from Asia and Africa, previously limited by the severe restrictions of the national origins quotas, has shown the sharpest increase (Table 1).[14]

The Economic Progress of Immigrants

To evaluate the impact of immigrants requires an understanding of their economic status in the United States, including their progress over time.

---

[13] A pamphlet distributed by the government of New Zealand says, "At present New Zealand is only accepting immigrants between the ages of 18 and 45 years who have certain professional, technical and trade skills for which there is a demand." Certain requirements may be waived, however, for the immediate family of New Zealand citizens. See New Zealand Government, "Immigration to New Zealand," March 1978, p. 1. For a comparison of U.S., Canadian, and Australian immigration policies, see Department of Justice, *Domestic Council Committee Report*, pp. 26–31.

[14] In fiscal year 1976, for example, only four Eastern Hemisphere countries had 15,000 or more immigrants charged to the country limit: China (19,244), India (16,642), Korea (19,852), and the Philippines (20,895). Department of Justice, *1976 Annual Report*, table 7.

An analysis of the earnings and occupational mobility of immigrants provides some insights into their adjustment to life in the United States. A similar analysis for the native born children of immigrants provides insights into possible second generation effects. That is, to what extent do immigrants pass on to their children characteristics that are favorable (or unfavorable) to receiving high earnings? The findings reported here are primarily from a series of research papers by the author on the earnings and occupational mobility of foreign born adult (age twenty-five to sixty-four) white men living in the United States, based on data from the 1970 Census of Population.[15]

Hypotheses. When they arrive, immigrants undergo an adjustment from life in their country of origin to life in the United States. They come from a variety of countries, some of which more closely resemble the United States than do others. A twenty-year-old high school graduate from Canada will not find the United States as alien an environment as will a twenty-year-old high school graduate from Russia or Mexico. Nor are immigrants from the same country necessarily alike. A fifty-year-old Russian immigrant who arrived last month will not have the same employment opportunities as a fifty-year-old Russian immigrant who came thirty years ago. Hence, in an analysis of the earnings and occupational status of immigrants, it may be important to know the person's country of origin and how long he has been in the United States.

Recent immigrants to the United States are likely to have fewer of the characteristics associated with high earnings or high occupational status than native born men have. The immigrants have less knowledge of the customs and language relevant to jobs in the United States; they have less information about job opportunities; and they have less training that is specific to the U.S. firm or industry in which they are employed. They are also less likely to have acquired the union card or occupational license needed in the United States to apply the skills acquired in their country of origin. As time passes, however, the immi-

---

[15] Unless indicated otherwise, the analyses and findings reported in this section are based on Barry R. Chiswick, "Sons of Immigrants: Are They at an Earnings Disadvantage?" *American Economic Review*, vol. 67, no. 1 (February 1977), pp. 376–380; Barry R. Chiswick, "The Effect of Americanization on the Earnings of Foreign Born Men," *Journal of Political Economy*, forthcoming, 1978; Barry R. Chiswick, "An Analysis of Earnings among Mexican Origin Men," *1977 Proceedings of the American Statistical Association, Business and Economics Statistics Section*, 1978, pp. 222–231; and Barry R. Chiswick, "A Longitudinal Analysis of the Occupational Mobility of Immigrants," in Barbara D. Dennis, ed., *Proceedings of the 30th Annual Winter Meeting, Industrial Relations Research Association*, Madison, Wisconsin, 1978.

grant may gain knowledge of the United States, acquire job specific training, and either acquire the union card or modify his skills accordingly.[16]

Hence, because knowledge and skills are not perfectly transferable across countries, immigrants would initially have earnings significantly lower than the native born, but the gap would narrow as the immigrants' years in the United States increase. If we trace the change in occupational status of immigrants from their last occupation in their home country to their early and later occupations in the United States, a U-shaped relationship would be expected. On average, they would experience downward occupational mobility when their last job in their country of origin is compared with their early jobs in the United States, and they would subsequently experience upward occupational mobility.

The U-shaped pattern of occupational change and the initially low earnings rising with time would be less intense for immigrants from countries similar to the United States (for example, Canada, Britain). The pattern would also be less intense for those who are conventional economic migrants rather than refugees. The latter tend to be older at the time of immigration and include a larger proportion of persons with skills that have little international transferability. Among professionals, for example, lawyers and judges, with skills that are very country specific, are seldom economic migrants, but they do appear in refugee populations. Even within occupations, refugees are less likely than economic migrants to have anticipated or prepared for the move.

If the foreign and native born have the same level of labor market ability and motivation, the earnings of the foreign born would approach and might equal, but would not exceed that of the native born. Economic theory suggests, however, that migration in response to economic incentives is generally more profitable for the more able and more highly motivated.[17] This self-selection in migration suggests that for the same schooling, age, and other demographic characteristics, immigrants to the United States would, on average, have more innate ability and motivation relevant to the labor market than the native born. If the effect on earnings of the self-selection in migration eventually outweighs any remaining earnings disadvantges from being of a foreign origin, the earnings of the foreign born would equal, and could then exceed, that of the native born.

---

[16] Job specific training is training that is useful only in the firm or industry in which it is acquired.

[17] In the simplest model, this arises from the assumptions that relative wages are approximately the same across countries and that there are costs of migration that are invariant with earning potential.

Table 4

CHARACTERISTICS OF ADULT WHITE MEN BY COUNTRY OF BIRTH AND PARENT'S COUNTRY OF BIRTH, 1970

Characteristic	Foreign Born	Native Born	Native Born	
			Foreign born parents[a]	Native born parents[b]
Earnings in 1969[c] ($)	9,662	9,738	10,568	9,442
Schooling (years)	10.8	11.9	11.9	11.9
Age (years)	46	43	47	42
Weeks worked in 1969	47	48	48	48
Rural (%)	11	30	18	33
Southern (%)	13	29	10	34
Years since migration	22	0	0	0
Married (%)	83	85	86	85
Father foreign born (%)	—	—	86	0
Mother foreign born (%)	—	—	74	0
Both parents foreign born (%)	—	—	60	0
Proportion of adult white men (%)	5.3	94.7	17.8	76.9

[a] One or both parents foreign born.

[b] Both parents native born.

[c] Earnings include income from wages, salary, and self-employment.

Source: 1970 Census of Population, 1/1,000 sample. Columns (1) and (2) from 5 percent questionnaire, columns (3) and (4) from 15 percent questionnaire.

Earnings of Immigrants. Overall, the annual earnings (wage, salary, and self-employment income) of the native born exceeds that of the foreign born by less than 1 percent (Table 4). The native born have about one additional year of schooling and worked one more week in the year, but they are three years younger and are more likely to live in low earnings areas, the South and rural areas. Among men of the same age, schooling, and area of residence, the foreign born have 3 percent higher earnings than the native born. The earnings of immigrants rise, though at a decreasing rate, with duration in the United States. The earnings of the foreign born are 9.5 percent lower than the native born if they have been in the United States only five years, 3.4 percent lower if they have been in the United States for ten years, equal after about thirteen years, 6.4 percent higher than the native born after twenty years, and 13.0 percent higher after thirty years. An analysis of citizenship indicates that, among the foreign born, naturalized citizens have higher earnings than aliens because the former have been in the United States for more years. Holding constant the number of years since immigration, as well as schooling level and the demographic variables, there is no significant difference in earnings between naturalized citizens and aliens.

The finding that immigrants reach earnings parity with their native born counterparts by ten to fifteen years after migration, and have higher earnings later on, is quite robust. It emerges when the data for immigrants are limited to those who came to the United States as adults, when Cuban born men are compared with native born white men, and when Mexican born men are compared with native born men of Mexican origin. This finding suggests that the greater innate ability and work motivation of immigrants, compared with their native born counterparts, eventually outweigh earnings disadvantages due to a foreign origin.

The steepness of the rise in earnings with duration in the United States varies by country of origin. It is flattest for immigrants from the developed English-speaking countries for whom the required adjustments are minimal. Indeed, the earnings pattern for immigrants from Britain and Canada with high levels of schooling resembles that of native born men who move within the United States because of a voluntary change in employment. The rise in earnings with duration in the United States is steeper for the Cubans, a refugee population, than for immigrants from other non-English-speaking countries.

Occupational Mobility of Immigrants. Since the 1970 Census of Population asked occupation in 1965 and in 1970, it is possible to trace the change in occupational status over this interval, and relate the change to duration in the United States and country of origin. The changes in earnings reported above are mirrored in the occupational mobility of immigrants.

For immigrants in the United States less than five years, their occupation in 1965 was in their country of origin. There is a tendency toward downward occupational mobility when the "last" (1965) occupation in their country of origin is compared with their "early" (1970) occupation in the United States. Among professionals and nonfarm managers in their home country, 22 percent were in lower level occupations in 1970. The net downward mobility was least for immigrants from the developed English-speaking countries (for example, only 6 percent of the professionals and managers were in lower level jobs), somewhat greater for immigrants for non-English-speaking countries other than Mexico and Cuba (19 percent), and greatest for the immigrants from Mexico (56 percent) and Cuba (58 percent).

After the initial fall in occupational status, immigrants begin an adjustment to U.S. labor market conditions. Among immigrants who had been in the United States at least five years in 1970, occupational mobility tended to be upward. The net upward mobility in the five-year period was greater for those here six to ten years than for those here eleven to twenty years. The extent of upward mobility, whether out of the lowest skilled jobs or into the highest skilled jobs, varies by country of origin. It is most intense for the Cubans (for example, 30 percent of the professionals in 1970 were in lower level jobs in 1965), less intense for immigrants from non-English-speaking countries (15 percent), and weakest for those from the English-speaking countries (12 percent).

Mexican Immigrants. In recent years, attention has focused on immigration, both legal and illegal, by Mexican nationals. It is, therefore, important to examine the earnings in the United States of Mexican immigrants. Mexico is the only important country of origin for which the earnings of white male immigrants differ substantially (and also significantly) from that of white men from the British Isles.[18] The earnings disadvantage of men from Mexico, even after accounting for their lower level of schooling, is not limited to first generation Mexican-Americans. First, second, and "third" (third and higher order) generation Mexican-Americans can be compared with other white men of the same generation. Other variables the same, Mexican-Americans earn about 15 to 25 percent less than other white men, and the differential does not seem to decline with the length of the family's residence in the United States.

The analysis indicates that the large proportion of first and second generation Americans is not the cause of the relatively low earnings and occupational status of the Mexican-American population. The reasons for their low earnings are as yet unknown. One hypothesis is that they have been subject to substantial discrimination, particularly in the Southwest. This interpretation, however, may not be consistent with the far greater economic progress made by the Chinese and Japanese Americans who were also subjected to substantial prejudice in the same states. An understanding of the reasons for the low earnings of the Mexican-American population is important in forming both domestic social programs and immigration policies. Yet, little research has been done on this subject.

---

[18] Using a regression analysis to control for the effects on earnings of schooling, years since migration, and demographic variables, the earnings of immigrants from the British Isles (the benchmark group) were compared with that of immigrants from other countries.

Indochinese Refugees. Considerable attention has focused on refugees from Indochina since the fall of South Vietnam, though refugees also continue to come to the United States from other places.[19] Since the fall of Saigon in April 1975, over 170,000 refugees from Vietnam, Laos, and Cambodia have entered the United States.[20] The very preliminary data on their first two years in the United States suggest that these refugees are experiencing a pattern of occupational change and economic progress similar to that of Cuban refugees and immigrants from other non-English-speaking countries.[21]

According to an August 1976 survey, the refugees tend to be employed in a lower status occupation in the United States than in Vietnam. Among heads of households who were professionals in Vietnam, 15 percent were professionals, 23 percent were clerical and sales workers, and 61 percent were blue collar workers in August 1976. Among those who were craftsmen in Vietnam, 45 percent reported they were craftsmen in the United States, and 48 percent were in lesser skilled blue collar jobs.

Compared with their situation when they first left the refugee camps, however, the Vietnamese have made substantial economic progress. Data for a panel of about 400 Vietnamese refugee households during the eleven months from August/September 1975 to July/August 1976 indicate that a larger proportion of the refugees were working, that a larger proportion of employed household heads were in white collar and craftsmen jobs, and that the wage and salary income of employed household heads had increased (Table 5). Most of the nearly 600 Vietnamese doctors and dentists in the United States are in training programs to acquire the necessary license, and some are already fully certified and employed in these occupations.

Children of Immigrants. The effect of immigrants on the country of destination depends on the characteristics not only of the immigrants

---

[19] From fiscal year 1946 to 1976 over 1.1 million other refugees were admitted to the United States under the several special refugee programs. These include 765,000 persons born in Europe, 72,000 born in Asia (27,000 in China and Taiwan), 264,000 born in Cuba, and 12,000 from other countries. Department of Justice, *1976 Annual Report*, table 6E.

[20] Over 85 percent of the refugees are Vietnamese. Although the Indochinese refugees were admitted under parole status, under recent legislation they are to receive permanent resident alien (immigrant) status without regard for the normal quota system. The change in status reduces their vulnerability to deportation, makes them eligible to obtain citizenship, and removes certain barriers to occupational licensing, employment, and "in-state" tuition at many public colleges.

[21] The data on the employment, earnings, and occupation of Indochinese refugees are from Opportunity Systems, Inc., 1976 Report, *Third Wave Report: Vietnam Resettlement Operational Feedback*, prepared for HEW Refugee Task Force (Washington, D.C., September 1976), particularly tables 14, 33, 35, 36.

Table 5
ECONOMIC PROGRESS IN THE UNITED STATES OF A PANEL OF VIETNAMESE REFUGEES, 1975–1976

	Survey I	Survey II	Survey III
	August– September 1975	November– December 1975	July– August 1976
Number of households	446	446	398
Employment ratio[a]			
Male employment ratio	66.9	82.8	86.1
Female employment ratio	49.4	73.3	79.6
Occupation[b]			
White collar	14.4	30.9	38.0
Craftsmen	20.5	16.3	33.2
Other blue collar	52.5	52.8	28.9
Not ascertained	2.6	—	—
Total	100.0	100.0	100.0
Earnings[c]			
$399 or less	37.6	36.8	22.5
$400 to $599	40.2	37.2	35.9
$600 and over	18.8	26.0	41.0
Not ascertained	3.4	—	0.6
Total	100.0	100.0	100.0

Note: Detail may not add to total due to rounding.

[a] Employed as a percentage of population, persons aged sixteen and over.

[b] Employed household heads—percentage.

[c] Monthly wage and salary income, employed household heads—percentage.

Source: Opportunity Systems, Inc., *Third Wave Report: Vietnam Resettlement Operational Feedback*, prepared for HEW Refugee Task Force (Washington, D.C., September 1976), tables 33, 35, 36.

themselves, but also of their children. The future economic progress of the children of the current foreign born population cannot be readily evaluated. However, the earnings and other characteristics of the adult native born children of an earlier generation of immigrants can be studied.

It appears that immigrants are self-selected persons with higher than average innate ability or work motivation. This tendency would be passed on to their native born decendants, through genetic inheritance or through the home environment, although presumably the tendency would be less pronounced the further removed a cohort is from its immigrant ancestors. On the other hand, the children of immigrants would be raised in a home less familiar with the English language, with the U.S. school system, and with labor market opportunities in general. In addition, second-generation Americans may be subject to adverse discrimination. The net effect of these factors can be determined by an analysis of the earnings of adult native born men, comparing the native parentage with the foreign parentage (one or both parents foreign born).

Adult white men of foreign parentage had annual earnings 12 percent higher than the native parentage in 1969 (Table 4). There was virtually no difference between the two groups in their level of schooling or weeks worked in the year. Although men of foreign parentage tend to be somewhat older, this would have a small effect on the difference in earnings. Most important is the different geographic distribution of the two groups. The foreign parentage are far more likely to live in urban areas and are less likely to live in the South.

Adjusting for differences in schooling and the demographic variables, foreign parentage men have earnings 5 percent higher than the native parentage. The earnings advantage is greatest if only the father is foreign born (8 percent), smaller if both parents are foreign born (6 percent), and weakest if only the mother is foreign born (4 percent).

The favorable effect on earnings of having a foreign born father and a native born mother is intriguing. It may reflect the effects on productivity of the different characteristics that sons acquire from their mothers and their fathers. It is reasonable to assume that in general mothers have a greater impact on their sons' knowledge of English. Having been raised in a home in which a language other than English was spoken is associated with lower earnings, other things being the same. On the other hand, fathers may have a greater impact on their sons' work motivation and occupational choice. And, the self-selection of immigrants on the basis of ability or work motivation is likely to be more intense for men than for women, many of whom accompany their husbands and do not anticipate a strong attachment to the labor market. Men with a native born mother and a foreign born father may then have the "best" possible combination.[22]

Not all sons of immigrants are equally successful in the United States. Using men of foreign parentage from the British Isles as the benchmark group, it is possible to examine the relative earnings, other

---

[22] On the other hand, the differential effect of parents' nativity may be a spurious finding. It could rise, for example, if the foreign born men who are financially the most successful marry native born women, and the income of the father influences the earnings of his sons.

things the same, of men with parents from other countries.[23] Among adult white men of foreign parentage, earnings differ substantially and significantly from the benchmark for only one major source of immigrants, Mexico. The earnings of men of Mexican parentage are about 18 percent lower than those with parents from the British Isles.

Thus, in terms of generating earnings, the advantages of having foreign born parents apparently outweigh any disadvantages of being raised in a home less familiar with the language and institutions of the country or from discrimination against the children of immigrants. The advantages may be due to the apparent higher-than-average innate ability and work motivation of their immigrant parents.

Summary. The economic success in the United States of male immigrants and their sons appears to be widespread. Whether measured by earnings or occupational status, the relatively low position of immigrants when they first arrive is temporary. Their earnings and occupational status rise with their duration in the United States, rapidly at first, at a slower rate later on. After ten to fifteen years the earnings of immigrants reach parity with those of native born men with similar characteristics, and afterwards they have higher earnings. This suggests that it would be inappropriate to base estimates of the impact of immigrants solely on their earnings or occupational status during their first few years in the country.

The rise in earnings and occupational status with time in the United States is less intense for immigrants from countries similar to the United States, such as Canada and Britain. It is most intense for refugees, such as the Cubans who came to the United States since the late 1950s.

Some of the characteristics of immigrants that contribute to their economic progress in the United States are apparently transmitted to the next generation. The native born white sons of immigrants have about the same schooling level as the adult white sons of native born parents, but, other things being the same, they have 5 percent higher earnings. Compared with other white men of the same "generation" in the United States, the Mexican origin population has a lower level of schooling and lower earnings, even when schooling and demographic variables are held constant.

The findings reported here indicate that in general white male immigrants are successful in the U.S. labor market. Additional work is needed, however, for black and Asian male immigrants, as well as

---

[23] Parent's country of birth is that of the father if he was foreign born; otherwise it is the mother's country of birth.

women of all races to ascertain whether they too are as successful as their native born counterparts.

Illegal Aliens

Illegal aliens have existed in the United States as long as the laws that restrict entry into the country. Over time, however, attention has shifted, from Chinese in the late nineteenth century to Mexicans in the 1970s.[24] A rational policy for dealing with the illegal alien issue requires an understanding of who they are, why they come to the United States, and what impact they have on the country.

The number of illegal aliens currently residing in the United States is unknown. Estimates range from 2 to 12 million, but the estimating procedures are necessarily crude and indirect because these aliens have an incentive to hide or to falsify their identity when approached by a survey interviewer. Unlike crimes that have a more direct effect on property or personal safety, violations of the immigration law are seldom reported. The enforcement of immigration laws is likely to be as effective as the enforcement of the laws restricting the production and sale of alcohol during Prohibition.

Data do exist, however, on the number of deportable aliens apprehended in a year, although the extent of multiple apprehensions of the same persons is unknown. Illegal alien apprehensions have increased sharply since the early 1960s: 71,000 in 1960; 110,000 in 1965; 345,000 in 1970; 767,000 in 1975, and over 1 million in 1977.[25] Of the 767,000 apprehensions in 1975, 680,000 were Mexican nationals, most of whom were arrested at the border and had entered the United States without inspection.[26]

---

[24] For a discussion of the current illegal alien issue, see Department of Justice, *Domestic Council Committee Report*, chap. 2, 3.

[25] Department of Justice, *1976 Annual Report*, table 23.

[26] Deportable Aliens Located by Nationality and Status of Entry, Fiscal Year 1975

Nationality	Number	Status of Entry (percent)		
		Entry without inspection	Other	Total
Europe	17,766	2.1	97.9	100.0
Asia	17,287	6.5	93.5	100.0
Mexico	680,392	96.2	3.8	100.0
Canada	9,048	43.8	56.2	100.0
Other Western Hemisphere	37,013	22.6	77.4	100.0
Other	5,094	0.9	99.1	100.0
Total	766,600	87.1	12.9	100.0

Source: Department of Justice, *1975 Annual Report*, table 27B.

Most apprehended illegal aliens entered the United States only shortly before their arrest. In 1975, 57 percent of the arrests were made within seventy-two hours of entry (primarily at the border), 15 percent within four to thirty days, 16 percent within one to six months, 4 percent within seven months to one year, and 8 percent over one year.[27] Among apprehended illegal aliens who had penetrated the border, the small proportion who had been in the United States more than six months prior to their arrest probably arises from two factors: (1) those illegal aliens with characteristics that result in a high probability of arrest tend to be arrested sooner rather than later, and (2) with time in the United States illegal aliens become less visible, reducing the probability of being arrested.

The increase in the number of arrests is primarily due to the increase in the discrepancy between the number wishing to enter the United States and the number allowed. The discrepancy appears to have increased most sharply for Mexicans for several reasons: the rapid population growth (3.5 percent annual rate of increase) and relatively sluggish performance of the Mexican economy; the end of the *bracero* (contract farm labor) program, in effect from 1942 to 1964, which resulted in a shift from legal to illegal status for many temporary farm workers;[28] numerical limits on Western Hemisphere immigration as of 1968; and, most recently, the prospect of amnesty (that is to say, the granting of temporary or permanent resident alien status) for those already in the United States before some arbitrary point in time.

For the reasons mentioned above, little is known about the characteristics of illegal aliens living in the United States. The data suggest that apprehended illegal aliens are predominantly young adults (primarily age eighteen to thirty), male (90 percent), recent arrivals, and from Mexico. The probability of being arrested, however, is not independent of these characteristics. For example, for the same Immigration and Naturalization Service budget, more arrests can be made if resources are concentrated along the Mexican border; young adults are more apt to come into contact with the police (an important source of referrals for the INS) and hence are more vulnerable to being detected; recent arrivals have had less experience in masking their identity; and it is alleged that the scarcity of INS detention facilities for women and policies for transporting women bias the agency's apprehensions towards men.[29]

Some insights into the earnings and earnings related characteristics of illegal aliens who have avoided detection may be inferred from a

---

[27] Department of Justice, *1975 Annual Report*, p. 13.

[28] At its peak over 400,000 Mexican workers were employed annually under the *bracero* program.

[29] Department of Justice, *Domestic Council Committee Report*, p. 126.

comparison of apprehended illegal aliens with the foreign born legally in the United States. The data on apprehended illegal aliens are, however, dominated by the 90 percent from Mexico, and Mexican immigrants (both legal and apprehended illegal) have a low average level of schooling and occupational status. It is important to stratify by country of origin, that is, to make the comparison of legal and apprehended illegal aliens separately for Mexican and non-Mexican immigrants. If, as is suggested by the data, legal and apprehended illegal aliens from the same country who have been in the U.S. the same length of time have similar earnings and earnings related characteristics, it is reasonable to assume that the nonapprehended illegal aliens also have the same general characteristics.

One of the richest sources of information on the characteristics of apprehended illegal aliens who have succeeded in penetrating the border is a sample collected by David North and Marion Houstoun.[30] In May–June 1975 they interviewed 793 illegal aliens (481 from Mexico, 237 from other Western Hemisphere countries, and 75 from the Eastern Hemisphere) over age sixteen who had worked in the United States for at least two weeks. Even though non-Mexican apprehended illegal aliens are "over-sampled," the sample appears representative of apprehended illegal aliens who have penetrated the border in that it is relatively young (average age 28.5 years), male (91 percent), and recently arrived.[31]

For the same country of origin and years in the United States, there does not appear to be a substantial difference in the schooling and occupational distribution of the foreign born legally in the United States and apprehended illegal aliens. The apprehended illegal aliens averaged 6.7 years of schooling, 4.9 years for those from Mexico, 8.7 years for those from other Western Hemisphere countries, and 11.9 years for those from the Eastern Hemisphere.[32] Among adult white men in the United States in 1970, the average level of schooling was 6.1 years for the Mexican born and 10.8 years for all foreign born, in contrast to 11.9 years for the native born.[33]

---

[30] David North and Marion T. Houstoun, *The Characteristics and Role of Illegal Aliens in the U.S. Labor Market: An Exploratory Study* (Washington, D.C.: Linton and Co., 1976, mimeo.).

[31] The respondents were asked: "About how many years in all did you work for wages in the U.S.?" There was a similar question for self-employment in the United States. Duration of employment is the sum of the two answers. Thus, the data are for all U.S. labor market experience, and not simply experience in the most recent episode in the United States. On average they worked in the United States for 2.1 years, 44 percent for less than one year, 27 percent for 1 to 3 years, 21 percent for 3 to 6 years, and 9 percent for 6 to 20 years. North and Houstoun, *The Characteristics*, Abstract, pp. A-1–A-2, and Appendix B, p. 5.

[32] North and Houstoun, *The Characteristics*, Abstract, p. A-2.

[33] Chiswick, "Americanization," table 1, and "Mexican Origin," table 2.

In Table 6 the occupational distribution in the United States of North and Houstoun's sample of apprehended illegal aliens is compared with that of foreign born men as reported in the 1970 Census of Population. Although there are some apprehended illegal aliens in all of the major occupational categories, they clearly have a lower occupational status. However, the difference in the occupational distribution is much smaller when the illegal aliens born in Mexico are compared with foreign born men from Mexico, and it is even smaller when the comparison is with recent Mexican immigrants. There is, however, an over-representation of farm workers among the apprehended illegal aliens from Mexico. The occupational distribution of the apprehended illegal aliens from other Western Hemisphere countries (primarily from Latin America) most closely resembles that of recent Mexican immigrants. The occupational distribution of the very small sample of apprehended illegal aliens from the Eastern Hemisphere closely resembles that of the foreign born who migrated between 1965 and 1970.

Some researchers have attempted to ascertain whether illegal aliens are paid lower wages than legal residents with the same skills. In his study of men in Mexico who had worked in the United States legally or illegally, Cornelius reported: "Illegal migrants are not necessarily paid at lower rates than legal workers at their place of employment—indeed, none of the illegals whom we interviewed claimed that they had been discriminated against in this way. Rather, wages paid for certain types of jobs (particularly in agriculture) are uniformly low, at least by U.S. standards."[34] North and Houstoun reported that only 16 percent of their sample felt they were paid lower wages as a direct result of their illegal status.[35] This belief was most common in the counties along the Mexican border. They note that "illegals who reported exploitation of this kind were almost twice as likely to have been in the U.S. less than two years (about half of the sample) than illegals who had been in the U.S. two or more years." The reported decline in "exploitation" with time in the United States could result from the recent illegal immigrants inappropriately comparing themselves with legal workers who have been in the United States for several years, rather than with recent legal immigrants. Alternatively, illegal aliens who have been in the United States for several years may be more effective in masking their illegal status, and hence may be less likely to be paid lower wages. These studies suggest, however, that if there is discrimination in wages against illegal aliens (that is to say, the payment of

---

[34] Wayne Cornelius, "Mexican Migration to the United States: The View from Rural Sending Communities," Migration and Development Study Group (M.I.T., June 1976, mimeo., p. 27).

[35] North and Houstoun, The Characteristics, pp. 132–134.

Table 6
U.S. OCCUPATIONAL DISTRIBUTION OF EMPLOYED FOREIGN BORN MALES AND APPREHENDED ILLEGAL ALIENS
(percent)

Occupation	Foreign Born			Born in Mexico			Born in Other W. Hemisphere Countries	Born in E. Hemisphere
	Illegal aliens (1975)	Legal immigrants (1970)	Recent (1965–70) immigrants (1970)	Illegal aliens (1975)	Legal immigrants (1970)	Recent (1965–70) immigrants (1970)	Illegal aliens (1975)	Illegal aliens (1975)
White collar	5.4	39.6	37.7	1.2	11.7	6.7	8.7	29.2
Craft	15.3	21.3	17.5	14.3	18.8	13.8	13.3	31.2
Operative	25.1	17.8	21.4	22.6	27.4	33.5	37.0	4.2
Nonfarm laborer	14.8	6.0	6.9	17.9	15.0	15.7	11.6	—
Service	20.6	12.1	13.6	16.9	11.5	13.4	24.9	35.4
Farm worker	18.8	3.2	3.1	27.0	15.6	16.7	4.6	—
Total	100.0	100.0	100.0	100.0	100.0	100.0	100.0	100.0
Sample size	628	a	a	407	a	a	173	48

Note: Data are for persons age sixteen and over who reported an occupation in the United States. Because of rounding, columns may not total 100 percent.

a The sample is very large: the data are from a 5 percent sample of the U.S. population.

Source: For apprehended illegal aliens, David North and Marion T. Houstoun, *The Characteristics and Role of Illegal Aliens in the U.S. Labor Market: An Exploratory Study* (Washington, D.C.: Linton and Co., 1976), mimeo., table V-5, p. 108; for the foreign born, 1970 Census of Population, Subject Reports, *National Origin and Language* (PC (2)-1A), table 18, p. 466.

lower wages to illegal than to legal workers of the same productivity characteristics) it is not common.

The North and Houstoun data can be used to compare the earnings of their sample of Mexican illegal aliens with the earnings of Mexican born men as reported in the 1970 Census of Population. The Mexican illegal aliens earned $2.34 per hour. Mexican born adult white men (age twenty-five to sixty-four) who responded to the census earned $5,115 in 1969 and worked forty-five weeks. Assuming that they worked forty hours in the weeks they worked (90 percent of Mexican born heads of households worked thirty-five hours or more in the reference week in April 1970) and adjusting their earnings for the rise in the adjusted hourly earnings index for the private nonfarm sector from 1969 to 1975, the hourly earnings of the Mexican born men in 1975 are estimated to be $4.33. Thus, the illegal aliens had hourly earnings 46 percent lower than the estimate for Mexican born men.

The extent to which the illegal aliens have lower earnings because of their earnings-related characteristics, rather than their illegal status per se, can be estimated. The regression coefficients from an analysis of the earnings of native and foreign born men of Mexican origin living in the Southwest reflect the influence on earnings of differences in: schooling, total labor market experience, years in the United States, and marital status.[36] If the North and Houstoun sample of Mexican illegal aliens

---

[36] In the regression equation the dependent variable is the natural logarithm of earnings. The difference between the natural logarithm of $4.33 (1.466) and $2.34 (0.850) is 0.616. The mean values of the explanatory variables and their effects on the difference in the natural logarithm of earnings are:

	Means of Variables		Partial Effect on the Log of Earnings of the Difference in Means
	North and Houstoun illegal aliens from Mexico	Mexican born men	
Schooling (years)	4.9	6.1	0.059
Labor market experience (years)[a]	18.0	30.0	0.051
Years since migration[b]	2.4	16.4	0.416
Proportion married	0.50	0.66	0.072
Total			0.598

Note: About 85 percent of the Mexican born men in each sample live in the five southwestern states. Seven percent of the sample of illegal aliens are women.

[a] Measured as age minus schooling minus 5.

[b] Years of total U.S. experience, not just in the most recent stay.

Source: North and Houstoun, *The Characteristics*, pp. 69, 75, 76, 85, 115; Chiswick, "Mexican Origin," tables 2, 3.

The antilog of 1.448, the sum of 0.850 and 0.598, is $4.25. Note that this procedure assumes that an earnings function computed for apprehended illegal aliens from Mexico would have the same regression coefficients as was obtained in the analysis for men of Mexican origin in the census data.

had the same values for these variables as Mexican born men in the Census, and if the effects of these variables on earnings were the same for both groups, the hourly earnings of the apprehended illegal aliens would be $4.25, within 2 percent of the hourly earnings of the Mexican born.[37] The dramatic narrowing of the earnings gap is largely due to the effects of time in the United States on earnings.[38] About two-thirds of the difference in hourly earnings is due to the shorter period of time the apprehended illegal aliens worked in the United States.

In summary, apprehended illegal aliens have low earnings, schooling, and occupational status because they are predominantly from Mexico and recently arrived in the United States. There are apparently no substantial differences in earnings, schooling, or occupational status between legal and apprehended illegal aliens from Mexico who have been in the United States for the same length of time, except for a greater proportion of illegal aliens engaged in farm work. This similarity also appears in a comparison of the schooling level and occupational status of legal and apprehended illegal aliens from other countries.

Illegal aliens are a non-random sample of persons wishing to enter the United States but who do not apply for or are denied immigrant visas. If the immigration policy favored those most likely to be financially successful in the United States, apprehended illegal aliens would tend to have lower earnings than legal immigrants. The analysis of earnings suggests that U.S. immigration policy is largely neutral with respect to skills and earning potential in the issuance of immigration visas, rather than favoring those most likely to have high earnings in the United States.

Impact of Immigrants

The immigration policy of the United States should be based, a least in part, on the economic impact of immigrants on the native population. An analysis of this impact should include not only the effect on the

---

[37] The earnings of the illegal aliens are lower by 9 percent if there is no statistical control for differences in marital status.

[38] North and Houstoun also report an important effect of time in the United States. Without controlling for country of origin or other variables, those in the country two or more years (averaging 3.4 years) earned $2.97 per hour while those here less than two years (averaging 0.5 years) earned $2.40 per hour, a 24 percent rise in hourly earnings for the three additional years in the country. This is larger than the effect for Mexican born men in the census data, when other variables are held constant—a 12 percent increase in earnings for an increase of from 0.5 to 3.4 years in the United States. (North and Houstoun, *The Characteristics*, p. 115; Chiswick, "Mexican Origin," table 3.)

aggregate income in the economy but also the distribution of this income among segments of the population. A program that would increase average income, but with the gainers outnumbered by the losers, may not be enacted unless income redistribution policies are adopted to spread the benefits more widely.

Simple Ricardian Model. In a simple Ricardian model of the economy there are two factors of production—say, capital and labor—that are not perfect substitutes for each other. The wage rate is determined, as in Figure 1, by the intersection of the labor supply curve and the downward sloping curve for the marginal product of labor. Initially the supply of labor is S_0, so the wage rate is W_0, aggregate labor income is Area OW_0AL_0. Since aggregate income is the area under the curve for the marginal product of labor, aggregate income is Area $ODAL_0$. The return to the capital stock in the economy is therefore the Area W_0DA.

Suppose there is an increase in the supply of labor (from S_0 to S_1) due to the immigration of workers who bring no capital with them. The increased supply of labor, capital stock held constant, lowers the marginal product of labor (that is, the wage) to W_1, raises aggregate income by the Area L_0ABL_1, and raises the aggregate income received by capital by Area W_1W_0AB. The total income of the original (native) population is their labor income OW_1CL_0 plus their capital income W_1DAB, a *net* increase of Area ABC. Thus, the aggregate income of the native population and hence the average income of the native population increases, but there is a change in the distribution of income as the owners of capital gain while native labor loses.

The native population as a whole and the immigrants gain because of the immigration. The aggregate native income increases by Area ABC. The immigrants move presumably because even a wage of W_1 is better than the alternative they left behind. Yet, data from the National Income Accounts or households samples will show a decline in average income, from L_0E to L_1F in Figure 1. Thus, aggregate data can convey the false impression that income falls as a result of immigration.

The simple Ricardian model points to a major divergence of interest regarding immigration. The changes in the "functional distribution" of income indicate that native labor loses and capital gains. If capital were equally distributed among the native workers, the average total income (labor and capital income) of each native worker would be higher and, ignoring other considerations, they would support the immigration. At the other extreme, if the vast majority of the population were workers who owned no capital, and a small proportion of the population owned the capital but did not work, the majority would find it in their direct economic interest to oppose immigration.

Figure 1

THE EFFECT OF IMMIGRATION ON THE LEVEL
AND DISTRIBUTION OF INCOME

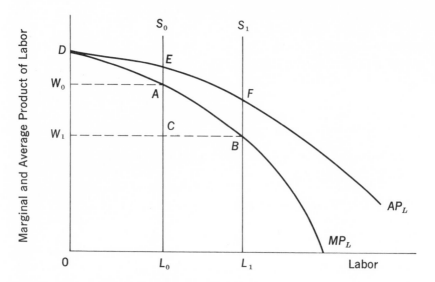

Note: S_i = Supply schedule of labor at time i
  MP_L = Marginal product of labor
  AP_L = Average product of labor
  L_i = Employment of labor at time i
  W_i = Wage rate at time i

Although the Ricardian model outlines the essence of the economic impact of immigrants, it diverges from the reality of the United States in several dimensions that warrant discussion. A three-factor rather than a two-factor view of the economy provides greater reality, there is a welfare system that transfers income from the taxpayers as a whole to those with low wages, and there are other public assets and public goods and services, such as social overhead capital and defense.

Three-Factor Model. Aggregate production functions are a useful means of describing the totality of the economy, even if the simple two-factor Ricardian model or a multifactor Cobb-Douglas functional form are inadequate. Recent research suggests that the U.S. economy can be well described by a three-factor constant elasticity of substitution (CES) production function. The three factors are high-level manpower (professionals), low-level manpower, and physical capital. The production function and the algebraic manipulations needed to obtain the implications of immigration that are summarized here are presented in the appendix to this paper.

An increase in the supply of unskilled workers due to immigration decreases the marginal product (wage) of unskilled labor and increases the marginal product of skilled workers and capital. As aggregate income in the economy increases by more than the total wages of the immigrants, the aggregate income of the native population is increased. Thus, immigration of unskilled workers widens wage differentials, increases the return to capital relative to the wages of the unskilled, and raises the aggregate income of skilled workers, capital, and the native population. However, the aggregate income of native unskilled workers declines. If the ownership of capital is concentrated, overall income inequality, measured by a Lorenz curve or any other conventional measure, is increased.

Suppose, however, the immigrants are skilled workers. This lowers skill differentials and lowers the aggregate income of the native born skilled workers, but raises the income of unskilled workers and capital. The aggregate income of the native population also increases. Income inequality in the lower end of the personal income distribution declines, but inequality in the upper end increases.

The analysis becomes somewhat more complex if it incorporates the finding that the skills of immigrants vary with their time in the United States. The initial impact of a cohort of immigrants, particularly from non-English-speaking countries, differs from its ultimate impact. In an extreme example, if the immigrants are initially all unskilled they widen wage differentials and lower the earnings of unskilled native workers. As the immigrants adjust to the United States, their productivity rises, and an increasing proportion (perhaps all) become skilled workers. As this occurs wage differentials narrow, and the earnings of unskilled native workers increase. Ultimately, if the ratio of skilled to unskilled workers becomes larger among the immigrants than among the native population, relative skill differentials are smaller and the earnings of unskilled native workers are higher than prior to the immigration.

When there is a time path to the skill distribution of the immigrants, who gains and who loses among native workers (in terms of the present value of future income) depends on the initial and ultimate skill distribution of the immigrants compared with the native workers, the time path of the change in relative skills of the immigrants, and the discount rate of native workers. The greater the initial and ultimate skill level of the immigrants relative to native workers, and the faster they reach their ultimate skill level, the greater the gains in income for native unskilled workers and the smaller the gains for skilled workers.

The higher the discount rate of unskilled native workers (that is, the smaller the present value of future income) the smaller the gain to them from the type of immigration just described. On the other hand, the higher the discount rate of skilled workers the more they would gain from a policy that raised their earnings initially, even though it lowered them in the future. Unskilled workers are likely to have a higher discount rate than skilled workers—different time preferences for consumption may account for the differential investment in human capital and discount rates may be negatively related to human and non-human wealth.[39] If the divergence in discount rates is sufficiently large, that is, if the unskilled place little value on the higher incomes received in the future while the skilled place little extra value on receiving higher incomes in the present, it is possible for both skilled and un-skilled native labor to lose because of the immigration. However, the total income received by the native population and by the owners of capital would be larger in each and every year, and hence the present values of these incomes would also be larger with the immigration.

The Welfare System and Compensating Income Transfers. Let us now introduce a welfare system into the schematic economy.[40] If the welfare system (that is, the criteria for eligibility and the schedule of benefits) is invariant with the immigration policy, the immigration of unskilled workers increases aggregate welfare expenditures in two ways. First, as the immigration depresses the wages of unskilled workers, a larger proportion of native unskilled workers qualify for some benefits, and those already receiving benefits receive a larger transfer. Second, the unskilled immigrants themselves may qualify for benefits. If the immi-grants are excluded from participating in the welfare system, enough income could be transferred from skilled workers and capital to the unskilled so as to make everyone at least as well off as before the im-

---

[39] See Gary S. Becker, *Human Capital* (New York: National Bureau of Economic Research, 1964), chap. 3.

[40] Contrary to the general view, as a result of food stamps and other programs, the United States does have a negative income tax or a guaranteed annual income even for two-parent working poor families. For the purpose of this discussion, any income- or earnings-contingent public transfer, including unemployment compensation, is treated as part of the welfare system. Reduced taxation of low income workers has the same effect as increased welfare payments. For a description and analysis of the major welfare programs, see Barry R. Chiswick, "The Income Transfer System: Impact, Viability and Proposals for Reform," in William Fellner, ed., *Contemporary Economic Problems 1977* (Washington, D.C.: American Enter-prise Institute, 1977), pp. 347–428.

migration.[41] This can occur because aggregate income among the native population has increased.

Suppose the welfare system is not permitted to differentiate between natives and immigrants.[42] If both native and immigrant unskilled workers are to be brought up to the income level of unskilled workers prior to immigration, the aggregate income (after taxes) of skilled workers and capital must be lowered. In the two-factor model in Figure 1, through a tax on capital each of the L_0 native workers can receive a subsidy of AC to raise their earnings to W_1, with capital still receiving a net increase in income, although it is reduced to Area ABC instead of Area W_1W_0AB. If all L_1 workers are to receive the subsidy of AC, the aggregate income of capital must be lower than before the immigration. (For the analysis using a three-factor model, see the appendix.)

The welfare system itself may serve as a means of attracting immigrants.[43] For some the calculus of the costs and benefits of migration to the United States is the comparison of earnings in the country of origin with welfare benefits in the United States. For others who intend to work in the United States, the potential availability of welfare acts as an insurance that cushions the loss of income due to unemployment.

Immigration of skilled workers causes a decline in the wages of native born skilled workers and a rise in the wages of native born unskilled workers. As a result of the rise in the latter's wages, aggregate net welfare expenditures received by low income native workers decline if the structure of the welfare system does not change. The additional revenues from the taxation of the higher income of capital and lower welfare expenditures could be used to lower the tax rate paid by skilled labor. In principle, native born skilled workers could be made at least as well off as before the immigration without eliminating the net gain to the other factors of production, as long as immigrant skilled workers are not substantial recipients of transfers.

---

[41] This assumes that there are no adverse labor supply or capital formation effects of the tax and transfer system.

[42] Under current U.S. law, legal resident aliens have the same legal entitlement to welfare benefits as citizens. The number of illegal aliens receiving welfare benefits of one form or another is unknown. Temporary (guest) workers in the United States, as under the former bracero program, are not eligible for welfare benefits. Legislation has been introduced in Congress, however, to bar most aliens from Supplemental Security Income (ssi) until they have lived in the United States for at least five years, unless the disability occurs after they arrive, and to make the sponsor legally responsible for the alien's financial support.

[43] For an analysis of the effect of regional differences in earnings and welfare benefits on geographic mobility within the United States, see Robert Reischauer, "The Impact of the Welfare System on Black Migration and Marital Stability," (Ph.D. diss., Columbia University, 1971).

In summary, if immigrants are not included in the income transfer system, the increase in the aggregate income of the native population means that, in principle, some income can be transferred from the native groups that gain to the native groups that lose as a result of the immigration, so that no native group loses. The welfare and tax systems can be the mechanisms for this transfer. However, this may not be accomplished if the immigrants themselves are to be substantial recipients of welfare benefits, that is, if they receive an income substantially in excess of their productivity. Immigrants are most likely to be welfare recipients if they are unskilled or disabled, if they bring their dependent family members with them, and if they remain in the United States when they are unemployed.

Public Goods and Services. Thus far the discussion has ignored the public provision of goods and services financed through the tax system or a growing public debt. National defense, police and fire protection, the court system, public schools, parks, roads, sewers, and the like are government provided goods and services that are financed by taxes and the public debt rather than by user-charges. In forming a view toward immigration, the native population would be concerned with the increase in their aggregate income *net* of the difference between the taxes paid by immigrants and the increased public cost of providing goods and services to the population augmented by immigrants.[44] Although it is an interesting topic for speculation, too little is known about the marginal cost to the native population of the use of public goods and services by immigrants.

One relevant consideration is the extent of economies of scale in the provision of public goods and services. The marginal cost of some publicly provided goods and services may be invariant with the size of the population. An extra 1 million people in the U.S., for example, is not likely to result in an increased Armed Forces, or an increased cost of maintaining the interstate highway system in Wyoming. The expenditure for some public goods and services (libraries) may be proportional to the population size. For other public goods and services (police and fire protection), costs may rise at a faster rate than the size of the population. On balance, it is not clear whether there are net economies of scale from an increase in the population by, say, 1 million persons. And, the answer may depend on the composition of the additional population. An extra 1 million persons over age eighty places a

---

[44] For a fuller analysis of this issue, and estimates for Great Britain, see Dan Usher, "Public Property and the Effects of Migration upon Other Residents of the Migrants' Countries of Origin and Destination," *Journal of Political Economy*, vol. 85, no. 5 (October 1977), pp. 1001–1020.

different demand on public services than an extra 1 million teenagers. Increasing the U.S. population by 1 million immigrants is not the same as a one-half percent increase in the population in all age groups. For example, as immigrants tend to be young adults, when they arrive or, more often, shortly after they arrive, they place a greater demand on the public school system, but little additional demand on the services of public nursing homes.

Empirical studies suggest that taxes in the United States are roughly proportional to earned income, that is, income from labor and nonlabor assets.[45] It is far more difficult to calculate the extent to which the marginal cost of public goods and services varies by income level. Although the poor may have more school-age children and use subsidized public transportation, the wealthy may place a higher demand on police and fire protection and subsidized higher education and public highways. In addition, immigrants may have a different pattern of use of public goods and services, limiting the transferability to them of the findings of a study of the marginal cost of public goods by income level for the population as a whole.

Synthesis—Progress and Impact

The largely empirical analysis of the economic progress of legal and illegal immigrants and the largely theoretical analysis of the impact of immigrants on the native population can be synthesized. The result is several preliminary points regarding immigrants and policy issues.

Immigrants. Immigrants can be selected in a manner that increases the aggregate income of the native population, although without income redistribution policies some groups will lose while others will gain. If the immigrants are unskilled and are substantial recipients of welfare benefits and social services, the income of the native population as a whole could decline.

The earnings and occupational status of immigrants, and hence the net benefits to the native population, increase the longer the immigrants are in the country. The earnings of white male immigrants equal that of the native born by ten to fifteen years after migration, and then exceed the native born. The net benefits are, therefore, greater if the immigrants come as young adults rather than older workers. The favorable impacts tend to continue in the second generation (native born children of immigrants).

---

[45] Joseph A. Pechman and Benjamin A. Okner, *Who Bears the Tax Burden?* (Washington, D.C.: Brookings Institution, 1974).

Schooling and occupational level in the home country can be used to predict, although imperfectly, the immigrants' ultimate success in the United States. Immigrants from Mexico, however, have much lower earnings than other white men for the same level of schooling, age, and place of residence in the United States. Although refugees initially have greater difficulty adjusting to the United States than other immigrants, this disadvantage apparently does not persist.

Legal and apprehended illegal aliens from the same country who have been in the United States for the same number of years do not appear to differ in earnings-related characteristics or in earnings. This suggests that illegal aliens are not "exploited" (that is, paid wages lower than legal aliens from the same country with similar productivity characteristics). In addition, it suggests that current immigration procedures do not disproportionately select those who are likely to be the most productive in the United States from among those wishing to immigrate.

Low-skilled immigrants with families eligible for welfare benefits and who use public services (for example, schools) are more likely to be a net cost to the native population. These costs are reduced under a guest worker program in which the worker comes to the United States without his family for a maximum fixed period of employment after which he must leave. Because of the relatively short duration of employment, guest worker programs are most likely to be successful for jobs that require little or no training specific to U.S. employment conditions.

Policy Issues. The analysis indicates that the income of the native population is more likely to be increased if preference in immigration is given to highly trained workers (without regard for the specific skill), whether they are refugees or economic migrants. This suggests a decrease in the relative importance of family reunification as a criterion for entry, and an increase in the importance given to the migrants' skills. The electorate, however, may be willing to sacrifice some money income for the psychic income of helping those in need. Humanitarian consideration will quite properly continue to influence immigration policy, with some scope for family reunification and special assistance for refugees.

The national origins quota system was inconsistent with an immigration policy based on humanitarian considerations or on facilitating the entry of the most skilled workers. Immigrants from some countries, however, do appear to earn less than those from others, even after earnings data are corrected for demographic variables. It would be most advantageous if the factors that result in their less successful economic progress could be identified and removed without substantial cost. Then, an immigration policy that is neutral with respect to country of origin would be consistent with a policy of maximizing the aggregate economic well-being of the native population.

Guest worker programs may be a means of acquiring the services of less-skilled workers, while minimizing the costs generated from their family's use of welfare benefits and public services.[46] Such programs have been widely used in Western Europe and to a lesser extent in the United States (primarily in agriculture). Guest worker programs are not without their disadvantages, however, as the workers cannot be used in jobs that require country specific skills, and they are often reluctant to return to their home country when their period of employment has ended.

There have been proposals to fine employers who "knowingly" hire illegal aliens in order to decrease the employment opportunities and the incentive for illegal immigrants. The illegal aliens who work, however, are likely to be net contributors to the native population. The productivity of these aliens will be lower if they must take employment that more effectively masks their illegal status or if they are forced further "underground" to find employers willing to hire them. It is noteworthy that there are no serious proposals to penalize those civil servants who "knowingly" provide public income transfers or social services to illegal aliens and their families—transfers that are more clearly net drains on the native population. Legislation to penalize employers who hire illegal aliens raises two serious concerns about possible infringements of civil liberties: (1) through increased discrimination in employment against persons of foreign origin (for example, Mexican-Americans with a legal right to be in the United States; and (2) ultimately through the development of an "internal passport" to facilitate enforcement of the law.

Immigration policy is likely to be subject to intensive review in the coming years. It has now been over a decade since the major changes in immigration policy introduced in the 1965 amendments have been in effect. The amendments were passed during a period of relatively low and declining unemployment and when changing attitudes made the national origins quota system anachronistic. The challenge to the American people is to balance the widely accepted objectives of an immigration policy that is humanitarian and equitable and that improves the economic well-being of the native population. The challenge to re-

---

[46] This is based on the assumption that it would not be desirable or feasible to have *permanent* resident alien workers and families who are denied access to the income transfer system in time of economic hardship or who are denied the use of certain publicly provided services, such as schooling for their children.

searchers is to develop further our understanding of the alternatives before us.

Appendix:
Aggregate Production Function Analysis of the Impact of Immigrants

Aggregate production functions are a useful means of describing the totality of the economy. Recent research suggests that the U.S. economy can be well described by a three-factor constant elasticity of substitution (CES) production function. The three factors are high-level manpower (professionals), low-level manpower, and physical capital, and the pairwise elasticities are consistent with a CES (σ) equal to about 2.5.[47] Aggregate output (Q) may be written as:

[1]
$$Q = [\beta_1 U^{-\rho} + \beta_2 H^{-\rho} + \beta_3 K^{-\rho}]^{-1/\rho}$$

where U = Low-level manpower
H = High-level manpower
K = Capital stock

$$\sigma = \frac{1}{1 + \rho} = \text{elasticity of substitution.}$$

The marginal product of each factor of production is:

[2]
$$\left| MPU = \beta_1 \left(\frac{Q}{U}\right)^{1/\sigma} , \quad MPH = \beta_2 \left(\frac{Q}{H}\right)^{1/\sigma} \right.$$
$$\left| MPK = \beta_3 \left(\frac{Q}{K}\right)^{1/\sigma} \right.$$

An increase in the quantity of unskilled labor, U, increases output (Q), but at a smaller rate than the growth in unskilled labor so $\frac{Q}{U}$ declines.

Then, an increase in U due to the immigration of unskilled workers decreases the marginal product of unskilled labor (MPU), and increases the marginal product of skilled workers (MPH) and capital (MPK). If the number of unskilled workers increases from U_0 to U_n, aggregate income in the economy increases by the integral $\int_{U_0}^{U_n} \beta_1 \left(\frac{Q}{U}\right)^{1/\sigma} dU$. After the n immigrants arrive, the marginal product of unskilled workers is $MPU_n = \beta_1 \left(\frac{Q}{U_n}\right)^{1/\sigma}$ and their aggregate wages are $(MPU_n)U_n$.

---

[47] Carmel U. Chiswick, "The Growth of Professional Occupations in U.S. Manufacturing: 1900–1973," *Research in Human Capital and Development* (Greenwich, Conn.: JAI Press, 1978, forthcoming).

Because of the decreasing marginal product of unskilled labor, the increase in aggregate income exceeds the total wages of the immigrants. The change in the aggregate income of the native population is

[3]
$$\int_{U_0}^{U_n} MPU_n \, dU - n(MPU_n),$$

which is necessarily positive for any elasticity of substitution between zero and infinity.

Thus, immigration of unskilled workers widens wage differentials, increases the return to capital relative to the wages of the unskilled, and raises the aggregate income of native born skilled workers, capital, and the native population. The aggregate income of native born unskilled workers declines. Parallel changes occur if the immigrants are skilled workers.

If the unskilled immigrants are excluded from participating in the welfare system, enough income could be transferred from skilled workers and capital to unskilled native workers so as to make everyone at least as well off as before the immigration. This can occur because aggregate income among the native population has increased.

If both native and immigrant unskilled workers are to be brought up to the income level of unskilled workers prior to immigration, the aggregate income (after taxes) of skilled workers and capital must be lowered. That is, the rise in the aggregate income of skilled workers and capital exceeds the transfer that would return native unskilled workers to their pre-immigration income (a transfer of $(MPU_0 - MPU_n)(U_0)$) but not the transfer that would be needed to bring the unskilled native workers and immigrants to the pre-immigration level of earnings for unskilled workers (a transfer of $(MPU_0 - MPU_n)(U_n)$).

Contemporary Health Policy: Dealing with the Cost of Care

Robert B. Helms

Summary

Justifications for National Health Insurance (NHI) have undergone a gradual but noticeable change in recent years. In the early 1970s the most common arguments for NHI were based on the need for improving access to medical care among people who did not have adequate insurance coverage or who could not otherwise afford adequate care. Since that time an argument has evolved that NHI is needed to control rapidly expanding costs for medical care.

The medical sector has not been spared the effects of the relatively high rates of inflation this country has experienced since 1968. But most indexes of medical prices have increased at a faster rate than indexes for the economy as a whole. These recent price increases have strengthened the political arguments in support of NHI and caused many to question traditional explanations of economic behavior in medical markets. It is not an exaggeration to say that in the popular view medical markets are somehow considered a special case among economic markets. Competitive forces and economizing decisions by consumers have seemed inadequate to the task of controlling medical costs. When medical markets are viewed in this way, it is not difficult to understand why a system of government finance under NHI is seen as an easy way to control an otherwise uncontrollable market.

But is this popular perception correct? It should be obvious that a clear understanding of how medical markets work is essential if we are to develop a national health policy that provides the kind of health care we want at reasonable cost. This paper looks at what we know about economic behavior in medical markets in an attempt to identify ways in which they differ from other markets. Specifically, the discussion deals

*with three broad aspects of medical markets that economists have iden-
tified to explain perverse economic behavior in those markets. These
are the role of tax subsidies for the purchase of medical insurance, lack
of consumer control of demand, and lack of market competition.*

*A central conclusion of this paper is that there is no inherent dif-
ference in medical markets that cannot be explained by standard economic analysis. The perverse effects of rapidly increasing expenditures
and prices are seen as consequences of rational behavior on the part of
consumers and providers of medical care in response to the distorting
effects of government subsidies. These subsidies (both tax subsidies
for the purchase of medical insurance and direct, government payments
through Medicare and Medicaid) have promoted a system in which consumers and physicians make decisions about the use of medical facilities and services with very little consideration of the costs of these decisions. It is argued in this paper that this situation of minimal cost-
sharing at time of treatment has pervasive effects on the performance
and structure of medical markets. It is also argued that our public policies to subsidize medical care are largely responsible for the development of other problems in medical markets, such as physicians' influence over consumers' medical decisions and the apparent lack of
competition in some medical markets. In other words, there are logical
economic explanations for what many perceive to be a "market failure"
in medicine.*

*The policy implication of this analysis is that the predominant
argument now being given for national health insurance is based on a
fundamental misunderstanding of how medical markets function—
why they have developed in the way they have and how they could be
expected to perform either under more extensive regulation or, alternatively, under a policy designed to increase consumer cost-sharing. If
we are interested in formulating a national health policy that avoids the
detrimental effect of regulation experienced in other industries, while
maintaining such strong features of our medical system as high quality,
rapid innovation, and freedom of individual choice, we should not so
readily abandon the principles of a market economy.*

Introduction

Given the public concern about the rising cost of medical care, it is not
surprising that health policy is now considered a principal policy issue.
President Carter ran on a platform promising the passage of national
health insurance and has stated that an administration bill will be in-

Table 1
PRIVATE AND PUBLIC HEALTH EXPENDITURES, 1929–1976
(billions of dollars)

Fiscal Year	Total Expenditures	Percent of GNP	Out-of-Pocket Private Expenditures			Public Expenditures		
			Total	Percent of total	Average annual percent change[c]	Total	Percent of total	Average annual percent change[c]
1929	3.6	3.5	3.1	86.7	—	0.5	13.3	—
1935	2.8	4.1	2.3	80.9	−4.9	0.5	19.1	2.2
1940	3.9	4.1	3.1	79.9	6.1	0.8	20.1	7.6
1950	12.0	4.5	9.0	74.5	11.2	3.1	25.5	14.6
1955	17.3	4.5	12.9	74.5	7.6	4.4	25.5	7.6
1960	25.9	5.2	19.5	75.3	8.6	6.4	24.7	7.7
1965	38.9	5.9	29.4	75.5	8.6	9.5	24.5	8.3
1970	69.2	7.2	43.8	63.3	8.3	25.4	36.7	21.6
1975[a]	122.2	8.4	71.4	58.4	10.2	50.9	41.6	14.9
1976[b]	139.3	8.6	80.5	57.8	12.8	58.8	42.2	15.6

[a] Revised estimates.
[b] Preliminary estimates.
[c] Average annual percent change in expenditures during period from previous entry.
Source: Robert M. Gibson and Marjorie S. Mueller, "National Health Expenditures, Fiscal Year 1976," *Social Security Bulletin*, vol. 40, no. 4 (April 1977), Table 1, p. 4; U.S. Department of Health, Education, and Welfare, *Health, United States, 1976–1977* (Washington, D.C., 1977), Table 140, p. 345.

troduced in 1978.[1] There also seems to be substantial congressional and popular support for some kind of national program to provide more extensive health coverage and to control costs. However, given what is currently known about the working of medical markets and the anticipated costs of more extensive medical coverage, a government program to control the rapid rise in medical costs is popularly perceived to be a prior condition for passage of national health insurance.

Thus policy makers are faced with the dilemma of wanting to pass politically popular programs to extend subsidies for medical care but not wanting to interfere with a responsible budgetary policy. Table 1 presents some summary data illustrating the relative growth in public

[1] Executive Office of the President, *The United States Budget in Brief, Fiscal Year 1978* (Washington, D.C., 1978), p. 53.

and private health expenditures. When Congress is faced with containing these increasing public expenditures, it has two broad choices: it can reduce the coverage provided by the policy or it can attempt to persuade (or require) the providers of that service to supply the given quantity and quality at controlled prices. The policies that might be adopted to carry out either of these choices involve important questions of "efficiency," a term which refers to the general concept of using scarce resources in such a way that the benefits of health services are kept in line with the benefits of alternative uses of those resources, such as for education, housing, or food.

This essay will look at the economics of this fundamental public policy choice now being debated by Congress, the medical profession, and the general public. What are the causes of medical cost increases and what are the likely consequences of increasing our reliance on planning and regulation as opposed to a greater reliance on market incentives?

This country is already well on the way to establishing an extensive system of economic regulation in health. What we are witnessing is a classic case of the political process overlooking the fundamental economics of the marketplace and ignoring the long-term consequences of an expedient policy. As we have seen with other cases of economic regulation such as natural gas, airlines, railroads, and trucking, the potential economic loss from such a regulatory approach is not insignificant.[2] Contemporary health policy, it is argued here, should not so readily abandon the principles of a market economy.

Regulation versus the Market: A Choice of Policies

The future of health policy is being debated in an atmosphere of increasing concern about government expenditures, deficits, and inflation, and growing skepticism about the efficacy of government regulation. While we are already in the process of establishing a system of health regulation with emphasis on planning, certification of additional capacity, and revenue controls, the ongoing debate about cost control and national health insurance still leaves room for some basic choices about the part market principles should play in health policy.

A theme often heard in the debate about medical care costs is that medical markets "do not work" and therefore that the government must control costs. Several important interim questions should be

---

[2] Roger Noll, "The Consequences of Public Utility Regulation of Hospitals," in *Controls on Health Care* (Washington, D.C.: Institute of Medicine, National Academy of Sciences, 1975), pp. 25–48.

asked about medical markets before a policy of government regulation is adopted by default: In what sense do medical markets perform differently from other markets? In what sense do they perform similarly? What forces can be identified that make people less cost-conscious in medical markets? This paper will discuss some of the economic forces at work in medical markets in an attempt to identify the causes of medical cost increases. The presumption is that if we can determine what is different about economic behavior in medicine, we can then propose policies that promote economic efficiency and individual freedom of choice while avoiding the costs of government regulation.

A premise of this paper is that the regulatory approach to controlling medical expenses is not likely to be successful in the long run. Controlling hospital capacity, some medical prices, or even the total revenue of hospitals may have some measurable success in reducing expenditures for medical care for a few years. But if we are to learn from predictions of economic theory and our experience with regulation in other industries, we can anticipate that a system of health regulation will be subject to strong political pressures that will dissipate the short-run effects of such regulation. The result will be a health care system that retains the inefficiency of the present one while protecting existing interests from competition and technological change. As has been shown with other regulatory programs, consumers (patients) will very likely to be worse off.[3] We do know from the history of regulation, however, that the elimination, or even reform, of an established regulatory system is extremely difficult to achieve. For that reason alone we should be extremely careful about abandoning market principles in favor of a regulatory approach to health care.

Do Medical Markets Work?

A widely held perception about medical markets is that they are so inherently different from other markets that they cannot be relied on to maximize consumer well-being in the absence of direct government interference. This perception is continually reenforced by statements of both economists and noneconomists that the laws of supply and de-

---

[3] Research into the effects of various types of health regulation is in an elementary stage. For some discussion of the probable effects, see Noll, "The Consequences of Public Utility Regulation of Hospitals"; Penny H. Feldman and Richard J. Zeckhauser, "Some Sober Thoughts on Health Care Regulation," in *Regulating Business: The Search for an Optimum* (San Francisco: Institute for Contemporary Studies, 1978), pp. 93–120; David Salkever and Thomas Bice, "The Impact of Certificate-of-Need Controls on Hospital Investment," *Milbank Memorial Fund Quarterly: Health and Society*, vol. 54, no. 2 (Spring 1976), pp. 185–214.

mand do not apply to medical markets.[4] Medical markets—like markets for everything from automobiles to zucchini—have certain distinctive characteristics. They are different in some respects from other markets. But this does not mean that the concepts of supply and demand are not useful tools of analysis. Attacks on these concepts are based on misconceptions about the use of abstract models and the role of prices as an equilibrating mechanism.

The economist's attention to price (and economic incentives) may seem inconsistent with casual observations about the apparent unimportance of prices to participants in medical markets. Prices refer to the cost of foregone alternatives, that is, what consumers must give up in other consumptive opportunities and what resources are required to produce that good or service. For example, the price of an operation may represent both the sacrifice of a vacation trip to a consumer and the necessary inducement to physicians and hospitals to "produce" the operation. Other factors that may affect the consumer's choices (such as taste, income, and prices of other goods), or the producer's willingness to supply what the consumer wants (such as the costs of inputs and technological knowledge), can be considered in an orderly fashion using the concepts of supply and demand. Even when certain market conditions relating to structure and the availability of information are not strictly met, the supply and demand model can be useful because, even as an abstract model, it allows for an analysis of a multitude of forces affecting the behavior of individuals in markets.

Before discussing those aspects of medical markets that may differ from other markets, consider for a moment the many changes in medical markets that are obviously consistent with the standard analysis. In an industry sometimes described as the third largest in the country (behind agriculture and construction), there are obviously many examples of medical markets responding to outside forces (such as changes in income or shifting population patterns), which are predictable from standard economic theory. Economists have provided some empirical backup for a few examples.

First, there is substantial evidence that physician supply is affected by population shifts.[5] For example, in such areas as the Sun Belt where

---

[4] "Health care is not and should not be considered a commodity, perceived to be the same kind as other goods and services. Health care is not governed by marketplace economics. People consider health services to be qualitatively different from other goods and services." Statement by Philip Caper, M.D., in W. S. Moore, ed., *Regulatory Reform: Highlights of a Conference on Government Regulation* (Washington, D.C.: American Enterprise Institute, 1976), p. 26.

[5] For example, see Lee Benham, Alex Maurizi, and Melvin Reder, "Migration, Location, and Remuneration of Medical Personnel: Physicians and Dentists," *Review of Economics and Statistics*, vol. 50, no. 3 (August 1968), pp. 332–347; and Henry B.

there has been a net migration of the population, physicians, dentists, nurses, and others serving medical markets are responding to the demand by moving there.

There is also evidence that the traditional fee-for-service medical profession responds to increased competition from an alternative form of delivery, just as would be predicted by the standard economic theory of the firm.[6] Goldberg and Greenberg have found that in response to the success of Kaiser Permanente (a health maintenance organization—HMO) in northern California, Blue Cross broadened its hospital and physician benefit packages (including maternity coverage) and established competing HMOs. Private physicians have also responded to the success of Kaiser by forming foundations for medical care (FMCS), which provide consumers with another form of prepaid coverage.[7]

Evidence also exists that physicians, even when acting as agents for their patients rather than for their own direct pecuniary gain, prescribe relatively more drugs in certain therapeutic markets where prices have declined.[8]

While few economists would dispute that there are many aspects of medical markets that work, these examples serve to remind us that, contrary to popular belief, strong economic forces do operate in medical markets. If the market seems to produce perverse effects, such as excessive price increases or a misallocation of certain resources, then what is required is not an abandonment of economic reasoning but a deeper

---

Steele and Gaston V. Rimlinger, "Income Opportunities and Physician Location in the United States," *Western Economic Journal*, vol. 3 (Spring 1965), p. 191.

[6] See Lawrence C. Goldberg and Warren Greenberg, *The Health Maintenance Organization and Its Effects of Competition* (Washington, D.C.: Federal Trade Commission, July 1977). Health maintenance organizations (HMOs) provide medical care in exchange for a fixed annual capitation payment. In contrast to the more traditional fee-for-service providers, HMOs bear the risk of providing complete medical care for their enrolled population. Foundations for medical care (FMCS) refer to a wide variety of organizations that in general provide a form of prepaid coverage to patients but retain the fee-for-service aspect of payment to private physicians. Financial discipline is imposed through a system of peer review.

[7] Goldberg and Greenberg, *The Health Maintenance Organization*, pp. 72–84. They have also found that similar but less dramatic competitive effects have been found in other areas of the country where HMOs have become established. See also Jon B. Christianson, *Do HMOs Stimulate Beneficial Competition?* (Excelsior, Minn.: InterStudy, 1978).

[8] See Douglas L. Cocks, "Product Innovation and the Dynamic Elements of Competition in the Ethical Pharmaceutical Industry," in Robert Helms, ed., *Drug Development and Marketing* (Washington, D.C.: American Enterprise Institute, 1975), pp. 225–254, and the discussion by Yale Brozen et al., pp. 281, 289–290. Similar evidence for the United Kingdom is presented by W. Duncan Reekie in *Pricing New Pharmaceutical Products* (London: Croom Helm, 1977) and, for the United States, in "Price and Quality Competition in the United States Drug Industry," *Journal of Industrial Economics*, vol. 26, no. 3 (March 1978), pp. 223–237.

look at what may be causing the perverse market behavior. Discussed below are three broad arguments considered by economists as more serious explanations of why medical markets are "different."[9]

Tax Subsidies and Insurance. The principal reason for what appears to be different modes of economic behavior by individuals in medical markets is the effect of tax subsidies for the purchase of health insurance. Tax exemptions for medical insurance have prompted the growth of insurance coverage, which in turn has had the effect of removing some financial constraints on decisions made by both medical providers and patients.[10] While these general effects are quite well known to economists and health policy analysts, the more pervasive effects on the behavior of individuals and the structure of the medical industry are generally unappreciated.

First, consider the role of tax exemptions in promoting the growth of medical insurance coverage. In an unsubsidized market, some rational consumers would choose to purchase insurance to protect themselves from the risk of large medical payments. But tax exemptions induce the purchase of more complete insurance than consumers would otherwise buy—that is, more complete in terms of the medical problems covered and the financial cost of treatment. These effects occur not only because individuals can deduct part of their expenditure for medical insurance from taxable income, but because the tax system promotes the purchase of medical insurance through employment-related

---

[9] For other discussions of how medical markets differ, see Mark V. Pauly, "Is Medical Care Different?" in Warren Greenberg, ed., *Competition in the Health Care Sector: Past, Present, and Future* (Washington, D.C.: Bureau of Economics, Federal Trade Commission, March 1978), pp. 19–48; Cotton M. Lindsay and Keith B. Leffler, "The Market for Medical Care," in Cotton M. Lindsay, ed., *New Directions in Public Health Care* (San Francisco: Institute for Contemporary Studies, 1976), pp. 66–82. It is sometimes argued that because medicine involves questions of life and death, it is in no sense a "market" with emphasis on price and therefore is not subject to the laws of supply and demand. But economic theory is an abstract model that can be applied as a tool of analysis to any situation where consumers and producers make choices and where scarce resources are used. The concept of elasticity of demand is capable of incorporating those few medical decisions (such as emergencies) where price is given little apparent consideration.

[10] The literature on health finance and insurance is now rather extensive. For a recent popular treatment, see Martin S. Feldstein, "The High Cost of Hospitals— and What To Do About It," *Public Interest* (Summer 1977), pp. 40–54; for a more technical treatment, see Martin S. Feldstein, "The Welfare Loss of Excess Health Insurance," *Journal of Political Economy*, vol. 81 (March/April 1973), pp. 252–280. See also Joseph P. Newhouse, Charles E. Phelps, and William B. Schwartz, "Policy Options and the Impact of National Health Insurance," *New England Journal of Medicine*, vol. 290 (June 13, 1974), pp. 1345–1359; Mark V. Pauly, "Health Insurance and Hospital Behavior," in Lindsay, ed., *New Directions in Public Health Care*, pp. 103–129.

group policies. Since the employer's cost of providing medical insurance is not considered part of the employee's taxable income, employees have an incentive to bargain for more insurance coverage rather than for more wages which can be taxed. Feldstein has calculated that the employee can gain about 50 percent more in benefits from nontaxable income spent for medical insurance than he can from an increase in wages. That is, instead of a $1.00 increase in wages which are subject to taxes, he can obtain $1.50 worth of medical insurance.[11] And the employer has an incentive to provide more insurance coverage rather than to increase wages because his expenditures for social security and state taxes would be higher if he increased wages. Enthoven has estimated the federal tax subsidy for fiscal year 1978 to be $10.1 billion, which consists of $5.84 billion for the exclusion of employee contributions to insurance premiums, $2.87 billion for medical expense deductions, and $1.43 billion from foregone social security taxes.[12]

To summarize developments since World War II: (1) there has been a great increase in the percentage of the population having some medical insurance; (2) the coverage has become more complete both in terms of medical events insured and in the proportion of medical costs covered—that is, there has been more "first dollar" or "shallow" coverage; and (3) the proportion of coverage provided through employment-based group policies has increased. Recent government surveys show that in 1974, 81.3 percent of the population had some hospital insurance and 63.3 percent of the population had some group coverage.[13] As would be expected from an income effect and from a subsidy system related to income, the amount of insurance coverage

---

[11] Feldstein, "The High Cost of Hospitals," p. 45.

[12] Alain C. Enthoven, "Consumer Choice Health Plan (CCHP): An Approach to National Health Insurance (NHI) Based on Regulated Competition in the Private Sector," unpublished memorandum to Joseph A. Califano, secretary of health, education, and welfare, dated September 22, 1977, p. 3 and Appendix 21, pp. 3–4. It is interesting to note that Mitchell and Vogel estimated the tax subsidy to be $2.5 billion for 1970, though they apparently did not allow for social security taxes as Enthoven has. Still this illustrates how inflation has pushed people into higher tax brackets, causing a rapid increase in tax subsidies to health insurance. See Bridger M. Mitchell and Robert J. Vogel, *Health and Taxes: An Assessment of the Medical Deduction* (Santa Monica: Rand Corporation, August 1973), Table 5, p. 16.

[13] Charles S. Wilder, *Hospital and Surgical Insurance Coverage, United States—1974* (Washington, D.C.: National Center for Health Statistics, August 1977), p. 5, Table A and Table 16. It should be noted that there are difficult problems of double counting when individuals are covered by more than one source of insurance or government program. Using a different procedure to count that part of the population covered under Medicare, Medicaid, and other government programs (VA and military hospitals), Sudovar and Sullivan estimate that 94.2 percent of the population now has some protection for health expenses. See Stephen G. Sudovar, Jr., and Kathleen Sullivan, *National Health Insurance Issues: The Unprotected Population* (Nutley, N.J.: Roche Laboratories, 1977), p. 3.

increased with the level of income.[14] For persons under the age of sixty-five with private insurance, only 37.2 percent of those with incomes less than $3,000 were covered while 91.8 percent of those with incomes more than $15,000 were covered.[15] Given the preponderance of work-related group policies, it is not surprising that the under-sixty-five age group also shows 85.3 percent coverage for those currently employed but only 64.0 percent coverage for those currently unemployed.[16]

Data illustrating the growth of shallow coverage are less precise because of the diversity in insurance policies. The Health Insurance Institute does show, however, that the percentage of insurance policies covering 80 percent or more of medical expenses has been above 85 percent since 1966 and above 90 percent since 1970.[17] Perhaps the best evidence of the growth of shallow coverage is found in Martin Feldstein's study of what has happened to out-of-pocket medical expenditures as hospital coverage has been extended.

> In 1950, when average cost per patient-day was a little less than $16, private insurance and government programs paid 49 percent of hospital bills. This meant that, on the average, the net cost to a patient of a day of care was just under $8. By 1975, average cost per patient-day had jumped to about $152—but private and public insurance were paying 88 percent of the hospital bill, leaving a net cost to the patient of only $18. Thus, although the cost of providing a day of hospital care had increased more than ninefold (from $16 to $152), the net cost to patients had only just about doubled (from $8 to $18). Moreover, the general increase in the prices of all goods and services meant that $18 in 1975 could only buy as much as $8 in 1950! So in real terms, the net cost to the patient at the time of illness has not changed at all during the past 25 years.[18]

While insurance companies pay about 27 percent of total expenditures for personal health care, the other large third-party payer (about 40

---

[14] For a discussion of this effect and evidence that the tax subsidy is strongly related to income, see Mitchell and Vogel, *Health and Taxes*, pp. 4–13.

[15] Wilder, *Insurance Coverage*, Table D, p. 6.

[16] Ibid., Table 9, p. 20. For those not in the labor force, 70.1 percent had hospital coverage in 1974.

[17] *Source Book of Health Insurance Data 1976–77* (New York: Health Insurance Institute, 1977), p. 38. See also the discussion of the completeness of coverage by Frech and Ginsburg, "Competition among Health Insurers," in Greenberg, ed., *Competition in the Health Care Sector*, pp. 216–219. They show some evidence that coverage by Blue Cross and Blue Shield is more complete than that provided by non-Blue companies.

[18] Feldstein, "The High Cost of Hospitals," pp. 41–42.

percent) is the government.[19] Medicare and Medicaid were passed in 1965 to provide coverage for the aged and poor. In 1975 Medicare covered approximately 24.2 million people and disbursed $15.6 billion. Medicaid provided $12.7 billion in fiscal year 1975 to an estimated 22.9 million people.[20] The latest federal budget includes $29.4 billion for Medicare and $12.1 billion for Medicaid.[21] Total federal expenditures for hospital and medical services have been growing at an average annual rate of roughly 16 percent since 1968 and roughly 18 percent since 1973.[22]

Table 2 shows some trends in medical prices and out-of-pocket private expenditures for three broad segments of medical markets. As can be seen in the table, prices have increased at a faster rate in those segments of medical markets (hospital and physicians' services) where insurance coverage has become more extensive than they have in less insured markets (other services). An explanation is that tax exemptions and government programs that have promoted the growth of third-party payments for medical care have removed most financial considerations from decisions about the use of medical facilities and services. This has led to a system that increases expenditures for medical care, increases both medical and insurance prices, and fosters a demand for alternative ways of controlling usage that do not rely on personal consumer choice. The individual behaves differently because the insurance coverage has changed what he perceives as the marginal cost of treatment. When a person becomes ill and seeks care, the tendency is to "get what's coming to me," that is, to seek the highest quality care, and larger quantities of care, up to the point where the marginal benefits are thought to be equal to the individual's marginal cost (including his time). Shallow insurance coverage, which lowers the individual's marginal cost, increases the amount of care demanded even though the additional cost may be much greater than its value to the individual. Thus, the individual not only seeks more care but he also has less incentive to be cost-conscious about the care sought.[23] The resulting higher prices for medical care in turn increase the demand for insurance because of the increase in the individual's financial risk.[24]

---

[19] Sudovar and Sullivan, *National Health Insurance Issues*, p. 4.

[20] *Source Book of Health Insurance Data 1976–77*, pp. 41–42.

[21] *United States Budget in Brief, Fiscal Year 1978*, p. 54.

[22] Calculated from the Office of Management and Budget's *Special Analyses of the Budget for Fiscal Years 1970–79*.

[23] Clark C. Havighurst and James F. Blumstein, "Coping with Quality/Cost Trade-Offs in Medical Care: The Role of PSROs," *Northwestern University Law Review*, vol. 70, no. 1 (March/April 1975), pp. 15–20.

[24] Feldstein, "The High Cost of Hospitals," p. 44.

Table 2
TRENDS IN MEDICAL COST-SHARING AND PRICES, 1955–1976

	Fiscal Year					
	1955	1960	1965	1970	1975	1976
Hospital Care						
Percent private direct payments[a]	23.6	18.6	18.5	12.3	9.8	8.9
Hospital service charges[c]						
Semiprivate room charges	6.9	6.3	5.8	13.9	10.2	13.8
Operating room charges	—	—	—	11.4	10.9	14.8
X-ray services	—	—	—	5.1	7.2	11.8
Physicians' Services						
Percent private direct payments[a]	71.2	66.0	63.2	44.9	39.0	38.7
Physician fees[c]						
Office visits	3.6	3.0	2.9	7.0	7.2	11.4
Tonsillectomy and adenoidectomy	2.6	3.1	2.5	5.2	6.9	9.7
All Other Services[b]						
Percent private direct payments	85.7	84.5	82.3	71.7	63.2	62.0
Selected indexes[c]						
Dentist fees	2.7	2.4	2.4	5.3	6.3	6.4
Eyeglasses	1.0	2.0	1.7	4.1	5.7	6.2
Drugs	1.4	2.0	0.8	0.7	2.8	6.1
Consumer Price Index[c]	2.2	2.0	1.3	4.2	6.8	5.3

[a] In addition to private direct payments, other sources of health care payments are private insurance benefits, private other, and public expenditures.

[b] All other services consist of dentist services, other professional services, drugs and drug sundries, eyeglasses and appliances, nursing-home care, and other health services.

[c] Figures refer to the average annual percent change in each index during the previous five years, except for 1976 where the period is 1975–1976.

Source: Robert M. Gibson and Marjorie S. Mueller, "National Health Expenditures, Fiscal Year 1976," *Social Security Bulletin*, vol. 40, no. 4 (April 1977), Table 7, pp. 19–20; U.S. Department of Health, Education, and Welfare, *Health, United States, 1976–1977* (Washington, D.C., 1977), Table 163, p. 377.

A system dominated by third-party payers also weakens the physician's incentive to resist the patient's demand for more extensive care. The physician does not bear the additional cost of the decision to provide more extensive care and may receive both financial and professional benefit from prescribing additional and higher quality care. In addition to the increased monetary reimbursement, additional tests or a longer hospital stay may increase the probability that a correct diagnosis has been made and thus lower the physician's risk of a malpractice suit.[25] Some of the effects of more complete insurance are translated into physician and hospital demand for more elaborate and expensive equipment whose use increases the cost of care.[26] The Congressional Budget Office estimates that almost half the 14.7 percent increase in the 1976 hospital cost per patient-day was attributable to increased services rather than to higher wages and prices paid by hospitals.[27]

Medical market behavior is also affected by a tax policy that induces people to obtain insurance coverage through employment-related group policies. There do seem to be some economies of scale in the purchase of group policies when compared with individually purchased policies.[28] But the preponderance of purchases of group policies has the effect of adversely selecting out those who do not work because they are less healthy, thus raising the price of individually purchased policies. The higher cost of individual policies and the tax subsidies on group policies lessen the chance for individuals to express their own preferences about the amount and kind of insurance they desire, a situation quite different from other insurance markets such as automobile, life, and fire insurance.[29] The effective demand on the part of those

---

[25] Michael D. Intriligator and Barbar H. Kehrer, "An Economic Model of Medical Malpractice," in Simon Rottenberg, ed., *The Economics of Medical Malpractice* (Washington, D.C.: American Enterprise Institute, 1978), pp. 89–98.

[26] See Martin Feldstein and Amy Taylor, *The Rapid Rise of Hospital Costs* (Washington, D.C.: Council on Wage and Price Stability, January 1977), pp. 20–28. For evidence that the level of insurance increases the rate of product innovation, which will in turn cause a higher rate of increase in expenditures, see Joseph P. Newhouse, "The Structure of Health Insurance and the Erosion of Competition in the Medical Marketplace," in Greenberg, ed., *Competition in the Health Care Sector*, pp. 270–287.

[27] Congressional Budget Office, *Expenditures for Health Care: Federal Programs and Their Effects* (Washington, D.C., 1977), p. 29.

[28] Mitchell and Vogel report that loading costs (premiums minus benefits) for group policies of even moderate-sized firms are only 8 to 10 percent while individual policies have loading costs of 50 to 100 percent. Mitchell and Vogel, *Health and Taxes*, p. 14.

[29] H. E. Frech III and Paul B. Ginsburg, *Public Insurance in Private Medical Markets: Some Problems with National Health Insurance* (Washington, D.C.: American Enterprise Institute, 1978).

who would prefer to have policies with higher deductibles and copayments (and lower premiums) is reduced. With less diversity in the type of policies offered, there is less pressure on the providers of care to be concerned about the cost-effectiveness of their care.

Another consequence of tying health insurance to employment is that some people lose their coverage when they become unemployed. While it is quite common for group policies to continue to cover an individual and his family for a limited period after the termination of employment, unless the unemployed worker takes definite action to purchase an individual policy, he and his family will be uncovered for some period of time. With the uncertainty of finding a new job and the financial strain of being unemployed, it is not difficult to understand why surveys show 34.3 percent of the unemployed do not have hospital insurance coverage.[30] The greater the number of uninsured people, the larger will be the financial strain placed on personal savings, relatives, Medicaid, or charitable institutions that attempt to pay for uninsured and unpaid medical care.

Several empirical studies show that a change in the consumer's copayment does affect the consumer's demand for care. Rosett and Huang use a 1960 Bureau of Labor Statistics survey of consumer expenditures to estimate a model that tests the effects of several variables on household medical expenditures. In a numerical illustration based on their findings, they show that for a family with an income of $7,000, 80 percent of all standard households would spend less than $834 per year when the coinsurance rate is 20 percent but that 80 percent of the households would spend less than $709 when the coinsurance rate is 30 percent. If the coinsurance rate were 40 percent, the figure would decline to $597. Furthermore, they estimate empirically that when the coinsurance rate is 20 percent, the $834 for medical expenses includes an additional amount of care that the family values at $325 but that costs an additional $634 to produce.[31]

Feldstein has estimated the effects of increasing the coinsurance rate from 33 percent to 50 and 67 percent. After allowing for the costs imposed by bearing increased risk, he finds that there would be a net gain to society in excess of $4 billion per year (based on 1969 private

---

[30] Wilder, *Insurance Coverage*, Table 9, p. 20. This compares with 12.7 percent not insured among the currently employed. The percentage of those not having surgical insurance was 14.5 percent for the currently employed and 36.0 percent for the currently unemployed.

[31] Richard N. Rosett and Lien-fu Huang, "The Effect of Health Insurance on the Demand for Medical Care," *Journal of Political Economy*, vol. 81, no. 2, part 1 (March/April 1973), pp. 296–297.

hospital expenditures of $12.6 billion) when reasonable assumptions are made about supply and demand elasticities.[32]

In a 1973 study of the effects of coinsurance, Phelps and Newhouse obtain evidence using insurance company data that when coinsurance rates are reduced from 25 percent to zero, total medical expenditures increase by 12 percent (an arc elasticity of 0.043). But when they measure separate responses to coinsurance in several different medical markets (hospital services, physician office visits, ambulatory ancillary services, physician house calls, and prescription drugs) and aggregate these (using expenditure weights), they find an arc elasticity of 0.10, which implies a 28 percent increase in expenditures from a decrease in coinsurance rates from 25 percent to zero. They conclude from these results that

> some persons feel coinsurance is irrelevant to decisions about consumption of medical services, because physicians make all the relevant choices. The results presented here are strong evidence against that hypothesis. Consistently, across a number of studies based upon diverse data, coinsurance has been found to exert an impact on utilization of various services.[33]

In a recent study of the effects of imposing a $1.00 per visit charge (strictly a deductible rather than a percentage copayment) on physician office visits among welfare patients in California, Helms, Newhouse, and Phelps found the charge reduced office visits by 8 percent. While the $1.00 charge reduced the program's cost for physician service by $1.04 per person per quarter, the experiment was not judged a success because it induced the patients who were eligible for hospital coverage to increase their hospital care by 17 percent. The switch to the more expensive hospital services cost the program an additional $2.64 per person per quarter.[34] While the authors conclude that the imposition of out-of-pocket payments for ambulatory care may not be effective in controlling costs in a welfare population, it should be noted that the experiment did not consider consumer behavior when cost-sharing was applied to both hospital and physician care.

---

[32] Feldstein, "The Welfare Loss of Excess Health Insurance," pp. 251–280, especially p. 277.

[33] Charles E. Phelps and Joseph P. Newhouse, "Coinsurance, the Price of Time, and the Demand for Medical Services," *Review of Economics and Statistics*, vol. 56, no. 3 (August 1974), pp. 337–341.

[34] Jay Helms, Joseph P. Newhouse, and Charles E. Phelps, "Copayments and Demand for Medical Care: The California Medicaid Experience," *Bell Journal of Economics*, vol. 9, no. 1 (Spring 1978), pp. 200–201.

In summary, it appears that there is nothing inherently different about the behavior of medical markets that cannot be explained by the effects of tax subsidies and direct government subsidies for care. Individuals are responding in predictable ways both to the tax subsidies that increase insurance coverage and to the direct governmental subsidy through Medicare and Medicaid. It is not a matter of "market failure" resulting from some fundamental difference in the pursuit of health, but only of efficient responses on the part of individuals to deliberate government policy to subsidize health. It is obvious that the intent of our public policies was to increase access to medical care among the aged and the poor and to reduce the financial burden of medical expenditures among all taxpayers. It is not so obvious that we intended these subsidizing policies to have such perverse and cost-increasing effects on individual incentives. But the fact remains that if we now want to revise public policies to control health cost increases in a way that maintains efficiency in medical markets, we must first take into consideration the effects of tax subsidies.

Even if we had fewer tax subsidies for the purchase of health insurance so that individuals would choose more cost-effective policies, there are other popular arguments about why medical markets will not work. The following two sections consider two of these arguments.

Lack of Consumer Control of Demand. If we assume for the moment that we can ignore the effect of overinsurance caused by tax subsidies, there are two varieties of criticisms of medical markets that are based on demand considerations: the apparent unresponsiveness to price of demand for medical services and physicians' influence over patients' demand for care.

Inelasticity of demand. The unresponsiveness (inelasticity) of medical demand refers to those situations where substitutes are not readily available or there is little time to make alternative arrangements. Consumers, under such circumstances, apparently give relatively little consideration to price. This is often illustrated by the case of the unconscious accident victim about to undergo emergency surgery.

If unresponsiveness to price is common across medical markets, the policy implications are that changes in supply will have little effect on the amount of medical services demanded but large effects on the revenue (income) of those being paid to deliver the services. It also follows that medical markets will be relatively immune from ordinary price competition because new entrants will have little chance to gain a larger share of the market by offering the consumer a lower price.

While there may be individual markets relatively unresponsive to price, it is highly simplistic to take this view of medical markets in general.[35] It would be expected from standard demand analysis that the elasticity of demand would vary among individual medical markets depending on consumer tastes, the availability of substitutes, and consumer knowledge about these alternatives. While emergency treatment may be an example of a market with a relatively inelastic demand, it is not characteristic of most medical situations where consumers have considerable time to decide among several available choices. These more ordinary medical choices involve such things as the choice of a family physician, whether or not to have minor surgery or a certain symptom investigated, or even an advance decision about which hospital one would prefer for emergency care should the need arise. Under such situations of deliberate choice, not only price but other aspects of the service, such as travel and waiting time, the quality of the care, and the "bedside manner" of the physician, all become more important.

In addition, there are numerous ways in which consumers may make substitutions in medical markets. For example, a consumer may follow a pharmacist's advice about an over-the-counter drug for a rash rather than consult a dermatologist, or a consumer may choose between living with a certain amount of pain as opposed to having a heart bypass operation. The greater the conceivable choices, the more elastic the demand.

Consumers can also make advance decisions to protect themselves from the risk of medical events requiring treatment when they can predict they would not want to be concerned at time of treatment with price or cost (that is, treatment having an inelastic demand). The market for insurance is a response to such situations. Even if there were no tax subsidies inducing people to purchase insurance, consumers could be expected to insure against the uncertainty of large medical expenditures in the event of an accident or a catastrophic disease.[36] It is not obvious, however, that consumers will purchase enough accident or catastrophic (deep) insurance to cover the total cost to society of such treatment if some individuals anticipate they will be taken care of once their own resources are depleted.

While obtaining empirical estimates of demand elasticities is a

---

[35] R. D. Fraser, *A Research Agenda in Health Care Economics* (Toronto: Ontario Economic Council, 1975), chapter 4, p. 2. See also Mark V. Pauly, "Is Medical Care Different?" pp. 20–27.

[36] The more inelastic the patient's demand for a particular medical service, the greater is the insurance company's role in controlling the cost of that service. See below for a discussion of limitations on insurance companies' ability to control costs.

complex task,[37] there is some evidence against the popular perception that prices for medical care are unimportant to patients. In the previously mentioned study, Rosett and Huang found consumers were more responsive to price changes for hospital and physicians' services when the coinsurance rate was increased. Specifically, they found the price elasticity of demand to be −0.35 when the coinsurance rate was 20 percent but −1.5 when consumers had to pay 80 percent of their bill.[38] Feldstein has found the elasticity of demand for hospital services to be −1.12.[39]

The previously mentioned study of the effects of coinsurance and time on medical demand by Phelps and Newhouse also contains findings of different elasticities among different kinds of medical markets. By converting a number of previous elasticity measures, they estimate elasticities which imply that for a decrease (increase) in the coinsurance rate from 25 percent to zero, the following approximate percentage increases (decreases) in expenditures could be expected:

physician house calls	108 percent
dental services	38 percent
physician office visits	33 percent
hospital expenses	17 percent
ambulatory ancillary services	15 percent
prescription drugs	15 percent
hospital admissions	8 percent[40]

These estimates are consistent with the argument that if consumers

---

[37] In addition to having adequate data, the principal problems are those associated with separating the effects of changes in prices from all other supply and demand factors affecting real world medical markets. In particular, there is the problem of separating price effects from changes in incomes and coinsurance rates. For a discussion of these complexities, see Joseph P. Newhouse and Charles E. Phelps, *On Having Your Cake and Eating It Too: Econometric Problems in Estimating the Demand for Health Services* (Santa Monica: Rand Corporation, R-1149-NC, April 1974).

[38] Rosett and Huang, "The Effect of Health Insurance," p. 301. The minus sign indicates the negative relationship between an increase (decrease) in price and a decrease (increase) in quantity demanded. A higher absolute value (1.5) indicates a greater quantity response (15 percent) for a given change in price (10 percent) than a lower absolute value (0.35).

[39] As reported by Rosett and Huang, "The Effect of Health Insurance," p. 301. For additional evidence, see Joseph P. Newhouse and Charles E. Phelps, "New Estimates of Price and Income Elasticities of Medical Care Services," in Richard N. Rosett, ed., *The Role of Health Insurance in the Health Services Sector* (New York: National Bureau of Economic Research, 1976), pp. 261–313.

[40] Charles E. Phelps and Joseph P. Newhouse, *Coinsurance and the Demand for Medical Services* (Santa Monica, Calif.: Rand Corporation, October 1974), table 12, p. 44.

paid a larger proportion of their medical bills directly rather than having them paid through third parties, they could be expected to reduce expenditures for such things as home visits, office visits, and dental care relatively more than for hospital services where more serious medical problems are treated.

Physician control of demand. The second argument about the consumer's "peculiar" behavior in medical markets concerns physician control over the demand for care.[41] In the medical context, the physician is seen to have such extensive influence over the individual that he determines the demand and hence the level of his own income. This perception of medical markets gains strength from observations that consumers have little technical information about medical choices and so put great (some would say, too much) faith in the physician's opinion. Medical training, peer pressure, and concern about malpractice liability encourage physicians to prescribe more care and a higher style of care. The policy implications are that medical markets may be less competitive and therefore less resistant to increases in prices and total expenditures.[42]

This reasoning explains much of the popular perception that medical markets "don't work." It is argued here, however, that this behavior is largely a function of the method of paying physicians through third parties. To the extent that it can logically be separated from the third-party payment effect, the propriety of physician control of demand becomes a question of the medical correctness of information supplied by physicians to patients. To what extent do physicians induce patients to consume more medical goods and services than they would buy with full and accurate information? Given the diversity of professional opinion that exists for almost any medical problem and the difference in the ways individual patients respond to treatments, not even a system of peer review could be expected to have much effect on whatever amount of inappropriate demand may have been created. To state the problem this way is to illustrate what a hopeless morass it would be to distinguish between appropriate demand and actual use.[43]

---

[41] This is conceptually a different point from the inelasticity argument because in this case the physician's influence is to increase a demand curve of a given elasticity. For an extended treatment of this topic, see Frank A. Sloan and Roger Feldman, "Competition among Physicians," in Greenberg, ed., *Competition in the Health Care Sector*, pp. 57–131.

[42] For a recent government report arguing this point, see Zachary Dyckman, *A Study of Physicians' Fees* (Washington, D.C.: Council on Wage and Price Stability, March 1978).

[43] For an analysis of the government's Professional and Standards Review Organizations (PSRO) program designed to control cost and quality of medical care, see Havighurst and Blumstein, "Coping with Quality/Cost Trade-Offs," pp. 6–68.

345

While an empirical attempt to measure inappropriate demand is not likely to be successful, economic analysis can be used to predict that physician control of demand (in the absence of the third-party payment effect) is not likely to be different from the system in other markets where agents are paid by consumers for information.

First, consider a medical market where there is a well-defined product or procedure such as the treatment of a skin disease, a pap smear, a hysterectomy, a heart bypass operation, or even the removal of a known tumor. The extent to which the physician can increase demand for these services will be a function of the information consumers have about the probable effectiveness of each procedure, the cost of the procedure (both in terms of time and money), and the availability of alternative sources of supply. As Pauly has pointed out, the consumer can be expected to be more informed about those procedures that are repeatedly purchased, either by the individual or his friends and relatives.[44] Thus, to the extent that the physician's control of demand can be logically separated from the third-party payment effect, such control should not be a problem for the great majority of medical procedures in which repeat purchases by the same person are common. The problem of physician control of demand can then be largely confined to those procedures that are rarely purchased, such as emergency operations and procedures of a more experimental nature.

Even in these cases, however, there are several constraints on physician behavior that may mitigate against the temptation to abuse patient trust. The first is the physician's role in supplying medical information. Consumer purchases of goods or services that are difficult to evaluate are not restricted to medicine. If there is a real demand for information, in the absence of restrictions or prohibitive costs, institutions can be expected to evolve to supply it. Middlemen traditionally perform this service in most markets (real estate, insurance, stocks) but other examples include the Consumers' Union, Good Housekeeping seal, technical magazines, and computer consulting firms. It is quite likely that there would be more of these if physicians were not so efficient in supplying information to consumers. Personal communication between physician and patient is obviously quite important.

Note that such a view amounts to dropping the assumption of a well-defined medical product. This suggests that medical markets should be more broadly defined in terms of what consumers are demanding and physicians are supplying.[45] It can be argued that one of

---

[44] Pauly, "Is Medical Care Different?" pp. 20–27.

[45] As Armen Alchian used to say in economic theory classes at UCLA, some of the biggest disputes in economics are over what is on the horizontal axis (of a supply and demand diagram).

the largest components of medical "output" is the information provided to consumers. For example, from the consumer's point of view, information that a disease is not present will obviously be productive in reducing anxiety. Because the value of medical information depends largely on personal perceptions of its worth, it is nearly impossible to measure objectively. This has led to considerable debate about the extent to which physicians overtreat patients and thus distort the ordinary workings of the market. There is no reason to believe that the demand for medical information is any less elastic than the demand for other information or that physicians have unusual powers to increase consumers' demand for information.

In addition, as Lindsay and Leffler point out, if consumers learn that a particular physician has a bias toward too much service, they may discount the physician's advice. The possibility arises that more skeptical consumers may then purchase too little medical care compared with some standard of optimal care. Other factors constraining the physician in his relations with his patients are his concern for his professional reputation among his peers, the importance consumer trust plays in building and maintaining a practice, and the availability of prepaid forms of care such as HMOs where physicians have stronger incentives to prescribe a cost-effective amount and quality of care.[46] Thus, it is argued, there are reasons to doubt the seriousness of concern over physician control of demand.

Lack of Competition. Because all markets deviate in some respects from an abstract model of perfect competition, it is not surprising that medical markets have been accused of a lack of competition. From a policy perspective, the important point is that this so-called lack of competition in medical markets is used as a justification for regulation. It is therefore important to determine in what respect competition may be lacking and why. If competition is lacking, economic theory predicts that some monopoly returns will be earned, prices will be higher than under more competitive conditions, and fewer services will be provided to consumers than they desire.

The issue of the competitiveness of medical markets cannot be separated from the effects of tax policies and insurance because the existence of third-party payments increases the demand for care and also decreases the elasticity of demand.[47] The more complete the insurance coverage, the less the incentive to search for a lower-cost pro-

---

[46] Lindsay and Leffler, "The Market for Medical Care," pp. 67–68.
[47] Mark V. Pauly, "The Economics of Moral Hazard," *American Economic Review*, vol. 53, no. 3 (June 1968), pp. 531–537.

vider of care. As stated earlier, a tax policy that promotes the purchase of complete medical insurance has pervasive effects on medical markets. Policies to reduce the effect could be expected to put more competitive pressure on medical markets because of the savings to consumers from lower prices and less waste of resources.

Still other considerations about competition are relevant to the discussion of how well medical markets perform or can be made to perform. These will be discussed under two broad headings, barriers to entry and competition among insurance companies.[48]

Barriers to entry. A "barrier to entry" is the term used to describe any factor tending artifically to raise the cost of entering a market. While there are many markets such as for hospitals, nurses, or blood where some barriers may be effective, we will start with the market for physicians. It has important effects on competition in other medical markets and is most commonly considered to be affected by barriers to entry.

The late Reuben Kessel in his 1958 article, "Price Discrimination in Medicine," reviewed the history of the American Medical Association's (AMA) attempts to strengthen its control over medical markets by controlling entry into medical schools, supporting more restrictive state licensing, and discouraging price competition among physicians and various modes of prepaid health care.[49] Dyckman reports that the number of physicians per 100,000 population declined from 146 in 1910 to 133 in 1959. Dyckman also points out that because of a change in both government and AMA policies, physician supply increased from 149 per 100,000 population in 1965 to 177 per 100,000 in 1975. He concludes that while earlier restrictions on physician supply may have been responsible for rapid fee increases, the dominant force affecting these fee increases in the 1960s and 1970s was the growth of insurance.[50]

In discussing physicians' incomes, Dyckman concludes from the evidence that physicians' incomes, which averaged $68,800 in 1976, are now higher than necessary to attract a sufficient supply of physicians. To support the finding he uses AMA figures showing that between

---

[48] For recent literature on competition in medical markets, see Warren Greenberg, ed., *Competition in the Health Care Sector.* A topic not considered here is the lack of the profit-maximizing motive in medicine. For discussion of this difference in medical market behavior, see Kenneth W. Clarkson, "Some Implications of Property Rights in Hospital Management," *Journal of Law and Economics,* vol. 15, no. 2 (October 1972), pp. 263–284; and Mark Pauly and Michael Redisch, "The Not-for-Profit Hospital as a Physician's Cooperative," *American Economic Review,* vol. 63, no. 1 (March 1973), pp. 87–89.

[49] Reuben A. Kessel, "Price Discrimination in Medicine," *Journal of Law and Economics,* vol. 1 (October 1958), pp. 20–53.

[50] Dyckman, *A Study of Physicians' Fees,* pp. 9–11, 43.

1965 and 1975 the ratio of medical school applicants to acceptances increased from 2.1 to 2.8 per person accepted even though actual first-year enrollments almost doubled. In addition, the quality of those accepted in medical schools is apparently increasing (as measured by grades), and a growing (but undocumented) number of Americans are now enrolled in foreign medical schools.[51]

It is obvious that higher incomes and other prestigious factors related to a medical career are still attracting medical students and foreign-trained physicians. It may be that while entry into medicine is now easier than before 1965, increasing insurance coverage and income (and perhaps the efficacy of care) is causing demand to grow faster than the increasing supply of physicians can accommodate. Even though organized medicine's control over entry may have declined, there is reason to suspect that state and federal policies may now be increasing barriers to entry. Among health policy analysts, there is a general acceptance that federal subsidies to medical education have now produced a surplus of physicians. The administration is proposing a reduction in these subsidies to medical schools with aid directed more to individuals as an inducement to practice in rural and urban areas now considered to be underserved.[52] Demand is growing for government policies to increase barriers to entry as a way of controlling costs. A more direct approach would be to deal with incentive-changing effects of tax subsidies, which would help restore more price competition among physicians.

Should government policy succeed in controlling the supply of physicians without reducing the inflated demand and price insensitivity that have resulted from insurance programs, physicians' incomes will increase even more, thus increasing political pressure for their direct control. Some parties are already calling for the replacement of the traditional fee-for-service system with a budget approach to control physicians' revenues under National Health Insurance.[53] This situation suggests that common phenomenon of one regulation begetting another, which McKie so aptly refers to as "the tar baby effect."[54]

---

[51] Ibid., pp. 73–93, especially pp. 78, 84–85.

[52] *United States Budget in Brief, Fiscal Year 1979*, p. 55.

[53] The Health Security Act (the Kennedy-Corman bill) would establish a national health budget in which, "Medical societies would be obligated to negotiate realistic fee schedules so that the budget for physician services could not be exceeded" (Statement of Bert Seidman, director, Department of Social Security, AFL-CIO in Government Research Corporation, *Controlling Health Care Costs: A National Leadership Conference*, Washington, D.C., June 27–28, 1977, p. 70).

[54] James W. McKie, "Regulation and Free Markets: The Problem of Boundaries," *Bell Journal of Economics and Management Science*, vol. 1, no. 1 (Spring 1970), p. 9.

Of the several other factors known to be increasing the cost of entry, professional restrictions on advertising deserve some mention. Kessel has analyzed the effects of these in medicine.[55] The usual justification for these restrictions is that they prevent such unethical behavior as making claims about the effectiveness of one's treatment or attracting patients by lowering prices. Regardless of the stated purposes of restrictions on advertising, they are seen by economists as reducing price competition and protecting those already established in a medical practice. A young physician wishing to enter a market has the option of establishing a new practice or purchasing an existing one. If professional restrictions prevent him from advertising, he will be at a disadvantage in attracting patients and will have to go through the slower process of building a practice through word-of-mouth. The result, whether intended or not, is that the cost of entry is increased and the market value of existing practices is protected.[56] Recent Supreme Court decisions regarding professional advertising as well as continuing pressure by the Federal Trade Commission and various consumer groups may have the effect of providing more information about prices and comparative performance to consumers. This should result in a lower cost of entry for new physicians, more direct price competition, and more alternative forms of care such as prepaid plans, nurse practitioners, or "surgicenters," which provide out-patient minor surgery.

Again the policy debate returns to the effects of tax exemptions on insurance. In a system of medical finance with less complete insurance and more direct consumer payment for medical care, a reduction in barriers to entry could be expected to bring about increased market competition and lower prices.

Competition among insurance companies. For policy purposes, the question must be raised of why insurance companies have not exerted more pressure on hospitals and physicians to restrain medical expenditures. These companies obviously have some incentives to keep the cost of reimbursements under control as they do in other insurance markets such as automobile and fire insurance. Why then has the market behavior of medical insurance been so different and why has the growth of insurance resulted in such large increases in medical expenditures and prices?[57]

---

[55] Kessel, "Price Discrimination in Medicine," pp. 43–44.

[56] Casual discussions with physicians indicate that a new physician can expect to retain a very large percentage (some say 90 percent) of the clientele of an ongoing practice.

[57] This discussion relies heavily on Frech and Ginsburg, "Competition among Health Insurers." For additional discussion of medical insurance, see Lawrence E. Goldberg and Warren Greenberg, "The Effects of Physician-Controlled Health In-

The health insurance industry has been described as consisting of two segments: (1) the commercial (for-profit and mutual) firms where entry is easy and the structure is unconcentrated, and (2) the Blue Cross and Blue Shield plans (referred to as "the Blues"), which are organized and controlled by hospitals and physicians. State laws sometimes give the Blues protection from new entrants and special tax treatments. Collusion among the plans to divide markets on a geographical and functional basis is common. Commercial firms offer a wider range of types of coverage while the Blues prefer more standardized policies with lower deductible and copayment (more complete) provisions.[58] Given the close ties between hospitals, physicians, and the Blues, it is not surprising that a system of reimbursement based on "usual, customary, and reasonable" (UCR) fees for physicians and cost reimbursement for hospitals has led to higher payments than under indemnity policies, which pay only a set amount for a given procedure.[59] Because the Blues provide about half the medical insurance, this deliberate policy of providing full reimbursement makes it more difficult for the non-Blue insurers to control cost. An individual insurer, such as Aetna, can be expected to have little success in negotiating lower fees with physicians and hospitals when it does not have a large share of the market. In addition, even though one company may succeed in reducing fees, it will not capture all of the gain because the reduced fee will benefit all insurers.[60]

Various proposals have been made to strengthen market competition among medical insurers. Some of these have been reform of state regulations of insurance, a change from retrospective cost reimbursement to prospective reimbursement, and application of antitrust laws to the Blues to diminish the influence of providers on the insurance companies.[61] The effectiveness of any of these policies would be increased if there were a change in tax policy that induced consumers to demand less complete coverage and gave them a greater incentive to search for

---

surance: U.S. vs. Oregon State Medical Society," *Journal of Health Politics, Policy and Law*, vol. 2, no. 1 (Spring 1977), pp. 48–78; Dyckman, *A Study of Physicians' Fees*, pp. 21–33; Pauly, "Health Insurance and Hospital Behavior"; and Clark C. Havighurst, "Improving the Climate for Innovation in Health Care Financing and Delivery" (paper presented at the American Enterprise Institute conference on "The Antitrust Laws and the Health Service Industry," Washington, D.C., December 19–20, 1977).

[58] Frech and Ginsburg, "Competition among Health Insurers," pp. 216–219.

[59] Dyckman, *A Study of Physicians' Fees*, pp. 25–27.

[60] Ibid., p. 31; and Pauly, "Health Insurance and Hospital Behavior," p. 116.

[61] Clark C. Havighurst, "Controlling Health Care Costs: Strengthening the Private Sector's Hand," *Journal of Health Politics, Policy and Law*, vol. 1, no. 4 (Winter 1977), pp. 471–498.

an insurance company that provided a plan more suitable to their desires. Insurance companies, including the Blues, could still sell insurance, but they would have to compete more vigorously by offering more cost-effective policies at lower premium costs. Under an insurance system with greater consumer cost-sharing, both consumers and insurance companies could be expected to put more pressure on providers to control costs.

To summarize, standard economic analysis is useful to identify those aspects of medical markets that are different and in this way help correct the popular perception that medical markets cannot be relied upon to maintain an efficient use of resources.

Conclusion

This paper has discussed the arguments behind the popular perception that economic behavior in medical markets is inherently different from behavior in more traditional markets. It has pointed to medical tax exemptions as the primary factor behind the increasing cost of medical care. The analysis indicates that if we want to establish a health policy that benefits consumers through greater efficiency and freedom of individual choice, we must face up to the role played by tax subsidies in promoting the spread of shallow insurance coverage. It is contended that if the individual consumer is given a greater role in sharing the cost of care, his economic behavior in the medical market will be more cost effective. Efficiency will be improved because reductions in expenditures will tend to be those which the consumer and his physician agree will be less productive.[62]

It should be noted that increasing the consumer's participation in the direct payment for medical care does not mean denying care to the poor or to those who experience catastrophic health expenses. We already have Medicare and Medicaid to provide care for the aged and the poor. These programs could be improved so that the lower the income of the individual or family, the smaller the proportion of direct payment. If we choose, at some cost we could even eliminate cost-sharing for the extremely poor by completely subsidizing their care. It would also be relatively inexpensive to eliminate cost-sharing for the

---

[62] For literature on proposals aimed at restoring consumer cost-sharing to medical markets, see Havighurst, "Controlling Health Care Costs"; Joseph P. Newhouse and Vincent Taylor, "How Shall We Pay for Hospital Care?" *Public Interest*, no. 23 (Spring 1971), pp. 78–92; Mark V. Pauly, *National Health Insurance: An Analysis* (Washington, D.C.: American Enterprise Institute, 1971), pp. 33–40; Feldstein, "The High Cost of Hospitals—and What To Do About It," pp. 40–54; Enthoven, "Consumer Choice Health Plan (CCHP)."

small number of cases experiencing a catastrophic health situation. (Approximately 1 percent of the population under age sixty-five have medical expenses over $5,000 annually.)[63] Because the relatively rare occurrences of catastrophic diseases are readily insurable, such insurance could be provided directly by the government or through private insurance if mandated in some way by the government. The obvious social concern for the well-being of the aged, the poor, or those facing catastrophic medical expenses should not be used as an excuse for not establishing policies that restore cost-conscious behavior among the much larger segment of the population that has both the income to pay for normal amounts of care and the willingness to make decisions.

The pessimistic view is that it will take a deliberate change in policy together with strong political leadership to make the case for a return to market principles in health. But perhaps it would be best to end on at least this grace note of optimism. It took the economics profession approximately thirty years to begin to develop the methodology to measure the costs and benefits of regulation established during the 1930s and before. It has taken approximately another ten years of hard work to begin to invoke a public awareness of the cost of regulation. Possibly health economists and others analyzing health markets have now enough of a headstart so that it will be somewhat less than forty years until this country begins to realize the economic and personal costs of health regulation and attempts to deal with the real factors affecting health costs.

---

[63] The aggregate expenses over $5,000 of that 1 percent of the population are about $13.1 billion. Congressional Budget Office, *Catastrophic Health Insurance* (Washington, D.C., 1977), p. xiv.

Cover and book design: Pat Taylor